The Pectol-Lee Artifacts
from Capitol Reef

RELICS REVISITED

New Perspectives on an Early
Twentieth-Century Collection

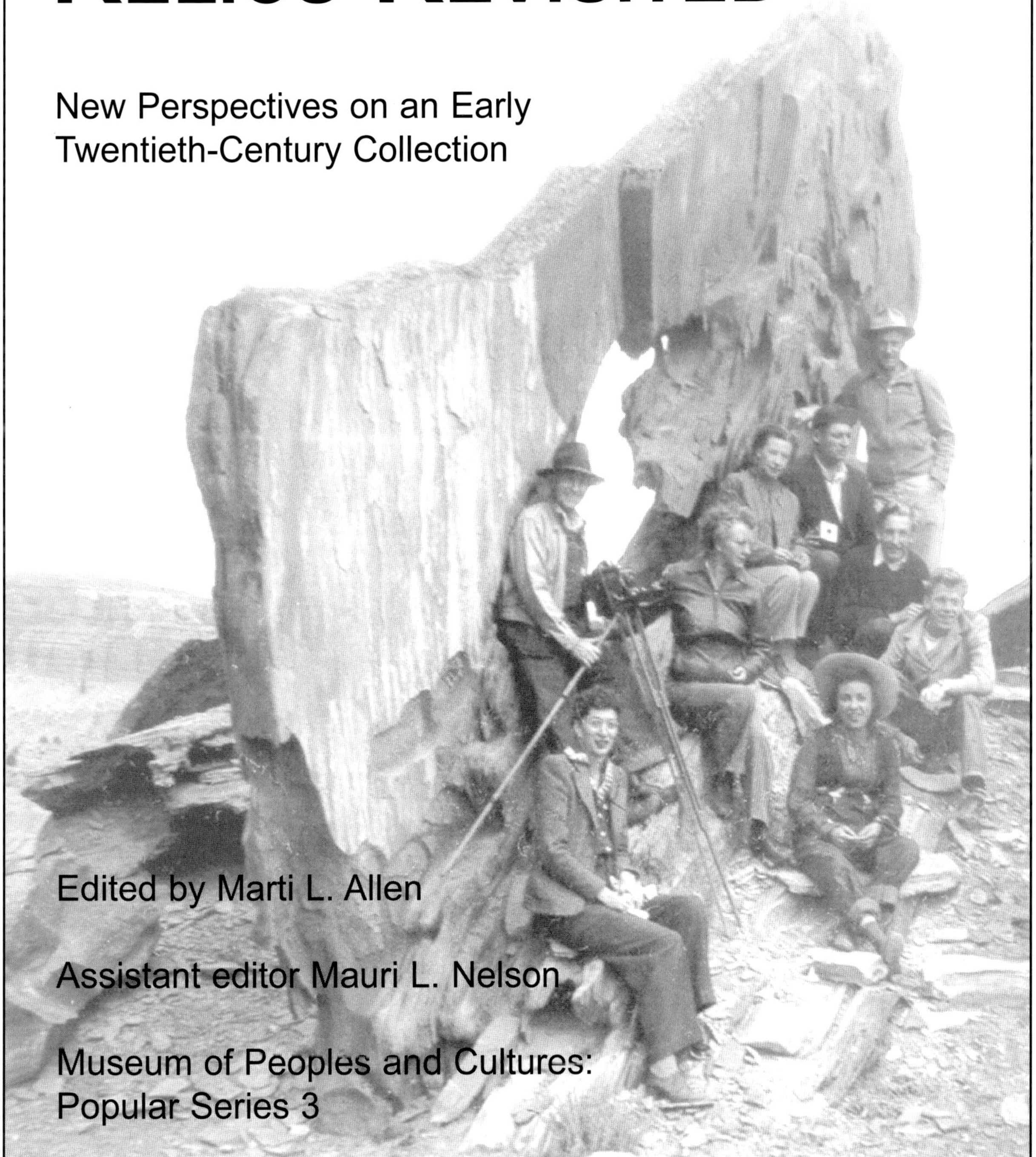

Edited by Marti L. Allen

Assistant editor Mauri L. Nelson

Museum of Peoples and Cultures:
Popular Series 3

ISBN # 0-87480-733-6

MUSEUM of
PEOPLES
and CULTURES

BYU's Teaching Museum

Cover image: Associates of Ephraim Pectol on excursion in Capitol Reef area, ca. 1930s. Photo courtesy E. P. and Dorothy Hickman Pectol Family Organization.

Funded in part by the Brigham Young University Office of Research and Creative Activities and the Utah Office of Museum Services.

Printed in the United States of America

TABLE OF CONTENTS

LIST OF FIGURES

Figure 44. Fremont pottery decorations. From Joel C. Janetski, Richard K. Talbot, Deborah E. Newman, Lane D. Richens, James D. Wilde, Shane A. Baker, and Scott A. Billat, *Clear Creek Canyon Archaeological Project Volume Five: Results and Synthesis*, Museum of Peoples and Cultures Technical Series 95-9 (Provo: Brigham Young University, 1997), 72–73.

LIST OF COLOR PLATES

Photo by Christopher D. DiCicco, 2001.
Color Plate 14. Bighorn sheep headdress with olivella shell pendants, College of Eastern Utah Prehistoric Museum, Price, Utah (CEUM 9462). Fremont (AD 400–1300)/Agricultural Period (AD 1–1300)? Photo courtesy College of Eastern Utah Prehistoric Museum.

Color Plate 15. Bison mask. Plains Indian, ca. 1860. From Madan, Fort Berthold Indian Reservation, North Dakota. Photo courtesy Buffalo Bill Historical Center, Cody, Wyoming (NA.203,359), Chandler-Pohrt Collection. Photo by Lucille Warters.

Color Plate 16. Bison headdress ("buffalo horn bonnet"). Gros Ventre Tribe, Great Plains, ca. 1880. Buffalo Bill Historical Center, Cody, Wyoming. Gift of Mr. and Mrs. Larry Larom (NA.203.136). Photo by Devendra Shrikhande.

Color Plate 17. Watercolor painting of Zia Buffalo Dance (untitled), by Velion Shije Herrera, Ma-Pe-Wi, Zia Pueblo, ca. 1918. Photo courtesy Museum of Indian Arts and Culture/Laboratory of Anthropology, Museum of New Mexico, Santa Fe, New Mexico (14220/13). Photo by Blair Clark.

Color Plate 18. Decorated basketry trays from the Pectol-Lee collection. Clockwise from top left: cat. nos. 29, 28, 31, 30. Photo by Leslie-lynne Sinkey, 2001.

Color Plate 19. Decorated basketry bowls from the Pectol-Lee collection. Left to right: cat. nos. 44, 35, 43. Photo by Leslie-lynne Sinkey, 2001.

Color Plate 20. Rod-in-bundle bulrush baskets from the Pectol-Lee collection. Left to right: cat. nos. 39, 38. Photo by Leslie-lynne Sinkey, 2001.

PROJECT PERSONNEL

Marti L. Allen, Ph.D., Director, Museum of Peoples and Cultures/Associate Professor (Administrative), Department of Anthropology, Brigham Young University. Allen was principal investigator of the Pectol project, which she conceptualized, designed, secured funding for, directed, and administered. She edited the catalogue and was principal author of two articles. As instructor of Anthropology 525, 526, and 596, she trained and directed the students in cataloguing the artifacts and closely mentored them in bringing their catalogue entries and papers to final form.

Shane A. Baker, M.A., Assistant Curator of Collections, Museum of Peoples and Cultures/Staff Archaeologist, Office of Public Archaeology, Brigham Young University. Baker was a faculty mentor for the project, guided the students in the research phases of their papers, and contributed an article to the catalogue.

Laurel Casjens, Ph.D., Curator of Collections, Utah Museum of Natural History, University of Utah, Salt Lake City, Utah. Casjens was a peer reviewer for the catalogue articles.

Kathy Kankainen, Anthropology Collections Manager, Utah Museum of Natural History, University of Utah, Salt Lake City, Utah. Kankainen was a peer reviewer for the catalogue articles.

Lee Ann Kreutzer, Ph.D., Park Archaeologist/Cultural Resources Program Manager, Capitol Reef National Park, Torrey, Utah. Kreutzer was a peer reviewer for one of the articles and the project's point person at Capitol Reef National Park.

Byron Loosle, Ph.D., Forest Archaeologist, Ashley National Forest, Vernal, Utah. Loosle was a peer reviewer for the catalogue articles.

Pamela Miller, M.A., Associate Director/Curator of Archaeology, College of Eastern Utah Prehistoric Museum, Price, Utah. Miller was a faculty mentor for the project and one of the peer reviewers for the catalogue articles. She checked the catalogue entries against the objects and closely advised in bringing the student (co-)authored papers to final form.

Michelle R. Munsey, undergraduate student, BYU History Department. Munsey wrote catalogue entries for the hide, bone, wood, antler, horn, pottery, clay, raw material, and miscellaneous artifacts and wrote a paper as part of curriculum for the Fall 2000 Anthropology 525 (Museum Registration and Collections Management), Winter 2001 Anthropology 526 (Museum Curation and Programming), and Spring 2001 Anthropology 596 (Museum Projects) classes. Her catalogue entries were developed and brought to their final form in consultation with the catalogue editor and Pamela Miller. Her class paper on the cradle board, the clay figurines, and the deer headdress, entitled "Ritual, Religion, and Abstract Thought in Prehistory," was reworked by the editor to become components of this volume's articles on the cradle board and the deer headdress.

Mauri (Liljenquist) Nelson, M.A., Assistant Curator of Education, Museum of Peoples and Cultures, Brigham Young University. Nelson was assistant editor of this catalogue and co-instructor of the Anthropology 526 and 596 classes. She supervised the installation of the exhibition *In Search of Relics: The Pectol-Lee Collection of Artifacts from Capitol Reef* and oversaw development of its promotion and accompanying educational materials.

Matthew T. Seddon, Ph.D., Principal Investigator, SWCA Inc., Environmental Consultants, Salt Lake City, Utah. Seddon was a peer reviewer for the catalogue articles.

Leslie-lynne Sinkey, master's student, BYU Department of Anthropology. Sinkey wrote catalogue entries for the basketry, stone, cordage, and agricultural materials and contributed an article on basketry to the catalogue as part of curriculum for the Fall 2000 Anthropology 525 (Museum Registration and Collections Management), Winter 2001 Anthropology 526 (Museum Curation and Programming), and Spring 2001 Anthropology 596 (Museum Projects) classes. These entries and the article were brought to their final form in consultation with the catalogue editor and Pamela Miller.

Richard K. Talbot, M.A., Director, Office of Public Archaeology, Brigham Young University. Talbot was a faculty mentor for the project, guided the students in the research phases of their papers, and contributed an article to the catalogue.

FOREWORD: THE TEACHING MUSEUM

The Museum of Peoples and Cultures is BYU's "teaching museum." The Museum's staff members participate in teaching classes that at once guide students through practical aspects of museum studies and ultimately generate all the Museum's programs. Under the staff's guidance, student aides inventory the collections and accomplish collections management duties, while students who take a series of museology courses participate in producing the Museum's exhibitions and developing associated educational and promotional programs. Accordingly, students who aspire to the museum and anthropology professions gain "real-life" experience and enter the job arena with marketable skills.

In the academic year 2000–2001, museum curriculum focused on the Pectol Project, which was designed to generate this catalogue and an accompanying exhibition of the Pectol-Lee collection of artifacts. This collection was amassed in the early years of the twentieth century by the Pectol and Lee families from the Capitol Reef region and has been on loan to the Museum from the E. P. and Dorothy Hickman Pectol Family Organization since 2000. The Pectol Project was among those selected and funded by the BYU Office of Research and Creative Activities as part of its new Environments for Mentoring Program. The students who benefited most directly from this project were Michelle R. Munsey, an undergraduate in the History Department; and Leslie-lynne Sinkey, a graduate student in the Department of Anthropology. They constituted the entire enrollment for the 2000–2001 museology classes series, that is, Museum Registration and Collections Management (Anthropology 525); Museum Curation and Programming (Anthropology 526); and Museum Projects (Anthropology 596).

Mentored student projects of this nature have inherent challenges for both students and mentors. Students with little background are immediately immersed in professional activities and require close, patient monitoring. The students must accomplish the work within the hard and fast time limitations imposed by the University's academic year and according to professional standards to which they have no prior exposure and perhaps little comprehension. Mentors must be willing to devote the extra time necessary to give training and must be responsive with feedback. To ameliorate the challenge facing them, Munsey and Sinkey were given extensive preparatory training in Fall 2000. The curriculum of the Museum Registration and Collections Management class provided substantial training in museum technical writing, such as artifact description, cataloguing, and condition reporting. The Museum also brought in several experts to help the students identify and describe various types of artifacts. Moreover, while other mentoring projects at BYU were being done wholly on volunteer time, Munsey and Sinkey had the benefit of class structure to minimize the volunteer commitment, thereby enabling them to use their professional involvement with the project to satisfy requirements of three separate classes. In the spring term, furthermore, they were hired as halftime curatorial interns, enabling them to be remunerated for some of their professional contributions.

The students put what they learned into immediate action as they described and completed condition reports on basketry, lithics, pottery, hide, and other artifacts in the Pectol-Lee collection. Beginning in Fall 2000 and continuing over the next two semesters, Sinkey worked on basketry, cordage, fiber, stone, and agricultural materials, while Munsey catalogued everything else, i.e., hide, wood, bone, antler, horn, pottery, clay, etc. The students turned in draft after draft of their catalogue entries for editing on accuracy and clarity. Each draft was checked against the objects and returned with corrections until the Museum's standard was achieved. Faculty mentor Pamela Miller made several trips from Price, Utah, to consult on the basketry entries with Sinkey, a basket maker herself who brought significant skills to the project. This close mentoring helped the students refine their technical writing skills and enabled the quality achieved in the catalogue section that concludes this monograph.

The students also benefited significantly from their association with the project's other faculty mentors, Shane A. Baker and Richard K. Talbot. In addition to contributing their own papers to the catalogue, Baker and Talbot played an important mentoring role in the early phases of the project. With their cooperation, the Winter 2001 Museum Curation and Programming class was custom-designed to accommodate the Pectol Project. During the first two months of the term, these two faculty mentors met weekly with the students, directing the initial phase of their research and supervising the first drafts of their papers.

From March 2001 on, the student papers were supervised by the volume editor in conjunction with a panel of external peer reviewers. In addition to Pamela Miller, these were Laurel Casjens, Kathy Kankainen, Byron Loosle, and Matthew T. Seddon. The rigor of this editing process introduced students to peer-review publishing and helped bring the papers to final form.

While the students elected to devote the lion's share of their energies to writing for the catalogue, they also participated in the production of a modest but commendable exhibition, *In Search of Relics: The Pectol-Lee Collection of Artifacts from Capitol Reef.* As part of the curriculum in the Museum Curation and Programming and the Museum Projects classes, co-instructed by Mauri (Liljenquist) Nelson and myself, the students learned how to organize and produce an exhibition. Working under the careful and discriminating guidance of their instructors, the students participated in every phase of exhibition planning and production. They received training in the technical aspects of how to design and mount an exhibition, from selecting the objects to mocking-up the cases consistent with the Museum's existing gallery style. They even built the object mounts needed for the exhibition in a workshop instructed by Gene Riggs, Head of Exhibition Fabrication, BYU Museum of Art.

In Spring 2001, as the students continued to work on their papers for the Museum Projects class, the Museum hired them as interns to install the exhibition. Before they could mount *In Search of Relics*, Munsey and Sinkey had to help the Museum's staff dismount the preceding kachina doll exhibition, which consisted almost exclusively of loans from other institutions and private lenders. They accordingly gained experience in preparing outgoing loans for shipment. The students received exposure to label writing and actually cut and mounted the labels and photodidactics. They learned aspects of conservation environment, such as how to create micro-environments in the exhibit cases, maintain proper humidity and lighting in the galleries, and ensure security in the design. Also as part of their paid internships, the students photographed most of the objects for publication in this volume. They also had the opportunity to observe the Museum's professional staff, most notably Mauri Nelson, design and launch the promotion strategy and develop educational materials accompanying the exhibition, such as the Museum's new scout activity patch. Consequently, every aspect of student involvement in mounting the exhibition and producing the programming was work for hire subject to the Museum's own internal protocols for evaluation and approval, and these standards had to be met—another taste of reality for the students.

In Search of Relics, on display through May 2003, focuses on the perspective of the "relic hunters" who amassed the collection in southern Utah during the early 1900s (see Introductory Remarks, p. xxiii, this volume). The exhibition has several objectives. It targets a general audience with the intention of serving BYU students, local school students, scouts, school teachers, home schoolers and, indeed, all audiences who seek introductory information about Utah's native cultures. In particular, the exhibition complements many courses at BYU in the departments of anthropology, history, art history, humanities, studio art, and geography, to name a few. The catalogue itself provides more in-depth content and seeks to serve students of anthropology, school teachers, and researchers. The catalogue entries will facilitate studies by regional archaeologists who have long wanted to see the Pectol-Lee collection published.

In many ways the theme, "In search of . . .," suggests a metaphor for the learning experience shared by the students in the 2000–2001 museum classes. While Pectol and Lee headed out in search of relics, these students began this series of courses in search of experience that would enable them to isolate their interests, determine their aptitudes, and find their way in the professional world. Those who choose the multifaceted world of museums learn they must wear many hats and cross many disciplines to fulfill a museum's purpose and public trust functions. Most importantly, they must learn to collaborate with professionals from diverse backgrounds, people who may share goals, but not necessarily methods for achieving the goals nor opinions of what constitutes a goal achieved. It is a hard lesson to learn, but a critical one, for a museum is a family of disciplines that must cooperate to succeed. The mentoring environment sponsored by the Office of Research and Creative Activities led the students of the 2000–2001 museology classes to this discovery most profoundly and most thoroughly. If their experience in these classes shall have guided them into careers that indulge their professional interests and engage their finest talents, the objectives of these classes—and those of BYU's Environments for Mentoring Program—will have been achieved.

Marti L. Allen

ACKNOWLEDGEMENTS

The Pectol Project not only provided a unique opportunity for students and professionals to collaborate, but also created a forum for professional interaction with other museums and scholars. It is my privilege to thank the parties who contributed time and support to this project. I am especially grateful to Mauri Nelson and Pamela Miller, both of whom brought needed special talents to the project and provided moral support throughout the project. Nelson, herself a former student in the museology course series, notably carried out the critical functions of overseeing installation of the exhibition *In Search of Relics* and the development and implementation of the associated promotional and educational programs. Owing to her background in history and her training and experience in museum studies, she brought significant insights to both the exhibition and the catalogue articles. Additionally, she ably served as assistant editor of this catalogue. Her ameliorating persona was especially effective during difficult moments in the collaboration.

Pamela Miller's academic expertise and her extensive firsthand experience with Utah's native material culture were essential to the success of the project, and every catalogue entry bears her scrutinizing mark. She collaborated closely with me to monitor the research, content, and academic viability of the three papers with student (co-)authors, devoting tens of hours executing a difficult but rewarding charge. Miller also joined me in checking and correcting the entire catalogue section to ensure accuracy in identification, attribution, description, and condition of the artifacts, and we together completed the comments accompanying many of the catalogue entries. The project, the Museum, and most of all, the students owe her an enormous debt of gratitude.

The Museum was fortunate to have the support of still other colleagues who played significant roles in realizing this project. The Museum was first made aware of the opportunity to borrow the Pectol-Lee collection through Assistant Curator of Collections Shane Baker's conversations with Park Archaeologist Lee Kreutzer of Capitol Reef National Park, Torrey, Utah and Neal Portman Busk of Richfield, Utah. We thank Lee Kreutzer, who brought the Museum's staff into contact with the Pectol Family Organization and facilitated the loan process in every way. She also gave the project's team members access to Pectol family correspondence held by Capitol Reef National Park and graciously served as an additional peer reviewer for the article on the history of the collection (Baker, p. 21, this volume). Albert J. Hendricks,

Superintendent, Capitol Reef National Park, generously gave permission to the project's team to examine and photograph the Pectol-Lee artifacts currently on exhibit at the Park's Visitor Center. Benson L. Lanford, a noted expert on Native American hide artifacts, flew in from Oregon to meet with the students for a full day, sharing his enthusiasm for hide artifacts, giving the students pointers on techniques of hide preparation, and helping us identify some of the more enigmatic specimens in the Pectol-Lee collection. Wesley ("Skip") Skidmore, Taxonomist and Curator of Animal Trophies, BYU Monte L. Bean Museum of Life Sciences, spent several hours with the students in an effort to identify the animal hides and pelts in the collection. Joel C. Janetski, Professor of Anthropology, Brigham Young University, shared with the class his knowledge of basketry construction and decoration. Phil Geib, Supervisory Archaeologist, Navajo Nation Archaeology Department, Northern Arizona University, Flagstaff, who studied two of the horn flakers in the Pectol-Lee collection, generously shared the results of his analyses (see cat. nos. 117–118). The Museum also thanks Lane Richens, Staff Archaeologist, Office of Public Archaeology, and Grant Smith, graduate student, Department of Anthropology, for identifying the pottery and projectile points in the collection, respectively.

Although the Pectol Project was designed specifically to provide specialized museum training for students aspiring to a museum career, it embraced other students whose contributions had significant impact. Photography student Helen Stevens did the graphics design for the exhibition's signage and for promotional and educational materials as well as produced all photodidactics for the *In Search of Relics* exhibition. She re-photographed some of the objects for this catalogue and digitally enhanced photographs not taken by professional photographers. She also laid out the initial design for the catalogue before leaving to pursue other interests. Design student Scott Ure, whose design talents were already memorialized in the Museum's last catalogue, *Of Earth, Stone, and Corn*, ably picked up where Stevens left off and is chiefly responsible for the present catalogue design and the digitally enhanced images. The project greatly benefited from his thoughtful advice on graphic presentation and its impact on thematic objectives. Student Office Assistant Heidi Livingstone was instrumental in implementing Nelson's promotional and educational agendas, earning a promotion to Promotion Manager in the process. MPC Student Aides Corinda Kelly and Camille Jolley as well as MPC Volunteer Christine Merrill contributed significant energies to the installation and associated collections management activities. Student Office Manager Michael Rasband and his summer relief Mike Khron kept the office afloat while Allen and Nelson threw themselves into the Pectol Project full time.

The Museum is indebted to Neal Portman Busk and all the members of the E. P. and Dorothy Hickman Pectol Family Organization for generously lending the Pectol-Lee collection to the Museum for research, publication, and exhibition. Their desire to share this important collection with students, researchers, and the general public made this project possible and, indeed, inspired it from beginning to end. Neal Busk was particularly responsive to the project's need for documentation from Ephraim Pectol's personal correspondence.

Finally, I wish to acknowledge Gary Hooper, Associate Academic Vice President for Research and Graduate Studies and author of the Environments for Mentoring Program, for his support of the Museum in this and other endeavors. The Museum endorses Hooper's mentoring ideals in spirit and action and is privileged to have been among the pilot projects of this commendable mentoring program. The Museum thanks the BYU Office of Research and Creative Activities for funding this project, including the majority of the printing costs. The Museum also gratefully acknowledges the Utah Office of Museum Services which provided additional funding for design and printing.

Marti L. Allen

INTRODUCTORY REMARKS: ON THE ETHICS OF STUDYING UNPROVENIENCED COLLECTIONS

Both *Relics Revisited* and its accompanying exhibition *In Search of Relics* touch upon an issue that may cause archaeologists, Native Americans, and indeed many people to bristle with discomfort. The Pectol-Lee collection was amassed during the era of so-called "cowboy archaeology," when artifacts representing the rich native cultures of the American West were extracted from lands by people having little or no knowledge of scientific methodology and even less appreciation for the feelings of living native peoples who feel culturally or spiritually symbiotic with these lands.

From the 1880s through the first several decades of the twentieth century, there was a great interest on the part of Euroamericans living in the American West to amass "relics," that is, souvenirs and artifacts perceived as tokens or even oddities of Native American peoples about whom they understood very little. Early Mormon settlers in particular saw native cultures through the unique lens of their faith, which finds connections between native cultures of the New World and the restored gospel of Jesus Christ as recorded in the *Book of Mormon*. It is evident in the writings of Ephraim Pectol that he, Charles Lee, and others in their circle were in part motivated to collect because they perceived native artifacts as demonstrative of these beliefs.

Regrettably, collecting practices of the late nineteenth and early twentieth centuries ran contrary to the type of scientific investigative techniques that have today become standard and are governed by law on public lands. Modern techniques of excavation provide a means of discriminating between layers or *strata* of earth that preserve discrete pockets of culturally and chronologically significant information. These techniques enable trained archaeologists to maintain an association between these layers and the artifacts retrieved from them. Thus, earth and artifacts removed from a pit or post hole are kept discrete from soils taken from an adjacent hearth or mud surface. Scientific excavations are typically conducted slowly and methodically, using trowels, spoons, brushes, and even dental instruments to prevent loss of critical evidence. Earth is screened through a mesh to recover tiny artifacts such as bone fragments and pieces of pottery, and samples of soil are floated in water to separate pollen and other microbotanicals from "just plain dirt," thereby enabling reconstruction of prehistoric environment. Even garbage dumps and human fecal materials can yield important information about daily life in prehistoric times and about the diet and health of the people. Radiocarbon dating and dendrochronology (counting and overlapping series of tree-rings)—especially when combined with stylistic analysis of the artifacts themselves—help archaeologists understand prehistoric time depth and interrelate information from geographically disparate sites. When archaeological sites are disturbed without the benefit of these painstaking and exacting methodologies, critical information is lost forever, and all of humanity loses a part of its collective past.

Today, moreover, federal law recognizes native interest in prehistoric material culture and sets forth procedures ensuring equitable consideration of native rights and "ownership" of native culture. The Native American Graves Protection and Repatriation Act of 1990 is the landmark legislation in this regard. NAGPRA not only requires archaeologists to consult with appropriate Native American groups when burials are encountered during excavation, but also provides for the repatriation or return of Native American human remains, funerary goods, and sacred and patrimonial items from federally funded museums. By raising the issue of who owns the past, this legislation is helping people understand that the past belongs to all humankind, and that every people's perspective on the past is valid and even critical to understanding it.

Thus, like many other collections amassed during the era of "cowboy archaeology," the Pectol-Lee collection survives today as an anachronism, reflecting archaeological practices and societal sentiments that are incongruous with the present. They sorely remind us how much precious knowledge has been irrevocably lost as a result of unscientific practices and confirm our desires to reform scientific ethics such that all peoples and all cultures have a meaningful role in the making of knowledge as well as a shared future in this land.

Despite the questionable methods by which the Pectol-Lee artifacts and other collections like it were amassed, the scientist still feels compelled to recapture as much information as possible from these contextually disassociated objects, and it is possible to do so. The Pectol-Lee collection includes some of the most fascinating artifacts ever recovered in Utah, such as a deer headdress from a late prehistoric hunting costume (cat. no. 71) and a one-of-a-kind cradle board nestling a remarkable Fremont figurine (cat. no. 61). [The famous hide shields were unavailable to the project for study due to a desire on the part of Capitol Reef National Park to respect the wishes of native groups pursuant to NAGPRA.] *Relics Revisited* also highlights new findings about Fremont basket-decorating and sheds light on a region in Utah with a rich multicultural prehistory. The catalogue not only presents new information but addresses academic concepts that both place the Pectol-Lee artifacts in context and contribute to our understanding of the Capitol Reef region and its history.

The Pectol-Lee collection is only one of many such collections that languish understudied and unappreciated in museums and private collections. Hiding these collections from view does not correct the errors of the past; but perhaps revisiting these artifacts, as we have attempted to do in this volume, will both fill gaps in our knowledge and help repair feelings among the many people who have mutual interests in them.

Marti L. Allen, Director
Mauri L. Nelson, Assistant Curator of Education
Museum of Peoples and Cultures

DATES USED IN THIS CATALOGUE:

Archaic	8000 BC–AD 1
Prehistoric	before 17th century AD
Agricultural Period [Does not distinguish between Anasazi and Fremont]	AD 1–1300
Anasazi	AD 1–1300
Fremont	AD 400–1300
Late Prehistoric	ca. AD 1250–1750
Numic	ca. AD 1250–1880
Historic	AD 1750–1900

IN SEARCH OF THE ANCIENT UTAHNS: THE PREHISTORY OF THE FREMONT RIVER DRAINAGE, AD 1–1800

Richard K. Talbot

> The work of July and August 1928 revealed an unexpected and interesting situation. To the southeast of the district under examination, across the Colorado River in San Juan County, a rich series of remains had long been known, ranging from the classic Basketmaker II sites of Grand Gulch to ruins of the Mesa Verde period. To the west, the explorations of Judd had also established the presence of a definitely Puebloan culture, while Nusbaum as well as Judd had found typical Basketmaker II remains. Consequently, we had every reason to believe that any remains found by us would fall readily into the established sequence of Southwestern cultures with only minor local variations. Quite to the contrary, the Fremont drainage proved to be the seat of a distinctive culture, to which nearly all the local remains are to be assigned. This culture was characterized by cave sites with a slab cist architecture similar to that of the Basketmaker and Pueblo I periods; by a distinctive unpainted black or gray pottery; by the exclusive use of a unique type of moccasin; by a cult of unbaked clay figurines obviously related to, but more elaborate than Basketmaker III figurines; by abundant pictographs of distinctive types; and by a number of minor features which tended to identify it as a Southwestern culture on approximately a Basketmaker III level, but which showed consistently a degree of divergence from corresponding features of orthodox cultures. The presence of small amounts of black-on-white and corrugated pottery, with other evidence, showed that this complex was contemporary with Pueblo II in other regions.[1]
>
> —Noel Morss 1931

Indeed, the Fremont River drainage *was* the seat of a distinctive archaeological culture, the remains of which from that point forward would be referred to as “Fremont.” Unwittingly, Morss gave name to a set of attributes in material remains and architecture now recognized throughout most of present-day Utah and into surrounding states. The name in essence defines an archaeological “tradition,” or a recognizably distinct lifeway that was practiced for a particular period of time and within a particular region. In this paper, the Fremont tradition refers to a lifeway practiced by people living north of the Colorado River whose archaeological remains date to about AD 1–1300 and who farmed as their primary subsistence strategy. This time period is referred to in this article as the Agricultural Period.

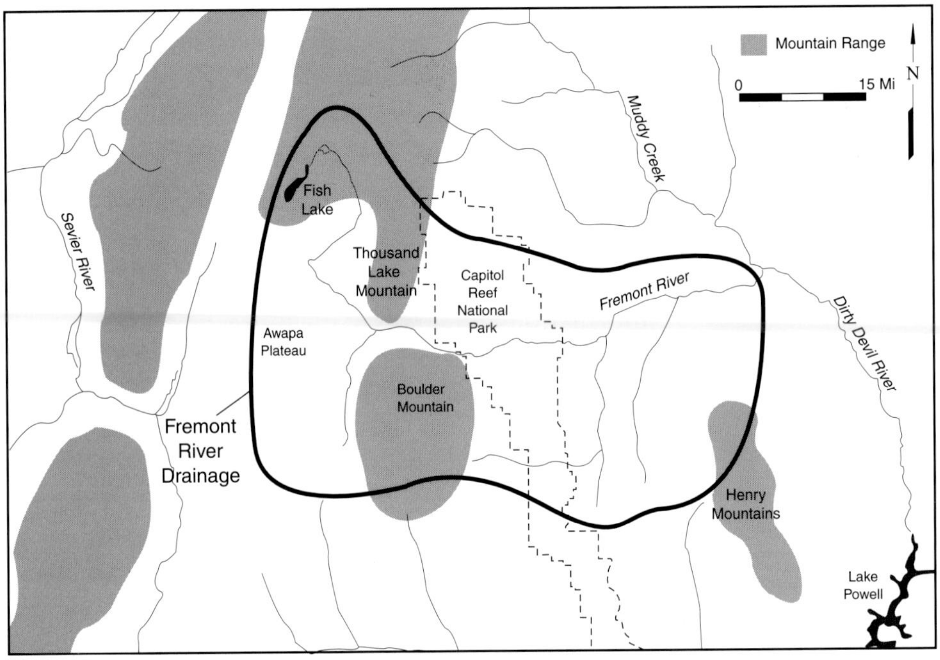

Figure 1. Map of the Fremont River drainage. Produced by Debbie Silversmith, 2001.

We can expect variability in the lives of farmers spread over such a wide physiographic area and over such a great expanse of time. Yet, as Morss recognized, if we look beyond these expected individualities, farming and other commonalities in Fremont remains over this vast area imply shared beliefs, traditions, and in a very broad sense, cultural identity.[2] Indeed, since prehistoric times, the Fremont River drainage, where the Fremont tradition was first defined, was a region of very significant cross-cultural activity. It is somewhat ironic then, that the prehistory of this area remains comparatively obscure.

At the same time Fremont groups occupied the Fremont River drainage, Anasazi farmers inhabited areas to the south.[3] The Anasazi tradition is archaeologically distinct from that of the Fremont, both in material remains and architecture. While neighboring Fremont and Anasazi farmers might have used the same types of plants, chosen similar rock sources, or used the bones from the same kinds of animals to make similarly functioning tools, their methods of construction often varied. Specialists are often able to distinguish Fremont and Anasazi artifacts such as pottery by studying the method of construction. However, other types of artifacts are more difficult to assign to a specific time period or tradition. For example, certain tools used by both Fremont and Anasazi farmers (e.g., forms of groundstone, certain bone instruments, and perishable wood objects) are stylistically and functionally generalized and display no significant variability. In such cases, it is difficult to determine cultural affiliation.

In the case of the Pectol-Lee collection, the challenge of determining cultural affiliation presents itself: are the artifacts Fremont or Anasazi? It has sometimes been assumed that the artifacts were mostly Fremont, owing to the fact that they are said to have been found in the Capitol Reef region, where Morss first defined the Fremont tradition. In fact, however, the artifacts lack specific provenience; that is, we have no precise information about where the artifacts were found or about their context or association with features or other artifacts. The artifacts comprising the Pectol-Lee collection date primarily to the Agricultural Period, and many of the artifacts display styles or characteristics that are definitively Fremont in origin, but in several cases it is not possible to distinguish whether some of the Pectol-Lee artifacts are Anasazi or Fremont.

In addition, the collection includes artifacts that post-date the Fremont and Anasazi occupations and are characteristic of Southern Paiute or Ute populations who inhabited the region after the Fremont. Some technologies and many kinds of material culture persisted for thousands of years right up to the ethnographic present. The collection's broader temporal affiliation, then, involves the Fremont/Anasazi occupation during the Agricultural Period as well as the Southern Paiute or Ute occupations during the Late Prehistoric Period.

Also complicating interpretation is the potential for prehistoric regional interaction. Were the Pectol-Lee artifacts made or obtained locally, or were they traded in? What about the modern history of the collection? Oral traditions among the collectors and their families hold that the artifacts were collected within the Fremont River drainage, but can this be confirmed; or is it possible Ephraim Pectol, Charles Lee, or their family members augmented the collection from other sources?

It is not surprising to find researchers scratching their heads in confusion. One of the objectives of this volume is to help sort out these questions through a careful study of the artifacts against the backdrop of the Fremont River drainage culture history. The overview presented below provides a summary of Fremont River drainage occupation from the Archaic Period to the present and serves as a cultural-historical framework for the Pectol-Lee artifacts.

THE ARCHAIC PREFACE: 10,000 BC–AD 1

The culture history of the Fremont River drainage does not begin with the Agricultural Period. For approximately ten millennia before that time mobile hunters and gatherers roamed the landscape. The early part of that period was very wet and favorable for big game and plant resources. However, through time the climate shifted toward warmer and dryer conditions, and resource exploitation patterns changed accordingly.

The earliest residents, typically referred to as Paleoindians or Paleoamericans, are least represented in the archaeological record. They are recognized by their distinctive styles of large, fluted projectile points, known as Clovis and Folsom points, and hence are often described as having been primarily hunters of large beasts, such as the wooly mammoth and other megafauna. This may be an over-generalization, since so little is known about these earliest lifeways. For example, none of the Paleoamerican sites on the northern Colorado Plateau or eastern Great Basin have revealed any direct evidence of economic strategies,[4] although the settings where some are found suggest both plant and animal resources may have been exploited.[5] The spatial distribution across the plateau of large animal remains and sites with fluted points suggested to Alan Schroedl that big game hunting initially was focused along the lower water courses, and that this strategy eventually spread to and persisted in the higher elevations, "while an Archaic lifeway . . . [was] evolving in the lowland canyon environments on the central Colorado Plateau."[6]

The next cultures established in the archaeological record are identified as people of the Archaic Period. The transition to an Archaic lifeway involved a broadening or generalizing of the economic strategy to include more varieties of plants and smaller game and occurred roughly about 8,000 years ago. Certainly it was a gradual transition, probably involving relative shifts in diet through time as environmental and social contexts changed. With a few exceptions, Archaic populations thereafter were probably not tied to any one ecosystem.[7] Through time, however, population increases and environmental stress undoubtedly affected the movement and strategy choices of hunter-gatherers. Tool kits were adjusted as needed. Projectile point styles and technology changed considerably through time. Atlatls (wooden spear throwers), as well as composite cane and hardwood shafts tipped with large stone dart points were used throughout the period. Other tools characteristic of the Archaic period include basketry, snares, netting, flat milling stones, digging sticks, curved wooden clubs, various bone tools, etc. People wore hide moccasins, fiber sandals, and furs. In addition, shells from the California coast were used in necklaces and as earrings. With the exception of stone tools, the majority of these remains have been best preserved in various cave deposits throughout the region, including Sudden Shelter to the north of the Fremont River,[8] Cowboy Cave to the east,[9] and Sand Dune Cave, Dust Devil Cave,[10] and Broken Arrow Cave to the south.[11]

Figure 2. View of the lower Fremont River drainage, looking east from Boulder Mountain. Capitol Reef National Park is in the middle of the photo, and the northern end of the Henry Mountains is in the distance, to the right. MPC photo archives.

In the Fremont River drainage, Archaic sites abound. Because Archaic peoples were transitory, the sites typically yield discard associated with short-term hunting or camping episodes, such as a few atlatl dart points or other bifacial tools that were broken while being made or refitted; an occasional piece of groundstone broken or otherwise left in place; and, of course, stone flakes in various stages, colors, and material, including mostly cherts, some quartzite, and occasional obsidian. Often the remains of hearths or small, temporary pole houses survive. Within these features, bone, seed, and pollen remains can be found, suggesting a variety of foods in the Archaic diet. Faunal studies show exploitation of just about every kind of animal of both significant and insignificant size. Small mammals such as rabbits were most commonly taken, but deer, mountain sheep, and other larger game were also exploited. Grasses, goosefoot, cactus, and sunflower predominate among plant remains. Obviously, Archaic peoples were skilled at exploiting any and all resources available to them. Still, as early as 300 BC and certainly by AD 1, a significant change occurred in the economic strategy of peoples living in the Fremont River Basin and elsewhere on the northern Colorado Plateau and eastern Great Basin. The change may have been inevitable, given similar changes occurring to the south. In any case, within a very short time, ten thousand years of hunting and gathering gave way to a lifeway focused on an important new food source—corn.

THE AGRICULTURAL PERIOD: AD 1–1300 (FREMONT TRADITION)

No single event had a greater long-term impact on Southwest prehistory than the arrival from the south of corn and its associated technologies. The mode and timing of this strategy shift are still in debate, but increasingly archaeologists are finding greater time depth to the earliest Southwest farming, on the order of 1000–2000 BC.[12] Currently, however, the earliest corn north of the Colorado River, found in Central Utah, is dated around AD 1.[13] Thereafter, the distinct tradition Morss called "Fremont" took form throughout central and northern Utah and vicinity. One of the most direct routes by which agriculture could have spread is through the Fremont River drainage.

Archaeologists long assumed that native Archaic Period groups learned to farm and obtained the initial corn seed from their Anasazi neighbors to the south. Dates from corn at various sites, including Cowboy Cave, fall into the AD 300–500 period, with ceramics also appearing in the archaeological record during the latter part of this period. Smiley recently developed a simulation for the diffusion of farming across large territories, suggesting the spread of technology and knowledge would be much more rapid than that associated with the creeping movement of an agricultural frontier (e.g., farmers gradually expanding their territory).[14] While this may be true at certain times and in particular situations across the American Southwest, recent DNA evidence from the Fremont region suggests it was people, and not just ideas, that were moving northward.[15] Other studies indicate that these people very likely were corn reliant at the time of their move and thereby quickened the spread of the strategy in their new locations.[16] More likely, then, small groups of early Anasazi farmers probably spread rapidly across the northern Colorado Plateau, settling in locations where conditions for agriculture were most favorable.[17]

A northward movement of farmers would explain much about the subsequent development of Fremont culture history. The increase in distance between these earliest farmers and their traditional homelands to the south would have encouraged greater interaction and development of traditions at the local level. Farming groups to the south became increasingly regionalized into what we now recognize as the major Southwest cultural traditions (Anasazi, Hohokam, Mogollon).[18] Similarly, the farmers north of the Colorado River, now falling under the Fremont label, would have developed regional characteristics. Hence, the cultural traits that Morss laid out as characteristic of the Fremont indeed separate these northern farmers from contemporary Anasazi.

From the beginning Fremont farmers seem to have favored certain areas more than others. These areas were on or near alluvial fans, where mountain streams emptying into warm valleys could be used to water cornfields and where access to both lowland and upland resources was good. The more fertile valleys of the Colorado Plateau/Great Basin transition zone were initially occupied by small, probably extended family groups, then later by larger populations living in small villages of 50–100 or more people. These were not large populations compared to the other contemporaneous Southwest traditions. In fact, the Fremont never had large, socially complex pueblos like those that developed to the south. Rather, small sites with pithouses, that is, houses constructed partially below the ground (Figure 3), were the norm during the early centuries of the Agricultural Period. These small sites gave way to villages in the AD 1200s, but pithouses remained the primary habitation features. Interestingly, while in most parts of Utah the Fremont were experienced in the use of adobe in their architecture, in some parts of the Colorado Plateau, including the Fremont River drainage, rocks were commonly used to line pithouses, and actual stone masonry is often found in certain types of surface habitations and in some storage structures.

Farming populations in the Fremont River drainage never achieved the significant levels common in the west and north. Residential sites tended to be small, consisting of one to five pithouses along with various other features but, interestingly, usually lacking the kinds of surface storage structures common at larger Fremont sites elsewhere. However, the general characteristics of Fremont settlement and subsistence strategies were the same. The Waterpocket Fold within Capitol Reef National Park is a transition zone between mountain and desert that was a particularly favored settlement location.[19] Sufficiently low in elevation, it accommodated the long growing season necessary for domesticated plants such as corn, beans and squash. In addition, many small drainages coming off Boulder and Thousand Lakes Mountains cut through the Fold and converge with the Fremont River, thus providing numerous choice locations for small-scale settlement. Resources in this lower pinyon-juniper-sage setting are abundant. From these locations the forested slopes of the mountains, with their many plant and animal resources, are easily accessible in the warmer months. To the east the Henry Mountains provide similar resources, though at a slightly farther distance. To the south, accessible through various drainages, are the canyons of the Colorado River, where additional resources are available.

The need to plant, tend, and ultimately harvest crops required that farmers live in one settlement at least for the growing season, perhaps six months of the year. This does not mean, however, that part of the population could not design special hunting or gathering trips away from the residence to collect plants that came in season at different times of the year, or take animals when and as they became available. Consequently, small campsites dating to the Agricultural Period (Figures 4–5) are

Figure 3. A rock-lined Fremont pithouse near Pleasant Creek, just east of Capitol Reef National Park. MPC photo archives.

common in the Fremont River drainage and are similar in many respects to Archaic Period sites. Still, throughout the Southwest (including the Fremont region) after the initial Basketmaker Period spread of agriculture, environmental conditions tended to deteriorate through the centuries, culminating in a significant large-scale drought in the late AD 1200s.[20] Throughout this time, the commitment of all Southwestern farming groups to farming intensified, with diets increasingly reliant upon domesticated plants. The Fremont River drainage farmers probably followed suit, but undoubtedly they also intensified efforts to exploit the local wild resources.

The Fremont artifact assemblage was rich in both perishable and non-perishable materials.[21] In rare cases some perishables have survived the centuries, primarily those left in well-sheltered caves and other dry, protected locations, and occasionally some of those make their way into the hands of archaeologists. Consequently, we know that Fremont single-rod-and-bundle basketry was common (e.g., cat. nos. 28–36). Artifacts constructed from grasses, reeds, hide (e.g., cat. nos. 129, 147–149), wood (e.g., cat. nos. 101–103), feathers, fur, and even human hair have been found.

One of the most important technological improvements during the Agricultural Period was the bow and arrow (e.g., cat. nos. 88–91). This weapon appeared in the Fremont area in the second or third century AD, replacing the well established atlatl technology with a more reliable, more

Figure 4. A seasonal Fremont campsite near Fish Lake near the head of the Fremont River, at an elevation of ca. 9000 ft. MPC photo archives.

accurate means of bringing down game, particularly small game. Pottery technology likewise contributed significantly to the artifact assemblage, though Fremont pottery production never reached the technological complexity or artistic caliber of other Southwest groups. Fremont pottery ranged from gray wares (e.g., cat. nos. 80–82), sometimes with unique forms of incising, punctate, and appliqué (including a "coffee bean" appliqué), to increasingly complex black-on-gray designs. Of course, perhaps the most commonly recognized, though rare, Fremont artifacts are unique figurines hand-modeled from clay and baked in the sun (e.g., cat. nos. 61, 65–70). Another well known Fremont artifact is the "Utah-type" metate, a trough metate or grinding stone with a secondary depression or shelf on one end. Finally, the Fremont use of deer skin moccasins contrasts with the fiber sandals common elsewhere in the Southwest.

Rock art is abundant throughout the Fremont River drainage, but in particular along some of the watercourses that have cut deep canyons through the Waterpocket Fold, such as the Fremont River (Figure 6), Pleasant Creek, and Capitol Gorge. To the north, an intriguing concentration of rock art is found among high sandstone monoliths on the east side of Thousand Lakes Mountain. In general, Fremont rock art throughout this region depicts elements highly suggestive of both the supernatural and the everyday, including scenes of deer and mountain sheep, bird-like figures, corn stalks, landscapes, and a variety of linear

Figure 5. A deep shelter in Capitol Reef National Park used by Fremont and other prehistoric groups for short-term camping. MPC photo archives.

and geometric designs. However, the most distinctive are trapezoidal human figures, often elaborately dressed, that parallel the classic styles of Fremont triangular-bodied figurines.

As mentioned, the genetic roots of the Fremont appear to lie at least in part within Puebloan groups to the south, so we should not be surprised to find important relationships between later Fremont and Anasazi farmers. In fact, the northern reaches of Anasazi settlement stretch into the southern portions of the Fremont River drainage. The most obvious, large scale intrusions are located at the well known Coombs Village site at Boulder, Utah, and at the Lampstand Ruins site at the northern end of the Circle Cliffs, both of which lie just outside the boundary of the Fremont River drainage, but well within the Fremont cultural sphere. Small Anasazi sites are scattered throughout the region of the Escalante River and Halls Creek drainages, which border the Fremont River drainage on the south. A few Anasazi sites, mostly small camp sites, but with some small residential sites as well, are found just south of the Fremont River. To the east, significant Anasazi influence is also seen at the Bull Creek sites at the northern base of the Henry Mountains.[22]

The exact nature of the Fremont-Anasazi relationship is still unclear. The presence of some decorative Anasazi ceramics at numerous sites within the southern Fremont area, including the Fremont River drainage, suggests the northward trade of those wares. Turquoise from mines in

Figure 6. Fremont rock art located near the Fremont River, in Capitol Reef National Park. MPC photo archives.

New Mexico, Arizona, and Nevada is also known to have been a desired trade item, along with shell from both the Pacific and Caribbean coasts. What items were moving southward from the Fremont is as yet unclear. Rich obsidian sources in Utah may have been an attractive resource. Most likely, however, the exchange of perishable materials such as foodstuffs and plant or animal materials, either in raw form or as constructed artifacts, constituted the bulk of cross-cultural exchange. Certainly within the Fremont River drainage and other areas where Anasazi and Fremont groups were in close proximity, the period after about AD 1000 was one of considerable contact, and there was probably significant movement of peoples across blurred cultural boundaries.[23]

The Fremont tradition generally disappeared from the archaeological record between AD 1300 and 1400, except in a small pocket in northwestern Colorado where some farming continued. Despite, or perhaps in part because of, parallel economic strategies, similar cultural trajectories, and even genetic roots (and therefore possibly perceived kinship ties), both Fremont and Anasazi farmers were probably impacted by events beyond their control. Primary among these were changes in the environment, such as a shift in the regional rainfall pattern that provided less water during the critical growing season, and a general decrease in annual precipitation culminating in an extended drought period in the late AD 1200s. In response to these changes and the resultant competition for increasingly scarce resources by growing populations, peoples to the north and south of the Fremont River drainage tended to congregate in larger communities, relying on group cooperation to stretch the strained resources as far as possible. Such large communities, for the most part, did not occur among Fremont River drainage farmers, so population pressure was probably less a contributing factor than the environmental shifts themselves. The prolonged drought may have been the final straw that brought the Agricultural Period to a halt. By the mid-AD 1300s, very few farmers remained in Utah. Many probably moved elsewhere in search of more favorable farming locations. Others may have reverted to a hunter-gatherer economy, joining groups of non-farmers who appear to have spread across the lands formerly inhabited by the farmers.

THE LATE PREHISTORIC AND EARLY HISTORIC PERIOD: AD 1300–1800 (UTE AND PAIUTE TRADITIONS)

The ancestors of the historic Southern Paiute and Ute may have begun to move into the region from the west and south as early as AD 1000.[24] These hunter-gatherers were efficient at exploiting the wide range of wild resources across the northern Colorado Plateau and often times were probably in direct competition with farmers for those resources. The abandonment of farming and probable depopulation that ensued left a void that was quickly filled by these groups.

The Fremont River drainage seems to have attracted relatively small numbers of hunter-gatherers. When found, their sites are typically small, often exhibiting small hearths or other evidence of overnight camping, but sometimes with evidence of larger features such as wickiups or roasting pits. Material remains are most commonly limited to flaked stone debris, including small arrow points; brown ware pottery; and open and close twined, usually multiple-rod basketry (e.g., cat. no. 50). Dry caves have sometimes yielded perishable materials from Late Prehistoric context, including some described in this volume (e.g., cat. no. 71), but these types of remains are relatively rare. Oral tradition suggests the best known of these, the Pectol-Lee shields, probably came from the Fremont River drainage (see Baker, pp. 21 and 28, this volume). Their cultural attribution, however, is as yet not definitive.[25]

Of major regional importance to native Plains and Great Basin cultures was the arrival of the horse sometime before AD 1700. For example, the Comanche quickly adopted the new mode of transportation. During the 1700s, the Comanche left western Wyoming after acquiring the horse and pursued buffalo onto the Great Plains.[26] The Utes adopted the horse as well but remained in their original territory.

Aboriginal occupation of the Fremont River drainage at the time of first Spanish and then later European intrusion included both Ute and Southern Paiute groups. Thus, understanding the history of these two groups is important to discerning precontact patterns. Both groups speak a form of Southern Numic of the Uto-Aztecan linguistic family.[27] Maps defining the distribution of Ute and Southern Paiute groups place most of the drainage within lands traditionally occupied by the Ute.[28] However, Southern Paiute ethnographies[29] and ethnohistory[30] indicate use of this general region by those groups as well, and the boundary between the two tended to be hazy. In addition, there is limited evidence for possible Navajo visits to the area.[31]

Like their ancestors, the Ute and most of the Southern Paiute were hunter-gatherers who ranged seasonally over established territories collecting wild plants and hunting various large and small animals. In the Fremont River drainage, Koosharem band Paiute groups apparently moved seasonally between Loa (winter), Fish Lake (late spring-summer), and Boulder Mountain (fall).[32] Kelly reports Paiute hunting on the Aquarius Plateau during the fall.[33] Movement was difficult in parts of the Fremont River drainage, however, and in particular through the Waterpocket Fold because of the rugged terrain. For this reason watercourses were probably the most commonly used routes. Little is known of the Ute population movements and subsistence strategies in the Fremont River drainage, but overall regional populations of both Ute and Southern Paiute were generally sparse, and Kelly has suggested occupation of the Circle Cliffs area (on the southern border of the Fremont River drainage) by just a "few families."[34]

The encroachment of Euroamerican settlers in the 1800s had a profound effect on the Southern Paiute and Ute groups throughout the Fremont River drainage and elsewhere. Traditional lands and, in particular, those with water sources and other conditions favorable to agriculture, were taken over by the settlers. Native Americans, restricted or denied access to those traditional lands, were forced to settle both on and off reservations and to make the radical shift from a hunter-gatherer to a market economy, a transition that was devastating to the people and the culture.

THE PECTOL COLLECTION IN PREHISTORIC CONTEXT

The overview of Fremont River drainage occupation given above provides a cultural-historical framework for the Pectol-Lee collection. Obviously the question of provenience is paramount to interpreting and contextualizing the collections, and the inadequate or conflicting records of artifact provenience (see Baker, p. 21, this volume) are not encouraging. On the other hand, clearly many of the artifacts are typologically (and, for the dated items, chronologically) consistent with Fremont, Anasazi, or one of the Late Prehistoric groups. Thus, while the physical context is lost, the hope is that some degree of meaning can be assigned to, and knowledge obtained from, the artifacts relative to their prehistoric context. That is one goal of this volume.

Any reconstruction of prehistory based on limited data sets must necessarily be simple, but an important value of the Pectol-Lee collection is that it includes perishable materials that normally do not survive the ravages of time. Since archaeologists must assume that the non-perishable artifacts they normally recover are but a fraction of a much broader range of material culture, the artifacts from Pectol collection—especially the perishable ones—help fill a very broad gap in our knowledge of this intriguing region of prehistoric Utah.

1. Noel Morss, *The Ancient Culture of the Fremont River in Utah*, Papers of the Peabody Museum of American Archaeology and Ethnology, vol. 12, no. 3 (Harvard University: Cambridge, 1931).

2. This definition differs somewhat from that recently offered by David B. Madsen and Steven R. Simms, "The Fremont Complex: A Behavioral Perspective," *Journal of World Prehistory*, vol. 12, no. 3 (1998): 255–336. They see the Fremont as encompassing a much broader "complex" of subsistence strategies that allows for a diversity of options, such that some may be much more intensive farmers than others, while some may not farm at all. As conditions change, some farmers may choose to opt out of farming in favor of hunting-gathering, and vice versa. The definition views prehistoric people from the individual or small group decision-making level, and in that sense archaeological labels such as "Fremont" falsely portray unity or commonalities Madsen and Simms do not believe existed.

3. Some Native American groups find the term "Anasazi" offensive, and archaeologists have begun to use "Ancestral Pueblo" or other designators, often names selected by particular Native American groups. However, for decades before the age of political correctness, "Anasazi" was used by archaeologists as a convenient and completely unbiased descriptor, and that function and intent are followed here. It should also be emphasized that terms used in this text, including Paleoamerican, Archaic, Fremont, Anasazi, and Late Prehistoric are used solely as abbreviated forms describing the archaeological traditions or time periods of the same name, and not as identifiers of ethnicity. The latter is very difficult if not impossible to tease out of the archaeological record.

4. Various site specific reports describe Paleoamerican finds in Utah. The majority of these are summarized by James M. Copeland and Richard E. Fike, "Fluted Projectile Points in Utah," *Utah Archaeology 1988*, vol. 1, no. 1 (1988): 5–28; and by Alan R. Schroedl, "Paleo-Indian Occupation in the Eastern Great Basin and Northern Colorado Plateau," *Utah Archaeology 1991*, vol. 4, no. 1 (1991): 1–15. A more recently excavated site is reported by William E. Davis, Dorothy Sack, and Nancy Shearin, "The Hell'N Moriah Clovis Site," *Utah Archaeology 1996*, vol. 9, no. 1 (1996): 55–70.

5. See especially Davis et al, "Hell'N Moriah Clovis Site."

6. Schroedl, "Paleo-Indian Occupation," 11.

7. Jesse D. Jennings, *Prehistory of North America*, 2nd ed. (New York: McGraw-Hill, 1974), 129.

8. Jesse D. Jennings, Alan R. Schroedl, and Richard N. Holmer, *Sudden Shelter*, Anthropological Papers No. 103 (Salt Lake City: University of Utah, 1980).

9. Jennings et al, *Sudden Shelter*.

10. Alexander J. Lindsay, Jr., J. Richard Ambler, Mary Anne Stein, and Philip M. Hobler, "Survey and Excavation North and East of Navajo Mountain, Utah, 1959–1962," *Museum of Northern Arizona Bulletin*, No. 45 (Flagstaff, 1968).

11. Richard K. Talbot, Lane D. Richens, Shane A. Baker, and Joel C. Janetski, *Broken Arrow Cave (42Ka4356): 1997 Testing Results*, Museum of Peoples and Cultures Technical Series No. 99-5 (Provo, Utah: Brigham Young University, 1999).

12. For a recent review on the dating of Southwest maize, see Francis E. Smiley and Michael R. Robins, eds., *Early Farmers in the Northern Southwest: Papers on Chronometry, Social Dynamics, and Ecology*, Animas-La Plata Archaeological Project Research Paper No. 7 (Flagstaff: Bureau of Reclamation, 1997).

13. For discussions of the antiquity of corn north of the Colorado River, see Richard K. Talbot and Lane D. Richens, *Steinaker Gap: An Early Fremont Farmstead*, Museum of Peoples and Cultures Occasional Papers No. 2 (Provo, Utah: Brigham Young University, 1996).

14. Smiley and Robins, eds., *Early Farmers in the Northern Southwest.*

15. Several recent descriptions of DNA studies relevant to both Fremont and Anasazi populations have become available. A summary is provided by Dennis H. O'Rourke, M. Geoffrey Hayes, and Shawn W. Carlyle, "Ancient DNA Studies in Physical Anthropology," *Annual Review of Anthropology* 29 (2000): 217–242; and a more detailed description of the results is given by Dennis H. O'Rourke, Ryan L. Parr, and Shawn W. Carlyle, "Molecular Genetic Variation in Prehistoric Inhabitants of the Eastern Great Basin," in *Understanding Prehistoric Lifeways in the Great Basin Wetlands: Bioarchaeological Reconstruction and Interpretation*, eds. B. E. Hemphill and C. S. Larsen (Salt Lake City: University of Utah Press, 1999), 84–102.

16. See in particular the recent work of Joan Brenner Coltrain, "Fremont Foragers and Farmers: A Stable Carbon Isotope Study" (paper presented at the 24th Great Basin Anthropological Conference, Elko, Nevada, 1994); and *idem*, "Stable Carbon and Radioisotope Analyses," in Talbot and Richens, *Steinaker Gap*, 115–122.

17. The concept of micro-migrations is summarized by Richard K. Talbot in "Fremont Farmers: The Search for Context," in *The Archaeology of Regional Interaction: Religion, Warfare, and Exchange Across the American Southwest and Beyond*, ed. Michelle Hegmon (Boulder, Colo.: University Press, 2000), 275–293.

18. Jonathan Haas, Edmund J. Ladd, Jerrold E. Levy, Randall H. McGuire, and Norman Yoffee, "Historical Processes in the Prehistoric Southwest," in *Understanding Complexity in the Prehistoric Southwest,*

eds. G. J. Gumerman and M. Gell-Mann, SFI Studies in the Sciences of Complexity, Proceedings Volume 16 (Reading, Mass.: Addison-Wesley, 1994), 210.

19. Joel C. Janetski and Lee Kreutzer, "Contrasts in Forager and Farmer Land Use Along the Waterpocket Fold, Capitol Reef National Park" (paper presented at the 62nd Annual Conference, Society for American Archaeology, Nashville, Tennessee, 1997).

20. Kenneth Lee Peterson, *Climate and the Delores River Anasazi,* Anthropological Papers No. 113 (Salt Lake City: University of Utah, 1988).

21. James H. Gunnerson, *The Fremont Culture: A Study in Culture Dynamics on the Northern Anasazi Frontier*, Papers of the Peabody Museum of Archaeology and Ethnology, vol. 59, no. 2 (Cambridge: Harvard University Press, 1969) provides an excellent summary of Fremont material culture.

22. Jesse D. Jennings and Dorothy Sammons-Lohse, *Bull Creek*, Anthropological Papers No. 105 (Salt Lake City: University of Utah, 1981). The Bull Creek sites remain unique in the archaeological literature with significant quantities of both Fremont and Anasazi material culture, as well as architectural styles that could be argued to represent influence from both groups.

23. Phil R. Geib, *Glen Canyon Revisited*, Anthropological Papers No. 119 (Salt Lake City: University of Utah, 1996).

24. A thorough consideration of the movement of Late Prehistoric groups can be found in David B. Madsen and David Rhode, eds., *Across the West: Human Population Movement and the Expansion of the Numa* (Salt Lake City: University of Utah Press, 1994).

25. Lee Ann Kreutzer, "The Pectol Collection, Capitol Reef National Park, Utah," *Utah Archaeology 1994*, vol. 7, no. 1 (1994): 104–116, gives a thorough summary of the shields, as well as the other artifacts in the collection. See also Benson Lanford and Pamela Miller, "Late Prehistoric Painted Rawhide and Leather Artifacts from Utah," *American Indian Art Magazine*, Summer (2000): 38–47. The Hopi and the Navajo are among the present-day tribes laying claim to the shields through the Native American Graves Protection and Repatriation Act on the basis of oral tradition.

26. Wick R. Miller, "Numic Languages," in *Great Basin,* ed. Warren L. d'Azevedo, vol. 11, *Handbook of North American Indians*, ed. William C. Sturtevant (Washington, D.C.: Smithsonian Institution, 1986), 98–106.

27. Ibid.

28. Julian H. Steward, *Basin-Plateau Aboriginal Sociopolitical Groups*, Bulletin No. 120, Bureau of American Ethnology (Washington, D.C.: Smithsonian Institution, 1938); Omer C. Stewart, *Culture Element*

Distributions XVIII: Ute-Southern Paiute, University of California Anthropological Records, vol. 6, no. 4 (1942): 231–355; and, *idem*, “Tribal Distributions and Boundaries in the Great Basin,” in *The Current Status of Anthropological Research in the Great Basin: 1964*, eds. Warren L. d’Azevedo, Wilbur A. Davis, Don D. Fowler, and Wayne Suttles, Technical Report Series S-H, Social Sciences and Humanities Publications No. 1 (Reno, Nev.: Desert Research Institute, 1966), 167–237.

29. Isabel T. Kelly, *Southern Paiute Ethnography*, Glen Canyon Series No. 21, Anthropological Papers No. 69 (Salt Lake City: University of Utah, 1964); Stewart, *Culture Element Distributions*.

30. Robert C. Euler, *Southern Paiute Ethnohistory*, Glen Canyon Series No. 28, Anthropological Papers No. 78 (Salt Lake City: University of Utah, 1966).

31. Lee Ann Kreutzer and M. R. Shaw, “Survey for Cultural Resources of Little Sand Flat in Capitol Reef National Park, Utah” (manuscript on file, Capitol Reef National Park, Utah, 2001).

32. Office of Public Archaeology, *Capitol Reef National Park Research Design: Phase 1*, Museum of Peoples and Cultures Technical Series No. 96-5 (Provo: Brigham Young University, 1996).

33. Kelly, *Southern Paiute Ethnography*, 151.

34. Ibid., 142.

IN SEARCH OF RELICS: THE HISTORY OF THE PECTOL-LEE COLLECTION FROM WAYNE COUNTY

Shane A. Baker

> We built a bonfire in front of the cave, and at ten o'clock [p.m.] we unearthed three of the most wonderful shields ever seen by man. For the space of two or three minutes, no one seemed to breathe as we were so astonished. We felt that we were in the presence of the one-time owner of that shield . . . .[1]

With these words, Ephraim Portman Pectol (Figures 7 8) described the compelling moment in 1926 when he and his wife discovered a stunning set of nearly perfectly preserved hide shields cached in a small, otherwise unremarkable, prehistoric archaeological site near Torrey, Utah. It was only one of a number of impressive finds that Pectol would make and that would lead him to become one of the preeminent collectors of early Native American material culture in southern Utah just after the turn of the century.

As the nineteenth century came to a close and the first decades of the twentieth century dawned, there were comparatively few professional archaeologists practicing in the western United States. Much of the investigation of the poorly understood archaeological resources from the remote areas of Utah, Colorado, New Mexico, and Arizona was being carried out by amateur explorers, entrepreneurs, or avocational archaeologists like the well-known Wetherills of Colorado.[2] Less well known than the Wetherills were people such as Platt Lyman, Charles Lang, Charles McLoyd, and Charles Cary Graham, who were actively involved in the pursuit of antiquities in the state of Utah. Some of these individuals worked in collaboration with professionals when opportunities permitted, but others were more motivated by financial aspirations and collected antiquities in an effort to amass materials for resale to museums and other institutions. Many prominent eastern museums owe a large portion of their prehistoric Ancestral Puebloan (Anasazi) collections to the efforts of such explorers and collectors.

Some of these early relic hunters, such as E. P. Pectol and Charles William Lee of Torrey, Utah, were drawn by the sense of mystery and

Figure 7. Ephraim Portman Pectol, ca. 1930. Photo courtesy E. P. and Dorothy Hickman Pectol Family Organization.

Figure 8. Ephraim Portman Pectol as a young missionary in New Zealand, ca. 1908. Photo by W. L. Joy Studio, Masterson, New Zealand, 1908. Courtesy E. P. and Dorothy Hickman Pectol Family Organization.

intrigue about the past. They collected primarily out of the same innate curiosity regarding history that many people share and with an eye towards making ancient "relics" available for others to enjoy. Although national laws had been passed protecting antiquities on public lands, there was little stigma attached to these generally well-intentioned early excavation and collecting practices carried out by private individuals on private land. It would take several more decades for Americans to realize how fragile and irreplaceable our national archaeological resources are and that they are best left preserved for future generations and studied only under carefully controlled scientific constraints.

Many of the early turn-of-the-century explorers/collectors left behind as their greatest legacy collections of priceless and unique prehistoric artifacts that provide a glimpse into the lifeways of long-vanished civilizations. Although the archaeological interpretation of these materials is often severely hampered by the lack of information about contexts, associations, and provenience, the objects themselves can still provide some exciting insights into the past.

The collection made by Ephraim Pectol is best known for the three large shields Pectol unearthed by the light of a blazing bonfire. Less well known is the fact that the collection includes literally hundreds of other artifacts collected by Pectol, Charles W. Lee, and several other early residents of south-central Utah in the area comprising present-day Wayne and Garfield counties. Although portions of the collection have been exhibited for many years at Capitol Reef National Park, the collection is primarily privately owned and has been little studied in the light of modern scientific methods and theories. This catalogue presents the first, complete, detailed publication of these materials together with radiocarbon dates and scientific analyses that shed new light on the collection and its significance.

The Pectol-Lee collection[3] came to the Museum of Peoples and Cultures at Brigham Young University in September of 1999. After several months of negotiations between the Museum and representatives of the E. P. and Dorothy Hickman Pectol Family Organization, the collection was made available to the university under a five-year loan agreement. The generosity of the Pectol Family Organization has made the collection available both for exhibition and study. This arrangement has allowed for the first intensive scientific examination and publication of the collection in its entirety.

The collection is a small but interesting assemblage of Fremont, Anasazi, and Late Prehistoric artifacts amassed primarily by Pectol and Lee, both early settlers and colonizers in the area of Torrey, Wayne County, Utah. It consists today of about 220 objects. Pectol noted in an early account, probably written sometime in the 1930s, that the number of objects he had in the collection was 210 and that "other items of interest are being added daily to the already wonderful collection . . . ."[4] It is clear that the collection originally may have included more objects than it does today. The history of the collection is an intriguing and complicated story involving movement of the objects from Pectol's and Lee's simple "museums" in Torrey to locations as far flung as the National Park Service conservation center in Harper's Ferry, West Virginia, and the Temple Square Museum in Salt Lake City, Utah.

Understanding the history of the collection is helpful in interpreting the materials and placing them in a proper context. This essay summarizes what is known about the history of the collection and relates a few of the circumstances and events in the lives of the two individuals most responsible for bringing the materials together.

EPHRAIM PECTOL

The majority of the artifacts making up the Pectol-Lee collection appear to have been gathered by Ephraim Portman Pectol and Charles William Lee. A few items may also have been found by other people who then donated or lent the objects to one or the other of these two individuals. The records are not good regarding these other possible contributors, but it seems clear that in most instances their intentions were that the prehistoric artifacts would end up as part of a single large collection that would eventually go to a public museum or exhibit somewhere in Wayne County.

Of the two principal collectors, Pectol certainly stands out as being the source of the largest number of objects and the one most possessed of a goal in his collecting. It is clear that from an early date Pectol was interested in promoting the economic interests of the local area by calling attention to its geological and archaeological wonders. He saw tourism as a way for the local people to derive some economic benefits from their proximity to the outstanding natural and historical resources of the Capitol Reef area. It appears the collection was kept together in large part by Pectol's determination to see that it played a role in this process.

Ephraim Pectol was born on May 16, 1875, in Glenwood, Sevier County, Utah (see map, Figure 9). His father, George Peter Pectol, was a member of the Church of Jesus Christ of Latter-day Saints[5] who had immigrated to Utah as a young man with his parents in 1850. After their arrival in Utah, George's family was called by the Church to be part of the directed efforts to settle southern Utah and to establish a cotton industry in the area of St. George. George moved to Glenwood, Utah, in 1864, where he settled for a while and began raising a family. Ephraim was the seventh of thirteen children born to George and Annina Pectol following their marriage in 1865. In about 1887, George and Annina moved the family to Caineville, Wayne County, where they would live until 1910.[6]

Ephraim grew up in Caineville, just to the east of Capitol Reef, and undoubtedly developed early on a deep love for this rugged country of slick rock and twisting drainages. It was while living in Caineville that he met and married his wife, Dorothy D. "Dot" Hickman, the daughter of Deseret N. and Dorothy A. Hickman.[7] The couple was married in the Manti Temple on June 21, 1899. For several years the young couple

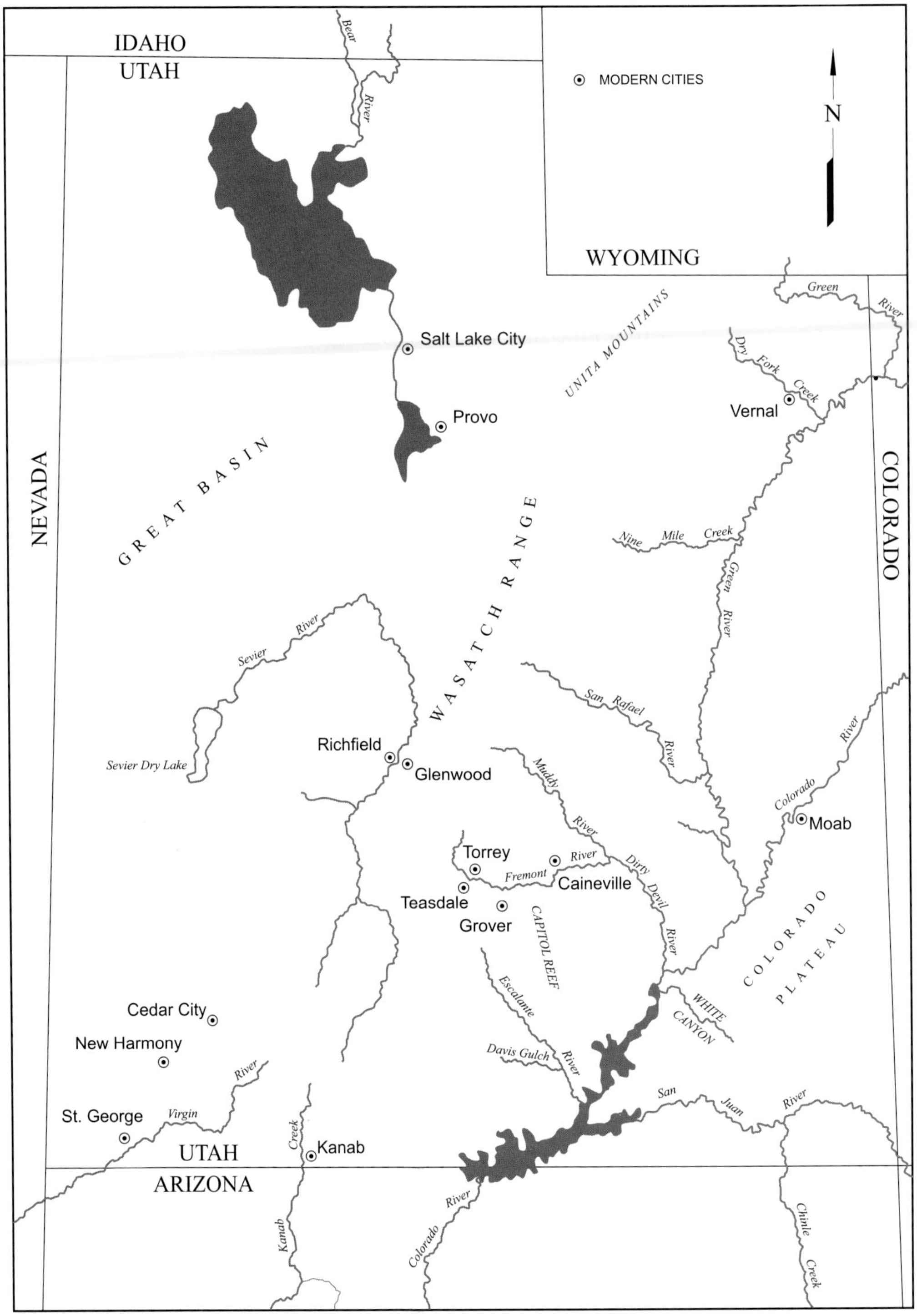

Figure 9. Map of Utah. Produced by Scott Ure, 2001.

struggled to make a living. For a while they boarded with relatives away from Caineville while Ephraim taught school and sold sewing machines for income. In the spring of 1906 they returned to Caineville, where Pectol assumed the post of superintendent of schools and accepted a contract to teach.

In August of 1906, Pectol was called by the Church of Jesus Christ to serve a mission to the New Zealand islands (Figure 8). He would be gone for two and one-half years, departing for service in August 1907 after completing his term as county school superintendent. During this time, Dot supported herself and four young daughters by running the small family farm, taking in boarders, operating the local post office, and running a Sears catalog business.[8]

It may be that Pectol first developed some of his love of indigenous tribal cultural materials while serving his mission, for this experience afforded extensive interaction with the native Maori people. When he returned from his mission he brought back native Polynesian artifacts.[9] One or two curious objects now in the Pectol collection not clearly attributable to the prehistoric cultures of Utah may in fact have come from New Zealand (e.g., cat. no. 181).

Pectol returned from his mission in New Zealand on Christmas Eve of 1909. The previous fall devastating floods had destroyed much of the prime farmland in and around Caineville, and the town was suffering through very difficult economic times. Ephraim and Dot sold their property and moved to Grover, Utah. A short time later the family sold their land holdings in Grover and Teasdale and used the proceeds to purchase a small general store in Torrey. The store, renamed "The Wayne Umpire" in 1912, provided a steady source of income for the family, who operated it continually until 1944. Dot shouldered much of the responsibility of running the store, freeing up Ephraim to teach and pursue his growing avocational interest in collecting antiquities. Over the years, Ephraim would be involved not only in the mercantile business, but also in ecclesiastical, civic, and political positions of responsibility. He was one of the key organizers of a Booster's Club in Torrey in 1921, serving as its first president, and was elected to the state legislature in 1933.[10] He became one of the most prominent men in Wayne County at the time and traveled widely in connection with his various public obligations and business interests.

Pectol recognized quite early the economic potential of the scenic, geological, and archaeological resources of the county. It became his dream to see official monument or park status granted to this area for which he coined the term "Wayne Wonderland." Pectol probably intended the artifacts he collected to be part of a museum or visitor attraction that would capitalize on these resources.

Figure 10. Ephraim Pectol and his daughters Golda (left) and DeVona (right) display the three painted hide shields, ca. 1930. Photo courtesy E. P. and Dorothy Hickman Pectol Family Organization.

It appears that most of the materials Pectol collected were amassed between his move to Torrey in 1910 and his death in 1947. As far as can be determined, Pectol never kept a written catalogue of his finds or any record of when or where each item came from. However, he wrote several, short, unpublished accounts about some of the various finds and spoke frequently at public gatherings about the collection and the significance he assigned to the items. Pectol felt a deep connection to the prehistoric people of the past and reverence for the artifacts he found. Many of his interpretations of the objects held religious significance, and he saw in the artifacts evidence for the Pre-Columbian cultures chronicled in the *Book of Mormon*, a volume of scripture accepted by the Church of Jesus Christ that recounts the history of a people in the Americas at the time of Christ.

The spectacular rawhide shields (Figure 10) were found late in the summer of 1926 at a known location not far from Torrey in a shallow rock alcove situated on a side drainage of Sulphur Creek. Little else is known about the location of most of the other finds that came to comprise the collection. The majority of the objects are assumed to have come from the area immediately around Torrey, but this is not known for sure. As Pectol traveled around the state, he may have collected or been given objects from areas distant from the Capitol Reef region. Only a few hints survive to suggest some interesting possibilities of the other locations where artifacts came from.

A significant stimulus to Pectol's interest in antiquities came from his involvement with professional archaeologists who began conducting research in the region in the mid-1920s. While working in the sparsely settled regions of southern Utah, professional researchers frequently retained the services of local settlers to act as guides, packers, and informants. These local people often had extensive first-hand knowledge of the ruins and geography of an area, and they became important contributors to many research expeditions.

In 1927, the Peabody Museum of Harvard University began a multi-year series of exploratory expeditions into the area of south-central Utah with the intention of documenting the prehistory of the rugged canyon country on the north side of the Colorado River. The 1928 expedition was led by Noel Morss, who focused his efforts on the Fremont River drainage near Torrey. It was based on the results of this work that Morss first defined the prehistoric Fremont culture and named it after the river where he initially identified it. During this trip, Morss employed Ephraim Pectol as part of the project team. It was probably Pectol's first exposure to field archaeology, and the experience may have been responsible in part for casting him in the role of local antiquarian and avocational archaeologist. Ephraim and Dot acted as hosts to Morss and his team and handled the crating and shipping of the artifacts back to Harvard following the expedition's return to the East Coast.[11]

An off-hand statement in Morss' report of the expedition provides a possible hint about the provenience of some of the Pectol artifacts. Morss reports briefly on his own excavations at a site he calls "Site 5" or "Image Cave," which today has been identified with a documented site in the Pleasant Creek drainage on lands now administered by Dixie National Forest. He notes that a portion of the cave had already been disturbed by previous digging, but that despite the damage his team's efforts still yielded "a moccasin, bone awls, arrowheads, manos, metates, a mortar, grains of corn, a bone pendant, and several small bone beads . . . and most important, a large collection of clay figurines."[12] He concludes his discussion by stating:

> Specimens probably from this cave in the possession of Bishop Pectol at Torrey include half the skin of a deer's head, dressed and sewed, which apparently was part of a headdress; snare sticks; and a few figurines.[13]

If we accept Morss' casual statement as accurate, this may indicate that the deer headdress (cat. no. 71) came from this site, perhaps as well as other objects in the collection such as the snares (cat. nos. 92–97) and some of the figurines (cat. nos. 65–70).

Although this summer of work on the expedition led by Morss may have been Pectol's first introduction to field archaeology, it was not the first exposure Pectol had to academic archaeology. As early as 1926, he was corresponding with Andrew Kerr, an archaeologist at the University of Utah, regarding the best method to clean calcium deposits off pottery.[14] About this same time Pectol began seeking ways to formalize his collecting into a more systematic and officially recognized effort. In January 1927, Pectol wrote Senator Reed Smoot making application for permission from the federal government to search for and collect antiquities. Senator Smoot forwarded the request to the Department of the Interior where the matter was addressed by John H. Edwards, Assistant Secretary of the Interior. Mr. Edwards responded that his agency could not grant permits for investigations on public lands outside the jurisdiction of the Department of the Interior and that such work could be conducted only for the benefit of "reputable museums, universities, colleges, or other recognized scientific or educational institutions."[15]

It is clear that the time Pectol spent working with Morss fired his interest in collecting archaeological materials. In a letter to Pectol written in October 1928, shortly after Morss returned to the Peabody, Morss told Pectol:

> By the way, I have looked into the Utah Compiled Statutes and find nothing except a provision punishing anyone who removes or defaces relics or hieroglyphics on public or private land without the land owner's permission, which we of course had. I have not looked through the laws passed at recent sessions, but I don't believe that anything has been passed which conflicts with federal law.[16]

Throughout the late 1920s and early 1930s Pectol appears to have been actively collecting artifacts. Three letters dated 1926, 1934, and 1938 give some hint at the quantity of materials Pectol had amassed. In December of 1926, Pectol wrote the Carnegie Museum in Pittsburgh asking whether they would be interested in the recently discovered shields. He elaborated further on the other items he sought to make available to them:

> three large prehistoric War Shields made from the buffalo hides . . ., some pottery of unusual cemetrical [sic] pattern and color designs, a number of baskets unusual in their designings and construction . . . . Many other trinkets such as bow strings of sinew, arrow points, weaving shuttle, sinew rope, bag of the cedar bark . . ., etc.[17]

A letter written in 1934 to a Mr. Joe Dubuicek of Chicago, Illinois, offered for sale a list of more than 25 artifacts including baskets, groundstone tools, and other perishable artifacts. The following is a copy of the list contained in the letter and the asking prices as noted by Pectol (spelling and punctuation as per the original document):

1 Petrified potatoe		$.50
1 Stone Crushe		1.00
1 Graining knife		1.00
Fire Stick		2.50
1 Piece Rope		5.00
Several small items included		2.00
1 Very Perfect Mano		5.00
3 good specimen Manos	@3.00 each	9.00
1 Jar with corn		10.00
1 Basket		25.00
1 Basket		20.00
1 Basket		20.00
1 Jug		100.00
2 fish hooks with line,		100.00
2 War Horns		10.00
1 Toilet set		50.00
1 Piece petrafied Bread		10.00
1 Clay image and Alter		1000.00
1 Bone Necklace		25.00
1 Antelope Spike Paint container		2.50
Several Bone Items		10.00
1 Hank of fibre used in ropes		25.00
1 Fox Hide Doile		5.00[18]

Recognizable in this list of artifacts for sale are several of the more impressive items now found in the Pectol-Lee collection, including (one assumes) the figurine in the cradle board (cat. no. 61), the bone fishhooks (cf. cat. no. 99), and the horns containing pigment (actually bighorn sheep horn: cf. cat. nos. 73–74). The total collection was offered to Dubuicek for sale at $1,438.50, with the encouragement that it "would be a source of revenue to the owner if living where you are, or in any large city." It appears that at the time of this letter, the collection already included material Pectol himself had not collected, for at one point he uses the pronoun "we" to refer to the owners of the collection: "*We* have considerable material unearthed in this place and some of it can be disposed of at the following prices."[19]

Interestingly enough, this letter to Mr. Dubuicek is on letterhead of the Associated Civic Clubs of Southern Utah. Since the offer was in response to a solicitation letter written by Mr. Dubuicek the previous year, Pectol's use of Civic Club letterhead may indicate he was acting in the capacity of spokesperson for a local group which had been organized to promote the county.

In a third letter dated April 26, 1938, Pectol responded to a request from a J. K. Oliver for information about the availability of fossils and small prehistoric artifacts Oliver wished to purchase for resale in an art and curio store he operated in Monterrey, California. Oliver's letter asks about the availability and asking price of fossils, "Indian arrow points," "spear heads," and "small indian [sic] pestles and mortars."[20] Pectol responded that he had not been successful in acquiring any fossil specimens for sale, but that he had "a very good collection of archaeological items, and will part with some very important items if you are interested in such." The letter goes on to list some of the objects offered for sale and their asking prices, including:

> 2 doz. Bone awls, 2 doz. prs. Moccason [sic] Half Soles, 1 hunting girdle, 1 set of 5 fish hooks and lines, 1 Double built jug, 2 baskets about 10 in., 3 baskets cerimonial [sic], 1 Clay Image on woven board.[21]

Again, this listing includes items that appear to be consistent with objects currently in the collection, namely, bone awls (cf. cat. nos. 151–155), moccasins (cf. cat. no. 129), fish hooks (cf. cat. no. 99), various baskets (cf. cat. nos. 28–50) and, of course, the cradle board with its figurine (cat. no. 61). The list notably includes items not mentioned in previous letters, suggesting the collection was still expanding. Noteworthy additions to the list included the moccasins and additional fishhooks, which may have been found after the 1934 letter to Dubuicek was written.

Three other letters recently found in Pectol family archives confirm that the materials collected by Ephraim were considered to be for sale over a period of several years. Two letters dated 1929 and 1930 from an individual in Salt Lake City inquire about the offering prices for materials in the collection.[22] A third letter dated 1937 from Ephraim to a potential client in Washington, D.C. offers guide services and also indicates that he is willing to sell artifacts from his collection. In the letter he states "I have many indian [sic] relics … the price of these depend on age, design and scarcity of the article."[23]

No evidence appears to have survived in the Pectol family's correspondence to indicate what the response was to Pectol's efforts either to interest the Carnegie Museum in the collection or to arrange the sale of any part of the collection to these other interested parties.

Significantly, the six letters noted above are the only indication the author found of Pectol himself seeking to sell any portion of his collection. It is also worth noting that for the most part, these few examples of Pectol offering portions of the collection for sale were written relatively early on, and during the height of the depression when the Pectols, like so many rural families all over the country, were struggling economically. They certainly do not characterize Pectol's thinking about the collection later in life.

Attached to the J. K. Oliver letter is a hand-written, undated list of objects that duplicates most of the items mentioned in the letter. At the top of the list appears the notation "E. P. Pectol and C. W. Lee, Owners." It is clear that from an early point in time, probably at least by the late 1930s, Pectol was collaborating with others in developing the collection, and notable among these others was Charles W. Lee, another prominent resident of Torrey.

Lee's involvement in building the collection is somewhat hard to assess, since records have not survived which clearly indicate the identity of the finder of each specific artifact. However, it is known that Charles Lee was the discoverer of the unique cradle board artifact now a part of the collection.

CHARLES W. LEE

Charles William Lee was born August 9, 1862, in New Harmony, Washington County, Utah, to Sarah Caroline Lee, the fourth wife of John Doyle Lee.[24] John D. Lee was, of course, one of the most famous and prominent early historical figures in southern Utah history. Lee joined the Church of Jesus Christ of Latter-day Saints in June of 1838 and became associated with the body of the church then founding the town of Far West, Missouri. Lee remained faithful through the trials and persecutions that members of the church endured first in Missouri and later in Illinois. Married when he joined the church, Lee later took several additional wives according to the doctrine of polygamy espoused by the early church. He married Charles Lee's mother, Sarah Caroline Williams (who usually went by Caroline) in Nauvoo, Illinois, in April 1845. However, Caroline was only fifteen at the time, and although ceremonially "sealed"[25] to Lee in Nauvoo, she did not become his wife in fact until nearly six years later. Apparently due to her very young age, Caroline was "sealed" to John D. Lee but continued to live with her own family. She was only one of several new wives Lee took while living in Nauvoo, the rest of whom actually resided with Lee.

Members of the Church of Jesus Christ faced increasing persecution in Nauvoo following the death of their leader Joseph Smith at the hands of a mob in June 1844. Eventually most of the members of the church were forced to flee Nauvoo. Brigham Young led the exiled refugees on an epic trek that culminated in the settlement of Salt Lake City. Caroline remained in Nauvoo with her family when John and the rest of his wives and children fled with other members of the church to seek refuge in temporary settlements in Iowa.

Lee's large family (five wives and five children) moved west to join Brigham Young and others of the Mormon faith in Utah in 1848. Lee was quickly given numerous significant responsibilities in settling the new territory and, by the winter of 1850, was called as one of the leaders in an expedition to help colonize southern Utah and establish an iron industry in the area of present-day Cedar City. A year later, in October 1851, he was called to lead the establishment of yet another new community at the junction of the Virgin and Santa Clara Rivers. During this period, Lee was reunited with Caroline. After a long absence and an intervening marriage to another man, Sarah Caroline made her way to Utah and rejoined John D. Lee, asking to be accepted as his wife.[26] She went with him to help establish this new community on the Rio Virgin and to colonize the area that would become Washington County.

Lee and his family ended up settling in the small community of New Harmony, just south of modern Cedar City, where he became busily engaged as a farmer, rancher, and local church leader. Late in 1857, complex circumstances led to his involvement in the tragic events culminating in the Mountain Meadows Massacre.[27] John D. Lee was the sole man tried and executed for his involvement in this event, although his execution would not come until some twenty years later. In the meantime, he continued in his efforts to establish a community in this remote, unsettled area of southern Utah. It was while still living at New Harmony that his wife Caroline gave birth to his sixth child, Charles William Lee, in the fall of 1862. Charles Lee was fifteen when his father was executed, and he was left with his mother and others of the large extended family to make a living without a father or husband in the home.

In January of 1881, Charles married Leah Arminda Young, a cousin of Brigham Young. He and Arminda, as well as Caroline, all moved to the Torrey area sometime after 1884 and became some of the earliest founders of the community. Lee engaged in sheep and cattle ranching as well as farming.[28]

While National Park Service archives are replete with correspondence from E. P. Pectol regarding the collection, far less documentation has survived regarding Lee's involvement in the origins of the Pectol-Lee

Figure 11. Ephraim Pectol's exhibit of artifacts at the family store, Torrey, Utah, ca. 1940. Ephraim and Dorothy Pectol show relics to Della Hickman. Photo courtesy E. P. and Dorothy Hickman Pectol Family Organization.

collection. It is clear that by the early 1930s both Lee and Pectol had assembled reasonably large collections of material which they were exhibiting publicly. Pectol maintained a "museum" in a small addition to the rear of his store in Torrey (Figure 11), while Lee ran an exhibit out of the basement of his home, charging visitors ten cents to view the artifacts.[29] None of the artifacts that appear to have been collected by Lee can now be traced back to identifiable archaeological sites. Like Pectol, Lee seems to have assembled the collection from many different localities and left behind no written catalogue or diary confirming the exact locations or circumstances of any of the finds.

An interesting document from 1930 indicates the origins of the cradle board were brought into question for a period of time. In an unsigned typescript of a letter which Pectol apparently received in November of 1930, an unidentified correspondent provided Ephraim a copy of the text of a letter from the famous archaeologist Neil Judd, then employed by the Smithsonian Institution.[30] Photographs of the cradle board and figurine had been submitted to Judd by a B.B. Howell at the request of someone (perhaps an associate of Pectol?). Judd responded with his assessment of the age and significance of the artifact and made a plea that the recipient of the letter "make inquiry of Mr. Lee, suggesting to him the desirability of having this specimen permanently preserved in the national collections here in Washington."[31] Judd also included in his letter a comment about the location where the object was found, and a reproof regarding the legal issues involved with collecting on the public domain.

> From the locality given, I judge this specimen was found on the public domain and there is, as you know, a law prohibiting the removal of antiquities without permission, from Federal lands. In other words, the government could confiscate this object . . . .[32]

This "judgement" could apparently not be confirmed and was not sustained (see below); but Judd's words were a forewarning of problems that would soon surface for both Pectol and Lee regarding the ownership of many of the antiquities they had collected. Although their intentions were probably good, there were suspicions that the two had violated the law by removing archaeological materials from public lands, and the federal government was shortly to take action in the matter.

THE FEDERAL GOVERNMENT INTERVENES

By 1932 federal government officials began to receive complaints that residents of Wayne County had amassed archaeological collections worth more than $50,000 from sites on public land in violation of the Antiquities Act of 1906. The federal government had begun considering the possibility of creating a national monument to protect the area of Capitol Reef, and officials were concerned about these reports. In September 1932, the General Land Office (GLO) dispatched geologist G. G. Frazier to investigate the claims. Frazier spent a week in Wayne County in an effort to verify the identities of the alleged violators and where the artifacts had been obtained, but he had little success in finding anyone knowledgeable about the materials that had been discovered. At the end of his investigation, Frazier concluded that E. P. Pectol and C. W. Lee were the only individuals under suspicion. Finding no other reliable sources of information, he finally interviewed both men to determine whether the law restricting removal of artifacts from public land had in fact been violated.[33]

With the cooperation of both Pectol and Lee, Frazier concluded that some of the prehistoric artifacts had indeed been removed from public lands. Frazier formally "confiscated" the materials on behalf of the federal government and attached tags to each item confirming this action and marking them as government property. However, Frazier's report of the investigation concluded that the value of the objects had been highly overstated and that the cost of crating them for shipment to the Smithsonian Institution would be prohibitive. Accordingly, he elected to leave all the seized material in the possession of Pectol and Lee. He reproved both collectors for their violation of the law and extracted a promise they would cease collecting activities on public lands.[34] Frazier felt little good would be accomplished in actually taking possession of the artifacts for the government or in prosecuting either person. He recommended they both be allowed to retain the relics until such time as the government established a local museum or park where the artifacts could be exhibited. Frazier suggested the two collections of both private and government-owned objects could form what he called "the nucleus of a museum" in the proposed park.[35]

Frazier's report of his investigation enumerated the items seized on behalf of the federal government. From Pectol's collection, the government asserted ownership of the three painted shields (see Figure 10), one tanned piece of buffalo hide, one planting stick, one mortar or grinding stone, and one stone ball. The list of items "confiscated" from Lee was more extensive and, notably, excludes the cradle board: "eight baskets, 2 jars [pottery vessels], one deer hide, one bundle of raw material for making baskets, 2 jars [pottery vessels], one 'grinder' [metate or mano], one jar of corn, one bundle of soles for moccasins, two pieces of deer legs, and three gaurds [probably gourds]." Frazier indicated he had no proof either person had sold any of the objects they had collected.[36]

THE COLLECTION GROWS

It appears that for the next several years Pectol's primary efforts were focused on lobbying for the creation of a national monument to protect and preserve the area around Capitol Reef. One gets the impression, however, that Pectol continued to have an active interest in the archaeology of the region and to collect materials from private land, and he gained a wide reputation for being an authority on the antiquities of the region. It appears that from time to time other local residents lent artifacts to Pectol for exhibit in the small "museum" attached to his store. This informal arrangement of accepting loans without documentation may have led to odds and ends collected by other persons actually remaining in the Pectol-Lee collection.

In particular, there is evidence that Earl Behunin of Torrey found some of the leather artifacts now included in the collection. Several memos written by Capitol Reef Park Superintendent Charles Kelly[37] name Behunin as having discovered the buckskin artifacts Pectol referred to as a "garment" or the "high priest's vestment."[38] These artifacts, consisting of several pieces of tanned leather with some sewn alterations and modest modifications, held particular significance to Pectol, who felt the assemblage was similar to ancient Biblical ceremonial clothing and modern religious clothing used by members of the Church of Jesus Christ of Latter-day Saints.[39]

In later years, Pectol wrote that the leather artifacts comprising the "vestment" were found at a location not far from where he discovered the shields, but he does not make clear who actually found them.[40] Today the collection includes a significant number of both large and small leather objects, some of which are incomplete. It is not possible to identify exactly which ones comprised the "vestments" that Pectol referred to.[41] Possibly both Pectol and Behunin separately found various leather objects that later came to be considered an associated set of related objects. It is not clear exactly which pieces Pectol found and which Behunin found, but there were at least enough objects in the collection found by Behunin that in the 1957 memo to the Regional Park Service Director, the superintendent of Zion National Park refers to the collection as the "Pectol-Buhanan [sic] collection."[42] In a notarized statement dated October 26, 1950, Pectol's widow Dorothy stated that in the collection:

> There are no relics belonging to Clarence Mulford, however, there are two jars belonging to E. F. Behunin. The skins or robes which are at the Bureau of Information because of certain marks on them, were given to my husband, the late E. P. Pectol and myself to put with our collection for display of articles found by us and others who have given different articles to us for this same purpose. These skins were a direct gift to us.[43]

The implication is that the Pectol-Lee collection came to comprise a variety materials, some of which were probably gathered by persons other than Pectol and Lee. This fact makes it even more difficult to be definitive about where all the objects originally came from and what their archeological provenience may be.

TEMPLE SQUARE MUSEUM

Sometime prior to 1939, Pectol lent his collection, including the government-owned objects, to the Temple Square Mission and Bureau of Information[44] of the Church of Jesus Christ of Latter-day Saints, which operated the Temple Square Museum in Salt Lake City. The Bureau of Information first requested that Ephraim consider lending some of his collections to the Church in August 1927.[45] The interest in the objects shown by representatives of the Church of Jesus Christ appears to have been prompted by letters Pectol wrote directly to President of the Church

Heber J. Grant and Joseph Eckersley of the Presiding Bishopric's Office in 1926.[46] It is not clear why the objects were not actually lent to the Church until many years later. The only insight seems to be Pectol's comments to President Grant that he felt the materials were most appropriately kept in Wayne County, where Ephraim was actively promoting them and showing them to all interested visitors.[47]

About the same time Pectol lent his material to the Church's Bureau of Information, Lee also lent his materials to the Church. It is not clear whether the two acted independently, or if perhaps Pectol transmitted the materials on behalf of both men to the Church.[48] At least a portion of the materials lent by the Pectols was put on display in the Temple Square Museum by the fall of 1939, but a government archaeologist reported the Lee collection was still on exhibit in the basement of Lee's home in November of 1939.[49] It may be that part of Lee's collection went to Salt Lake City and part remained in his home, but the division of objects and the timing of any movement of objects to Salt Lake City are uncertain.

By early 1941, Charles Lee was in declining health and desired to regain possession of the artifacts he had lent to the Church of Jesus Christ, apparently hoping to sell them to make some extra money. Pectol wrote Joseph J. Cannon, the director of the Bureau of Information on Temple Square in April, indicating Lee had asked him to "get the relics he left with you."[50] Lee's health continued to decline, and he died in Torrey on May 7, 1941. Following Lee's death, Pectol wrote the Bureau of Information with the news Lee had died and said he still intended to have a freighting company pick up both his and Lee's artifacts to return them to Wayne County. At this time Pectol reported that "one third" of the materials belonged to him and that he was willing to purchase the balance of the collection.[51] Dorothy Pectol later told Park Superintendent Charles Kelly that before Lee died he had sold a half interest in his collection to Ephraim Pectol.[52] Other evidence suggests the artifacts in question were offered to Pectol as collateral for a loan or against credit at Pectol's store.[53]

Within a day of making the request to the Bureau of Information to take possession of the artifact collections, Pectol wrote a second time informing them that Lee's heirs had produced a document instructing that artifacts belonging to Lee be delivered to S. E. Tanner, an attorney in Loa, Utah, for distribution to his survivors.[54] Apparently, the transfer of some of Lee's artifacts to Pectol had not been documented in writing, and Lee's descendants were now advancing their own claim to those objects. Pectol agreed both collections would be left in the care of the Temple Square Museum until after the attorney had examined them and deliberated the disposition of the materials in question in light of the various claims. Although Pectol was never able to produce a written statement of what

Lee had transfered to him, the question of ownership concerning some of the artifacts had now arisen. None of the Pectol or Lee collections was claimed at this time, and the materials remained in the care of the Temple Square Museum, ostensibly awaiting a settlement of the ownership issues.

With the onset of World War II, the Museum became anxious to have the collections returned to the owners, both to free up space and to be relieved of responsibility for them. John H. Taylor, Temple Square Mission President and Director of the Bureau of Information, made several written requests to expedite a legal settlement on the disposition of the materials.[55] Finally, Taylor threatened to have the materials removed into commercial storage and eventually sold if necessary to satisfy the storage fees.[56] Despite these efforts by the Temple Square Museum to resolve the matter, the collections remained in the care of the Church and languished there. There is no evidence, however, that any of the materials were ever sent to outside storage or sold.

By the time the Pectol and Lee families resumed efforts to get the collection released from the Temple Square Museum in the late 1940s, the clouded issue of legal title, i.e., which family owned what, caused the Museum to dramatically reverse its position on the disposition of the collection. Probably due in large part to a turnover in staff and a loss of records on the matter, the Museum took the official position that they could not release the collection until all questions of ownership were properly settled. This was also due in large part to a new complication in the form of a request from the government that the Museum turn over to federal authorities the portion of the collection that was government property. The Temple Square Museum found itself in the awkward position of admitting that it did not have documents to support ownership of any of the items or the legal status under which the items had been originally donated or lent to the Museum.

The United States government granted national monument status to Capitol Reef on August 2, 1937, bringing to fruition part of the dream Pectol worked so hard for over so many years.[57] Historians have noted the tremendous contribution that Pectol's efforts made to the establishment of the monument, with one recent scholar recognizing Pectol's instrumental role by calling him "the father of Capitol Reef."[58] Unfortunately, he did not live to see the creation of a museum facility or the return of the artifact collections to Wayne County. Ephraim Pectol died in Elsinore, Utah, on October 8,1947. Although the Monument had been in operation for 10 years before he died, the collections Ephraim hoped would reside in Wayne County had not found a permanent home or exhibit space, and they remained in Salt Lake City. Following Pectol's death, his widow and daughters continued efforts to get the artifacts released by the Temple Square Museum.

During the late 1940s and early 1950s, the federal government became concerned about the status of the collections and, in particular, about the disposition of the objects claimed by the government in 1932. Capitol Reef National Monument custodian Charles Kelly was directed to begin negotiating for the release of the government-owned materials from the Temple Square Museum so that they could be returned to the Park.[59] Kelly's investigations confirmed that much of the Pectol collection was still on exhibit or being held at the Temple Square Museum, but that Lee may have sold part of his collection prior to his death to raise money.[60] It is not clear what items may have been sold. Kelly simply noted that the best pieces of the collection, including the baskets, were gone. It is possible Lee divided up his collection prior to his death, selling some pieces, lending some to the Temple Square Museum, and perhaps using others as collateral against his debt to Pectol. It may never be possible to determine exactly what the entire Lee collection originally consisted of, and what part of it is now in the Pectol-Lee collection. Some of the objects Kelly assumed were sold may actually have been those items transferred to Pectol as collateral as per the loan arrangement described above. Other items, however, may have been sold and were now altogether missing from collections under consideration.

By the latter part of 1950 or early 1951, most of the legal issues about ownership of the collections being held in Salt Lake City had been resolved. The Lee and Pectol families agreed to claim all of the artifacts that were not government property and have them returned for exhibit in Wayne County. Their plan appears to have been to donate the materials comprising the Pectol-Lee collection to the federal government to become part of an exhibit as soon as the government could provide a suitable facility. The National Park Service began making plans to have the materials housed temporarily in the old Pectol store in Torrey, which was by then owned by Mr. Bernard Tracy.[61] However, Dorothy Pectol died in August 1951 before transferring title of the materials to the National Park Service, and the plan was never brought to fruition.

Shortly after Mrs. Pectol died, the Lee and Pectol families jointly asked for release of the materials in the Temple Square Museum. At about the same time, the federal government also asked the Museum to release the objects from the collection that were federal property to Charles Kelly of Capitol Reef National Park.[62] The Temple Square Museum found itself again in the awkward situation of having received what appeared to be possibly conflicting claims for the artifacts. The Museum reevaluated its position and requested all parties to provide proof of ownership. Richard L. Evans, Director of the Bureau of Information and Temple Square Museum, wrote the Pectol heirs and expressed the opinion that the Church believed it had been Ephraim

Pectol's intent to donate the materials. At the same time, the Museum asked the government to confirm which specific objects were the ones that had been seized by the government, for the government tags had by this time been removed from the objects. In the absence of clear records detailing ownership, the Temple Square Museum refused to release any of the artifacts.

Attorneys for all parties began marshaling for a showdown. At the eleventh hour, however, original correspondence between Pectol and the Bureau of Information was discovered by Fontella Webster, one of Pectol's daughters living in Loa, Utah. The old letters, kept for years by the Pectol family with Ephraim Pectol's papers, confirmed the objects had only been lent to the Church of Jesus Christ and not donated. Evans reluctantly agreed to release the collections but requested that several of the objects be left on loan with the Museum to continue on exhibit.[63]

The months of protracted negotiations finally culminated in an agreement among all parties that the National Park Service would take possession of the entire Pectol-Lee collection from the Temple Square Museum and move it to Wayne County for storage and possible exhibit. It was made clear at the time, however, that the families would retain ownership of all items that had not been specifically named in the 1932 government action. The heirs of Ephraim and Dorothy Pectol and Charles Lee all signed an agreement clearing the way for the materials to finally return to Capitol Reef.[64]

CAPITOL REEF NATIONAL PARK

On November 30, 1953, Mr. Paul R. Franke, Superintendent of Zion and Bryce National Parks, accompanied by representatives of both the Pectol and Lee families, picked up the collection from the Temple Square Museum. The receipt for the collection lists a total of 27 items, including the three shields, two jars, eight baskets, and several leather items. At the urging of Department of Interior archaeologist Jesse Nusbaum, the National Park Service agreed to leave several items on loan to the Temple Square Museum, including one of the shields, one leather belt, one deer skin, one pair of moccasins, and a few other small items.[65] The use of these materials by the Museum was formalized as a loan in December 1953.[66]

At about this same time, the Pectol and Lee families submitted to Charles Kelly a typewritten inventory of the materials they were lending to Capitol Reef National Park. This list is much more inclusive and itemizes 80 individual artifacts, including baskets, pots, a wood flute (cf. cat. no. 75), arrowheads, hides and leather fragments, other artifacts, and rock specimens.[67] Possibly, the families added other materials at that point which had been part of the collection, but which had not gone to the Temple Square Museum. This document also indicates the Lee family withheld the cradle board (cat. no. 61), one braided strand of bark (cf. cat. nos. 13–14), and several bone fishhooks with line (cat. no. 99), which were lent back to the Temple Square Museum. The latter list prepared by the families is much more extensive than the receipt prepared by the National Park Service.

From this point on, the collection remained in the care of the National Park Service. However, since no adequate facilities had yet been constructed at the Park, the collection was placed on exhibit at the Tracy store in Torrey. The materials remained on exhibit there until the storeowners asked the government to remove them in 1957 so that the store could be expanded and renovated.[68] Charles Kelly, who by this time had been made superintendent of Capitol Reef, suggested renovating a small building in the Park to house and exhibit the collection. Instead, the National Park Service elected to have all the materials moved to Globe, Arizona, to be stored in a regional curation facility there. The transfer of the materials took place in March 1958.[69] In January of 1961, in anticipation of the construction of a new visitor facility and interpretive exhibits, the artifacts were again transferred back to Capitol Reef.

In 1963, construction began on a new visitor center at Capitol Reef National Park, and an inventory was completed of all the materials in the Pectol-Lee collection that might be available for the new exhibit. This included both the materials held by the Park Service at Capitol Reef and those still held by the Church of Jesus Christ of Latter-day Saints. On February 28, 1964, at the request of the National Park Service, the Temple Square Museum returned the objects that had been on loan to it. Apparently, however, some of the objects lent to the Temple Square Museum by the Lee family, including the cradle board with its figurine (cat. no. 61), had inadvertently been given National Park Service catalogue numbers when the Church, acting under instructions from the Park Service, had labeled the loan objects in 1960.[70] The history of negotiations between the Temple Square Museum and the Lee and Pectol families had indicated these objects did not belong to the federal government, and it became clear that their receiving Park Service numbers was a mistake. However, the mistake served to once more cloud the issue of ownership. The Temple Square Museum declined to release these objects to the Park Service at this time, maintaining that they were not in fact government property.

As preparations for the new exhibit at Capitol Reef began in earnest, some of the objects were transferred to the Western Museum Laboratory in San Francisco to be prepared for exhibition. These included a basket, an antler artifact, a hide artifact, and a pair of moccasins.[71] The new visitor center in the Park opened in 1965 with exhibits of many of the objects from the Pectol-Lee collection. Materials not placed on exhibit were stored at the Park. In 1977, sixteen baskets from the collection were transferred from Capitol Reef National Park to Harper's Ferry Center in West Virginia for conservation and were later returned to the Park.[72] On May 11, 1989, the cradle board and its figurine were conveyed to the Park by the LDS Museum of Church History and Art, the successor to the old Temple Square Museum. These objects had never been returned to the Lee family, and now, 35 years after refusing the Park Service's 1964 request, the Museum returned the objects to the Park, probably on the basis of the National Park Service numbers that had been mistakenly affixed to these objects in 1960. A second transfer of the fishhooks originally lent by Glen Lee, son of Charles Lee, was made to the Park in October of 1993 along with several other small basketry cradle board fragments (cf. cat. nos. 62–64).[73]

In subsequent years, the collection variously resided at Capitol Reef or was moved elsewhere as curation needs dictated. Portions of the collection were transferred by the Park Service to the Western Archaeological Conservation Center (WACC) in Tucson, Arizona, because storage conditions in the Capitol Reef visitor center were not ideal. Some of the pieces developed an insect infestation and were sent to Arizona for conservation. In 1994, Park archaeologist Lee Kreutzer moved all of the artifacts not on exhibit to WACC so that they could be stored in a better conservation environment.

It seems there was a clear desire on the part of the families to donate the collections to the Park, but it was never done. With the passage of time, nearly all of the persons immediately involved with the original loan to the Park died, and the matter was left unresolved. The collections resided at the Park for so long that both the Park Service and the families came to think of the collections as the property of the Park Service. In fact, ownership was never conveyed through any formal legal transaction, so the issue of the permanent disposition of the Pectol-Lee collection remained unaddressed for decades.

The collection remained in that functional but legally ambiguous status until 1990. In that the year the Native American Graves Protection and Repatriation Act (NAGPRA) was passed into law. This new legislation provided for the repatriation of ancestral Native American human remains and certain classes of sacred and ceremonial objects held by museums. The National Park Service, along with all other federally funded museums, was required to assess their collections for possible sacred objects, funerary objects, and objects of cultural patrimony as a prelude to possible repatriation. The Pectol-Lee collection came under scrutiny as possibly containing artifacts subject to the provisions of the law. As Capitol Reef National Park pursued the review process, Park archaeologist Lee Kreutzer discovered that the artifacts in the Pectol-Lee collection had never been formally donated. This meant that they were not the property of the Park Service and, therefore, not subject to the law. Sometime during 1993 or 1994 Kreutzer began negotiations with the Pectol and Lee families to determine the disposition of the materials in the collection. The families chose to have the Park Service return the artifacts to the control of the Pectol family rather than risk having any of the items dispersed from the collection under the provisions of the law.

Accordingly, in August 1996 the entire Pectol-Lee collection was returned to Capitol Reef from the WACC facility in Tucson,[74] and on August 23, 1996 the National Park Service formally returned to the Pectol family the majority of the Pectol-Lee collection that had been on loan to the federal government since 1953. A second small transfer consisting of some corn, a braid of plant fibers (cf. cat. nos. 13–14), fishhooks and twine (cf. cat. no. 99), and a sheep horn with ochre (cf. cat. nos. 73–74) occurred in August of 1997.

One final problem arose in the process of the transfer. Although Park Service archival records gave general descriptions of the artifacts seized in 1932 by the GLO investigator, G. G. Frazier, none of the objects could be conclusively identified on the basis of the descriptions alone. The identification tags attached by Frazier had long since been removed, making it nearly impossible to establish beyond reasonable doubt which of the very similar baskets and bits of leather were owned by the federal government. Accordingly, the decision was made by government legal experts to return all of the collection, with the exception of the shields, which were easily identifiable as government property. The family in turn executed a loan that enabled 36 objects still on exhibit at the Park to remain there. This small collection of materials remained on loan to the Park until February 1999, when several objects, including moccasins (cf. cat. no. 129) and a fringed apron (cf. cat. no. 145), were removed at the request of the Zuni Tribe and returned later that month to the Pectol family. Other objects were lent by the family to replace the objects taken off display.

On May 19, 1998, the National Park Service notified its regional units that all materials subject to the requirements of NAGPRA would have to be removed from exhibit.[75] Accordingly, two shields that had been on exhibit at the Park since the new visitor center had opened in 1965 were removed and sent to WACC for temporary storage pending a decision on ownership and right of disposition under the new law. Deliberations based on studies of cultural affiliation and consultation with interested Native Americans are under way at the present time.

The ownership of the cradle board and figurine as well as the fishhooks remained unresolved for several months beyond the return of the rest of collection while Park Service attorneys attempted to sort out the still muddled issue of ownership. The cradle board was clearly part of the original Lee collection, but the subsequent history of this celebrated object clouded the issue. In April 1998, the National Park Service returned the cradle board to the Pectol's after concluding the preponderance of documentation—notably information indicating the Lee family had relinquished all claims prior to Mrs. Pectol's death—supported their title.

Today, the Pectol-Lee collection is in the ownership of the E. P. and Dorothy H. Pectol Family Organization, with the exception of the shields, which remain the property of the federal government. Several artifacts remain on loan to Capitol Reef National Park where they are on exhibit in the visitor center. The bulk of the collection is on loan to the Museum of Peoples and Cultures for research and exhibition until 2005. The family is concerned about the long-term deposition of the materials. Ephraim Pectol always dreamed they would find a permanent home in Wayne County, and the family still hopes to make that dream a reality.

Ephraim also hoped these precious "relics" might be seen and appreciated by many people and that they would lead people to a better understanding of the prehistoric inhabitants of his beloved "Wayne Wonderland." The publication of this catalogue, together with the newly completed research on the collection, makes data about these artifacts widely available to professional researchers for the first time since they were discovered. In this way, at least part of Ephraim Pectol's dream has been realized.

1. Elaine Christensen Southwick, arr., *". . . And I Went Home Rejoicing:" The Background, Life and Posterity of Edward Southwick III* (Provo, Utah: J. Grant Stevenson, 1971), 123. See also E. P. Pectol, *The Shields*, unpublished manuscript in possession of Neal Busk, Richfield, Utah, n.d.

2. B. K. Wetherill and his sons, Richard, Alfred, John, Clayton and Win, were ranchers in the Mancos River valley of southeastern Colorado during the 1880s. In December 1881, Richard and Al Wetherill along with their brother-in-law, Charlie Mason, made the discovery of a lifetime. While searching for stray cattle they happened upon the spectacular "Cliff Palace" cliff dwelling that is now part of Mesa Verde National Park. This discovery launched the family's long-term involvement with the archaeology of the Southwest. Richard Wetherill would later become extensively involved with research in the Chaco Canyon area in collaboration with professional archaeologists from several eastern universities.

3. The two people primarily responsible for the collection as it exists today are Ephraim Pectol and Charles Lee, and this catalogue will refer to the composite body of materials as it now exists as the "Pectol-Lee" collection in recognition of the role both played in bringing the collection into existence.

4. E. P. Pectol, "Wonders of Wayne's Wonderland" (unpublished manuscript in possession of Neal Busk, Richfield, Utah, n.d.).

5. In the past a number of nicknames or shortened forms have been used for Church of Jesus Christ of Latter-day Saints, including "Mormons," LDS Church, or Latter-Day Saints. Recently the Church itself requested the shortened designation be simply the "Church of Jesus Christ."

6. Andrew Jenson, *Latter-day Saint Biographical Encyclopedia* (1901; reprint, Salt Lake City: Western Epics, 1971), 483–484.

7. Ibid., 482–483.

8. Judy Shell Busk, "E. P. Pectol" (unpublished manuscript in possession of Neal Busk, Richfield, Utah, n.d.).

9. Neal Busk, personal communication, 2001.

10. Judy Shell Busk, "E. P. Pectol," 5; Miriam B. Murphy, *A History of Wayne County* (Salt Lake City, Utah: Utah State Historical Society, 1999), 347.

11. Noel Morss, letter to E. P. Pectol of Torrey, Utah, August 26, 1928; *idem*, letter to E. P. Pectol of Torrey, Utah, November 6, 1920; *idem*, letter to E. P. Pectol of Torrey, Utah, November 18, 1928; *idem*, letter to E. P. Pectol of Torrey, Utah, October 7, 1928 (copies in possession of Neal Busk, Richfield, Utah).

12. *Idem, The Ancient Culture of the Fremont River in Utah: Report on the Explorations Under the Claflin-Emerson Fund, 1928–1929*, Papers

of the Peabody Museum of American Archaeology and Ethnology, Harvard University, vol. 12, no. 3 (Cambridge, Massachusetts: Peabody Museum, 1931), 5.

13. Ibid.

14. Andrew A. Kerr, Department of Archaeology and Western History, University of Utah, Salt Lake City, Utah, letter to Ephraim Pectol, November [date unclear], 1926 (copy in the possession of Neal Busk, Richfield, Utah).

15. John H. Edwards, Assistant Secretary of the Interior, letter to Senator Reed Smoot, Washington, D.C., January 20, 1927 (copy in the possession of Neal Busk, Richfield, Utah).

16. Noel Morss, letter to E. P. Pectol of Torrey, Utah, October 7, 1928 (copy in possession of Neal Busk, Richfield, Utah).

17. E. P. Pectol, letter to the Carnegie Museum of Pittsburgh, Pennsylvania., December 3, 1926 (copy in possession of Neal Busk, Richfield, Utah).

18. E. P. Pectol, letter to Joe Dubuicek of Chicago, Ill., July 2, 1934 (copy in possession of Neal Busk, Richfield, Utah).

19. Ibid., emphasis added.

20. J. K. Oliver, letter to E. P. Pectol of Torrey, Utah, March 10, 1938 (copy in possession of Neal Busk, Richfield, Utah).

21. E. P. Pectol, letter to J.K. Oliver of Monterrey, Calif., April 23, 1938 (copy in possession of Neal Busk, Richfield, Utah).

22. Irvin T. Nelson, Salt Lake City, letter to E. P. Pectol, Torrey, Utah, July 18, 1929; *idem*, Salt Lake City, letter to E. P. Pectol, Torrey, Utah, August 16, 1930 (copies in possession of Neal Bush, Richfield, Utah).

23. E. P. Pectol, Torrey, Utah, letter to Harold H. Hart, Washington, D.C., May 11, 1937 (copy in possession of Neal Busk, Richfield, Utah).

24. Juanita Brooks, *John Doyle Lee: Zealot, Pioneer Builder, Scapegoat* (Logan, Utah: Utah State University Press, 1992).

25. It was a common practice in the Church of Jesus Christ of Latter-day Saints during the latter half of the nineteenth century for women to be "sealed" to prominent male leaders in the church. These ceremonial "sealings" were meant to ensure salvation in the life hereafter and often did not equate to a temporal marriage relationship or living arrangement.

26. It appears that since the earlier marriage to Lee was a "spiritual sealing" and never consummated, Caroline was free to marry someone else during the lengthy time she was not associated with John D. Lee. Only much later did she seek to formalize a spousal relationship with Lee.

27. The Mountain Meadows Massacre was the only event associated with a brief period of hostilities, known historically as the "Utah War,"

that resulted in the loss of life. A group of approximately 120 immigrants from Arkansas and Missouri were massacred by Mormon militia and their Indian allies at a location approximately 35 miles southwest of Cedar City, Utah, in September 1857. The immigrants, who were headed to California, arrived in Utah during a period of war hysteria occasioned by misunderstanding and hostilities between the U.S. Government and the Latter-day Saint settlers in Utah. President Martin Van Buren dispatched a force of 2,500 army regulars to suppress what was being painted in the eastern press as a "Mormon insurrection." In the midst of these difficult circumstances and heightened emotions, the Baker-Fancher wagon train from Arkansas appears to have become embroiled in a disagreement with local citizens in the southern portion of the state as they traveled from Salt Lake City towards modern-day Cedar City. Hostilities mounted and armed conflict broke out with the immigrants being attacked at a camping spot called Mountain Meadows, just south of the modern community of Enterprise, Washington County. After a seven-day standoff, the members of the immigrant party were lured from their defensive breastwork of wagons and rifle pits by a false promise of safe escort back to Cedar City. The entire group of travelers, with the exception of 17 or 18 young children, was then brutally massacred. For a complete discussion of this complex and tragic event and the circumstances that caused it, see Juanita Brooks, *The Mountain Meadows Massacre* (Norman, Okla.: University of Oklahoma Press, 1970); and Donald R. Moorman and Gene A. Sessions, *Camp Floyd and the Mormons: The Utah War* (Salt Lake City: University of Utah Press, 1992).

28. Glen Lee of Salt Lake City, Utah, personal communication with the author, March 16, 2001.

29. G. G. Frazier, letter to Commissioner, General Land Office, Washington, D.C., December 9, 1932 (Capitol Reef National Park, museum accession file no. 3, copy).

30. Unsigned typescript of letter to Bishop [Pectol], November 13, 1930 (copy in possession of Neal Busk, Richfield, Utah).

31. Ibid.

32. Ibid.

33. G. G. Frazier, letter to Commissioner, General Land Office, Washington, D.C., December 9, 1932 (Capitol Reef National Park, museum accession file no. 3, copy).

34. Ibid.

35. Ibid.

36. Ibid.

37. Charles Kelly, a noted western historian, was appointed custodian of the new Capitol Reef National Monument in 1944. He was made

Superintendent of the Monument in 1951. In the interim period, Kelly acted as the government authority stationed at the Monument, but the facility was under the official administration of Zion National Park and overseen by various superintendents stationed there to whom Kelly reported.

38. Charles Kelly, memo to Superintendent, Zion National Park, December 11, 1952 (Capitol Reef National Park, museum accession file no. 3, copy); *idem*, memo to Superintendent, Zion National Park, January 27, 1953 (Capitol Reef National Park, museum accession file no. 3, copy); Jesse Nusbaum, National Park Service Archaeologist, memo to Director, National Park Service, Region Three, Santa Fe, New Mexico, June 5, 1953 (Capitol Reef National Park, museum accession file no. 3, copy).

39. E. P. Pectol, "The Shields" (unpublished manuscript in possession of Neal Busk, Richfield, Utah). See also, Elmer C. McGavin, *"Mormonism" and Masonry* (Salt Lake City: Bookcraft, 1947), 80–83; and Frank Beckwith, "The High Priest's Vestments used by the Ancient Cliff Dwellers of Wayne County Centuries Ago," *Improvement Era* (September 1927): 1029–1037.

40. E. P. Pectol, "The Shields."

41. [Editor's note: cf., however, several hide panels (cat. nos. 134–137), which undergraduate student Michelle Munsey observed resembled certain elements of the hide set pictured in McGavin, *"Mormonism" and Masonry*," 72 and referred to as priest's vestments. These panels exhibit chatter marks on the inner face, the result of the skinning and tanning process, as well as scattered (fortuitous) stains and pigment. Cf. also an article of hide clothing showing numerous enigmatic alterations suggesting a ruse (cat. no. 138).]

42. Paul R. Franke, Superintendent, Zion National Park, memo to Regional Director, Region Three, National Park Service, August 16, 1957 (Capitol Reef National Park, museum accession file no. 3, copy).

43. Dorothy H. Pectol, notarized document to Stiner Busk, October 26, 1950 (original in possession of Neal Busk, Richfield, Utah).

44. The Bureau of Information was a visitor information facility located at Temple Square in Salt Lake City and was operated by the Church of Jesus Christ of Latter-day Saints under the auspices of the Temple Square Mission. It would expand over the years to include an exhibit facility that would become known as the Temple Square Museum.

45. L. E. Young, Bureau of Information, Salt Lake City, Letter to Bishop E. P. Pectol, Torrey, Utah, August 29, 1927 (copy in possession of Neal Busk, Richfield, Utah).

46. Joseph Eckersley, Office of the Presiding Bishopric, Salt Lake City, letter to Bishop Ephraim P. Pectol, Torrey, Utah, September 14,

1926; Heber J. Grant, Salt Lake City, Utah, letter to Bishop Ephraim P. Pectol, Torrey, Utah, November 29, 1926; E. P. Pectol [copy not signed], Torrey, Utah, letter to President Heber J. Grant, Salt Lake City, December 9, 1926 (copies in possession of Neal Busk, Richfield, Utah).

47. E. P. Pectol [copy not signed], Torrey, Utah, letter to President Heber J. Grant, Salt Lake City, December 9, 1926 (copy in possession of Neal Busk, Richfield, Utah).

48. Lee Kreutzer, "The Pectol Collection, Capitol Reef National Park, Utah," *Utah Archaeology* 7, no. 1 (1994): 104–116.

49. Joseph J. Cannon, Bureau of Information, Salt Lake City, letter to Bishop Ephraim P. Pectol, Torrey, Utah, October 18, 1939 (copy in possession of Neal Busk, Richfield, Utah). Jesse Nusbaum, Archaeologist, memo to Superintendent Finnan, Zion National Park, Utah, March 5, 1940 (Capitol Reef National Park, museum accession file no. 3, copy).

50. E. P. Pectol, letter to Joseph J. Cannon, Bureau of Information, Salt Lake City, Utah, April 25, 1941 (copy in possession of Neal Busk, Richfield, Utah).

51. E. P. Pectol, letter to John H. Taylor, Bureau of Information, Salt Lake City, Utah, May 9, 1941 (copy in possession of Neal Busk, Richfield, Utah).

52. Charles Kelly, Superintendent, Capitol Reef Park, memo to Chas. J. Smith, Zion National Park Superintendent, March 30, 1948 (Capitol Reef National Park, museum accession file no. 3, copy).

53. Kreutzer, "The Pectol Collection."

54. E. P. Pectol, letter to John H. Taylor, Bureau of Information, Salt Lake City, Utah, May 10, 1941 (copy in possession of Neal Busk, Richfield, Utah).

55. John H. Taylor, Mission President, Temple Square Mission and Information Bureau, Salt Lake City, letter to E.P. Pectol, Torrey, Utah, September 4, 1941 (Capitol Reef National Park, museum accession file no. 3, copy); *idem*, Mission President, Temple Square Mission and Information Bureau, Salt Lake City, letter to E. P. Pectol, Torrey, Utah, February 19, 1942 (Capitol Reef National Park, museum accession file no. 3, copy); *idem*, Mission President, Temple Square Mission and Information Bureau, Salt Lake City, letter to E. P. Pectol, Torrey, Utah, April 27, 1942 (Capitol Reef National Park, museum accession file no. 3, copy); *idem*, Mission President, Temple Square Mission and Information Bureau, Salt Lake City, letter to E. P. Pectol, Torrey, Utah, September 8, 1942 (Capitol Reef National Park, museum accession file no. 3, copy).

56. *Idem*, Mission President, Temple Square Mission and Information Bureau, Salt Lake City, letter to E. P. Pectol, Torrey, Utah, July 17, 1943 (Capitol Reef National Park, museum accession file no. 3, copy).

57. Bradford J. Frye, *From Barrier to Crossroads: An Administrative History of Capitol Reef National Park,* Cultural Resources Selections No. 12 (Denver, Colorado: National Park Service, 1998).

58. Ibid., 63.

59. Chas. J. Smith, Superintendent Zion and Bryce Canyon National Parks, memo to Charles Kelly, Custodian, Capitol Reef National Park, February 13, 1948 (Capitol Reef National Park, museum accession file no. 3, copy); Jesse L. Nusbaum, Archaeologist, National Park Service, memo to Superintendent, Zion and Bryce Canyon National Parks, February 4, 1948 (Capitol Reef National Park, museum accession file no. 3, copy).

60. Charles Kelly, Custodian, Capitol Reef National Park, memo to Chas. J. Smith, Superintendent, Zion National Park, March 2, 1948 (Capitol Reef National Park, museum accession file no. 3, copy).

61. Charles Kelly, Acting Superintendent, Capitol Reef National Park, letter to Gilda Bush, Elsinore, Utah, April 27, 1951 (Capitol Reef National Park, museum accession file no. 3, copy); *idem*, Acting Superintendent, Capitol Reef National Park, memo to Superintendent, Zion National Park, April 27, 1951 (Capitol Reef National Park, museum accession file no. 3, copy); *idem*, Acting Superintendent, Capitol Reef National Park, memo to Superintendent, Zion National Park, August 22, 1951 (Capitol Reef National Park, museum accession file no. 3, copy); Jesse L. Nusbaum, Archaeologist, National Park Service, Santa Fe, New Mexico, letter to Floyd E. Dotson, Chief Clerk, National Park Service, Washington, D.C., September 14, 1951 (Capitol Reef National Park, museum accession file no. 3, copy); A. E. Demaray, Director, National Park Service, Washington, D.C., memo to Chief Clerk Dotson, National Park Service, October 1, 1951 (Capitol Reef National Park, museum accession file no. 3, copy).

62. Paul R. Franke, Superintendent, Zion and Bryce Canyon National Parks, letter to Richard L. Evans, Church Museum Temple Square, Salt Lake City, October 6, 1952 (Capitol Reef National Park, museum accession file no. 3, copy).

63. Richard L. Evans, Director, Bureau of Information, Salt Lake City, letter to Paul R. Franke, Superintendent, Zion and Bryce National Parks, Springdale, Utah, January 8, 1953 (Capitol Reef National Park, museum accession file no. 3, copy); Paul R. Franke, Superintendent, Zion and Bryce National Parks, letter to Richard L. Evans, Temple Square Museum, Salt Lake City, March 10, 1953 (Capitol Reef National Park, museum accession file no. 3, copy); Richard L. Evans, Bureau of Information, letter to Conrad L. Wirth, Director, National Park Service, Washington, D.C., May 8, 1953 (Capitol Reef National Park, museum accession file no. 3, copy).

64. Document granting permission for National Park Service to take

possession of Pectol-Lee collection for exhibit purposes, March 25, 1953 (original in possession of Neal Busk, Richfield, Utah). This document was signed by representatives of the Pectol and Lee families.

65. Jesse L. Nusbaum, Archaeologist, National Park Service, memo to Director, Region 3, National Park Service, Santa Fe, New Mexico, June 5, 1953 (Capitol Reef National Park, museum accession file no. 3, copy).

66. Paul R. Franke, Superintendent, Zion and Bryce National Parks, letter to Richard L. Evans, Director, Temple Square Museum, December 4, 1953 (Capitol Reef National Park, museum accession file no. 3, copy).

67. Undated list of loan objects, signed by Glen E. Lee, son of Charles W. Lee (carbon copy in possession of Neal Busk, Richfield, Utah).

68. Paul R. Franke, Superintendent, Zion and Bryce National Parks, memo to Director, Region Three, National Park Service, Santa Fe, New Mexico, August 16, 1957 (Capitol Reef National Park, museum accession file no. 3, copy).

69. John F. Turney, Archaeologist, National Park Service, Globe, Arizona, memo to Superintendent, Capitol Reef National Park, March 4, 1958 (Capitol Reef National Park, museum accession file no. 3, copy).

70. Russel C. Harris, Director, Temple Square Information Bureau and Museum, Salt Lake City, Utah, letter to William T. Kreuger, Superintendent, Capitol Reef National Park, August 29, 1960 (Capitol Reef National Park, museum accession file no. 3, copy); *idem*, Director, Temple Square Information Bureau and Museum, Salt Lake City, Utah, letter to Gilbert R. Wenger, Western Museum Laboratory, San Francisco, California, February 1, 1965 (Capitol Reef National Park, museum accession file no. 3, copy).

71. Barbara A. Grater, Museum Curator, Western Museum Laboratory, memo of receipt to Superintendent, Capitol Reef National Park, March 25, 1964 (Capitol Reef National Park, museum accession file no. 3, copy).

72. David E. Warthen, Harper's Ferry Center, Harper's Ferry, West Virginia, memorandum of receipt to Superintendent, Capitol Reef National Park, December 12, 1977 (Capitol Reef National Park, museum accession file no. 3, copy).

73. LDS Museum of Church History and Art, transfer letter, May 11, 1989; T. Michael Smith, Historic Sites Registrar, transmittal letter to National Park Service, Capitol Reef National Park, October 5, 1993 (Capitol Reef National Park, museum accession file no. 3, copy).

74. Receipt for Property, August 22, 1996 (Capitol Reef National Park, museum accession file no. 3, copy).

75. Kate Stevenson, Associate Director for Cultural Resources and Partnerships, National Park Service, May 19, 1998, memo to regions or units (Capitol Reef National Park, museum accession file no. 3, copy).

IN SEARCH OF FUNCTION: THE PECTOL-LEE CRADLE BOARD

Marti L. Allen and Michelle R. Munsey

The Pectol-Lee cradle board (Color Plate 1–3, 5, cat. no. 61) is unparalleled in the archaeological record and, of all the artifacts in the collection, is perhaps the one scholars and others are most eager to know more about. The need for study is especially great because the cradle board has been restricted to storage for years owing to the long, complex history of the Pectol-Lee collection, particularly with regard to title and ownership issues (see Baker, pp. 35–37, 43–46, this volume).

Its future disposition, moreover, is uncertain. Ideally, a suitable long-term repository will be identified to ensure its continued availability for exhibition and study. The interests of native groups pursuant to the Native American Graves Protection and Repatriation Act (NAGPRA) may have an impact on this concern. Although the cradle board resides in private hands and is therefore exempt from NAGPRA, some tribes residing in Utah and the Southwest may consider it sacred or patrimonial. The evidence of scientific analysis in conjunction with native practices and oral traditions should be brought to bear on this notion.

These concerns determine one objective of this volume: to present a thorough description and photographic documentation of the Pectol-Lee cradle board in the public domain, so that all parties may be able to study it within whatever theoretical or cultural framework they deem most relevant or appropriate.[1] A thorough description of the cradle board with its figurine is provided in the catalogue section of this volume. Thanks, moreover, to Munsey's methodical examination of the figurine (see cat. no. 61 and below), Sinkey's analysis of basketry construction techniques (see cat. no. 61 and pp. 157–158, this volume),[2] and radiocarbon dating, the dating and attribution of this artifact seem secure. This article also describes physical aspects of the artifact never reported before, namely, the figurine itself and its step-by-step attachment to the cradle board.

Finally, this paper examines comparanda that may help elucidate how the cradle board functioned and considers these comparanda in light of several of the cradle board's features described here for the first time.

Noel Morss' 1954 publication *Clay Figurines of the American Southwest*[3] discussed numerous comparanda and advanced compelling theories regarding the cradle board's function, all worthy of close review. Hopefully, this article will bring attention to an area of research that has lain dormant for several decades but that richly deserves revisitation.[4]

DATE AND CULTURAL AFFILIATION

It will be beneficial to lead this article with the evidence by which we have dated and attributed the cradle board with its figurine. The evidence points to Fremont attribution. The figurine's size (16 centimeters in height) and its facial features (Color Plate 2 and Figure 12) are analogous to a Fremont figurine found in the Huntington Canyon excavations[5] and others described by Morss,[6] leaving little doubt of Fremont affiliation. In terms of its iconography the Pectol-Lee cradle-board figurine is modest as compared to the celebrated Pilling figurines[7] but, as will be discussed presently, this comparative plainness may simply reflect an intention on the part of the craftsperson to represent an infant. The stylistic dating of the figurine corresponds to the radiocarbon date of the basketry cradle board (ca. AD 1000).[8] The sample analyzed was taken from a section of the close wrapped twining comprising the backboard; thus there seems little question but that the unusual basketry construction employed is contemporary with the figurine itself, ruling out the possibility that an heirloom figurine was placed inside a more recent cradle board as suggested by Morss.[9]

It is possible the cradle board itself (Color Plate 3), constructed through a technique previously undocumented among the Fremont, was exotic to the Fremont and imported for use with the figurine. Possible sources would be areas in Nevada where the close wrapped twining technique has been documented (see Sinkey, pp.163–164). Yet there appear to be at least two other examples of close wrapped twined cradle boards said to be from areas with strong Fremont presence. One is a full-size cradle board, intact with its human baby, found by a rancher in Nine Mile Canyon and lent to the College of Eastern Utah Prehistoric Museum in Price, Utah from approximately 1961 to 1966.[10] Its current whereabouts are uncertain, but living witnesses at the CEU Prehistoric Museum vouch for its existence and its provenance, and an image of it appears on a postcard formerly marketed by that museum (Color Plate 4).[11] The backboard of another full-size cradle board in the Museum of San Rafael, Castle Dale, Utah, also shows the same technique (Figure 13).[12] Living witnesses recall its discovery some miles west of Ferron, Utah.[13] Given the small size of the Pectol-Lee cradle board, it seems

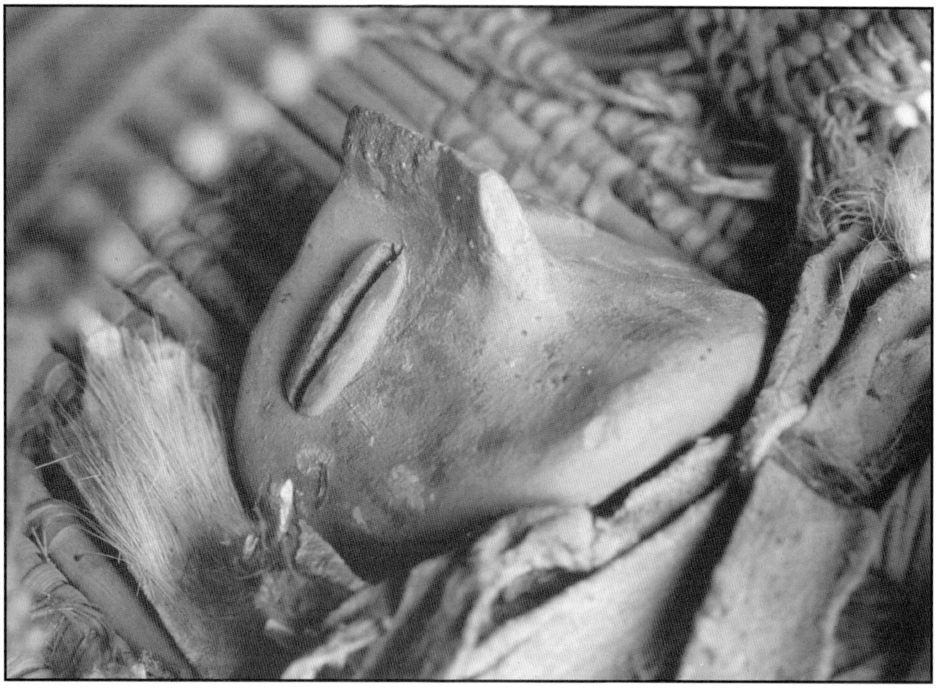

Figure 12. Pectol-Lee model cradle board (cat. no. 61), detail of face. Photo by David Hawkinson, 2001.

probable it was custom-made for this clay figurine, further strengthening Fremont affiliation. Thus, this example of close wrapped twining may, after all, not be singular among the Fremont. Additional parallels for the close wrapped twining may remain undocumented in museums and private collections.

A swatch of cotton textile is integral to the artifact but probably does not pose a contradiction to Fremont attribution (Color Plate 2). Woven cotton textile is normally believed not to have circulated north of the Four Corners region (Anasazi culture area); but in light of anomalies in the Pectol-Lee basketry suggesting Fremont-Anasazi cross-influence or interaction in the Capitol Reef region (see Sinkey, p. 164), it seems advisable not to preclude Fremont association based on the textile swatch alone. Rather, it is more prudent to allow for prehistoric exchange of woven cotton products or cotton-weaving technology in this region where overlap in Fremont and Anasazi occupation is known to have existed (see Talbot, pp. 10–12). Clearly, more comprehensive research addressing the question of Fremont-Anasazi interaction in the area is indicated and would be welcome.

Figure 13. Full-size cradle board said to be found west of Ferron, Utah, obverse (left) and reverse (right). Fremont? Museum of San Rafael, Castle Dale, Utah. Photos by Leslie-lynne Sinkey (right) and Scott Ure (left), 2001.

Whatever the source of the cotton textile and regardless of whether the board itself was made by a Fremont basket maker, it seems most likely the Fremont possessed and used it for the explicit purpose of cradling a Fremont-made clay figurine.

DESCRIPTION

The Cradle Board

As the basketry cradle board is fully described in the catalogue section (cat. no. 61), we will here describe only features relevant to our discussion. The cradle board consists of an elongated, lyre-shaped frame made of willow sticks worked in close wrapped twining that yielded richly decorative basketry. The backboard exhibits a visually striking checkerboard pattern achieved through close wrapped twining two colors of flexible wefts, light and dark brown, the darker of which were structurally dyed (Color Plate 3). The basketry sunshade spanning the upper portion of the cradle board also exhibits close wrapped twining, this time worked in a diamond pattern. The careful workmanship of the shade is not immediately apparent, however; a thin length of tanned hide extends across the exterior of the shade. This hide cover also drapes over the back, affording additional protection from the elements when the cradle board was in a vertical or hanging position. There are sinew stitch repairs on both ends of the hide cover. Perhaps the maker used a pieced panel to begin with, or perhaps the panel was damaged during its lifetime as part of the cradle board and was repaired rather than replaced.

The diamond design of the sunshade may carry significance. Among historic groups over a broad area, designs worked into the sunshade of cradle boards designated the gender of the infant. Among the Northern Paiute, for example, slanted lines were used for boys and zigzag lines for girls; among the Monache, slanted lines for boys and zigzags or diamonds for girls; and among the Washoe, diagonal lines for boys and rhomboids for girls.[14] Wheat reports the Paiute considered the sunshade to be the personal property of the baby, with great care being taken to preserve it.[15] The Fremont may have had similar customs.

The basketry "bassinette" nestling the figurine was constructed of rabbitbrush using techniques markedly different from those in the rest of the cradle board (Color Plate 1). The upper edge, a variation on a simple twined selvage, yields a decorative cornice that visually unifies the strong verticals of the open, multiple warps extending to the toe. Two rows of simple twining are worked across these warps, stabilizing and giving shape to the warps. As Sinkey noted in the catalogue description (p. 241, this volume), the bassinette is secured to the cradle board by two lengths of yucca cordage anchored to the reverse at their knotted ends and then tied together on front with slip-knots (viewer's left). As a result, the bassinette has ample "wiggle room" and could, in fact, have been removed without much effort. To Sinkey this suggested the bassinette was constructed last and only partially completed.

Other possibilities exist for why the bassinette construction differs from the rest of the cradle board. The bassinette of the Nine Mile Canyon cradle board (Color Plate 4) also exhibits a similar technical incongruency when compared to the construction technique used for the rest of the cradle board. Perhaps the seemingly temporary aspect of the bassinette was an intentional design feature of life-size cradle boards. A removable bassinette with "wiggle room" would have enabled the child to be more easily maneuvered in and out of the cradle board—indeed, as will be discussed below, the attachment method would have enabled the bassinette to be opened like a door, from left to right. The bassinette may have been viewed as more or less disposable, that is, intended to be replaced more frequently—less work would have been required to achieve the open warp construction. Perhaps the bassinette was intentionally left in an open weave to address the likely need for ventilation in this area. Finally, the open warp construction is by no means artistically inferior to the rest of the cradle board and may have been an aesthetic preference. Similar open warp construction has been the technique of choice among the historic Ute for cradle-board sunshades even on the finest, most intricately finished examples.[16] An aesthetic likely borne of utility, the open warp design of the Pectol-Lee bassinette is functionally appropriate and visually complementary to the rest of the cradle board.

The Pectol-Lee cradle board is equipped with a carrying strap—a strip of tanned bighorn sheep hide fastened to the board by means of looping through the rigid wefts (Color Plates 1 and 3). It is covered with a great deal of grime, apparently accreted through use. In addition, red ochre coloring lies both under and over the grime, indicating the red ochre was "freshened" from time to time. A line of yucca cordage twined through the base of the cradle board also preserves reddish coloring that appears to be ochre (Color Plate 1). Red ochre, and especially the color red, may have had special significance. Wheat reports that among the Paiute, the color red had protective or curative powers and the ability to bring good luck. The Paiute used it, for example, to repel rattlesnakes and to cure and prevent ailments, and mothers applied red coloring to the chafed skin of their babies' buttocks.[17]

A unique feature of this cradle board is its small size. Compared to the life-size examples mentioned above, the Pectol-Lee cradle board, at less than 42 centimeters in length, is about one half life-size. The backboard in the Museum of the San Rafael is 86 centimeters long and 48 centimeters at its widest point (Figure 14). A living witness recalls the example from Nine Mile Canyon (Color Plate 4) as being about 75 centimeters long and 50 centimeters wide.[18]

Despite its modest size, the Pectol-Lee cradle board is substantial and is, in fact, equipped with the same principal features deemed necessary for life-size cradle boards. Like the full-size examples, this cradle board has the lyre-shaped frame. Its sunshade is shaped and constructed similarly to the cradle board from Nine Mile Canyon (Color Plate 4). The only difference is that the Pectol-Lee specimen has the additional leather panel—a necessary precaution against rain, perhaps, since its unfired clay occupant would have been exceptionally vulnerable to water. As mentioned, the bassinettes of both the Pectol-Lee and Nine Mile

Figure 14. Comparison of Pectol-Lee cradle board (cat. no. 61) with cradle board from Museum of San Rafael. Photo by Leslie-lynne Sinkey, 2001.

Canyon cradle boards were each constructed differently from the rest of the cradle board and have a makeshift appearance (compare Color Plates 1 and 4).

The Pectol-Lee cradle board also has features in common with the San Rafael backboard (compare Color Plate 3 with Figure 13, right). The latter preserves pieces of hide that may be remains of a carrying strap and anchoring materials for a travois and sunshade. While the zig-zag design in the San Rafael example is a variation on the close wrapped twining used for the checkerboards in the model cradle board, the backboard does show the same construction technique along the bottom edge and the sides. Like the Pectol-Lee cradle board, the San Rafael backboard exhibits close wrapped twining "over two" across the lowest portion on the obverse, and its wefts or horizontal elements are attached to the vertical rods (warps) by wrapped twining in a chevron pattern on the back.

In sum, this model cradle board, which was obviously never intended to carry a real baby, has the basic accoutrements of a fully functional, life-size version. Indeed, it seems apparent its maker deliberately mimicked a full-size cradle board. This holds important clues about its intended function (see below).

The Figurine

The figurine in the Pectol-Lee cradle board cannot be fully seen (Color Plate 2). In addition to being nestled within a bassinette, it is almost completely swaddled in animal skins and textile from the neck down. The authors examined the figure tactilely as well as with x-ray images (Figure 15) and were thus able to discern several features unnoticed or at least not noted by previous examiners.

The figurine is fashioned of unfired, reddish-brown clay and is thirteen centimeters in height. The head closely resembles those of the Pilling figurines. It is pancake-shaped and roughly circular except for the wide, flat brow ridge delimiting the upper contour of the face. Like the Pilling figurines, there is a marked separation between the lower edge of the plane of the face and the torso, or as Morss preferred to say, the chin is "disengaged."[19] The eyes consist of "coffee-bean" appliqués with black painted lids and red dots at the inner corners. Unlike the Pilling figurines, it has an exceptionally prominent, ridge-like, pinched nose that slopes down steeply to the plane of the face. The head lacks a coiffure and any applied adornments; however, the lower half of the face itself is decorated with two tiers of short, vertical lines alternating in red and white pigment,[20] highly reminiscent of the one tier of red and white lines seen on most of the faces of the Pilling figurines.

The torso is a rather curvilinear trapezoid that narrows sleekly from broad shoulders to a small, low-placed waist before widening to hips. Based on x-ray images of the figurine (Figure 15), it lacks any indication of genitalia and has no sign of breasts, perhaps because the representation of an infant was intended.[21] There was no sign of a necklace or other personal adornment in modeled or applied clay, but x-ray imaging does not preclude the possibility that such elements were rendered in paint. Therefore the question remains open whether the figurine underlying its swaddling clothes is wholly unadorned.[22]

Because the bassinette is affixed loosely, visual and tactile examination of the lowest extremities was possible. The figurine terminates in substantial, stump-like appendages that are 3.8 centimeters in length and 1.3 centimeters in diameter and set at right angles to the body (Color Plate 5). Feet or legs are unusual for Fremont figurines, but not unheard of. Some of the figurines found during the Huntington Canyon excavations have lower extremities,[23] and Morss appears to have been familiar with examples of this unusual terminate.[24] The appendages

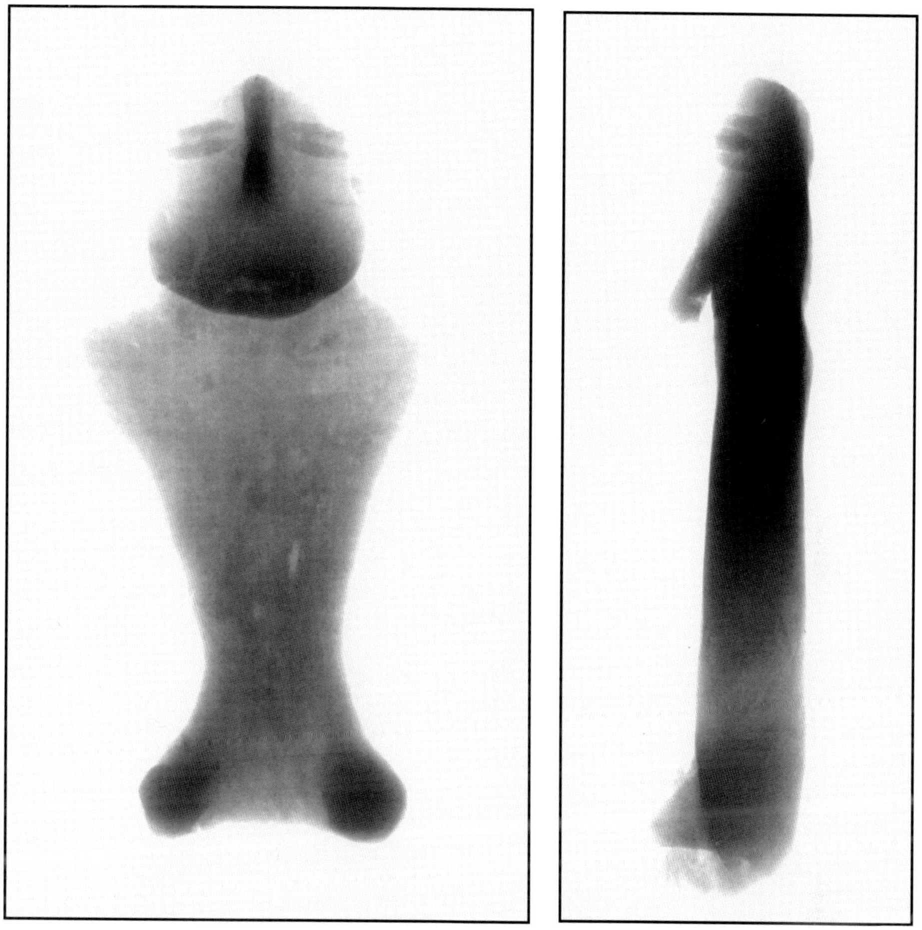

Figure 15. Figurine in Pectol-Lee model cradle board (cat. no. 61), obverse (left) and profile (right). Xrays by Brigham Young University Student Health Center, 2001.

of the Pectol-Lee cradle-board figurine are volumetrically substantial as compared to those of other clay figurines and are likely to be legs. They give the immediate impression of a child sitting with legs straight out. Considering the context of the figure, however, a more compelling interpretation is that of a very young infant reclining on its back with legs curled as a baby's legs would naturally do in life.[25] Of course, the abstract rendition makes it impossible to be definitive regarding the craftsperson's intentions.

Attachment of the Figurine to the Cradle Board

Through a careful study of the figurine in relation to the cradle board and its swaddling wraps, Munsey was able to reconstruct the steps through which the figurine was prepared for attachment to the backboard.

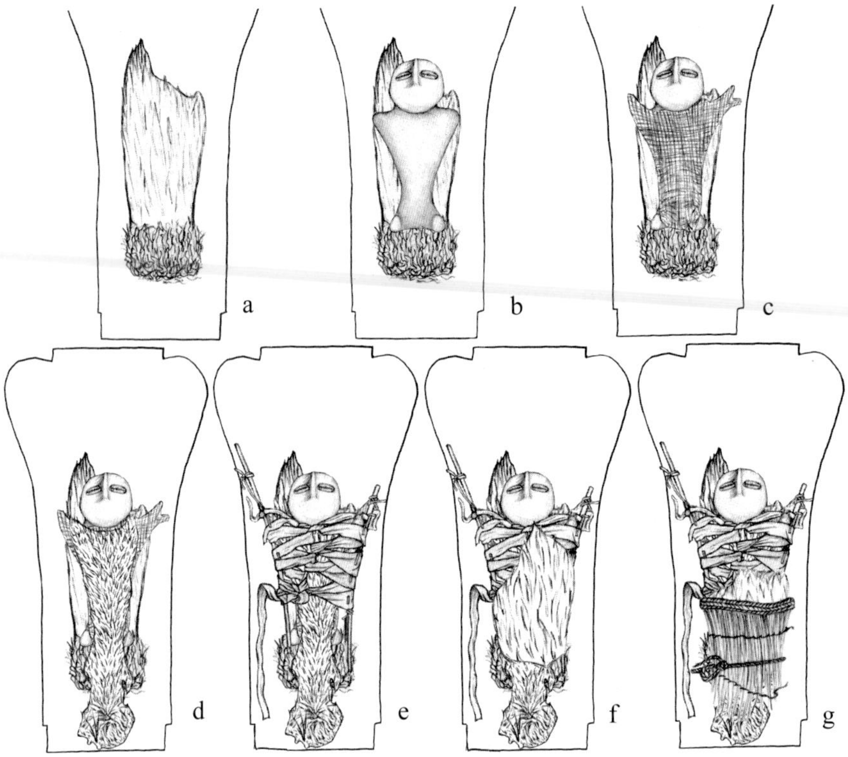

Figure 16a-g. Step-by-step process by which the Pectol-Lee cradle-board figurine (cat. no. 61) was attached to the board. (a) Animal skin bedding and shredded juniper bark pad; (b) figurine placed on top of animal skin bedding and shredded juniper bark pad; (c) cotton textile placed over figurine; (d) rodent skin pelt placed over figurine and cotton textile; (e) willow stick "travois" placed over swaddled figurine, laced with hide thongs, anchored at viewer's right by sinew stitches and at viewer's left with two cordage slip knots; (f) swatch of tinted deer fawn or bighorn sheep pelt laid over travois; and, (g) bassinette "closed." Drawing by Debbie Silversmith, 2001.

A review of these steps indicates nothing makeshift or cursory in this process: the clay infant was carefully swaddled and attached with deliberation to the cradle board.[26]

The steps of attaching the figurine began with laying a bedding of animal skin and placing at its base a pad of shredded juniper bark that had been worked until it was soft (Figure 16a). The clay infant was then placed on the skin bedding, its feet and buttocks overlaying the pad (Figure 16b). A swatch of cotton textile overlays the figure (Figure 16c). The cotton textile preserves its natural brown coloration and has a rolled hem with a red running stitch along the viewer's right. Next, a complete or nearly complete rodent hide, preserving at least the body with its hind legs, face, and whiskers, was placed over the figurine (Figure 16d). This pelt is oriented with the rodent head down. Its hind legs cup the figurine's lower face; its ribcage passes between the figurine's legs; and the rodent head extends beyond the figurine's body and through the bottom edge of the bassinette.

After the infant was covered with the rodent skin, an inverted A-frame "travois" was constructed of willow rods and laced together by two strips of tanned hide (Figure 16e). These two hide laces interlock around a third entering from the viewer's left and then pass down the sternum area and terminate in a knot on the viewer's left. The right side of the travois is anchored to the cradle board by means of sinew threads. On the viewer's left, the travois is affixed to the cradle board back in a more temporary fashion with two cordage slip knots, so that the travois could easily be "opened" from left to right and thereby free the clay baby. The willow rod travois with its hide lacings is thus an efficient restraining flap that would enable access to the child.

Following attachment of the travois to the backboard, an angular swatch of deer fawn or bighorn sheep pelt was laid across the figurine fur side out, with one of the corners directed toward the chin (Figure 16f).[27] Red ochre tints the flesh side of the pelt (Color Plate 5), recalling the Paiute beliefs, mentioned above, regarding the color red, and the corner of the pelt was folded under the bassinette, fur side out. The last step in securing the clay baby was to close the bassinette (Figure 16g).

Several of these features warrant emphasis and further discussion: the shredded juniper bark pad and its positioning relative to the figurine; the swaddling wraps in general and the cotton blanket and fawn or sheep pelt in particular; and the travois and its infant-restraining capabilities independent of the bassinette.

The juniper bark pad is located directly under the area of the clay infant that would correspond to the buttocks of a real baby (Figure 16b) and consequently may have been intended as expendable "diaper" material. The use of shredded juniper bark for diaper material corresponds to practices recorded among both the Anasazi and the Ute for their cradle boards.[28] In his 1942 listing of Ute and Southern Paiute "cultural elements," Omer C. Stewart chronicled numerous bands of Ute and Southern Paiute who reportedly used diapers of shredded bark.[29] According to Wheat, the Historic Paiute wrapped their babies in rabbit skins, dry algae, and sagebrush rubbed soft.[30] Juniper and sagebrush may well have been obvious choices for diaper material, owing to their natural scented oils and ability to be softened as well as to their medicinal value.[31]

The swaddling wraps used in the Pectol-Lee cradle board reflect general prehistoric customs for wrapping human infants. For example,

Wormington reported similar materials used in Basketmaker II cradle boards:

> The cradles were padded with juniper bark and covered with fur-cloth blankets, often made of the white belly skins of rabbits. Babies were tied in the cradle with soft fur cord . . . . Pads were used to prevent umbilical hernia. These were made of wads of corn husks or grass or a piece of bark, wrapped in a piece of prairie dog skin and tied in position with a fur cord.[32]

Some of the swaddling materials used in the Pectol-Lee cradle board, however, may have carried special significance. We have already mentioned the cotton blanket, which was probably exotic to the Fremont and most likely had to be procured from the Anasazi through trade. The swatch of pelt forming the uppermost layer of swaddling wraps (Figures 16f) may also be significant—if it is deer fawn as opposed to bighorn sheep. A pelt extracted from a baby deer may have been more highly valued than a pelt from an adult animal, perhaps of special significance. The use of fawn pelt for swaddling wraps is not a singular occurrence in the archaeological record. The mummy of a prehistoric human infant, recovered from a cave west of Ferron, Utah, was wrapped in the pelt of an antelope fawn before being placed in a woven bark mat.[33] Stewart reported that among several Ute and Southern Paiute bands fawn skin blankets were used to wrap babies.[34] A connection between infant human and infant animal may be suspected, or possibly the animal whose pelt was used as swaddling was perceived to convey to the infant some special trait of the animal.[35]

Finally, mention of the travois is pertinent owing to its design features. It effectively has a "hinge" which, in conjunction with the removable bassinette, would have enabled one to "open" the bassinette and change the juniper diaper but leave the travois "closed" so that the arms of the infant remained restrained (see Figure 16e). Given the realism the artisan observed in making the cradle board itself, and the correlation of the juniper bark pad to a real-life convention in the prehistoric and ethnographic records, it is reasonable to suspect that these design features of the cradle board were intended to reflect an actual practice. In a full-size cradle board or real-life situation, the use of a travois or other intermediate structure would have enabled the parent or other steward to change and clean the baby without freeing the arms of the infant.

Thus, the figurine in the cradle board represents exactly what it logically should, a baby—indeed, one whose legs, if we have interpreted them correctly, evoke an animate infant. The use wear on the cradle board is restricted to areas where one would expect use had it been handled analogously to a full-size cradle board in a real-life situation. The handling strap exhibits grime from carrying, and its red coloring was maintained through freshening. The edges along the sides of the cradle board show polish and grime at the narrowest point of the frame, a natural point for gripping while picking it up and laying it down. It shows grime where the knots of the travois and the bassinette would have been repeatedly tied and untied. In her condition report of the bassinette (p. 242, this volume), Sinkey reports that it "exhibits abrasion, particularly of the selvage and three succeeding rows . . . . [the] lowest course of twining [is] loose and separating from warps, . . . [and there is] loss of some warp elements or portions thereof, particularly on the viewer's right." Generally speaking, this wear corresponds to what one would expect if the bassinette had been repeatedly opened and closed in the manner described. It is also apparent that this use wear developed in prehistory, when the textile, fur, and basketry components were still supple and not in recent times, as through handling by the Pectol or Lee families or by researchers over the decades. Due to the embrittlement of these materials, such handling in modern times would have resulted in the destruction of these components of the artifact.

That the cradle board was used analogously to a full-size cradle board is further indicated by the lack of wear one would expect if it had been handled it in a manner incongruent with that function. The prominent features do not show contusions; the loose elements that attach the bassinette and the travois to the cradle board are intact despite the delicate nature of the cordage; and the delicate cotton textile is embrittled but otherwise undamaged except for minimal fraying and unraveling. Notably, the whiskers and nose of the rodent skin, which are fully exposed at the toe of the bassinette, are intact. Indeed, although the artifact saw noticeable use, it was apparently maintained in good condition throughout its use life, was not carelessly treated, and was used consistently with full-size examples.

IN SEARCH OF FUNCTION

The Cradle Board's Context

The cradle board is exceptional in the Pectol-Lee collection owing to the fact that Ephraim Pectol recorded some information about its provenience according to the finder, Charles W. Lee. For most artifacts, archaelogical context holds the best chance of elucidating function. In an unpublished history dated 1947, Ephraim Pectol wrote:

> A Clay Image [sic] with hawk and human features, and a true representation of Egyptian art—placed in a basket or (cradle board) [sic] with fine fur around it and of very fine workmanship was found by C. W. Lee. An alter [sic] found near by [sic] had falled [sic] into a fire place under neath [sic] it and was broken beyond repair.[36]

This description, clearly derived from Lee after the fact, is as intriguing as it is frustrating. One dismisses the fanciful comparison to attributes of the hawk-headed deity Egyptian Horus—whom the clay figurine resembles in no substantive way—and yearns in vain for a description of the altar and how closely (if at all) the cradle board was associated with it. Regrettably, nothing is said regarding what other artifacts might have been found in the vicinity to help define the context.

Despite the vagueness of the description, the compulsion to speculate about what Lee saw when he found the cradle board is great. Lee's reference to an altar is especially intriguing, even though he did not explain how he arrived at this interpretation nor specify the materials or construction of this collapsed feature. One is tempted to wonder if this feature was actually an earthen bench and hence find a comparison in a feature Montgomery and Montgomery found in Huntington Canyon, a Fremont site south of Price, Utah (42Em2095).[37] While excavating in a pit house dated ca. AD 1150 (Structure 1), the Montgomerys discovered what they described as a temporary earthen "shelf" (Feature 10-D) constructed in turn upon an earthen "bench" encircling the pit house interior. Numerous clay figurines had been placed—and in some cases inserted into—the earthen shelf near materials, such as food-stuffs, miniature clay burden baskets, a resin store, a leather string, a bone basket-making tool, and chipped and ground stone implements.[38] One cluster of these "special use" materials included a miniature clay cradle board into which a contextually unassociated clay figure "fitted nicely," an example of a so-called babe-in-cradle (see next section).[39] The presence of such exotic materials inclined the excavators to conclude the site had ceremonial or ritual purposes, and they interpreted the shelf as an altar or shrine, as opposed, for example, to a storage repository.[40] Noting the lack of comparisons in Fremont material culture, they compared the bench to features in Anasazi pithouses in the Four Corners, and both bench and shelf to benches and altars constructed by historic and modern Puebloan peoples for ritual purposes involving such items as fetishes, figurines, and miniature vessels.[41]

The comparison to the Huntington Canyon site led us to no firm hypothesis about its comparability to the cradle board's ill-defined context. The point of presenting such an enticing comparison is this: the Pectol-Lee cradle board is a classic and especially poignant example of an important cultural artifact irreparably robbed of contextual significance.

Pectol did not say what the mysterious altar was made of, and it was already "broken beyond repair" when Lee saw it. We cannot assume the features seen by Lee reflected an intact context. Pectol did not give the geographic location where Lee found the cradle board. Given the cradle board's state of preservation, the location was probably a dry cave. The contents of dry caves can be of multiple origins and time periods, and it is impossible to associate features without proper excavation. Literature contemporary to Lee and Pectol also indicates that the caves they knew in the Capitol Reef area were also known, visited, and apparently ransacked by other relic hunters (see Baker, p. 21). It is therefore conceivable the cradle board was in no way associated with the altar, if that feature can, indeed, be identified as such. The strata may have been disturbed before Lee visited the cave, or Lee himself may have disturbed the strata while rummaging for relics. In sum, Pectol's secondhand description is insufficient to enable reconstruction of the feature he described as a collapsed altar, to relate this feature to known features from other sites, or even to associate the cradle board with this unidentifiable feature.

Parallels in the Archaeological Record

The lack of stratigraphic context for the cradle board necessitates a search for iconographic and stylistic comparanda that may give insights to function. The most extraordinary feature of the Pectol-Lee cradle-board figurine is that it was carefully and deliberately placed within an ornate, intricately fashioned cradle board. One might expect the cradle board with its clay baby, being such a meticulously crafted artifact, to have developmental antecedents, that is, to be part of a substantial tradition of such artifacts; yet the cradle board appears to be an isolated occurrence in the archaeological record. The significant corpus of analogously large but elaborately decorated clay figurines, such as the Pilling figurines, affords unlikely comparisons. As Morss pointed out, it would seem contradictory to decorate a figurine carefully, only to obscure the decorations in wrappings and then lash the figure to a cradle board, especially given how prone clay appliqués are to detachment.[42]

On the other hand, the iconography itself of a figure combined with a cradle board does not constitute a singularity in prehistory. If we disregard size, function, and the multiple media used in the Pectol-Lee cradle board and consider alone the motif of a baby in a cradle, a prehistoric parallel, first noted by Morss, comes to mind.[43] This is a small genre of cradle-board figures, termed by Morss and others "babes-in-cradles." Babes-in-cradles are miniature figures modeled in clay, most of which have been attached to the handles of pottery bowls or ladles before firing, so that they are an integral part of the handle (Figure 17).[44]

Figure 17. "Babe-in-cradle" Ladle, Jeddito Yellow Ware, from Homolovi No. 1, Jeddito Valley, Arizona; top (left), profile (right). Pueblo IV, probably late fourteenth century AD. The Field Museum, Chicago, neg. #A93713 (left); neg. #A93714 (right). Scanned with permission of The Field Museum, Chicago, from Noel Morss, *Clay Figurines of the American Southwest*, Papers of the Peabody Museum of American Archaeology and Ethnology, Harvard University, vol. 49, no. 1 (Cambridge, Mass.: Peabody Museum, 1954), 92, fig. 18.

Babes-in-cradles are not plentiful in the archaeological record. Morss cited five pottery specimens hailing from (Kayenta) Anasazi sites in northeastern Arizona dated to the Pueblo III and Pueblo IV Periods (twelfth–fourteenth century AD): Young's Canyon (probably twelfth century), Homolovi (late fourteenth century), Big Hawk Valley (probably before AD 1250), Wupatki (twelfth or thirteenth century), and Awatovi (late thirteenth century).[45] An example from Mummy Cave in Canyon del Muerto is the earliest, dating to the Basketmaker III Period (AD 500–750),[46] while an unfired clay baby tied on its cradle board, reportedly excavated at Pueblo Grande de Nevada, would probably date, along with the site, to AD 900–1100.[47] We have already mentioned the miniature, unfired cradle board found in Huntington Canyon.[48] These latter two clay examples were apparently not attached to ladles, but share the iconography. The babes-in-cradles bear discussion, since Morss associated them with the Pectol-Lee cradle board, and subsequent references in scholarly literature to babes-in-cradles have perpetuated this association.

The function and significance of the babes-in-cradles can only be hypothesized, but scholarly opinion has leaned toward an association with shamanism or a concern for fertility among women. The pottery babe-in-cradle from Young's Canyon and the clay specimen recovered by Montgomery and Montgomery at Huntington Canyon (see above) may warrant special note since they were found in intact contexts that suggest a connection to shamanism. The Young's Canyon specimen was reportedly retrieved from the intact burial of an adult male whom one scholar referred to as "a man of great importance," although confirming information about this context was not readily available.[49] The Huntington Canyon specimen was found on an earthen bench in a pithouse. There may have been some connection between the ritual or "special use" materials in the pithouse, dated ca. AD 1150, and the burial of an adult male (Feature 10-G), which was discovered in the floor of the pit house and which postdated a hearth (Feature 10-F), a charcoal sample from which radiocarbon dated to AD 1015. The Montgomerys concluded that the person commanded importance and power in his community—perhaps as a chief or shaman. The building ("Structure 1") containing this burial and figurines was burned to the ground in a manner that led the excavators to conclude this was an intentional or ritual burning.[50] Indeed, the ritual nature of the Huntington Canyon site seems unquestionable, although its exact nature cannot be determined. The presence of the figurines led the Montgomerys to suggest "the houses were those of specialized religious practitioners," and they proposed the figurines were part of a "ritual tool kit."[51] If so, the clay babe-in-cradle would presumably have been one of several such "tools" at the disposal of the religious practitioner.

Morss hypothesized the connection of the babes-in-cradles with fertility concerns, suggesting that babes-in-cradles had relevance to what he termed an "increase cult," by which he seems to have meant a cult governing human fecundity (sexual fertility).[52] He developed this theory based on what he referred to as an "obvious" connection between the babes-in-cradles and modern cradle-board effigies used among Puebloan people to foster pregnancy in barren women or women who had miscarried.[53] He stated a similar connection between babes-in-cradles and the Pectol-Lee cradle board and proposed an indirect, ideological connection between the two genres, that is, that the babes-in-cradles were peripheral symbolic references to a larger cultic complex to which, in his mind, the Pectol-Lee cradle board also belonged.[54]

Certainly, some ethnographic examples of cradle boards with figurines have played key roles in ritual aimed at fertility in women. They also provide ready visual parallels for the Pectol-Lee cradle board and will be discussed below as valid comparanda. Whether or not the babe-in-cradle and other artifacts found in the earthen bench of the Huntington Canyon pithouse relate to the subfloor burial of the supposed religious practitioner could perhaps be debated, but a number of the cached artifacts themselves could be interpreted as references to *agrarian* fertility and productive activities normally associated with women.[55] These artifacts include the mano, used for grinding corn; the miniature clay burden baskets, one of which was filled with juniper fruit, reflecting the gathering task;[56] and perhaps the "bone matting/basketry tool," presumably an awl, used to make basketry food containers. Babe-in-cradle ladles were presumably made by women, who are normally assumed to have been the potters in the prehistory of this region; and the cradle board subject itself is an emphatic reference to female productivity. Therefore, a case might be made for interpreting the babes-in-cradles as cultic paraphernalia associated with a fertility cult focused on the well-being of women who were so closely connected physically to sexual fecundity and food processing.

Yet in many ways the leap between the pottery babes-in-cradles and model cradle boards, whether prehistoric or modern, seems a substantial one. As compared to the Pectol-Lee cradle board, the babes-in-cradles are generically, artistically, and typologically disparate. They are truly miniature, ranging in length from about five to fifteen centimeters. Affixed to their pottery handles, they have a fundamentally different visual and functional impact than the Pectol-Lee cradle board with its lifelike materials and features. The highly abbreviated, artistic renditions of cradle boards holding babies have no true-to-life presence whatever; in fact, their attachment to pottery ladles constructs an artificial context for a baby and cradle and leads one to suspect they had symbolic or decorative value. Babes-in-cradles were obviously specialized for functions quite different from the model cradle board. The pottery babes-in-cradle ladles would logically have been used for feeding or serving, although one could expend a good deal of energy hypothesizing specifically how they functioned in a fertility cult—were they "baby spoons" used to feed children? were they used to debouch substances deemed to increase a woman's chance of becoming pregnant? and so forth. The unfired examples from Pueblo Grande de Nevada and Huntington Canyon, being fragile, must have functioned more esoterically. The Pectol-Lee cradle board, along with its clay baby, on the other hand, was apparently physically used to mimic the care of an infant.

Moreover, the type of cradle board represented by the babes-in-cradles differs in three main ways from the Pectol-Lee cradle board, suggesting the two artifact types represent different cultural, or at least different ideological, traditions. First, the babes-in-cradles exhibit cradle boards with sunshades attached to the backboard along one long edge like an awning, such that there is no gap when the cradle board is in the vertical position, as in a "reclining U" (Figure 17), whereas the sunshade of the Pectol-Lee cradle board is attached by the short ends and extends over the baby's head, more like a free-standing canopy or a "standing" U (Color Plate 1). Second, the cradle boards on the pottery ladles are equipped with a wide brace across the chest to secure the baby, where as the clay baby in the Pectol-Lee cradle board is secured by means of the travois attached to the backboard. Third, the babes-in-cradles are supported from below by a flat ledge rather than a bassinette, as in the case of the Pectol-Lee cradle board. Given the precedence, demonstrated above, of mimicking the details of full-size cradle boards when crafting smaller versions, the differences in cradle board type noted here are probably culturally or ideologically significant.

In sum, the babes-in-cradles establish a prehistoric precedent in the Anasazi iconographic repertoire for the motif itself of a cradle board with figure and, it seems, in the Fremont repertoire as well, unless the single example from Huntington Canyon is anomalous, as in an Anasazi (Puebloan) interpolation based on the Montgomerys' comparanda for the associated architecture (above, p. 68). The tiny renditions of the cradle board subject appearing on the pottery ladles and as clay figurines are not close comparisons to the Pectol-Lee cradle board stylistically, typologically, or functionally. That there appear to be no intermediate, artistic developmental stages between the abstracted babes-in-cradles and the physically functional Pectol-Lee cradle board does not compromise the Fremont attribution of the cradle board ensemble, since the figurine alone is highly diagnostic. The artistic disparity and especially the functional differences seem strong deterrents to Morss' theory of an ideological connection between the two. Whether or not, moreover, there is sufficient evidence to support the use of the babe-in-cradle effigy ladles in shamanism or the existence of a larger, overarching, fertility cult in prehistoric times would need substantially more evidence than has been provided to date and is beyond the scope of this paper. Thus the babe-in-cradle artifacts must remain enigmatic to us for the time being. While they may have contributed symbolically to the significance of the ladles to which they were attached, and while the clay example from Huntington Canyon may have functioned esoterically in a shaman's "tool kit," the Pectol-Lee cradle board goes beyond motif and symbol—unlike the babes-in-cradles, it could be grasped within arms and carried like a real cradle and apparently was.

Parallels in the Ethnographic Record

Model cradle boards with and without model babies occur in the material culture of numerous modern-day native peoples in the Greater Southwest and beyond. In terms of size, materials, detail, and visual impact, these model cradle boards are much more comparable to the Pectol-Lee cradle board than the pottery babes-in-cradles appliqués and hence seem more likely to provide clues about the meaning and function of the Pectol-Lee cradle board. Model cradle boards have various functions among modern native peoples. The authors encountered three different possibilities: dolls or toys, fetishes for barren women, and funeral pyres for cremating the dead.

Dolls or Toys

Among Native Americans, model cradle boards are most broadly considered "dolls" or "toys." In native language, these terms imply "teaching tools" rather than devices of distraction or entertainment such as yoyos, tops, bubble blowers, or modern electronic toys. These terms do not refer to games of chance, such as board, stick, or ball games, which are often associated in Native American cultures with gambling. Even within traditional Western understanding, many "toys" and certainly "dolls" are, as most people would probably acknowledge, commonly intended, among other things, to aid in the indoctrination of children into gender- or culture-specific roles, with domestic skills formerly being associated with female roles and hunting, war, and careers outside of homemaking and caretaking associated with males.[57]

The traditional Western definition seems similar to native perceptions of "dolls" or "toys." In 1995 Clifford Duncan, then commonly recognized as a ceremonial leader among the Northern Ute, examined numerous Ute dolls in the Dillman Collection in the Museum of Peoples and Cultures. According to Duncan, dolls dressed in traditional Ute clothing were intended to teach Ute children "how to dress, how to *be*, and how *not* to be like other Indian children."[58] Among native peoples whose religion tend to be inextricably intertwined with daily life functions, "toys" might also help indoctrinate children about religious concepts—or even into religious societies. This fuller sense seems to correspond to what Morss meant when he described native cradle-board figures used as children's toys:

> Toy cradles are the most common and most prized possession of the little [Hopi] girls. [However,] the dolls of the Hopi children are regarded, at least by their elders, as educational toys and not mere idle playthings, and represent supernatural personages.[59]

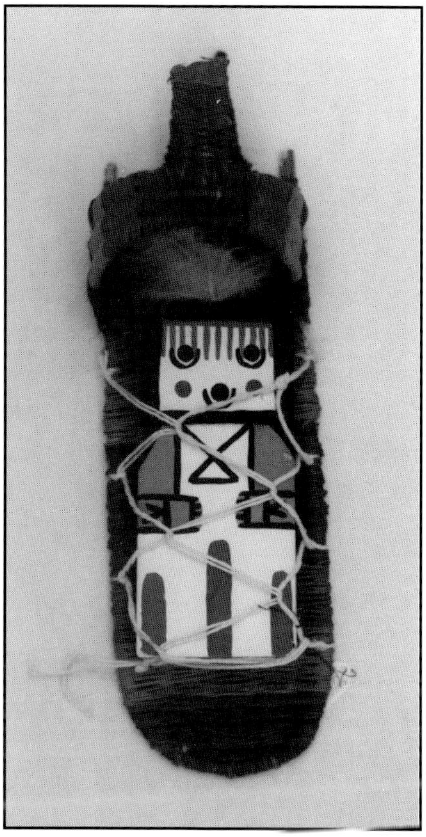

Figure 18. Cradle-board Kachina (Hahai-I Wuhuti, Kachina Mother). Hopi, twentieth century. Utah Museum of Natural History (ET 300.395). Photo courtesy Utah Musuem of Natural History, Salt Lake City.

Indeed, serious studies frequently define Hopi kachina dolls as "teaching tools."[60] The dolls help familiarize children with the forms assumed by the many kachina spirits who inhabit the San Francisco Peaks and visit Hopi communities seasonally. They also foster a sense of belonging within tribe and clan. Kachina dolls have a complex significance that goes beyond "teaching:" as one of the three manifestations of Hopi kachina spirits, each doll embodies a supernatural being.

Kachina dolls have four different physical forms, each considered to reflect one of the four stages of *Tihu*, or physical development of the child, from baby to adolescent, the first stage being the flat cradle-board babies given to toddlers (Figure 18).[61] The dolls representing the first stage of *Tihu*, therefore, are most relevant to the present study, yet these do not offer a close visual comparison to the Pectol-Lee cradle board. Traditional Hopi kachina dolls are constructed entirely of painted

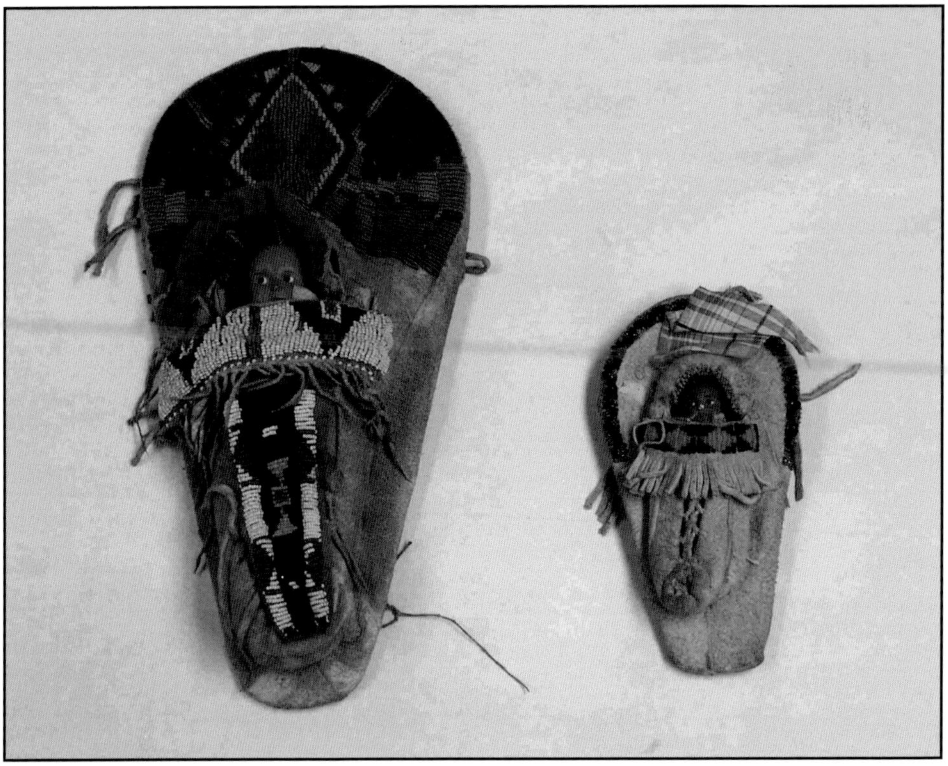

Figure 19. Toy cradle boards with Skookum dolls, obverses. Ute, ca. 1930. Museum of Peoples and Cultures, 87.130.176 (left) and 87.130.120 (right). Photo by Camille Jolley, 2001.

cottonwood, although as the craft developed over the years, some painted details were elaborated upon by a range of trappings applied in various materials, such as leather belts, yarn armlets, cloth sashes, vinyl kilts, and so forth.[62] Cradle-board kachinas, however, rarely consist of more than the painted wood with a feather on the head, and the cradled babies are not swaddled, although they are at least sometimes detachable, as in the example we have illustrated here. Rather, these dolls—as with all kachina dolls—were made primarily for viewing and were often suspended on walls.

Thus, while cradle-board kachinas are considered to have the properties of "teaching tools," they also have symbolic functions. The wooden cradle boards do not closely imitate the appearance or materials of actual cradle boards used by Hopi women, nor do they physically function in a way that is analogous to how the Pectol-Lee cradle board experienced handling.

Most visually, technically, and functionally comparable to the Pectol-Lee cradle board are model cradle boards made for use more purely as

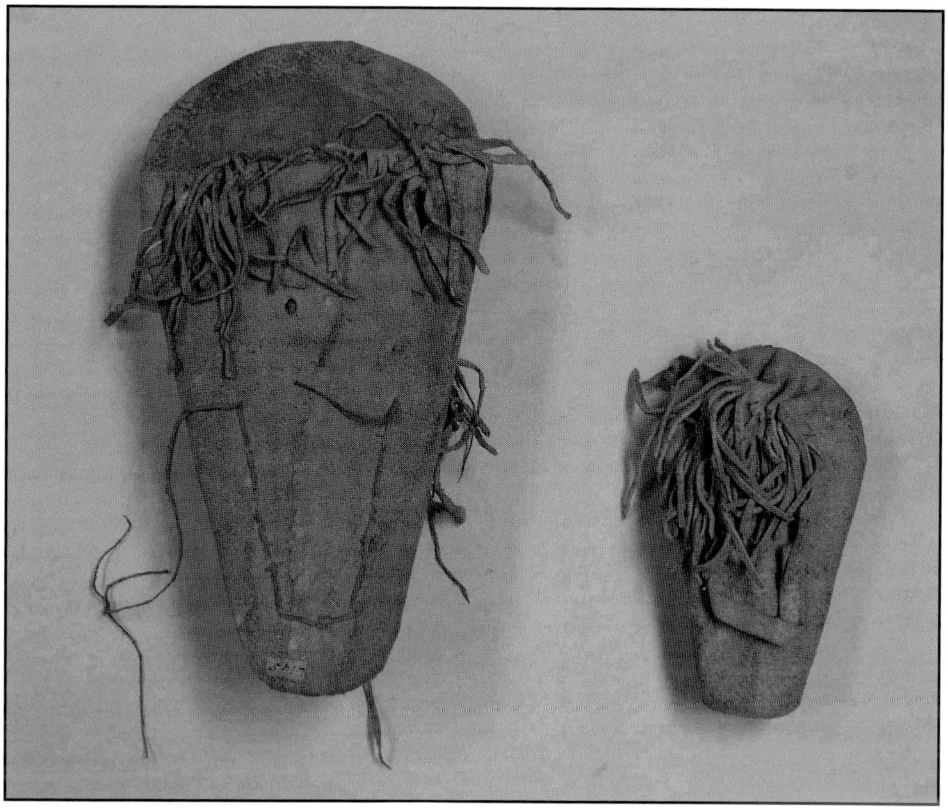

Figure 20. Toy cradle boards with Skookum dolls, reverses. Ute, ca. 1930. Museum of Peoples and Cultures, 87.130.176 (left) and 87.130.120 (right). Photo by Camille Jolley, 2001.

dolls or toys in the sense we have defined, that is, instruments that indoctrinate children into gender and cultural roles but lack symbolic or supernatural powers. Model cradle boards with babies closely resembling the Pectol-Lee cradle board in critical respects are documented in many cultures, for example, among the Northern Plains Indians, the Shoshone-Bannock, Great Basin cultures, the Navajo, the Apache, the Dakota, and the Cheyenne.[63] In each case documented here, the cradle boards are constructed similarly and with the same materials as full-size cradle boards made for real babies; and the dolls, commonly made of cloth or tanned hide, are entirely removable, enabling use or "play" that closely mimics real-life practice as a mother with her child.[64]

For example, two model cradle boards in the Museum of Peoples and Cultures, collected by Mildred Miles Dillman from the Northern Ute reservation near Duchesne, Utah, have removable Skookum dolls probably dating around 1930 (Figures 19–20).[65] The larger cradle board is 34 centimeters in height and 17 centimeters at its widest point; while the smaller is 19 centimeters in height and 10 centimeters at the widest point. Like the life-size cradle boards they closely imitate, these model cradle boards have beaded plackets that can be untied, giving access to the laced front where the dolls can be removed. To gain access to the doll in the larger example (Figure 19, left), one first unties the fringed, horizontal placket, which is secured by tanned hide thongs at the viewer's left, and "opens" the placket from left to right. The anchor stitches at viewer's right appear to be more permanent. Then one unties the vertical placket which is secured by tanned hide thongs at any of the four corners and lifts the placket completely away if desired, exposing the tanned hide laces up the front. These latter untie from the bottom up. To remove the doll from the smaller cradle board (Figure 19, right), one unties the fringed, cross placket and "opens" it, again from left to right, gaining access to the laces, which unlace from the top down. Like full-size cradle boards, the model examples have loops for suspension on the reverse. The larger of the two has one small, sturdy loop at the point of the baby's head and a second, longer but flimsy loop at the point of the buttocks (Figure 20, left). The small cradle board has a single, sturdy loop opposite the buttocks sufficiently generous to accommodate the hand and wrist of a child for carrying (Figure 20, right). Both cradle boards exhibit a fringed mass on the reverse at the top.

An example of an earlier model cradle board, which the principal author did not have an opportunity to examine firsthand, is in the San Diego Museum of Man (Figure 21). Made in ca. 1890, this Apache cradle board consists of a wood backboard and a standing "hoop" canopy, both covered with tanned, beaded hide stitched up the front and cradling a removable, swaddled, cloth baby with painted facial features and bead earrings.

Fertility Fetishes

In his well known work *Clay Figurines*, Morss surveyed the ethnographic record and compiled references to historic model cradle boards with associated doll babies that appear to have been used as fetishes by women desirous of having a child—indeed, this class of cradle board appears to have inspired his suggestion that the almost wholly dissimilar babes-in-cradles were connected to an "increase" cult.[66] He cited model cradle boards among certain Puebloan tribes of the Southwest (Zuni, Cochiti, Hopi, Laguna, and Jemez) and attributed (although without explanation) analogous practices among the Pomo and Coastal Miwok of California to Pueblo origin.[67] Morss' accounts, actually summaries of accounts made by earlier ethnographers, are provocative and warrant quoting:

Figure 21. Toy cradle board with cloth doll, obverse. Apache, ca. 1890. San Diego Museum of Man 1968-71-60. Scanned with permission of San Diego Museum of Man from Don and Debra McQuiston, *Dolls and Toys of Native America: A Journey Through Childhood* (San Francisco: Chronicle Books, 1995), 43, left.

> A clay "baby" may be placed over a Zuni Rain Chief's winter solstice altar by a woman desirous of offspring. More commonly the 'baby' is made of wood and dressed like a kachina. During a dance a woman who has suffered a miscarriage may be given one of these kachina dolls by a kachina dancer . . . . Subsequently, the *whia* (doll), together with the cradle board sometimes given with it, may be carried by the woman secretly under her blanket when she goes out of doors.[68]

> At the Hopi Powamu ceremony appear masks representing old women who carry doll babies partly hidden in spruce twigs. Childless women throw corn meal to these dolls, throwing to the male doll if a boy is desired, to the female doll, if a girl. Possibly these dolls are given to the women.[69]

> At Cochiti also a pregnant woman or one who desires a child receives from a priest a doll baby in a cradle, and cares for it and talks to it as she would a real baby. Here the cradle is of wood and the baby or *o'aka* is simply a wooden cylinder with a crude face at the top.[70]

> [In Pomo "increase rites"] the dolls were made of white clay and wood. The eyes were made of wampum. The dolls had heads, but no arms and legs . . . . The figures themselves were not sacred, for children played with similar toys. The dolls, however, acquired mana after they were blessed by the head priest (yomta) . . . . The women knew what was being done, and if they wished children they set about making baby baskets . . . from dogwood shoots . . . . Each woman received a male or female doll according to her desires. She put the doll into the cradle, took it to bed with her, suckled it, and in every way treated it as if it were a child."[71]

A weakness of Morss' discussion of fertility fetishes and therefore of the present study, is the lack of specific information about the physical characteristics of his comparanda, that is, the dolls mentioned in the excerpts quoted above. Most visually evocative of the Pectol-Lee cradle board among his comparanda were examples constructed of composite materials (wood, wicker, and pottery or clay). He illustrated a sketch of a small Hopi wicker cradle board with a pottery figure wearing a cloth shawl and reported it accurately mimicked a [full-size] Hopi cradle board; and he reproduced a sketch of a Zuni cradle board, reportedly about nine inches in length, made of willow with a wooden baby that appears to be wrapped in a textile or hide.[72] His other comparanda, however, were not described in details sufficient to aid comparison with the Pectol-Lee cradle board. Information essential for a comparison between these modern cradle boards and the Pectol-Lee cradle board would be overall size of the object, use wear, physical aspects of the figurine itself, the nature of the swaddling clothing, and whether the baby was removable. Therefore, a thorough examination of how closely the Pectol-Lee cradle board compares physically to known fertility fetishes will not be possible here.

Nevertheless, it is apparent that numerous native peoples have traditions of using cradle boards with babies in rites intended to help ensure the fertility of women, and these suggest one interpretation for how the Pectol-Lee cradle board was used. Indeed, Leigh [Jenkins]

Kuwanwisiwma, director of the Hopi Tribe Cultural Preservation Office, who examined the Pectol-Lee cradle board in March 2000, stated that, based on Hopi oral tradition, he would interpret the cradle board as a community fetish for barren women desirous of having children.[73] The Zuni cradle-board kachinas Morss made reference to may have been the same or similar to Hopi kachinas representing the first stage of *Tihu* (Figure 18); yet—on analogy with the Pomo rites converting simple toys to sacred items—perhaps they could have acquired additional powers as fertility fetishes after having been properly blessed. Since normally only toddlers received the first stage dolls, at least among the Hopi, the presentation of one to a married woman who had recently miscarried would indeed seem to carry a special meaning. In fact, the Pomo practice, cited above, of treating the cradle-board baby "in every way . . . as if it were a child," is evocative of the manner in which the Pectol-Lee example was handled.

Thus it seems reasonable to conclude that, even if the Pectol-Lee cradle board with its baby was originally made to function as a toy, a ritual performed by a shaman could have at any time "transformed" it into something more, that is, a fertility fetish. Morss made this hypothesis about the Pectol-Lee cradle board half a century ago without considering the most critical points of the evidence that could possibly connect the ancient piece to the modern practice, that is, the method of attaching the figurine to the cradle (Figure 16a–g), the use wear, and how closely the model cradle board mirrors full-size examples. This interpretation, therefore, can and should be made on the basis of use wear of the cradle board and modern ethnographic practices rather than the superficial iconographic connection hypothesized by Morss between the babes-in-cradles and the Pectol-Lee cradle board.

Dolls/Funeral Pyres

A third class of model cradle board is used among the present-day Mohave, a Yuman-speaking people who lived aboriginally in the lower Colorado River basin along the modern-day state boundary between California and Arizona.[74] Numerous examples at the School of American Research in Santa Fe illustrate the physical characteristics comparable to the Pectol-Lee cradle board (Figure 22).[75] Perhaps most significant for our comparison is the fact that the Mohave cradle boards, like the Pectol-Lee example, are fairly literal interpretations of the subject—model basketry cradle boards nestling removable clay "infants" swathed in contemporary clothing.

Many Mohave model cradle boards replicate life-size cradle boards,[76] but on a smaller scale, ranging in length from about 20 to 40 centimeters.[77] They are made of wood, fiber, clay, or basketry and hold unfired clay figurines with simple, hand-modeled features and facial paint. Details of the construction technique of Mohave cradle boards

Figure 22. Model cradle board with clay baby, obverse. Detached sushade in foreground. Mohave, late nineteenth-early twentieth century. Artist: Annie Fields. School of American Research 1994-4-261. Photo courtesy School of American Research, Santa Fe. Photo by Bettina Raphael, Conservator/Owner, Southwest Conservation Laboratory, Santa Fe, 2001.

differ significantly from the Pectol-Lee cradle board. The underlying backboards of examples with multiple materials are constructed of a stick bent into a hairpin shape and lashed with widely spaced crossbars, giving the appearance of a trellis or ladder (Figure 23). Overlaying this is a bed of padding constructed of bundled ribs of willow or mesquite bast coiled

Figure 23. Model cradle board, drawing of backboard. Mohave, mid–late nineteenth century. United States National Museum, Colorado River, Arizona, cat. no. 241146. From Otis T. Mason, "Cradles of the American Aborigines," *Report of the National Museum, 1886-'87* (Washington, D.C.: Smithsonian Institution, Government Printing Office, 1889), 183, fig. 15.

about themselves concentrically (compare the ribs protruding from the top of the cradle board in Figure 22).[78] A pad of finely shredded bast directly underlies the clay baby, but this is cushioning rather than a "diaper," *per se*. According to Felton Bricker, a Mohave elder residing in Mohave Valley, Arizona, who is regionally recognized for his traditional knowledge, diapers were not used among the Mohave, because proximity to the river enabled frequent cleansing with water.[79] Textile cordage resembling historic cotton shoelaces were commonly used to lash the baby to the backboard.

The Mohave had a standing tradition of making cradle boards, but beginning about 1850 they began making model cradle boards with clay babies for use as "teaching tools" among tribal children as well as for sale to tourists and collectors.[80] Cradle boards also continue to play an important role in ceremonies related to death and death rites among the Mohave: they are actually akin to funeral pyres to which the human corpse is bound for cremation, and for this purpose cradle boards are made in every size to accommodate infants and adults alike. Cradleboard dolls made with human hair attached are associated with mourning, since the Mohave only cut their hair when they are in mourning.[81] It is also a tradition among the Mohave to cremate all the belongings of the deceased,[82] thereby creating a problem in cases of toy cradle boards and clay babies sold to collectors and museums by tribal members who have since passed away.

In sum, there are two salient points of comparison between the Pectol-Lee cradle board and Mohave model cradle boards. Both closely imitate life-size cradle boards, and in each case they could have been used by children, presumably little girls, in "play" that closely imitated a mother caring for her baby. There are also obvious differences. First, Mohave cradle boards differ significantly in type and construction from the Pectol-Lee cradle board. Second, their use as funeral pyres is culturally disparate from what we know of Great Basin peoples prehistorically as well as in modern times. While among the Mohave, a cradle board that began its life as a child's toy was expected to follow the child's soul into the next life, a transmittal achieved through burning of all the deceased's personal possessions, the authors found no evidence that this has ever been a practice among Great Basin peoples.

CONCLUSION

The maker of the Pectol-Lee cradle board deliberately mimicked a full-sized cradle board and placed a removable clay doll in it. We conclude that the figurine in the cradle board represents exactly what it logically should, a baby. That would explain the figurine's placement within a cradle board that mimics in every way cradle boards made for the purpose of carrying human infants, as well as why it is gender nonspecific, and why it appears to lack coiffure, necklaces, and other symbols of status commonly seen on Fremont figurines of this size but more appropriate to adults. Based on patterns of use wear and the design of the cradle itself, it also appears the artifact was used in a manner consistent with the use of a real-life, full-size cradle board. As suggested above and on the basis of ethnographic analogy, the sunshade with its diamond pattern may have indicated the intended or perceived gender of the doll. Moreover, the extra protection afforded by the leather sheeting over the sunshade suggests its long-term care was a concern, and indeed it seems to have experienced use, as the repairs in the sunshade covering and grime on the carrying handle suggest.

The Pectol-Lee example corresponds closely to model cradle boards used ethnographically as toys in the sense of an instrument of learning—

the best physical and visual comparanda encountered in the present study are in fact classified as such toys among the native groups to whom they are attributed. Playing with a cradle board was probably deemed educational in that it indoctrinated girls into gender- and culture-specific roles of mothering. Since the Pectol-Lee cradle board cradles a doll and is too small ever to have held a human infant, the Mohave would view it as a toy, rather than a funeral pyre, but would consider it ultimately destined to have been cremated along with its deceased owner in keeping with tribal customs.

Even if the Pectol-Lee cradle board was originally created as a toy, it could have been transformed through a rite into something more symbolic or esoteric, such as a fertility fetish, as Morss suggested. Or, it could have been created specifically as a fertility fetish and never used as anything else. If one accepts this interpretation, then Morss' reports of barren women treating cradle doll babies in every respect like a human infant would bring a compelling meaning to the use wear noted on the Pectol-Lee cradle board and to the noted reaction Leigh Kuwanwisiwma had to the cradle board when he saw it. Given the use of exotic materials on the model cradle board, along with the careful and deliberate attempt to mimic a real-life practice right down to clay baby, juniper diaper, and "authentic" travois and bassinette, one may indeed suspect the Pectol-Lee cradle board had meaning beyond its outward appearance of a toy. It seems various cultures hold traditions that make transformation from toy to symbol possible, although we do not know what ceremonies would have been required, what words spoken, songs sung, or spirits invoked to achieve transformation.

We question Morss' connections between the Pectol-Lee cradle board and the babes-in-cradles, but do not reject his conclusion. If an ancient fertility cult did exist, and if the babes-in-cradles were indeed references to this cult—hypothetical points both in need of considerably more investigation than undertaken or reported by Morss—then one might identify the Pectol-Lee cradle board as an instrument of that cult, that is, a prescribed "medicine" for women desirous of having a baby. So far, however, the best evidence presented for this conclusion appears to lie in the ethnographic rather than prehistoric record. Much more research on the possible existence of an ancient fertility cult and the significance of the babes-in-cradle is warranted and will, hopefully, be stimulated by the discussion presented here. The more complete description of the Pectol-Lee cradle board provided in this catalogue should aid in the identification of additional prehistoric and ethnographic comparanda and enable a more comprehensive assessment of the resulting data. Detailed, object-focused publications of comparanda—even poorly provenienced examples in museums and private collections—would facilitate the inquiry.

1. The cradle board was published earlier by Julian H. Steward, "Pueblo Material Culture in Western Utah," *The University of New Mexico Bulletin*, no. 287, Anthropological Series, vol. 1, no. 3 (1936), 28, pl. 7, who provided a photograph and an undetailed description of the cradle board and the head of the figurine. Noel Morss, *Clay Figurines of the American Southwest*, Papers of the Peabody Museum of American Archaeology and Ethnology, Harvard University, vol. 49, no. 1 (Cambridge, Mass.: Peabody Museum, 1954), published a small sketch of the cradle board and brought it into a discussion of the meaning and significance of clay figurines in general. Some of his opinions and suggestions will be brought into the text of this paper. Several scholars referred back to Morss, such as Keith R. Montgomery and Jackie A. Montgomery, "Utah Department of Transportation State Route-31, Huntington Canyon Project: Archaeological Excavations at Sites 42Em2109 and 42Em2095, Emery County, Utah, UDOT Project No. RS-0282 (4), Prepared for Utah Department of Transportation and The Federal Highway Administration, Utah Division," vols. 1 and 2 (unpublished manuscript, Bluff, Utah: Abajo Archaeology, 1993), 455.

2. Sinkey was responsible for describing the basketry and textile components, while Munsey described all other elements. Faculty mentor Pamela Miller checked the descriptions for accuracy, and the editor of this volume integrated the information into the single catalogue entry.

3. This publication is fully cited in note 1.

4. This article had its origins in a paper written by undergraduate student Michelle R. Munsey on ritual, religion, and abstract thought, as guided by BYU faculty mentors Richard K. Talbot and Shane A. Baker. In that paper she postulated that prehistoric people perceived a transference of power between horned headdresses, horned anthropomorphs in rock art, figurines, and the figurine in the Pectol-Lee cradle board based on aspects of Zuni ceremonialism and iconic motifs in Puebloan art. A significant contribution on Munsey's part was her description of the nonbasketry elements of the Pectol-Lee cradle board and her innovative attempt to discern the step-by-step placement of the figurine onto the cradle board. The principal author takes responsibility for revising this descriptive material and discerning its significance for interpretation within the context of the present paper. Other portions of Munsey's original paper devoted to the cradle board were heavily indebted to Noel Morss, *Clay Figurines*, and to key references provided by (among others) Pamela Miller, Curator of Archaeology, College of Eastern Utah Prehistoric Museum; and Bettina Raphael, Conservator/Owner, Southwest Conservation Laboratory, Santa Fe, who had examined a number of Mohave model cradle boards for the American School of Research, Santa Fe. Late in the project, and in accordance with

the project goal of having object-focused papers, the catalogue editor redistributed the information presented in Munsey's meritorious paper to this article and to the article on the Pectol-Lee deer headdress (see Allen and Munsey, p. 99, this volume). This paper draws upon the description of the basketry portions of the cradle board done by graduate student Leslie-lynne Sinkey and from her attribution of the basketry. The principal author is responsible for the premise, prose, and compilation and organization of data for this article as well as for all additional reference material and comparanda. This paper benefitted from a review by the student editorial services organized and supervised by Professor Don Norton, Department of English, Brigham Young University.

5. Montgomery and Montgomery, "Huntington Canyon Project," vol. 2, 435–454.

6. Morss, *Clay Figurines*, 23–25; and, *idem*, *The Ancient Culture of the Fremont River in Utah: Report on the Explorations Under the Claflin-Emerson Fund, 1928–1929*, Papers of the Peabody Museum of American Archaeology and Ethnology, Harvard University, vol. 12, no. 3 (Cambridge, Massachusetts: Peabody Museum, 1931), 46–50.

7. Morss, *Clay Figurines*, 113, himself dated the Pectol cradle to "about the 11th century, possibly later," although it is not clear what criteria he used to arrive at this date.

8. Beta 154227, AMS date (plant material), 1040 +/- 40 BP. Calibrated dates (two sigma range) AD 910–920 and AD 960–1030.

9. Morss, *Clay Figurines*, 25, suggested the cradle board might be later than the figurine by virtue of the excellent state of preservation of the basketry portions.

10. The authors are grateful to Pamela Miller, Curator of Archaeology, College of Eastern Utah Prehistoric Museum, for bringing the Nine Mile Canyon cradle board to their attention.

11. Among the witnesses are Don Burge, Director, and Pamela Miller, Curator of Archaeology, College of Eastern Utah Prehistoric Museum: Burge and Miller, personal communications, April 2001.

12. The authors are grateful to Pamela Miller, Curator of Archaeology, College of Eastern Utah Prehistoric Museum, for bringing the cradle board in the Museum of the San Rafael to their attention.

13. Among the witnesses is Dixon Peacock, Director, Museum of the San Rafael, Castle Dale, Utah: personal communication, June 2000.

14. Northern Paiute: Catherine S. Fowler and Sven Liljeblad, "Northern Paiute," in *Great Basin*, ed. Warren L. D'Azevedo, vol. 11, *Handbook of North American Indians,* ed. W. C. Sturtevant (Washington, D.C.: Smithsonian Institution, 1986), 449. Northern Paiute and Monache: Catherine S. Fowler and Lawrence E. Dawson, "Ethnographic Basketry," in *Great Basin*, ed. Warren L. D'Azevedo, vol. 11, *Handbook of North*

American Indians, ed. W. C. Sturtevant (Washington, D.C.: Smithsonian Institution, 1986), 710, 714. Washoe: Warren L. D'Azevedo, "Washoe," in *Great Basin*, ed. Warren L. D'Azevedo, vol. 11, *Handbook of North American Indians,* ed. W. C. Sturtevant (Washington, D.C.: Smithsonian Institution, 1986), 486. Omer C. Stewart, *Culture Element Distributions: XVIII Ute-Southern Paiute*, Anthropological Records, vol. 6, no. 4 (Berkeley: University of California Press, 1942), 275, nos. 1910–1917, enumerates various Ute and Southern Paiute customs for designating a baby's gender, including zigzags and parallel diagonal lines for boys and a diamond chain for girls on the sunshade, color of the cradle board (white for boys, yellow for girls), and the nature of the lashings used to close the leather flap in front; but he records that all of these were "recent" or post-European—they may have been borrowed from other tribes. According to one custom practiced by the Northern Ute, gender was designated by the shape of the umbilical cord bag attached to the cradle board, whether lizard- or tortoise-shaped: Clifford Duncan, Ceremonial Leader, Northern Ute, personal communication, June, 1995.

15. Margaret M. Wheat, *Survival Arts of the Primitive Paiute*, 4th ed. (1986, Reno, Nev.: University of Nevada Press, 1967), 101–102. Some cultures consider the entire cradle board to be inalienable from the child for whom it was made. The Northern Paiute abandoned previous cradle boards as the child grew, hanging them high in a juniper tree in the mountains: Fowler and Liljebad, "Northern Paiute," 449. According to Zigmond, the Kawaiisu (westernmost branch of the Southern division of Uto-Aztecan) of south central California hung a boy's cradle board on a ponderosa pine when it was outgrown and a girl's on any tree, and if a jealous person destroyed the cradle, the child would die: Maurice L. Zigmond, "Kawaiisu," in *Great Basin*, ed. Warren L. D'Azevedo, vol. 11, *Handbook of North American Indians,* ed. W. C. Sturtevant (Washington, D.C.: Smithsonian Institution, 1986), 404. Among the Wintu of northern California, when a baby's cradle was outgrown, it was hung in a tree until it disintegrated: Frank R. Lapena, "Wintu," in *California*, ed. Robert F. Heizer, vol. 8, *Handbook of North American Indians,* ed. W. C. Sturtevant (Washington, D.C.: Smithsonian Institution, 1986), 327. Believing a display of grief over a deceased child's death would attract ghosts, the Mescalero Apache of present-day southeastern New Mexico and northwestern Texas placed the cradle board—and all other property—belonging to a deceased baby in a tree to disintegrate, while the infant's body was buried: cf. Morris E. Opler, "Mescalero Apache," in *Southwest*, ed. Alfonso Ortiz, vol. 10, *Handbook of North American Indians,* ed. W. C. Sturtevant (Washington, D.C.: Smithsonian Institution, 1983), 437, fig. 14. The Mohave are perhaps the most extreme in perceiving an inalienability between a person and his/her belongings: they cremate a

person along with all his/her possessions when the person dies, thereby transmitting these things "to the land of the dead along with the soul:" Kenneth M. Stewart, "Mohave," in *Southwest*, ed. Alfonso Ortiz, vol. 10, *Handbook of North American Indians,* ed. W. C. Sturtevant (Washington, D.C.: Smithsonian Institution, 1983), 66–67. As pointed out by Stewart, ibid., pp. 59 and 68, this custom has resulted in an unusally barren archaeological record for this people as well as an indifference to craftsmanship in material possessions.

16. Catherine S. Fowler, "Great Basin Affiliations of the Ute Peoples of Colorado," in ed., William Wroth, *Ute Indian Arts and Culture from Prehistory to the New Millennium* (Colorado Springs: Colorado Springs Fine Arts Center, 2000), 134–141, nos. 53–67. The Ute "board cradles" with their hide-covered wooden frames and open warp sunshades superceded an earlier, traditional cradle board made of bent and woven willow rods: Donald Callaway, Joel Janetski, and Omer C. Stewart, "Ute," in *Great Basin*, ed. Warren L. D'Azevedo, vol. 11, *Handbook of North American Indians,* ed. W. C. Sturtevant (Washington, D.C.: Smithsonian Institution, 1986), 347, caption to fig. 7.

17. Wheat, *Survival Arts of the Primitive Paiute*, 27.

18. Don Burge, Director, College of Eastern Utah Prehistoric Museum, personal communication, June 2001: "thirty inches long, eighteen to twenty inches wide."

19. Morss, *Clay Figurines*, 24.

20. As Munsey discovered in her research, these stripes were incorrectly described as black and white stripes in Morss, *Clay Figurines*, 25.

21. Cf. Morss, ibid., 55, who, in reference to Southwestern clay figurines in general, held the opinion that "pronounced adult [sex] characteristics . . . are inconsistent with their being infant effigies. Montgomery and Montgomery, "Huntington Canyon Project," vol. 2, 451 also suggested small figurines lacking ornateness represent infants.

22. As Munsey discovered in her research, some scholars believe the extent of ornateness in Fremont figurines provides insights regarding who Fremont figurines represented. For example, Gunnerson suggested that ornate figurines represented a different type of being or were used for different purposes than the plain or modest ones: James H. Gunnerson, *The Fremont Culture: A Study in the Cultural Dynamics of the Northern Anasazi Frontier*, Papers of the Peabody Museum of American Archaeology and Ethnology, Harvard University, vol. 59, no. 2 (Cambridge, Mass.: Peabody Museum, 1969), 160. Associating elaborate trappings with the ability to command prestige or power, other scholars have suggested the more ornate examples represent deities, shamans, and/or other powerful personages: see Montgomery and Montgomery,

"Huntington Canyon Project," vol. 2, 634, who interpreted plainer anthropomorphs as "citizens" as opposed to deities or shamans, etc., which they suggested were represented by the more ornate figures. In the case of the Pectol-Lee cradle-board figurine, however, there seems every reason to suspect an infant is represented.

23. Montgomery and Montgomery, "Huntington Canyon Project," vol. 2, 427–444.

24. Munsey concluded the Pectol-Lee cradle-board figurine fit into either the stump-leg or squatting/seating variety. Figurines with the "stump-leg terminus," of which Morss published eleven examples, were described as having "a slight crotch [which] . . . terminate[s] in two points, or rudimentary legs, pointing slightly forward or downward:" see Morss, *The Ancient Culture*, 49.

25. Munsey pointed out that in side view, the cradle-board figurine could possibly be interpreted as kneeling, although this seems unlikely given its context.

26. The principal author had the privilege of examining Munsey's conclusions (as summarized by Silversmith's illustrations) and assessing the pattern of use wear in conjunction with Pamela Miller, Curator of Archaeology, College of Eastern Utah Prehistoric Museum. Insights and observations arising from this joint examination were key to interpretation as presented in this section.

27. The authors are grateful to Wesley Skidmore, taxonomist and curator of animal trophies at the Monte L. Bean Museum of Life Science, for identifying this pelt. He inclined toward deer fawn, but could not rule out bighorn sheep.

28. Anasazi (Basketmaker II): H. M. Wormington, *Prehistoric Indians of the Southwest*, The Denver Museum of Natural History, Popular Series No. 7 (rev. ed., Denver, Colo.: Denver Museum of Natural History, 1970), 46. Ute: Callaway et al., "Ute," 347.

29. Stewart, *Culture Element Distributions*, 275, no. 1929: Shoshone Goshute, Pahvant Ute, Southern Ute, Shivwits Southern Paiute, Kaibab Southern Paiute, San Juan Southern Paiute. The type of bark was not specified.

30. Wheat, *Survival Arts of the Primitive Paiute*, 98.

31. The Hopi believed that the ashes of juniper and sage brush softened skin and "cause hair to grow only in the right places;" that corn cooked with juniper twigs made the mother's milk flow; and that the new mother should eat only food cooked with juniper leaves for the first twenty days after childbirth (it seems) to prevent blood clots in the womb: Leo W. Simmons, *Sun Chief: The Autobiography of a Hopi Indian* (1970 reprint, New Haven and London: Yale University Press, 1942), 28–29, and cf. also 31 for additional uses of juniper. See James

Dwyer and David Rattray, sr. eds., *Magic and Medicine of Plants* (9th ed., 1997, Pleasantville, New York: The Reader's Digest Association, Inc., 1986), 227, for juniper twig tea as a cure among Native Americans for stomachaches and colds; hot packs of juniper twigs and boiled juniper berries as a pultice for sores and aches; juniper berries as a diuretic, blood tonic, and for hemorrhaging; and, more recently among Euroamericans as a urinary antiseptic, especially for treating cystitis.

32. Wormington, *Prehistoric Indians of the Southwest*, 46.

33. Dixon Peacock, Director, Museum of the San Rafael, personal communication, June 2001. The current whereabouts of the (Basketmaker?) mummy, long held by the Pioneer Museum of San Rafael, are unknown to the authors but were reportedly transferred to the Office of the Utah State Archaeologist pursuant to NAGPRA.

34. Stewart, *Culture Element Distributions*, 275, no. 1923: Shoshone Goshute, White River Ute, Uncompaghre Ute, Moache Ute, Southern Ute, Antarianunt Southern Paiute, San Juan Southern Paiute. Other pelts used: rabbit skin, ground squirrel, woodchuck, wildcat, and buffalo, 275, nos. 1924, 1925, 1926, 1927, and 1928, respectively.

35. On analogy with ethnographic accounts of such practices as placing umbilical cords of female infants in ant hills to make the girls industrious: Clifford Duncan, Ceremonial Leader, Northern Ute, personal communication, June 1995. Cf. also: Fowler and Liljebad, "Northern Paiute," 449, who report that the Northern Paiute place a girl's umbilical cord in a mole hole to ensure her ability to dig roots and gather seeds.

36. E. P. Pectol, "Wayne County: Wayne Wonderland and Its Ancient Culture" (unpublished manuscript in possession of Neal Busk, Richfield, Utah, 1947), 5. [Pectol apparently intended this manuscript eventually to become chapter three of a book on the history of Wayne County. The Pectol papers in the possession of Neal Busk include another manuscript on the history of Torrey, probably intended as another chapter in this history.]

37. Montgomery and Montgomery, "Huntington Canyon Project."

38. Ibid., vol. 1, 174–176; vol. 2, 635. Other items found were maize pollen, corn cobs and kernels, beans, wild plant taxa, wolf berry seeds, a complete obsidian Bull Creek arrow point, basketry, worked bone tool, a mano, a large nodule of red-yellow ocher, miniature clay vessels (small seed jars?), a dome-shaped clay object (plume holder?) and other indeterminate clay materials.

39. Ibid., vol. 2, 634; cf. also, vol. 1, 176, 454–455, fig. 11.13; and vol. 2, 632–633.

40. Ibid., vol. 1, 31; and, in vol. 2 they cited various points of evidence for this conclusion, such as their opinion that some of the figurines had been made by the same hand, presumably for use associated

with the site (623), the presence of corn pollen (to the Hopi, sacred meal) and wild plant taxa with medicinal qualities (634–635).

41. Ibid., vol. 1, 177.

42. Morss, *Clay Figurines*, 55.

43. Ibid., 41, 54, and 86–92 with figs. 15–18 and 30q.

44. Ibid., figs. 15–18 and 30q.

45. Ibid., 39–40; 112, figs. 30q and q prime; 92, fig. 18; 91, fig. 17; 88, fig. 16a–b; 82, fig. 15b, b prime, and b prime prime. Two fragments, from Pueblo Bonito in Chaco Canyon and Awatovi (87, fig. 15a and c, respectively) are human figures supposed to be from cradle boards but preserving no trace of a cradle board. For a figurine without a cradle board interpreted as an infant found in the Shrine House of the Old Woman site, see Jesse D. Jennings, *Prehistory of Utah and the Eastern Great Basin*, Anthropological Papers No. 98 (Salt Lake City: University of Utah Press, 1978), 200.

46. Morss, *Clay Figurines*, 9. In this specimen, the babe had detached from the cradle, but "fits nicely into the cradle, whether by design or by coincidence." The babe and cradle were found along with other figurines inside a crushed jar. The babes, made separately from the cradle board and inserted into the cradles, are meant to stick to, but are easily detached from, the cradle boards: Morss, ibid., 38, 39.

47. Ibid., 42, citing M. R. Harrington, "Excavation of Pueblo Grande de Nevada," *Bulletin of the Texas Archaeological and Paleontology Society*, vol. 9 (1937), 138.

48. Montgomery and Montgomery, "Huntington Canyon Project," vol. 2, 454–455, structure 10-D. The specimen recovered had lost its baby, but impressions in the clay indicated the original composition. Morss, *Clay Figurines*, 41, perceived "relations, both morphological and functional" between the babes-in-cradles on fired ladles and, for example, the handle terminus class of unfired Fremont figurines, which he noted were similar in shape.

49. Young's Canyon: Morss, *Clay Figurines*, 54, reported the Young's Canyon burial contained "objects of considerable value," but did not describe or list any of them. Morss then cited J. Walter Fewkes, "An Archaeological Collection from Young's Canyon, Near Flagstaff, Arizona," *Smithsonian Miscellaneous Collections*, vol. 77, no. 10 (1926), 11, who referred to the buried man as a "person of great importance." The authors had no other information on the Young's Canyon burial or the babe-in cradle found there.

50. Montgomery and Montgomery, "Huntington Canyon Project," vol. 1, 32; vol. 2, 451.

51. Ibid., vol. 1, 35.

52. Morss, *Clay Figurines*, 41, 54–55, 61–62.

53. Ibid., 54: here Morss states, "It is obvious that the babe-in-cradle effigies on the handles of pottery vessels of the Kayenta Branch from the twelfth century onwards refer to the increase cult which has survived among the Hopi descendants of the potters and their neighbors in the Rio Grande Pueblos."

54. Ibid., 41, 52, where Morss suggested the babes-in-cradles might be references to a larger fertility cult.

55. This statement does not entirely contradict that made by the Montgomerys—perhaps in an effort to connect the subfloor burial of an adult male to the clay cradle board and other materials found in association with the above-ground bench—that the contextual data of Structure 1 "indicates that certain male–oriented endeavors such as the manufacturing of several types of arrow points and other formal chipped stone implements was a focus:" Montgomery and Montgomery, "Huntington Canyon Project," vol. 2, 635. The basketry/matting tool could have been used by either gender to make netting and cordage in addition to basketry or matting. Religious practitioners of either gender may have been responsible for gathering herbs or plants for ceremonial use.

56. Montgomery and Montgomery, ibid., vol. 1, 175.

57. Cf. the discussion of toys in Don and Debra McQuiston, *Dolls and Toys of Native America: A Journey Through Childhood* (San Francisco: Chronicle Books, 1995), 13–17. Of course, such toys also aid children in honing motor skills, visual acuity, and many other abilities.

58. Clifford Duncan, personal communication to principal author, 1995.

59. Morss, *Clay Figurines*, 53.

60. Mauri Liljenquist, "The Commodification of Twentieth-Century Hopi Kachina Dolls" (master's thesis, Brigham Young University, 2001), chapter 4 along with relevant references.

61. On the four stages of *Tihu*, see Helga Teiwes, *Kachina Dolls: The Art of Hopi Carvers* (Tucson: University of Arizona Press, 1991), 39–40. The authors are grateful to Mauri Liljenquist Nelson, Curator of Education, Museum of Peoples and Cultures, for this reference.

62. For a good summary of the stylistic development in kachina manufacture, see Liljenquist, "The Commodification of Twentieth-Century Hopi Kachina Dolls," chapter 4.

63. Cf., for example, McQuiston, *Dolls and Toys of Native America*, 43 (Apache, ca. 1890 and ca. 1910) and 47 (Shoshone-Bannock and Apache, ca. 1900 and ca. late 1800s); and, Judi Johnson, *Native American Dolls and Cradleboards*, Illinois State Museum Handbook of Collections, No. 4 (Springfield, Ill.: Illinois State Museum, 1983), 23, fig. 13, left (Northern Plains, 1900); 25, fig. 15 (Northern Paiute or Cheyenne,

1880–1900); 58, fig. 48 (Dakota, ca. 1875, removable doll missing); 60, fig. 50 (Cheyenne? 1890); 61, fig. 51 (Navajo, 1952); and 62, fig. 52 (Apache, 1885–1900).

64. These observations are based on a study of published photo images and descriptions of the cradle boards, not firsthand examination. Further observations would necessitate a study of the dolls dismounted from their cradle boards.

65. For Skookum ("Bully Good") dolls, the creation of Mary McAboy of Missoula, Montana and commercially manufactured from 1913 into the 1950s, see Johnson, *Native American Dolls and Cradleboards*, 8–9 and 48–53 with figs. 38–43. The dolls in these Ute cradle boards were not removed for examination, so it is not known whether the Skookum ("Bully Good") trademark adheres to the feet. In any event, the plastic faces, the treatment of the eyes, and the swaddling blankets are in keeping with the Skookum style.

66. Morss, *Clay Figurines*, 53–54.

67. Ibid. Morss drew connections between disparate corpores of materials. Following his discussion of ethnographic cradle boards and the hypothesized connection with the prehistoric babes-in-cradles, Morss proceeded to a more theoretic and expansive discussion of Southwestern figurines, based largely on analogy with Old World figurines of the Paleolithic period, regarding the meaning or significance of specifically female figurines and their possible relation to a mother goddess cult.

68. Ibid., 53, citing Elsie Clews Parson, "Increase by Magic: A Zuni Pattern," *American Anthropologist*, vol. 21, no. 3 (1919): 279–186; and Elsie Clews Parson, *Pueblo Indian Religion* (Chicago: University of Chicago Press, 1939), vol. 1, 317–318, 574. The particular cradle-board kachina described here may be analogous to Hopi first stage *Tihu* kachina dolls as described in our text.

69. Morss, *Clay Figurines*, 53, citing Parsons, *Pueblo Indian Religion*, vol. 1, 318. Cf. also, Simmons, *Sun Chief*, 195 and 259.

70. Morss, *Clay Figurines*, 53, citing Father Noel Dumarest, "Notes on Cochiti, New Mexico (translated and annotated by Elsie Clews Parsons)," *Memories of the American Anthropological Association*, vol. 6, no. 3 (1919), 141. Cf. also Charles H. Lange, *Cochiti: A New Mexico Pueblo, Past and Present* (Austin: University of Texas Press, 1959), 398: "pregnant women and also those who desired a child received carved wooden images (*o'ak*^{a}) from the *Shi'wanna,* or *Ka'tsinas.*"

71. Morss, *Clay Figurines*, 53, citing E. M. Loeb, "Pomo Folkways," *University of California Publications in American Archaeology and Ethnology*, vol. 19, no. 2 (1926), 246. More recent general information on the Pomo: Lowell John Bean and Dorothea Theodoratus, "Eastern Pomo and Southeastern Pomo," in *California*, ed. Robert F. Heizer, vol.

8, *Handbook of North American Indians,* ed. W. C. Sturtevant (Washington, D.C.: Smithsonian Institution, 1986), 289–305; and, Sally McLendon and Michael J. Lowy, Eastern Pomo and Southeastern Pomo," in *California*, ed. Robert F. Heizer, vol. 8, *Handbook of North American Indians,* ed. W. C. Sturtevant (Washington, D.C.: Smithsonian Institution, 1986), 306–323.

72. Morss, *Clay Figurines*, 113, figs. 30s and 30t.

73. Personal communication to principal author.

74. The authors are grateful to Bettina Raphael, Conservator/Owner, Southwest Conservation Laboratory, Santa Fe, for bringing these cradle-board figures to our attention. For an introduction to the Mohave, cf. Stewart, "Mohave," 55–70.

75. The authors are grateful to the School of American Research, Santa Fe, for granting permission to publish photographs of these model cradle boards. Thanks also to Kathy Whittaker, Director of the SAR, who allowed the principal author to examine the Mohave cradle-board figures in June 2001. Cf. also the similar model cradle boards with clay babies made by the Quechan, another Yuman-speaking group: Robert L. Bee, "Quechan," in *Southwest*, ed. Alfonso Ortiz, vol. 10, *Handbook of North American Indians,* ed. W. C. Sturtevant (Washington, D.C.: Smithsonian Institution, 1983), 90, fig. 4d.

76. Cf. a life-size cradle board at the School of American Research: 1994.4.489.

77. Estimates based on author Allen's examination of about fifty examples of clay babies in the American School of Research, Santa Fe. Most of the clay babies were eighteen to twenty centimeters in length, some being complete with their clay cradle boards; others were apparently separated from their multimedia cradle boards.

78. The use of mesquite in the construction of the cradle boards is important, for the plant relates in certain ways to the Mohave cycle of life and is considered to have medicinal properties: Christy Strum, Director, Poeh Museum, Santa Fe, personal communication with principal author, June 2001.

79. Personal communication with principal author, September 2001.

80. Christy Strum, Director, Poeh Museum, Santa Fe, personal communication with principal author, June 2001. The principal author is grateful to Strum, who has worked very closely with the Mohave regarding the use and nature of their cradle boards, for explaining the function to me as reported in this paragraph.

81. Christy Strum, Director, Poeh Museum, Santa Fe, personal communication with principal author, June 2001.

82. Stewart, "Mohave," 66–67.

IN SEARCH OF MEANING: THE PECTOL-LEE DEER HEADDRESS

Marti L. Allen and Michelle R. Munsey

This article examines the deer headdress Ephraim Pectol collected in the Capitol Reef region (Color Plates 6–9, cat. no. 71).[1] The headdress was originally part of a larger costume and as such belongs to the expansive genre of Southwestern native costume, a subject richly deserving of comprehensive study. When one considers representations of costumes and headdresses in prehistoric rock art, pottery, and kiva wall paintings in conjunction with the customs and ceremonial practices of historic and modern-day native peoples in the greater Southwest, hints of a vast and continuous prehistoric tradition of costume-wearing emerge.[2] This paper, which looks closely at a single example of animal costuming, demonstrates that even this fragmentary, unprovenienced deer headdress provides a surprisingly acute focus for discussion of traditional native costuming.

The first objective of this paper is to describe the headdress and suggest an attribution. Noel Morss and at least three other early researchers referred to the headdress, yet none published it in detail or perhaps had the benefit of firsthand examination.[3] The detailed documentation of the headdress in the catalogue section of this volume will help remedy this situation (see cat. no. 71). With this basic information, scholars will be able to conduct more comprehensive studies. The date and cultural affiliation of the headdress seem secure, thanks to radiocarbon dating and the general attribution to the Capitol Reef area.

The second objective is to reconstruct the original appearance of the headdress and how it was worn in prehistory. We begin by looking at several actual examples of prehistoric and historic animal headdresses. Then, in accordance with the well established methodology of drawing analogies between the practices of modern and prehistoric native peoples, we will consider late nineteenth- and early twentieth-century Native costumes that provide insights into the original appearance of the headdress. Then, we will investigate animal costumes and their use contexts as represented in Utah rock art, where portrayals of animal costumes and "horned" anthropomorphs provide prehistoric parallels for the Pectol-Lee headdress. In doing so, we will present and test a rather radical—but, we hope, provocative—hypothetical methodology for interpreting rock art images and demonstrate its potential for further elucidating the appearance and use contexts of animal costumes in prehistory.

As one looks at the Pectol-Lee headdress, one wonders who wore it and what meaning it held for those who wore it or saw it worn. As a third objective, this paper explores these questions, seeking to identify symbolism, native perceptions of inherent power, or other significance the headdress may originally have held for its wearers. The complete absence of archaeological context leaves us little to go on; yet most scholars would likely agree that native headdresses, as components of costume, imply "performance" of some kind. Animal costumes probably had symbolic or ritual value, with layers of meaning known only to those knowledgeable about performances for which they were worn. Our discussion draws upon the connection several scholars have proposed between "horned" anthropomorphs in rock art and shamanism. Basic art historical principles rarely used in studies of rock art images may aid in interpretation. We also employ modern theories regarding native perceptions of power resident in symbols and artistic motifs in general.[4]

Thus this paper begins with the concrete and moves increasingly toward the hypothetical.[5] It remains to the reader to evaluate our success in the search for *meaning* in the Pectol-Lee headdress.

DESCRIPTION, DATE, AND CULTURAL AFFILIATION

The deer headdress is an extraordinary cultural artifact. It preserves the proper right half of a flayed deer *face* (Color Plates 6–7). A single eye socket, one ear, and the proximal portion of an antler remain. While this headdress has at times been referred to as a "mask," it is apparent that it never served as such, for the eye socket is stitched shut. The perimeter of the ear is equipped on its interior surface with a twig armature that keeps the ear erect, and the thin skin shell of the ear is stuffed with grass and secured with sinew (Color Plate 8). The antler remains in its socket at the natural angle but is precariously perched, being heavier than the skin in which it is loosely anchored.

The antler, along with the stitched, shriveled eye socket and the pricked ear, impart an eerie but provocative visage; yet what survives of this embrittled headdress is only a remnant of what once was. Originally, the headdress comprised the entire face of the deer. This is indicated by diagonal sinew stitches running along the dorsal line of the head (Color Plate 9), for these stitches would have been unnecessary if the other half of the face had not been included. The headdress originally had an attached component sewn on at the nape of the neck, as evidenced by red-ochre tinted hide stitches passing through the headdress at the nape of the deer's neck (Color Plate 6, observable along side at viewer's lower left; and Color Plate 7, observable along edge at viewer's right). Notably, faint, patchy yellow pigment is discernible near the eye, indicating color was originally a visual force in this costume along with any significance this coloration may have carried.

The Pectol-Lee deer headdress is Late Prehistoric in date. A sample of hide taken from the reverse of the headdress radiocarbon dates to AD 1470–1660.[6] The Late Prehistoric date, in conjunction with the general provenience of the headdress, most likely indicates attribution to one of the Numic-speaking tribes of the region, that is, the Ute or Southern Paiute, as there is sparse evidence for Late Prehistoric presence of Navajo and Hopi in this region. To our knowledge, this is the first and only demonstrably Late Prehistoric animal headdress to come to light in this region.

PARALLELS PROVIDING EVIDENCE FOR ORIGINAL APPEARANCE

Actual Native Animal Headdresses

The Pectol-Lee deer headdress is similar to another deer headdress excavated over fifty years ago in Castle Park in northwestern Colorado.[7] The Castle Park example (Color Plates 10–11) also consists of a tanned scalp of a deer with the hair removed, and it has artificially stiffened ears, in this case held erect by feather quills rather than sticks (Color Plate 12). A stitched slit on the obverse (Color Plate 13) appears to be either the eye socket, as Gunnerson suggested, or an ancient repair or skinning cut;[8] the shriveled state of the skin makes this difficult to determine.[9] The Castle Park headdress has not been radiocarbon dated, but Robert F. Burgh and Charles Scoggin, who excavated the site, reported the headdress to be contemporaneous with a Fremont moccasin and established the ninth century AD as the terminal date for Fremont occupation at the site.[10] The fragmentary state of this headdress makes it difficult to say what it looked like when complete.

Another possible prehistoric antecedent is a partial bighorn sheep headdress, tentatively believed to be Fremont, now in the College of Eastern Utah Museum, Price, Utah (Color Plate 14).[11] It consists of the sheep horns secured to the base of the horn core by a fiber cordage that passes through holes correspondingly drilled through the horns and core. Pierced olivella shells decorate the base of the headdress, suspended on the same cordage. By the positioning of the olivella shells, it appears the horns and horn core at the immediate base of the horns constituted the principal elements of a stand-alone headdress, that is, unattached to the remainder of the animal's body hide. The headdress is said to be from the Canyonlands area, west of Moab in east central Utah.[12] The stated provenience, along with olivella beads—a known Fremont trade commodity—yielded the tentative prehistoric date[13] which, in the absence of radiocarbon dating, could be debated. Even the Fremont attribution could be debated, considering possible Anasazi presence in this area.[14] In the absence of more information we should perhaps follow Talbot's example (p. 1, this volume) and simply attribute it to the Agricultural Period (AD 1–1300).

Bison headdresses dating from the mid 1800s are held in the Plains Indian Museum in Cody, Wyoming.[15] These consist of both masks (Color Plate 15) and the so-called "buffalo horn bonnets" (Color Plate 16). The former are true "masks," with reinforced holes for the wearer's eyes and nose or mouth. The horns have been extracted from the animal and reconfigured to achieve the unnatural proximity and verticality. The buffalo horn bonnets (Color Plate 16) consist of the uppermost portion of the animal's head and maintain the natural placement of the horns relative to the intervening tuft of wooly hair.[16] Jingle bells, long beaded hide strips, feathers, and hair braids hang from the bottom edge. Both types are stand-alone headdresses, but they could be worn in conjunction with separately made costuming.

The flayed skin of an antelope head, collected prior to 1876 among the Western Apache of Arizona, attests to another type of stand-alone animal headdress (Figure 24).[17] Although the treatment of the antelope's eyes suggests the headdress was worn as a mask, it was not. Rather, the head skin was designed to be stuffed with grass and mounted on the shoulder as part of a hunting disguise (see below for more discussion of hunting disguises), so that when the hunter bent over, the animal's head was brought forward in imitation of a standing antelope (Figure 25). A stick lashed to the antelope's neck with hide thongs held the stuffed headdress erect on the hunter's shoulders.

Animal Costumes in the Ethnographic Record

Ethnographic parallels for the Pectol-Lee headdress, at least those for which we have adequate descriptions, consist of animal costumes being

Figure 24. Antelope head hunting disguise, horns missing. Apache, Historic Period, collected in Arizona prior to 1876. Photo courtesy Smithsonian Institution, Department of Anthropology (catalogue no. 21525; neg. 72–232).

worn as hunting disguises and as ceremonial garb for dancers mimicking animals. The costumes can consist of the animal head alone or all or part of the flayed body, as well as feathers and additional elements.

In his 1942 listing of Ute and Southern Paiute "cultural elements," Omer C. Stewart chronicled numerous Utah natives who reported using animal disguises to hunt deer, elk, antelope, and bighorn sheep.[18] He noted the use of deer costumes among several bands of Ute and Southern Paiute, as well as the Northwestern Navajo (among whom a small number of Southern Paiute lived) and Shoshone Goshute.[19] D'Azevedo reported that the Washoe of western Nevada used antler and deerskin cloak disguises to stalk deer.[20] According to Murphy and Murphy, the Northern Shoshone and Bannock in Idaho used antelope disguises to hunt antelope,[21] and, as we have seen, the Apache did as well (Figures 24–25). The authors did not come across a visual record of deer disguises from these cultures. One-line descriptions in Stewart's lists, however, suggest how Ute and Southern Paiute animal disguises *in general* were designed.[22]

Figure 25. Western Apache hunter posed to stalk antelope. Photo by D. F. Mitchell, probably early 1870s. Courtesy Sharlot Hall Museum, Prescott, Arizona (InA 174p).

While some bands reported using the heads alone, several others incorporated the whole skin into the costume, and there was overlap between the two practices, suggesting the same band could use either or both designs.[23] Some bands further enhanced the realism of their disguises by leaning forward on sticks or bows and arrows to mimic the legs of the animals.[24]

Apparently, animal disguises were deemed desirable for hunting the fastest game, since none of the bands investigated by Stewart reported using disguises for hunting bison or bear (but see below).[25] Deer, elk, and antelope appear to have been the animals normally mimicked by disguises, sometimes even during hunts for other animals. For example, Stewart notes the Shoshone Goshute used antelope disguises to stalk ducks: reportedly, the ducks liked antelope and would flock around hunters when they wore antelope disguises.[26]

Studies in the ethology of bighorn sheep suggest practical reasons to avoid wearing sheep costumes, at least while in the presence of rams. According to Fowler, historic native groups considered it dangerous to wear sheep costumes when hunting sheep because the full-grown rams were prone to charge the disguised hunters, whether the disguises derived from male or female sheep.[27] Matheny et al. published a rock art scene depicting the apparent victory of a ram over a horned anthropomorph.[28] Stewart noted several Ute bands who considered sheep hunting dangerous, as well as a Ute band and a Paiute band who used only the female sheep skin in disguises.[29] During the rutting season, when the rams were distracted by the females, or in the absence of rams, as when hunting ewes during the remainder of the year, however, this danger would not prevail. It follows that the bighorn sheep headdress in Price discussed above (Color Plate 14) may have been worn primarily for hunts during the rut season, hunts in pursuit of ewes only, or ceremonies when no sheep were present at all.

Historic rock art also provides informative parallels for hunting costumes. A panel in Dry Fork Canyon near Vernal, Utah, for example, pictures a person wearing what appears to be a bear costume (Figure 26a).[30] He crouches and holds a bow and arrow as though in the act of stalking or hunting. The animal costume appears to extend over the back in the full-body composition: the bear snout extends over the forehead of the wearer, and the body hide extends over the back. This panel appears to be a pastiche; that is, it has images dating from more than one period or culture. The crouching figure differs stylistically from the two figures to the viewer's right. These two latter figures, with their static, trapezoidal bodies delineated in a sure line, appear to be Fremont in style. The fluid line and spontaneous, sketchlike quality of the crouching figure are more reminiscent of Late Prehistoric or Historic Ute rock art, an attribution consistent with the geographic location. It was probably pecked over the preexisting Fremont panel.

Also evocative of the Pectol-Lee headdress are visual records of headdresses used in ceremonial dances among modern Puebloan people, such as at the Santa Ana, Zia, and San Juan Pueblos. The configuration of the Santa Ana and Zia headdresses may be fairly close to the original appearance of the Pectol-Lee headdress. As seen in a sketch by an unnamed artist portraying a deer dancer at Santa Ana between 1928 and 1941 (Figure 27)[31] and in a 1918 painting by Zia artist Hererra of the Zia Buffalo Dance published by J. J. Brody (Color Plate 17),[32] the animal costumes retain the whole head of the deer (or elk) or, perhaps, a stuffed

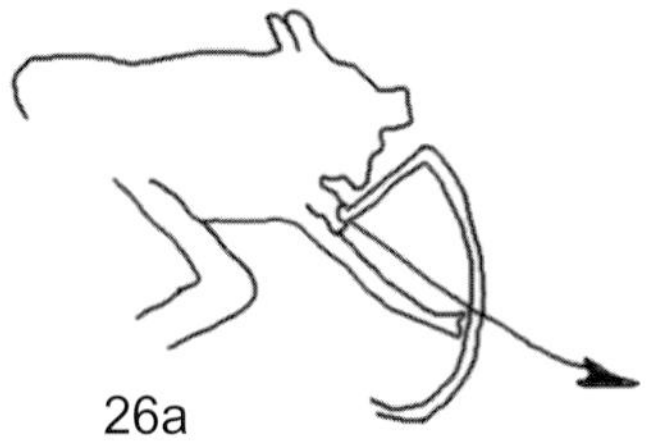

26a

Figure 26. Rock art panel, Dry Fork Canyon, Vernal, Utah. Historic Ute (ca. AD 1750–1880). Anthropomorph in (bear?) costume has been excerpted as 26a. Scanned with permission of Jean McConkie McKenzie from Jean McConkie McKenzie, *Rock Art: Dry Fork Canyon, Vernal, Utah* (Vernal, Utah: Mansfield Publishing, n.d.), 15.

version thereof, as seems to be the case for the deer and elk in the Zia painting (Color Plate 17a). The Zia ceremony is particularly elucidating because it involves dancers wearing four different kinds of animal headdresses, all clearly distinguishable from each other. In addition to elk (Color Plate 17a) and deer (Color Plate 17, viewer's upper right), the painting depicts antelope costumes consisting of just the upper portion of the head animal's head and, draped over the wearer's back, the animal's remaining body skin (Color Plate 17b); and partial bison masks in which the horns appear to have been reconfigured to stand erect in a mass of bison hair that extends nearly to the shoulders (Color Plate 17c).

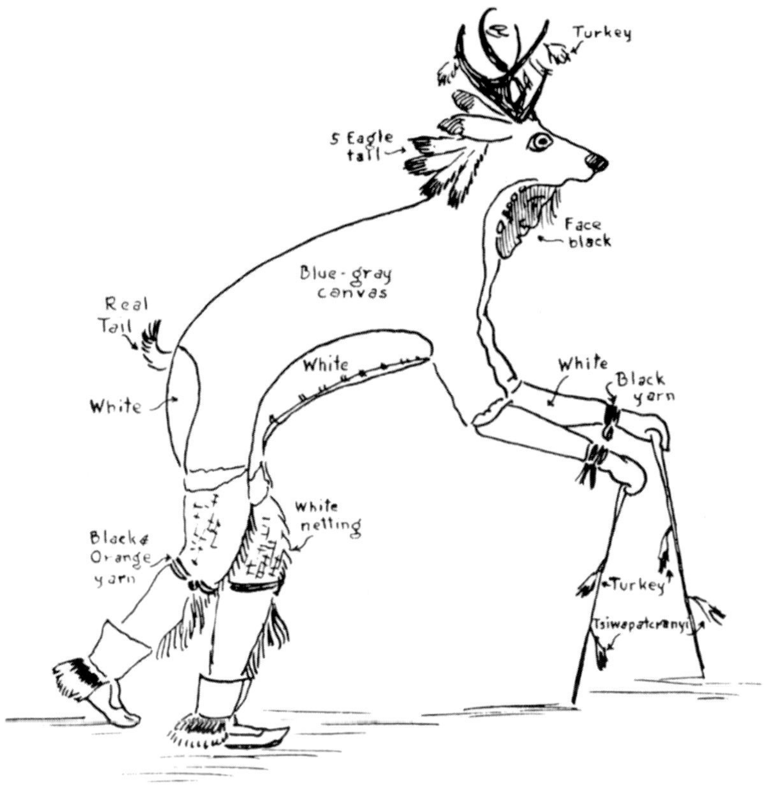

Figure 27. Sketch of deer dancer in the Buffalo Dance by unnamed Santa Ana artist, 1928–1941. Note the antlers, propped ear, snout, eye, and caped attachment. From Leslie A. White, *The Pueblo of Santa Ana, New Mexico*, Memories of the American Anthropology Association 60 (Menasha, Wis., 1942), fig. 31.

The antler headdresses worn by the Santa Ana and Zia dancers, which comprise the entire head of the deer or elk along with antlers, are worn on the pinnacle of the dancer's head, while his face protrudes below, painted all or partially black. When the dancer bends over, the deer head is carried forward and presented in the natural position, reminding of the Apache antelope disguise already mentioned (Figures 24–25) and the bear disguise depicted in Dry Fork Canyon (Figure 26). If the dancer were to stand up, the deer's head would be upside down with the ears hanging down. The illustrations of both the Santa Ana and Zia costumes depict the deer and elk heads with a wide-open eye, rather than a stitched socket (Figure 27 and Color Plate 17).

These representations show feathers were commonly part of animal costumes. According to the artist's notes in the sketch of the Santa Ana dancer (Figure 27), small turkey feathers were attached to the antlers, and the long tail feathers of an eagle were attached at the back of the head. The painting of the Zia deer and elk dancers shows an analogous design (Color Plate 17). Antler headdresses used in the San Juan Pueblo game-propitiation ceremony (Figure 28) have similar feather attachments but otherwise differ significantly in appearance. Only the antlers, rather than the whole deer head itself, were mounted, and the San Juan headdresses also included a tall visor of split cane that obscured the lower part of the headdress.[33]

The Santa Ana deer costume attempts to imitate the deer closely by including an extension of blue-gray canvas that extends snugly over the back of the dancer, and apparently, the deer's real tail was attached to the buttocks (Figure 27). The deer and elk costumes worn below the neck at both Zia and San Juan Pueblos (Color Plate 17 and Figure 28, respectively), on the other hand, do not attempt to mimic the animals in this detail, but rather consist of manufactured clothing, such as white shirts and embroidered kilts. The Zia painting, however, shows dancers in antelope costumes with fuller body costumes (e.g., Color Plate 17b). Both the Santa Ana deer dancer and the Zia deer, elk, and antelope dancers, moreover, are depicted bending and leaning on sticks held in their hands, evoking the front legs of the animals. This recalls other historic examples, mentioned above, in which Ute, Southern Paiute, and "Northwestern" Navajo dancers tried to emulate the front legs of prey with sticks.[34] Numerous other native groups, not listed here, stage dances or ceremonies in which the participants assume deer costumes consisting of part or all of deerskin hides with the heads.[35]

In sum, the actual examples of prehistoric and historic headdresses discussed above afford evidence for what the Pectol-Lee headdress may originally have looked like, while historic representations suggest there was much variety in details. The examples of actual headdresses examined were variations upon stand-alone headdresses, and similar designs appear in Puebloan ceremonial dances. The design could be a cap or bonnet, such as the sheep headdress in Price (Color Plate 14), the antler headdress worn by the San Juan deer dancer (Figure 28), and the Northern Plains buffalo horn bonnet (Color Plate 16); a mask, such as the Northern Plains bison mask (Color Plate 15);[36] or a stuffed or, perhaps the actual, animal head extending over the wearer's head, such as the Apache antelope headdress (Figure 24), the deer dancers at Santa Ana Pueblo (cf. Figure 27), and the elk and deer dancers at Zia Pueblo (Color Plate 17). Lengths of headdresses could vary, whether limited to the cranium as in the sheep headdress in Price (Color Plate 14); extending to the shoulders, as in the bison headdresses worn in the Buffalo Dances at Zia Pueblo (Color Plate 17c); or fully concealing the face, for example, as the Northern Plains Indian bison masks do (cf. Color Plate 15).

Figure 28. Deer dancer from San Juan Pueblo. Photo by T. Harmon Parkhurst, about 1935. Photo courtesy Museum of New Mexico (Neg. No. 3860).

The Pectol-Lee headdress had something lashed to the nape. If it was a stand-alone headdress, the lashed element may have been a stick similar to that on the Apache stuffed antelope head skin (Figure 24). Or, the headdress may have had a short extension, such as a feather collar or eagle tail attachments like those worn in historic Puebloan ceremonial dances (cf. Color Plate 17). Alternatively, the hide lashes along the nape may indicate the Pectol-Lee headdress was not a stand-alone type, but rather a full-body costume. The extension may have been lashed to the deer's remaining body hide, analogously to the antelope dancers at Zia Pueblo (cf. Color Plate 17b) or the hunting costumes described in numerous ethnographic reports. The Santa Ana deer costume provides a good idea of the visual impact the complete Pectol-Lee deer costume may have had if it included the deer's body skin over the back (Figure 27). The figure in the bear costume depicted in the rock art panel from Vernal shows such a body costume in use (Figure 26).

The Castle Park headdress, although too fragmentary to reconstruct in appearance, is the closest prehistoric precedent for the Pectol-Lee headdress, suggesting continuity of making and wearing animal headdresses through a long period of time, i.e., from at least ca. AD 400 to the ethnographic present. In light of the historical rock art panel discussed above, it seems probable that the late nineteenth- and early twentieth-century customs, practiced by many tribes, of wearing hunting disguises may be part of a much longer tradition. Ceremonial practices of wearing animal costumes among the Pueblos have an established recent history, but may also go back much further in time. More detailed interviews with native groups about their oral traditions may provide additional insights and data. A thorough examination of (heretofore understudied) Late Prehistoric and Historic rock art would supplement oral traditions.

The next section examines prehistoric rock art to see if the designs described above are borne out representationally in rock art and attempts to glean further details about appearance.

Animal Costumes in Prehistoric Rock Art

The best surviving prehistoric precedents for the Pectol-Lee headdress are not rendered in hide but pecked into and painted on rock faces. Images of anthropomorphic beings, common in the prehistoric rock art of Utah, show both stand-alone headdresses and fuller body costumes. We did not resort to this corpus of evidence above, because rock art interpretation is considered highly speculative, nor was the evidence of rock art needed to establish a general range of possibilities for the original appearance of the Pectol-Lee headdress. This section examines Utah rock art representations of animal costumes using a hypothetical approach to interpretation of the images. The hypothesis is that Fremont rock art artists, aware of the limitations of their craft, used both linear detail and the petroglyphic silhouette more judiciously and masterfully than previously recognized in an effort to attain their pictorial purposes. One purpose was to distinguish between characters both human and animal. Another was to portray costuming distinctive or appropriate to human characters, such as headdresses, masks, and voluminous body wraps, resulting in a figural style that appears abstract to modern viewers unfamiliar with the costumes depicted.

As a word of caution, other approaches and other interpretations are admittedly possible, and the present work does not claim to be definitive. Indeed, the extent to which this hypothesis bears out would require firsthand examination of the rock art images themselves rather than reliance upon published images alone as here. For the convenience of readers, the authors have made an effort to limit references to the rock art photos and illustrations published in a single book, the 1994 edition of Polly Schaafsma's *The Rock Art of Utah: A Study from the Donald Scott Collection*.[37] We also note here that we will be making a distinction between the term *horns*, that is, permanent bony or keratinous protuberances that grow from the head, as in cattle, sheep, and antelope; and the term *antlers*, that is, branched, bonelike projections that grow from the head but are deciduous or shed annually, as in deer, elk, and moose.

Based on rock art images, antler headdresses were known and worn by Fremont people. They were variously represented. Some rock art depictions of antler headdresses exhibit unmistakable antlers, complete with tines. For example, an anthropomorph rendered in a rock art scene in Panel P 88A in Ashley-Dry Fork Valleys near Vernal, Utah (Figure 29b),[38] and another on a panel in Spanish Valley near Moab, Utah (Figure 30),[39] both wear a distinct antler headdress.[40] In other cases antlers appear to have been represented as a pair of one or more vertical, curved elements with short, fringelike extensions. An anthropomorph wearing such a headdress is found in Panel P88A near Vernal, just mentioned (Figure 29a). Two others appear on Fortification Rock in Hill Creek Canyon (Figure 31) and Panel NP 7 in Nine Mile Canyon (Figure 32). The former shows two anthropomorphs (Figure 31a–b) wearing headdresses consisting of a pair of tall, curved, fringed elements,[41] while in the latter the headdress consists of a pair of two incurving, fringed elements (Figure 32a).[42] A fringed, curved element surmounting the body of a deer or elk on Panel P 76 in Ashley-Dry Fork Valleys demonstrates this particular mode of representation was, indeed, sometimes intended to represent antlers (Figure 33), although this particular representation was possibly executed in the Historic Period.[43] Artists sometimes distinguished between distinctly "horned" headdresses and headdresses with these fringed elements even in the same panel (Figures 29 and 31),[44] suggesting something other than horns were intended.

29a 29b

Figure 29. Panel P88A, Ashley-Dry Fork Valleys, Vernal, Utah. Fremont, Classic Vernal Style. Anthropomorphs possibly wearing antler headdresses have been excerpted as 29a and 29b. Photo scanned with permission of Publications Department, Peabody Museum of Archaeology and Ethnology, from Polly Schaafsma, *The Rock Art of Utah: A Study from the Donald Scott Collection*, Papers of the Peabody Museum of Archaeology and Ethnology, vol. 65 (Salt Lake City: University of Utah Press, 1994), 18, pl. 7. Copyright 1971 by the President and Fellows of Harvard College.

In still other cases, the fringed elements were omitted, yet the headdress still resembles that of a deer or elk. A good example is a "horned" anthropomorph in Panel P 72 in Ashley-Dry Fork Valleys (Figure 34b).[45] This headdress has a pair of three vertical, incurving elements visually analogous to horns. When considered in tandem with the narrow, triangular component surmounted by the horns, however, the head of a deer or elk is evoked.[46] If this is, indeed, an antler headdress, then the figure at the viewer's far left in this same panel may also be wearing an antler headdress (Figure 34a), although configured differently, i.e., without the intact face of the animal drawn over the wearer's face.

Figure 30. Panel with anthropomorph wearing antler headdress, Spanish Valley, Moab, Utah. Fremont, AD 900–1150. Photo courtesy of Polly Schaafsma; published with permission of University of Utah Press.

It is evident that paying close attention to such linear details in Fremont rock art is a productive exercise, indeed, that the artists themselves were paying close attention. In scenes representing multiple "horned" anthropomorphs and/or multiple horned or antlered animals, artists made careful distinctions between the horns or antlers of headdresses and animals. For example, an antlered anthropomorph in Ashley-Dry Fork Valleys (Figure 29b), already discussed, is portrayed standing amidst bighorn sheep and other animals, as well as other anthropomorphs, each wearing a different headdress. The artist clearly

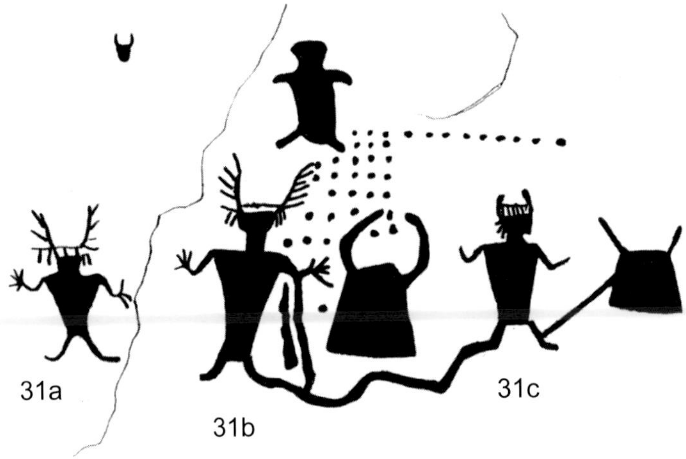

Figure 31. Drawing of petroglyph panel at Fortification Rock, Hill Creek Canyon, ET-6-7, Utah. Fremont, Northern San Rafael Style, AD 900–1150. Anthropomorphs salient to discussion in the text have been labeled 31a, 31b, and 31c. Photo scanned with permission of Publications Department, Peabody Museum of Archaeology and Ethnology, from Polly Schaafsma, *The Rock Art of Utah: A Study from the Donald Scott Collection*, Papers of the Peabody Museum of Archaeology and Ethnology, vol. 65 (Salt Lake City: University of Utah Press, 1994), 31, fig. 27. Copyright 1971 by the President and Fellows of Harvard College.

meant for these headdresses and the various horns and antlers of the animals to be distinguishable from each other. This is by no means a singularity in the rock art record. The attempt to distinguish both between horned and antler headdresses—indeed headdresses of all kinds—as well as between the horns and antlers of animals appears to be the norm.[47] Matheny et al., moreover, have demonstrated the tendency among rock artists to accurately portray animal ethology in their work,[48] and Schaafsma has noted the care with which Fremont rock artists depicted the details of shields.[49]

The use by rock artists of artistic literalism in certain aspects of their work demands an equal degree of literalism in rock art interpretation. Thus, when specific visual discriminatory details abound in prehistoric contexts, the modern researcher should utilize appropriate methodologies for quantifying and cataloguing the subtleties in variety as well as the overall visual program in which these forms appear. It appears this mode of analysis works especially well in representations of animals and animal costuming. The authors suspect most humans depicted in Fremont rock art were, in fact, intended to be understood as wearing specialized costumes, as opposed to mundane clothing. The attempt to depict costuming within a visual vocabulary limited largely to graphic line and

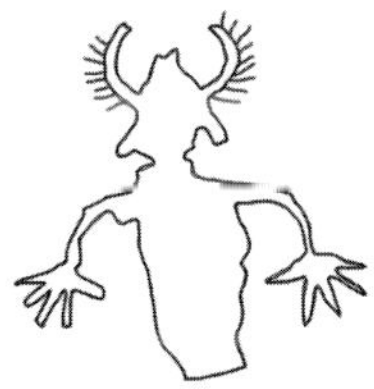

32a

Figure 32. Petroglyph panel with antlered anthropomorph, Nine Mile Canyon, Panel NP 7, Utah. Fremont, AD 900–1150. Anthropomorph possibly wearing antler headdress has been excerpted as 32a. Photo scanned with permission of Publications Department, Peabody Museum of Archaeology and Ethnology, from Polly Schaafsma, *The Rock Art of Utah: A Study from the Donald Scott Collection*, Papers of the Peabody Museum of Archaeology and Ethnology, vol. 65 (Salt Lake City: University of Utah Press, 1994), 30, pl. 11. Copyright 1971 by the President and Fellows of Harvard College.

the petroglyphic silhouette may sometimes account for the striking abstraction of human physique so notable in the genre. Pictographs, on the other hand, enabled a less restricted, painterly technique but are fewer in the Fremont rock art record. If one bears in mind the limitations of the craft and focuses on line and shape in "horned" anthropomorphs, it seems evident that rock art artists attempted to portray and discriminate between the details of costumes well beyond just horns or antlers. While graphic

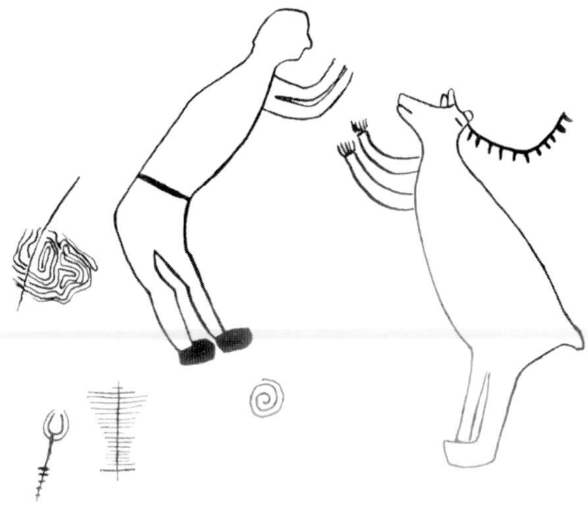

Figure 33. Drawing of petroglyph panel with deer or elk depicted with "fringed" antlers, Panel P 76, Ashley-Dry Fork Valleys, Utah. Fremont, Classic Vernal Style, AD 900–1150 or possibly Historic (AD 1750–1900). Photo scanned with permission of Publications Department, Peabody Museum of Archaeology and Ethnology, from Polly Schaafsma, *The Rock Art of Utah: A Study from the Donald Scott Collection*, Papers of the Peabody Museum of Archaeology and Ethnology, vol. 65 (Salt Lake City: University of Utah Press, 1994), 22, fig. 14. Copyright 1971 by the President and Fellows of Harvard College.

line worked well for appendages like horns, antlers, and headdresses which break the petroglyphic silhouette and protrude from the body mass, shape of mass was key to representing details *within* the body contour, and this would especially apply to costuming below the neck when the figures were rendered as solid masses. Thus, the shapes of these silhouettes may sometimes provide evidence of costuming.

Two good examples demonstrating the general principle are the Cottonwood panel (Figure 35), perhaps the best known of all hunting scenes in Fremont rock art, and the Sheep Hunter's House panel (Figure 36). Both are dated AD 900–1150 and are in Nine Mile Canyon, Carbon County, Utah. Each panel shows a prominent figure wearing the most common headdress depicted in Fremont rock art, that is, a pair of horns, although scholars apparently do not agree on what animal, if any, it represents.[50] In the Cottonwood panel, the figure is the large one standing in frontal aspect just to left of center at the top of the scene (Figure 35a). In the Sheep Hunter's House panel, it is the figure at top left shown in three-quarter view stepping into the scene (Figure 36a). In both cases the headdress consists of a pair of single, vertically deployed, inwardly

Figure 34. Drawing of Petroglyph Panel P 72, Ashley-Dry Fork Valleys, Utah. Fremont, Classic Vernal Style, AD 900–1150. Anthropomorphs salient to discussion in text have been labeled as 34a, 34b, and 34c. Photo scanned with permission of Publications Department, Peabody Museum of Archaeology and Ethnology, from Polly Schaafsma, *The Rock Art of Utah: A Study from the Donald Scott Collection*, Papers of the Peabody Museum of Archaeology and Ethnology, vol. 65 (Salt Lake City: University of Utah Press, 1994), 11, fig. 6. Copyright 1971 by the President and Fellows of Harvard College.

splayed horns which we will henceforth classify as the "classic horned" headdress.

For the moment, the silhouettes of the heads of these "classic horned" anthropomorphs are the focus of our demonstration. In the Sheep Hunter's House panel, the head of the "classic horned" anthropomorph resembles an animal's head. If the head is shown in the same three-quarters view as the body, the bulkiness of the face makes sense only if it represents an animal headdress which retains the face of the animal, probably a bison in this case, given the scale and shape of the head depicted. The head of the "classic horned" anthropomorph in the Cottonwood panel is a rounded trapezoid set directly on the body, with no apparent neck. This may not have been mere abstraction, but rather an attempt to depict a fuller headdress, such as a hood or mask, extending to the shoulders and thereby obscuring the neck.

Indeed, "classic horned" and other anthropomorphs are often rendered with heads seemingly devoid of natural shape—both triangular (cf. Figure 34a) or blocklike (cf. Figure 31b); or they may appear generally misshapen (cf. Figure 35b) or abstract (Figure 30); and, like the example in the Cottonwood panel already mentioned (Figure 35a), they often have

Figure 35. Cottonwood Panel, Nine Mile Canyon. Fremont, AD 900–1150. Showing horned anthropomorphic figures hunting bighorn sheep. Anthropomorphs salient to discussion in text have been excerpted as 35a and 35b. From Ray T. Matheny, Thomas S. Smith, and Deanne G. Matheny, "Animal Ethology Reflected in the Rock Art of Nine Mile Canyon, Utah," *Journal of California and Great Basin Anthropology* 19, no. 1 (1997), 86, fig. 10. Reprinted with permission of *Journal of California and Great Basin Anthropology*.

no indication of a neck (cf. also Figure 31a). Significantly, the geometric or abstract rendition of the heads of these anthropomorphs differs from that used to represent the heads of animals, which are usually shaped to facilitate identification (cf. the various animals in Figure 29 and the sheep in Figures 35 and 36). A seeming contradiction in perceptive abilities or aesthetic preferences on the part of the artist, this abstraction may be merely an artistic convention reserved for depicting human forms, as scholars have long assumed. It could, on the other hand, reflect an attempt to portray rather accurately how these headdresses were worn as visualized within the constraints of the petroglyphic silhouette.

This hypothesis could potentially have significant impact on the study of headdresses. The headdresses described in rock art literature as

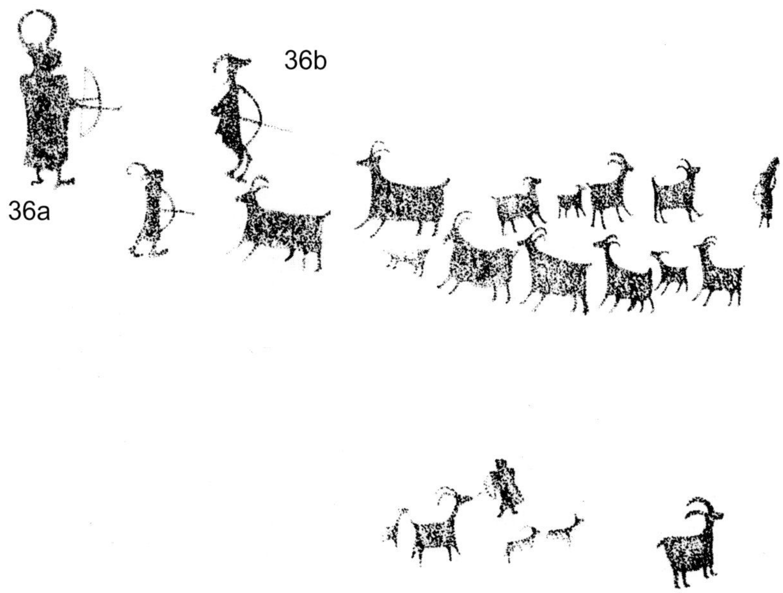

Figure 36. Sheep Hunter's House Panel, Nine Mile Canyon (Site 42Cb891). Fremont, AD 900–1150. Petroglyph panel showing five horned anthropomorphic figures hunting bighorn sheep. Anthropomorphs salient to discussion in text have been excerpted as 36a and 36b. From Ray T. Matheny, Thomas S. Smith, and Deanne G. Matheny, "Animal Ethology Reflected in the Rock Art of Nine Mile Canyon, Utah," *Journal of California and Great Basin Anthropology* 19, no. 1 (1997), 90, fig 12. Reprinted with permission of *Journal of California and Great Basin Anthropology*.

"bucket" or "helmet-type" headdresses[51] probably represent hood masks extending down to the shoulders in some cases and completely obscuring the face of the wearer. When eyes and noses or mouths are shown (cf. Figure 34a), these may represent perforations in the mask, as in the case of bison masks worn by Northern Plains Indians already mentioned (Color Plate 15). Rectangular faces on a defined neck (cf. Figures 31b–c) could be partial masks—perhaps even of wood—while rectangular or triangular faces with no defined neck could, again, represent hood masks (cf. Figures 31a, 34a, 35a). The absence in the archaeological record of wood masks, paralleling the paucity of animal headdresses, may reflect a cultural practice—that of disposing of costuming when its use life was deemed over, a custom observed by certain Puebloan peoples of the Southwest even today.[52]

The principle that abstraction in silhouetted heads may reflect portrayals of headdresses should perhaps be extended further. What has been presumed to be abstraction in the bodies of anthropomorphs *below the neck* may also be rather accurate silhouette portrayals of costuming. Sometimes "classic horned" anthropomorphs are represented without arms and/or with only the feet or a short length of the legs showing. For example, the legs of the anthropomorph with the "classic horned" headdress in the Cottonwood panel (Figure 35a) appear to be rendered from the knee down and the figure appears to be armless; while the analogous figure in the Sheep Hunter's House panel shows only the lowest portion of the legs and, perhaps, the hands (Figure 36a). It may be significant that the lower body is rendered as a solid, trapezoidal blank, for artists frequently demonstrated great interest in portraying the details of costuming below the neck when a linear rather than silhouette mode of representation was selected. For example, it is noteworthy that the artist consciously chose to present the "horned" anthropomorphs in one of the panels in Ashley-Dry Fork Valleys in frontal positions and to execute them in a linear manner rather than in petroglyphic silhouettes (Figure 34)—this technique increased the field of decoration, enabling the artist to show beaded pectorals and waistbands, necklaces, and other adornments and possibly body paint or tattoos as well. It follows that silhouette portrayals of horned anthropomorphs whose limbs appear to be omitted were intentionally not shown and may in fact depict figures wearing a cape or other body wrap which would partially or entirely obscure the limbs. Possibly, costuming below the neck in these cases was pieced together from hides and/or plant materials.[53]

We will now apply the principles demonstrated above in an effort to determine possible variations in types of antler headdresses and below-the-neck costuming associated with them. When examined with a methodology in which both linear details and the contours of the petroglyph are closely scrutinized, Fremont rock art portrayals of antler headdresses demonstrate at least three different ways a stand-alone antler headdress may have been worn: a cap or bonnet, a hooded mask, and a design incorporating the animal's head—all identified as possible designs in the previous section based on independent evidence. Because these rock art images depict the whole anthropomorphic figure, they may provide additional evidence for below-the-neck costumes.

The antler headdress worn by the anthropomorph in the Spanish Valley panel appears to be a cap design (Figure 30). It shows no indication of extensions below the head, and the fact that arms and legs are delineated free of the body silhouette suggests only the torso was costumed or that there was no meaningful below-the-neck costuming. Two anthropomorphs in the panel at Fortification Rock (Figure 31b–c) may also be wearing a stand-alone antler headdress, as the necks are clearly discernible. The two figures in the Fortification Rock panel may also wear shin- and thigh-length cloaks, respectively, based on the shape of the body silhouettes.

The second kind of stand-alone antler headdress appears to have been hoodlike, extending to the shoulder, probably a mask. Hoods or masks may be represented by a figure in the Fortification Rock panel (Figure 31a) and by others in the Ashley-Dry Fork Valleys panels discussed above, that is, a figure in Panel P88A (Figure 29b), who also appears to be cloaked to the ankles; and one in Panel P 72 (Figure 34a), who appears to wear a beaded necklace or pectoral and a short garment belted at the waist—details rendered in a linear technique over the reserve body silhouette. In all three anthropomorphs, there is no neck or it is ill-defined or the line of the jaw is not distinguishable from the neck, suggesting the headdress extended to the shoulders.

A third kind of stand-alone antler headdress—that corresponding most closely to the Pectol-Lee headdress—appears to retain the full deer or elk face, which may or may not be pulled down over the wearer's face. The wearer's options for this type of headdress may explain the curious way in which the artist represented the head of one of the anthropomorphs in Panel NP 7 in Nine Mile Canyon (Figure 32a). The anthropomorph may be wearing the headdress with the animal's head situated on the pinnacle of his own head, such that if he were to hunch over, as though to mimic the animal, the animal's face would appear at the natural orientation. With the anthropomorph standing straight up as depicted, however, the animal's head would be tilted back and oriented upside down. Taking the silhouette at face value, the snout of the animal head is oriented up and the ears hang down.[54] Such a headdress may also be represented in Panel P 72 in Ashley-Dry Fork Valleys (Figure 34b), with the exception that the face of the animal appears be pulled down over the face of the wearer. Only the linear rendition makes it possible to discern this. This latter headdress may also be more like a hood or mask, depending on how one interprets the lines extending to the shoulders at left and right.

In still other cases, headdresses depicted in rock art appear to have been integral to full-body hunting disguises. The Cottonwood panel may show such a full-body disguise, apparently a hunting costume (Figure 35b). This large figure lunging into the scene from the viewer's right seemingly wears the costume of a bighorn sheep.[55] His headdress consists of a curved element arcing over the head toward the viewer's left and possibly another protruding from the right, resulting in what appears to be a distortion in the shape of the head. His body is depicted in distinct three-quarter view and, based on the shape of this mass, his head and headdress carry this position through. The protuberances on the head, therefore, possibly represent the outwardly splayed, forward-curving horns of a bighorn sheep headdress, but depicted foreshortened, as in a three-quarter view. The horn on the viewer's left, which does not overlap the silhouette of the head, curves into the background; while the other horn curves into the foreground and across the face, thus overlapping the silhouette of the head and resembling a knob.

This would not be an isolated occurrence of foreshortening and three-quarter views utilized in the depiction of bighorn sheep.[56] The three-quarter view used to portray the "classic horned" anthropomorph in the Sheep Hunter's house has already been mentioned (Figure 36a). The neck of the disguised hunter in the Cottonwood panel (Figure 35b), moreover, is discernible, suggesting the horned headdress was a stand-alone type. It appears to be worn in conjunction with (albeit unconnected to) the body of an animal skin, the tail of which may be hanging between the legs.[57] The arm holding the bow and arrow appears to be partially cloaked by the body costuming.

Less of the hunting disguise is left to the imagination in the Sheep Hunter's House panel (Figure 36). The head of the third figure from the left (Figure 36b) is rendered in the same way as the heads of the nearby sheep, complete with the snout and downward sloping horns.[58] He may be wearing a sheep costume that includes the full head of the sheep and, possibly, a separate component that falls like a cape over the back and may be flipping up at just about hip level. Notably, the horns emerging from the head of the disguised hunter do not resemble the distinctly rendered "classic horned" headdress worn by the dominant figure in the scene (Figure 36a),[59] indicating the "classic horned" headdress in this case does not represent a sheep headdress but some other animal. We have already suggested the headdress may be bison head mask.

In sum, Fremont rock art affords numerous antecedents for animal costumes and multiple ways of configuring them, and also suggests how pervasive the practice of wearing them was prehistorically. The types recognizable were the same basic designs we arrived at independently through ethnographic analogy. The evidence of rock art suggested an additional interpretation for the Pectol-Lee headdress, that is, a design incorporating the whole face of the deer that could be pushed back on the head of the wearer or pulled down over the face. We also considered evidence for elements of fuller costumes wrapped around and obscuring large areas of the body. These results suggest our hypothetical methodology for interpreting rock art for evidence of costume design may warrant further testing and perhaps more vigorous application.

ANIMAL COSTUMES: USE CONTEXTS AND MEANING

By definition, a costume does not stand as a finished work in and of itself, but is brought to completion when worn during a "performance" of some sort. As demonstrated by the above discussion, Fremont rock art scenes with anthropomorphs wearing animal costumes provide insights into what the Pectol-Lee headdress would have looked like when worn.

The apparent care with which artists portrayed these details indicates animal costuming held great importance for the people who used it and for their ceremonies and other "performances:" the act of assuming an animal headdress or the costume of an animal, whether bison, antelope, deer, elk, bighorn sheep, or other animal, had purpose. This section examines rock art for evidence of the use contexts of animal costumes, i.e., who wore them and in what capacities. The final part of this section speculates about what it meant to prehistoric people to put on a costume, in a word, *why* costumes were worn.

Pictorial Hierarchy in Rock Art: Insights into Use Contexts of Animal Costumes

We have seen that close scrutiny of graphic line and petroglyphic silhouettes of anthropomorphs may aid in extrapolating details of headdresses and below-the-neck costuming, and that these extrapolations coincide with modern era Puebloan deer-dancer costumes and other ethnographic parallels. This section focuses on two well known rock art panels and examines certain visual devices that indicate artists sometimes portrayed social or authoritative hierarchy between the figures. Such artistic conventions as form, pose, and proportion of anthropomorphs as well as the relative placement of the anthropomorphs within the compositional field may help elucidate the identity or social capacities of costumed individuals relative to each other and to other characters in the composition, especially when considered in light of historic native customs and modern-day theories about shamans.

Frontally rendered, anthropomorphic beings wearing the "classic horned" and other headdresses are usually afforded positions of dominance in rock art compositions. The Cottonwood and Sheep Hunter's House panels (Figures 35 and 36, respectively) are good examples of this tendency because they were apparently executed by accomplished artists. The Cottonwood panel depicts an elaborate scene of several anthropomorphic figures amidst a herd of bighorn sheep, including males, females, and their young (Figure 35). The most prominent figure in the scene is the one literally heading the composition (Figure 35a): rendered in full frontality and devoid of motion, he is flanked by the visually dominant male sheep at the top of the composition and wears the "classic horned" headdress. The hunt scene depicted on the Sheep Hunter's House panel in Nine Mile Canyon (Figure 36) is a compositional corollary to the Cottonwood panel. Here, the dominant figure (Figure 36a) again heads the scene and wears the "classic horned" headdress. Entering the scene diagonally from higher ground and holding a bow and arrow, he is the largest figure in the scene, despite the fact that he is represented as being the farthest from the viewer.

Throughout the history of art—especially in religious or political works depicting historical or mythological subjects—static, aloof poses and compositional dominance have been used to reflect hierarchical distinctions between prestigious, authoritative, heroic, or divine figures and those considered ordinary or mundane.[60] It follows that compositionally dominant personages in rock art—such as the "classic horned" figures discussed above—may have been intended to be perceived as more prestigious or authoritative than subordinate figures, possibly even heroic or divine. The art historian recognizes that these "classic horned" figures appear so frequently and are rendered with such similar stylistic conventions in Fremont rock art as to assume an iconic quality, leaving little doubt that special persons or beings were intended and would have been readily recognized as such by anyone familiar with the genre. It seems likely singular "classic horned" anthropomorphs as well, when frontally portrayed, would also have been readily recognized as a special person or being. Figures wearing antlers would also have been recognized and understood.

Rock art researchers often interpret horned anthropomorphs as shamans, the term "horned" in these cases being used indiscriminately for horns and antlers. In one of her studies of rock art, for example, Polly Schaafsma, an authority on rock art iconography, conjectured that scenes bearing horned anthropomorphs reflected shamanic involvement in the hunt:

> Fremont art is replete with imagery that may be interpreted within a shamanic framework. The ceremonial attire of the anthropomorphs, especially their horned and other types of ornate headdresses, suggest that these are figures with supernatural powers . . . . In the rock art of San Rafael and Sevier regions, the association of horned anthropomorphs or shamans with mountain sheep and the presence of actual hunting scenes in which horned men participate suggest a specific function for some rock art. It would appear that . . . these petroglyphs are involved with rituals associated with hunting large game."[61]

That the compositionally dominant, "classic horned" anthropomorphs in the Cottonwood and Sheep Hunter's House scenes may represent shamans brings into question who the compositionally *subordinate* figures are. In the Cottonwood panel they mingle with the ewes and lambs in the lower tiers of the scene, some bearing shields, some taking aim with their bows and arrows. Our earlier discussion of this panel identified the figure armed with a bow and arrow and lunging into the scene from the viewer's right as possibly wearing an animal disguise (Figure 35b). He is second in the compositional hierarchy defined by the artist. Depicted in three-quarter perspective and shown with flexed knees, he is posed much more naturally than the "classic horned" anthropomorph. In the Sheep Hunter's House panel, the third figure from the left, identified earlier as wearing a bighorn sheep costume, is also second in the compositional hierarchy (Figure 36b). While depicted on the same plane as the "classic horned" anthropomorph, he is smaller in scale and has a more relaxed, striding posture, with flexed knees and slightly hunched shoulders. Three other armed figures occur in the lower tiers of the composition. Their silhouettes are carefully rendered, with two being in strong three-quarters perspective and two apparently taking aim: their smaller sizes suggest a lower status still.

Showing a subject naturalistically and engaging it in earthly pursuits are artistic devices often intended to define the subject as being of the earth, rather than divine. That the artists of the Cottonwood and Sheep Hunter's House panels used such artistic devices to make distinctions in status between these disguised hunters and the "classic horned" figures probably has significance. It implies a pecking order of authority in the hunt strategy, one in which the "classic horned" anthropomorph—possibly a shaman perceived as having divine or supernatural powers—oversees hunters with, in these cases, diminishing levels of authority.

According to a compelling study by Matheny et al., both the Cottonwood and Sheep Hunter's House panels depict a hunt at a particular time of year, one corresponding to the rutting season, the approximate two-week period in late fall and early winter when the male sheep join the females and their young for the purpose of mating.[62] Thus the hunters deliberately maximized upon the behavioral pattern of the sheep to encounter great numbers and ensure a lucrative kill with minimal risk to the safety of the hunters. Such an undertaking—especially given the apparent aggressive nature of rams—would have required cooperation between the hunters, perhaps under the leadership of one or more authority figures. Citing Schaafsma, Matheny et al. took the visually dominant figure with the "classic horned" headdress to be the lead hunter, possibly a shaman,[63] but did not comment on the roles of the subordinate figures.

What the artists of these panels may be representing are distinctions between a lead shaman or head strategist of the hunt and second in command. Native oral traditions record that more than one leader might be involved in the hunt and that a pecking order of authority could exist. Among various bands of Ute and Southern Paiute, for example, Stewart listed under "Deer and Elk Hunting" the practice of assigning a "formal hunt chief" or an "informal hunt chief;" he also listed "magic" as a feature, implying shamanic overtones in the proceedings.[64] Under "Communal Antelope Hunting," he reported three separate hunting chiefs and a ceremony preceding the hunt that featured such things as a "shaman smoking," "antelope masks and costumes," and a "special antelope dance."[65]

The subordinate figures who appear to be actively hunting in the Cottonwood and Sheep Hunter's House panels illustrate the most utilitarian function of an animal costume—their use as hunting disguises as practiced historically among the Ute, Southern Paiute, Northwestern Navajo, Shoshone Goshute, and other tribes. The use of headdresses and costuming for practical or utilitarian functions does not preclude the presence of ritualism or "shamanic involvement," however. Indeed, reality could have been inextricably intertwined with surreality: native cultures often perceive dimensions of the spiritual and ritualistic as necessary for understanding and controlling the events of reality. Among the Western Shoshone of Nevada and western Utah, a shaman reportedly aided antelope drives by capturing the souls of the animals through dreams, songs, and other ritual methods and also charmed the animals into a corral; and an antelope shaman in addition to deer disguises were sometimes used to hunt deer.[66] Stewart chronicled dreams in association with deer hunting among some Ute and Southern Paiute bands.[67] The leaders of Washoe deer-hunting parties had often dreamed of deer.[68] That figures reasonably identified as shamans were often depicted in prehistoric hunt scenes supports the view that shamanism was part of the hunting venture and strategy in prehistory as well.

In addition to being worn during hunts, animal headdresses and costumes were, according to the ethnographic record, worn in ceremonial dances associated with the hunt, whether before or after the hunt. Reference was made above to such dances among various Numic peoples and to game-propitiation dances at San Juan Pueblo. In fact, antler headdresses, in particular, had numerous ceremonial applications in dances among Puebloan people, as cited in our examples of deer and other animal dances at Santa Ana and Zia Pueblos. One suspects a connection of dance to the hunt, with the ultimate purpose being to successfully secure the animals or to ensure an abundance of animals. These ceremonial deer dances may be living vestiges of a long history of such practices.

Many more examples of hunt scenes in the Fremont rock art record could be cited in this discussion, but a comprehensive review of the rock art record is not needed here. The Cottonwood and Sheep Hunter's House panels attest animal costumes served two main purposes, and this conclusion does not depend on how one interprets the headdresses or below-the-neck costuming in detail. One purpose was to provide appropriate attire for a shaman or other authoritative personage. A second was to serve as animal disguises among subordinates in the hunt. A third purpose for animal costuming, not attested in rock art but which was inferred above through analogy with historic Puebloan deer dances, may have been for performance in ceremonial dances, a function perhaps linking shamanism and the hunt.

Thus, it appears artists were concerned about showing a distinction in the status of costumed individuals performing different roles. They not only distinguished between headdresses and other costuming, but also used such formal devices as pose, proportion, and composition to ensure the identities of the figures and their respective roles would be understood by the viewer. Perhaps the same costume could have multiple functions, necessitating the use of such artistic devices to help clarify their use contexts. Given the role of shamanism in the hunt among historic tribes, however, subordinate personages might still be perceived as having or using shamanistic powers to secure the kill.

It also remains possible that prehistoric hunting costumes were purely utilitarian in nature, devoid of all connection to shamanism and magic. They would simply have enabled hunters to disguise themselves or mimic their prey and thereby get closer to the animals without startling them into flight. This strategy would have ensured better accuracy in the kill. There seems no reason to doubt the basic efficacy of this practice, and there is likewise every reason to suppose that animal disguises would have been equally useful to all cultures that hunted. As we will see in the next section, however, researchers have seldom been satisfied with this simple, unilateral interpretation, and utilitarianism in function does not appear to be the trend among anthropologists. The notion that shamanic magic may have figured into the hunt, in particular, opens the door to multiple levels of interpretation for the wearing of animal costumes.

Images of Power in the Pueblos: Speculations about the Meaning of Wearing Animal Costumes

Costume-wearing among native peoples may have had multiple layers of meaning that went beyond the purely practical and even the purely physical. Indeed, the "performance" aspect of costume-wearing may have been pivotal to metamorphosis or translocation into a metaphysical realm where common reality was suspended.[69] In this "other world," portraying the animal could have been synonymous with "becoming" or "being" the animal portrayed, and portraying a successful hunt in rock art could have been "good medicine" for bringing a successful hunt to pass. By identifying with the animal, one might attain its actual personality or its perspective along with a broadened knowledge base capable of enhancing survival or spiritual power and insight.

The use of costumes to impersonate the subject represented by the costume has analogy in the ethnographic record. Indeed, ethnographic analogies largely drive this interpretation. In modern studies of Puebloan groups, a common motif begins to emerge—a belief that one can obtain powers by surrounding oneself with images or objects possessing the desired power. In her study of Zuni ceremonialism, for example, Ruth Bunzel coined the term "compulsive magic" to describe the attempt to affect or, more accurately, *effect*, the outcome of events either by graphically depicting the desired outcome in, for example, a painting; or by acting it out in a dramatic performance.[70]

A subsequent study of Zuni ritual systems and cultural symbolism by M. Jane Young elaborated on the notion that "images" could hold the power to affect or effect events, in particular, images that repeatedly appear in multiple media and different contexts.[71] Young observed that certain distinctive figures and symbols in Zuni rock art tend to figure prominently in other media as well. For example, she reported that representations of stinging insects in rock art had beneficial connotations among her Zuni informants. On the one hand, the insect might sting the enemy or, on the other hand, because it was sticklike in shape and could therefore camouflage itself, it might make the Zuni invisible to their enemies.[72] This instance of "see powerful image = receive power of image" was not isolated. According to Young,

> the Zunis would most naturally surround themselves with those elements regarded as potentially powerful and capable of bringing benefits to them, whatever the artistic mode, [and audiences who relate to these images believe] a result occurs because of the iconic power of the figure, [or conversely that this power] can lead to the prevention of [an] undesired outcome.[73]

Hence, according to Young, it seems reasonable to think that images evoking the idea of power tend to become favored in representation and eventually take on the quality and force of icons; that is, they become something more than mere representations, in a phrase, symbols or portents of power.

A living application of Young's thesis may be visible among adherents of the kachina religion in the Southwest. Within Hopi kachina societies, spirit beings possessing influence and supernatural powers are at once represented through the medium of dolls, impersonated by initiated tribal members who perform ceremonial dances and rites in identifiable costumes, and perceived as all-caring supernaturals who dwell in sacred places surrounding the pueblos—a trinity of divine manifestation. Through dance and the dolls, an abstraction is dynamically portrayed or impersonated by members of a community and recalled in physical objects.

Young's thesis has a counterpart in an earlier study of Puebloan painting by J. J. Brody.[74] In studying painting of various pueblos over the ages, Brody was struck with how frequently "visual attributes"—as, for example, motifs and even the compositional devices within which the motifs were embedded—appeared in a variety of media. He observed that artists used the same elements in a variety of contexts, both domestic and sacred. For example, two instances in recent times illustrated the transference of motifs and compositional devices between pottery and watercolor painting. He noted that male artists working after 1922 in San Ildefonso were lifting motifs used by women potters and translating them into watercolor. He also reported that earlier artists at the same pueblo, working in both pottery and painting, had adapted similar compositional devices to portray subjects in both their pots and paintings. For example, they might show a bird striding along a register in a pot and then transfer the bird, along with its confined perspective, to a painting by providing the watercolor bird with a floating ground line to walk along.[75] Brody, observing continuity in this tendency over two thousand years of Puebloan history, maintained that these long-lived "visual attributes" could be fully understood only in connection with activities like ritual dances and theatrical spectacles.[76] Characterizing the Puebloan view, he said the pictures themselves often took on the "personalities, vitality, and power of the sacred beings" they represented.[77]

Far from being just uninspired copying, the practice of lifting and repositioning certain motifs—along with the artistic conventions used to render them—may reflect a perception that they are inviolable. One should perhaps think in these terms when observing the horned or antlered anthropomorphs so ubiquitous in Fremont rock art. Indeed, a transference of meaning between media through symbolically loaded images, along with the ideological complexities this implies, is completely imaginable for earlier native peoples as well. These studies by Bunzel, Young, and Brody, in conjunction with theories proposed by Schaafsma and others regarding shamanic inference in rock art hunt scenes, lead one to suspect that animal headdresses and costumes in general could, indeed, have held multiple layers of meaning for prehistoric people. It seems plausible that the wearing of costumes among native peoples in prehistoric times may have been pivotal to comprehensive, other-worldly "performances" in which spirit beings, namely those represented by the costumes, had the starring roles.

Therefore, rock art hunting scenes showing anthropomorphic figures with horned or antler headdresses may need to be understood as complex "performances" with ritualistic overtones, and may even have been examples of "compulsive magic." Animal costumes may have aided hunters both in getting close to the animals and even closer to the spirits of the animals, providing the wearer with a medium by which to transcend the human realm and cross over into the animal world—indeed, to come and go as prescribed. The Pectol-Lee deer headdress may have brought this drama to life for a shaman or a hunter, enabling the wearer to assume the attributes, power, or spirit of the animal portrayed and thereby enact or effect the desired outcome, which was the same regardless of how one interprets the headdress: a successful hunt.

CONCLUSION

The dating of the Pectol-Lee headdress (AD 1470–1660) is critical because it provides information about the Late Prehistoric period, which is poorly understood. It suggests continuity in regional native practices of wearing animal costumes through at least fifteen centuries, i.e., from ca. AD 400 to the ethnographic present, when deer costumes still figure prominently in the ceremonial dances of some tribes.[78] A few animal headdresses from the culture regions of prehistoric Utah have survived the passage of time and offer ready antecedents for the Late Prehistoric Pectol-Lee headdress. Native oral traditions, especially of the Ute and Southern Paiute, along with ceremonial practices of modern Puebloan and Plains people, help establish the range of possible designs for the Pectol-Lee headdress. Images in rock art compositions may help refine this range and may provide insights into who was appropriately allowed to wear such costumes and for what purposes.

Indeed, an examination of Fremont rock art using a hypothetical methodology for interpreting the images indicates headdresses had many varieties, were highly specialized, and were meant to be distinguishable; yet they appear to have been just one component of costuming. Below-the-neck costuming was also frequently depicted in rock art—indeed, perhaps more often than previously recognized. This becomes clear once one is alerted to the unexpected literalism some rock art artists used for depicting both linear detail and the contours of mass, i.e., the silhouette, even from multiple perspectives. Shapes frequently dismissed as abstraction or ascribed to incompetence on the part of the artists may actually hold clues for interpretation when taken at face value. Literal interpretation of certain details of anthropomorphs in Fremont rock art seems to yield evidence for the appearance of both headdresses and below-the-neck costuming with which headdresses were combined.

A more comprehensive examination of "horned" anthropomorphs in rock art, using a methodology of systematic inspection for evidence of costumes, is indicated and would undoubtedly reveal much more about native costuming than was possible here. The hypothetical and art historical approaches taken in this paper may be viewed as somewhat controversial among traditionalist rock art scholars, but they have significant implications for the study of rock art in general and for the interpretation of anthropomorphs specifically. It would be particularly useful to investigate how consistently the tendencies noted in our limited study occur in a broader sample. It would also be necessary to study the original rock art images themselves in an attempt to discern evidence of relief details within petroglyphic "silhouettes." Subtle gradations in the plane of the pecked or sunken areas may reveal attempts on the part of the artists to indicate the contour of form within the "silhouettes" not observable in published photographs and sketches of rock art—such as a horn extending across an animal's face in three-quarter perspective or an arm cloaked against the torso of a fully frontal anthropomorph. Above all, one must approach the study of rock art with the realization that some rock artists were truly accomplished and that, as such, they would have prevailed upon every means within the limits of their medium to accomplish their visual purposes. These works thus need to be examined from an art historical perspective, to the end that quantitative studies are supplemented with qualitative ones.

In an effort to better understand the implications of costume wearing in prehistory, this paper initiated a theoretical foray into the possible meaning of the "horned" anthropomorphs that appear so ubiquitously in rock art. Who do they represent? What significance do they have relative to the scenes in which they appear? Why do they occur so frequently? We'll probably never know. Yet this cruel reality did not deter the researchers from acting on the desire to understand. In our concurrent search within the rock art and ethnographic records, we have attempted to build a case for "meaning" based both on an analysis of known bodies of evidence and a good deal of informed extrapolation that suggests a hunt may have been more than a "hunt" in prehistory.

The native custom of wearing deer and other animal costumes in Utah and the Southwest crossed cultural boundaries and has persisted to the modern era. As expressions of native spirituality, these costumes and the animal spirits that inhabit or travel through them tantalize the uninitiated Westerner with hints of spiritual dramas silenced by the passage of time and the taboos of living native oral traditions.

1. The headdress, along with everything in the collection, is said to be from the Capitol Reef area. Noel Morss, speculating in one of his publications, stated it "probably" came from "Site 5, Image Cave," which corresponds to a site in the Pleasant Creek drainage of Dixie National Forest: see Baker, p. 29, this volume, and Noel Morss, *The Ancient Culture of the Fremont River in Utah: Report on the Explorations Under the Claflin-Emerson Fund, 1928–1929*, Papers of the Peabody Museum of American Archaeology and Ethnology, Harvard University, vol. 12, no. 3 (Cambridge, Massachusetts: Peabody Museum, 1931), 5. It is tempting to suppose Morss was sure about this provenience when he referred to the headdress, but his own words do not reflect surety.

2. See Polly Schaafsma, *Indian Rock Art of the Southwest* (Albuquerque: University of New Mexico Press, 1980); J. J. Brody, *Anasazi and Pueblo Painting* (Santa Fe: School of American Research, 1991); and various articles on the modern pueblos in Alfonso Ortiz, ed., *Southwest*, vol. 9, *Handbook of the North American Indians,* ed. W. C. Sturtevant (Washington, D.C.: Smithsonian Institution, 1979).

3. Morss, *The Ancient Culture of the Fremont River*, 5; James H. Gunnerson, *The Fremont Culture: A Study in the Cultural Dynamics of the Northern Anasazi Frontier*, Papers of the Peabody Museum of American Archaeology and Ethnology, Harvard University 59, no. 2 (Cambridge, Mass.: Peabody Museum, 1969), 156; Robert Burgh and Charles Scoggin, *The Archaeology of Castle Park Dinosaur National Monument*, University of Colorado Studies Series in Anthropology, No. 2 (Boulder, Colo.: University of Colorado Press, 1948), 41–42. One assumes that when Taylor stated "feather and deer skin headdresses" were made by the Fremont, he was referring either to the Pectol-Lee headdress or to the Castle Park example (see below in text), or both: see Dee C. Taylor, *Two Fremont Sites and Their Position in Southwestern Prehistory*, University of Utah Anthropological Papers 29 (Salt Lake City: University of Utah Press, 1957), 155–156. H. M. Wormington, "A Reappraisal of the Fremont Culture," *Denver Museum of Natural History*, no. 1 (1955), may also have been referring to one or both of the headdresses when she stated "Headdresses of feathers and of deerskin have been found" (p. 174).

4. The principal author here refers to an aspect of discussion based on a paper written by undergraduate student Michelle R. Munsey: see next note.

5. The discussion of comparanda and their relevance to the original appearance and possible use contexts of the headdress, the sections and hypotheses based on art historical analyses, as well as the use of animal costuming as the conceptual foundation of the article and all text, are the work and responsibility of the principal author, Marti L. Allen. The

discussion of speculations on the purposes of wearing animal costumes (p. 127, this volume) is based on the research and original ideas of Michelle R. Munsey. Munsey's original paper topic focused on ritual, religion, and abstract thought in prehistory. By analogy with aspects of Zuni ceremonialism and iconic motifs in Puebloan art (see text below), she suggested, among other things, that prehistoric people perceived a transference of power between horned headdresses, horned anthropomorphs in rock art, figurines, and the figurine in the Pectol-Lee cradle board. The development and integration of this meritorious concept into the more manageable discussion of costume-wearing and its relation to the spiritual transformation implied in costumed performance are the contribution of the principal author. This paper benefited from reviews by the student editorial services organized and supervised by Professor Don Norton, BYU Department of English; by Professor Cynthia Finlayson, BYU Art History Department; and MPC Assistant Curator of Education Mauri Nelson.

6. Beta 152519, AMS date (animal hide sample); measured age, 230 BP; conventional age, 310 BP; error, +/- 40 BP. Calibrated dates (2 sigma range) AD 1470 to 1660.

7. Gunnerson, *The Fremont Culture*, 41–42, pl. 20a.

8. Ibid.

9. Deborah Confer, University of Boulder Museum, personal communication, June 2001, who examined the headdress in person and commented that the stitched slit might be too high on the head to have been the eye socket.

10. Burgh and Scoggin, *The Archaeology of Castle Park Dinosaur National Monument*, 76, 85.

11. The accession number of this sheep headdress is CEUM 9462. The headdress was published previously by Ray T. Matheny, Thomas S. Smith, and Deanne G. Matheny, "Animal Ethology Reflected in the Rock Art of Nine Mile Canyon," *Journal of California and Great Basin Anthropology*, vol. 19, no. 1 (1997), 74, fig. 2.

12. Pamela Miller, Curator of Archaeology, College of Eastern Utah Prehistoric Museum, personal communication, July, 2001, whom the donor himself told he had found it in the "Canyonlands."

13. Pamela Miller, Curator of Archaeology, College of Eastern Utah Prehistoric Museum, personal communication, July, 2001.

14. Richard K. Talbot, Director, Office of Public Archaeology, Brigham Young University, personal communication, September, 2001.

15. The authors are grateful to Pamela Miller, Curator of Archaeology, College of Eastern Utah Prehistoric Museum, for bringing these headdresses to their attention.

16. Emma Hansen, Curator, Plains Indian Museum, personal communication, July 2001.

17. Morris E. Opler, "The Apachean Culture Pattern and Its Origin," in *Southwest*, ed. Alfonso Ortiz, vol. 10, *Handbook of North American Indians,* ed. W. C. Sturtevant (Washington, D.C.: Smithsonian Institution, 1983), 371, fig. 1, below.

18. Omer C. Stewart, *Culture Element Distributions XVIII: Ute-Southern Paiute*, *Anthropological Records,* vol. 6, no. 4 (Berkeley: University of California Press, 1942), 240–242.

19. Ibid.: Moanunt Ute, Timpanogos Ute, Pavant Ute, Antarianunt Southern Paiute, San Juan Southern Paiute. We take Stewart's exacting account over the general statement in Anne M. Smith, *Ethnography of the Northern Utes*, Papers in Anthropology, no. 17 (1974), 52, that the Utes knew of deer head decoys but did not use them.

20. Warren L. D'Azevedo, "Washoe," in *Great Basin*, ed. Warren L. D'Azevedo, vol. 11, *Handbook of North American Indians,* ed. W. C. Sturtevant (Washington, D.C.: Smithsonian Institution, 1986), 478.

21. Robert F. Murphy and Yolanda Murphy, "Northern Shoshone and Bannock," in *Great Basin*, ed. Warren L. D'Azevedo, vol. 11, *Handbook of North American Indians,* ed. W. C. Sturtevant (Washington, D.C.: Smithsonian Institution, 1986), 293.

22. Stewart, *Culture Element Distributions*: compare 240, no. 23, which refers to nos. 448–456 as though he meant deer, against 248, nos. 448–452, described only as "disguises" and not referring specifically to deer. Cf., also, the photo of an Apache hunter wearing a partial antelope disguise in Opler, "The Apachean Culture Pattern and Its Origin," 371, fig. 1, top.

23. Stewart, *Culture Element Distributions*, 248: (heads only): Shoshone Goshute, Moanunt Ute, Timpanogos Ute, Pavant Ute, Uncompaghre Ute, Southern Ute, Antarianunt Southern Paiute, Shivwits Southern Paiute, San Juan Southern Paiute, Northwestern Navajo; (whole skin) Shoshone Goshute, Moanunt Ute, Timpanogos Ute, Pavant Ute, Uncompaghre Ute, Southern Ute, Antarianunt Southern Paiute, Shivwits Southern Paiute, and San Juan Southern Paiute.

24. Stewart, ibid., 248: (sticks as front legs) Shoshone Goshute, Moanunt Ute, Pavant Ute, Southern Ute, San Juan Southern Paiute, Northwestern Navajo; (bows and arrows as legs): Shoshone Goshute, Timpanogos Ute, Antarianunt Southern Paiute, San Juan Southern Paiute.

25. Opler, "The Apachean Culture Pattern and Its Origins," 371, caption to fig. 1, stated that antelope, which are well known to be the fastest and whose huge lungs are adapted for speed, are "even more difficult to approach than deer." The size of the animal and relative risks of stalking would also have been concerns. For example, hunting bison

on foot would have been dangerous because of their size and their propensity to stampede when spooked as a herd—before the advent of the horse in the New World, native hunters capitalized upon the panic of the stampede by driving the animals over cliffs in mass killings.

26. Stewart, *Culture Element Distributions*, 244, no. 219; 336, no. 219.

27. Catherine C. Fowler, "Subsistence," in *Great Basin*, ed. Warren L. D'Azevedo, vol. 11, *Handbook of North American Indians,* ed. W. C. Sturtevant (Washington, D.C.: Smithsonian Institution, 1986), 79, 82.

28. Matheny et al., "Animal Ethology," 89, fig. 11. Note the anthropomorph appears to be wearing what the present article terms a "classic horned" headdress and it is depicted in foreshortened perspective.

29. Stewart, *Culture Element Distributions*, 242, no. 109 (dangerous) and 248, no. 456 (female skins only).

30. From Jean McConkie McKenzie, *Rock Art: Dry Fork Canyon, Vernal, Utah* (Vernal, Utah: Mansfield Publishing, n.d.), 15. But cf. also, Schaafsma, *The Rock Art of Utah*, 22, pl. 10, who pictures this same scene, albeit reversed, and who discusses it on p. 20, where she seems to identify the figure as a "bearlike" animal and identifies it as Fremont. Her attribution should be reconsidered, because the zoomorphs in question have Ute stylistic traits and appear to superimpose the Fremont anthropomorphs.

31. Pauline Turner Strong, "Santa Ana Pueblo," in *Southwest*, ed. Alfonso Ortiz, vol. 9, *Handbook of the North American Indians,* ed. W. C. Sturtevant (Washington, D.C.: Smithsonian Institution, 1979), 403.

32. J. J. Brody, *Pueblo Indian Painting: Tradition and Modernism in New Mexico, 1900-1930* (Santa Fe: School of American Research Press, 1997).

33. Alfonso Ortiz, "San Juan Pueblo," in *Southwest*, ed. Alfonso Ortiz, vol. 9, *Handbook of the North American Indians,* ed. W. C. Sturtevant (Washington, D.C.: Smithsonian Institution, 1979), 285, fig. 7 (left).

34. Sticks as legs: see note 24 for reference to Stewart, *Culture Element Distributions*, who apparently recognized a regional group of Navajo.

35. Many dances among Pueblo people entail wearing animal costumes, including deer, elk, antelope, buffalo, eagles, etc.—cf., for example, the calendar of Cochiti dances in Charles H. Lange, *Cochiti: A New Mexico Pueblo, Past and Present* (Austin: University of Texas Press, 1959), 324–329. A particularly interesting ceremony involving deerskins is practiced by the Hupa of northwestern California in their White Deerskin Ceremony: the complete skins of albino or other oddly colored deer are brandished on poles as a show of wealth—see William J.

Wallace, "Hupa, Chilula, and Whilkut," in *California*, ed. Robert F. Heizer, vol. 8, *Handbook of North American Indians,* ed. W. C. Sturtevant (Washington, D.C.: Smithsonian Institution, 1986), 169 and 171, fig. 11; and, Malcom Margolin, ed., *The Way We Lived* (rev. ed., Berkeley: Heydey Books, 1993), 96. Drawing on the ceremony of tribes in northern California for comparanda to Numic practices is not far-fetched, as a recent DNA study has shown: See Frederika A. Kaestle and David Glenn Smith, "Ancient Mitochondrial DNA Evidence for Prehistoric Population Movement: The Numic Expansion," *American Journal of Physical Anthropology* 115 (2001): 1–12. The authors are grateful to Pamela Miller, Curator of Archaeology, College of Eastern Utah Prehistoric Museum, for bringing this study and the Hupa White Deerskin Ceremony to their attention.

36. Cf. also numerous types of Apache masks covering the entire head not representing animals, e.g., in Louise Lamphere, "Southwestern Ceremonialism," in *Southwest*, ed. Alfonso Ortiz, vol. 10, *Handbook of North American Indians,* ed. W. C. Sturtevant (Washington, D.C.: Smithsonian Institution, 1983), 748, fig. R, bottom right; 749, fig. 5; 750, fig. 6; 751, and fig. 7; Morrise E. Opler, "Chiricahua Apache," in *Southwest*, ed. Alfonso Ortiz, vol. 10, *Handbook of North American Indians,* ed. W. C. Sturtevant (Washington, D.C.: Smithsonian Institution, 1983), 415, fig. 12. Navajo examples: Leland C. Wyman, "Navajo Ceremonial System," in *Southwest*, ed. Alfonso Ortiz, vol. 10, *Handbook of North American Indians,* ed. W. C. Sturtevant (Washington, D.C.: Smithsonian Institution, 1983), 540, fig. 3, bottom (a–c); 541, fig. 4. Cf. also, Griffith, "Kachinas and Masking," in *Southwest*, ed. Alfonso Ortiz, vol. 10, *Handbook of North American Indians,* ed. W. C. Sturtevant (Washington, D.C.: Smithsonian Institution, 1983), 765, fig. 1 (Zuni); 767, fig. 3 (Hopi); 770, fig. 5 (Papago), who also states (p. 764) that prehispanic masking among the Pueblo, Apache, Navajo, and Papago is related.

37. Polly Schaafsma, *The Rock Art of Utah: A Study from the Donald Scott Collection* (Salt Lake City: University of Utah Press, 1994).

38. Schaafsma, ibid., (Fremont, Classic Vernal Style, Ashley-Dry Fork Valleys) 18, pl. 7.

39. Schaafsma, ibid., (Fremont, Spanish Valley, Moab) frontispiece. Cf. also animals, presumably deer or elk, with antlers portrayed with distinct tines: Schaafsma, ibid., (Fremont, Nine Mile Canyon) 35, fig. 33; (Fremont, Cottonwood Canyon) 39, fig. 39; (Fruita) 47, fig. 45; (Fremont, junction of Muddy River and Rochester Creek) 64, fig. 66; (Fremont, Glen Canyon Style, Dry Fork Valley) 66–67, fig. 67; (Fremont, Pumice) 101, fig. 104; (Eastern Virgin Kayenta Style, Oak Canyon) 115, fig. 121; (Western Virgin Kayenta Style, Lost City, Nevada) 123, pl. 54.

40. The antlered anthropomorphs on both panels also exhibit nearly circular or spherical objects dangling from the sides of the head. Similar objects are depicted as being worn by anthropomorphs wearing other headdresses in many other scenes, but this paper has not made a systematic examination of these. Perhaps they were feathers attached to the headdress, ear ornaments, or the drooping ears of the animal itself.

41. Schaafsma, ibid., (Fremont, Fortification Rock, Hill Creek Canyon) 31, fig. 27.

42. Schaafsma, ibid., (Fremont, Nine Mile Canyon) 30, pl. 11. Other examples of fringed-element headdresses not illustrated in this article: Schaafsma, ibid., (Fremont, Classic Vernal Style, Ashley-Dry Fork Valleys) 19, pl. 8; (Fremont, Nine Mile Canyon) 31, fig. 26; (Fremont, Kane Springs, Clark County, Nevada) 104, pl. 52; and, (Fremont, Kachina Rock Shelter, north of Baker, Nevada) 107, fig. 112 (three examples). It is also tenable, however, that when appearing on anthropomorphs, curved fringed elements sometimes represented horns with feathers, and that fringed elements, when rendered straight rather than curved, represented feathers alone or branches of plants rather than antlers.

43. Schaafsma, ibid., (Fremont, Classic Vernal Style, Ashley-Dry Fork Valleys) 22, fig. 14, where Schaafsma's Fremont dating may be in error. Other examples of animals, presumably deer or elk, with antlers portrayed as fringed: Schaafsma, ibid., (Fremont, Nine Mile Canyon) 35, pl. 15; (Fremont, Cottonwood Canyon) 39, fig. 39. Cf. also the representation of deer or elk with fringed antlers in Horseshoe Rock Shelter, Barrier Canyon, which Schaafsma (p. 50, fig. 49) identified as Fremont but which may be Ute: Pamela Miller, Curator of Archaeology, College of Eastern Utah Prehistoric Museum, personal communication, July 2001.

44. Schaafsma, ibid., (Fremont, Nine Mile Canyon) 31, fig. 27.

45. Schaafsma, ibid., (Fremont, Classic Vernal Style, Ashley-Dry Fork Valleys) 11, fig. 6.

46. But cf. the mask of the dancer impersonating the Navajo slayer twin in an eighteenth-century pictograph in Pine River Canyon Navajo Reservoir district, New Mexico, on which appears an inverted triangle: James Seavey Griffith, "Kachinas and Masking," 752, fig. 8.

47. See for example, Schaafsma, *The Rock Art of Utah*, (Fremont, Classic Vernal Style, Ashley-Dry Fork Valleys) 16, fig. 8 (excerpted images with various headdresses); (Fremont, Classic Vernal Style, McKee Spring, Dinosaur National Monument) 17, pl. 6 (three different headdresses); (Fremont, Ashley-Dry Fork Valleys) 24, fig. 19 ("classic horned" headdress distinguished from horns of bighorn sheep); (Fremont, Nine Mile Canyon) 30, pl. 11 ("classic horned" headdress distinguished from fringed antler headdress and from horns of bighorn sheep);

(Fremont, Nine Mile Canyon) 31, figs. 26 (two different headdresses distinguished from horns of bighorn sheep), 27 (antler headdresses and "classic horned" headdresses distinguished), 29 ("classic horned" headdress distinguished from bighorn sheep headdress); (Fremont, Nine Mile Canyon) 32, pl. 12 (several different headdresses distinguished from horns of bighorn sheep); (Fremont? Nine Mile Canyon) 34, pl. 14 (horns of bison distinguished from horns of bighorn sheep); (Fremont, Nine Mile Canyon) 35, fig. 33 ("classic horned" headdress distinguished from horns of bighorn sheep and from antlers of deer or elk); (Fremont, Nine Mile Canyon) 36, fig. 35 (horns of bison distinguished from horns of or ears of smaller quadrupeds); (Cottonwood Canyon) 39, fig. 39 (antlers of deer or elk distinguished from horns of bighorn sheep?); (Fremont River, Fruita) 45, fig. 43 ("classic horned" and other headdresses distinguished from horns of bighorn sheep); (Fremont, Capitol Wash Gorge) 47, pl. 25 (antler headdress distinguished from various other headdresses); (Fremont, Fruita) 47, fig. 45 ("classic horned" headdress, horns of bighorn rams, horns of bighorn ewes, and antlers of deer or elk all distinguished); (Fremont, Pleasant Creek, Image Cave, south of Fruita) 48, fig. 46 (antelope headdress, antler headdress, "classic horned" headdress distinguished from other headdresses); (mouth of White Canyon) 51, fig. 51 (excerpts of anthropomorphs wearing various headdresses and carrying variously decorated shields); (Fremont? Moab) 55, fig. 56 (distinctions between horns of bighorn sheep, antelope, and "classic horned" headdress); (Fremont, Davis Gulch, Escalante drainage) 58, pl. 28, lower register ("classic horned" headdress distinguished from bighorn sheep headdress); (Fremont, Vermillion Cliffs, south of Kanab) 59, fig. 62 ("classic horned" headdress distinguished from horns of bighorn sheep); (Fremont, Muddy River and Rochester Creek), 64, fig. 66 (distinctions made between "classic horned" headdress, insect antennae headdresses, horns of bighorn sheep, and antlers of deer or elk); (Fremont, Glen Canyon Style, Dry Fork Valley) 66–67, fig. 67 (distinctions made between "classic horned" headdress, other headdresses, horns of bighorn sheep, and antlers of deer or elk); (Fremont, Clear Creek Canyon) 90, fig. 88 (excerpts of anthropomorphs wearing headdresses, all distinguishable); (Fremont, Sevier Style, Clear Lake) 91, fig. 89 (various headdresses distinguished from horns of bighorn sheep and horns of antelope?); (Fremont, Summit Canyon, Santaquin) 92, fig. 92 (horned headdress distinguished from horns of bighorn sheep); (Great Basin Curvilinear Style, Pumice 95, fig. 96 ("classic horned" headdress distinguished from horns of bighorn sheep); and, (Fremont? Pumice) 101, fig. 104 ("classic horned" headdress distinguished from antlers of deer or elk). Cf. also Schaafsma, ibid., (Horseshoe Canyon, Barrier Canyon) 50, fig. 49 (elk or deer antlers distinguished from horns of bison), which Schaafsma identified as Fremont but which may be Ute (Pamela Miller, Curator of Archaeology, College of Eastern Utah Prehistoric Museum, July 2001).

48. Matheny et al., "Animal Ethology," 70–103.

49. Schaafsma, *Indian Rock Art of the Southwest*, 168–171.

50. From casual conversations with numerous colleagues, it seems the horns of the "classic horned" headdress are most often thought to be bison horns or bighorn sheep horns, the former because of the appearance of the horns, the latter because so many anthropomorphs shown wearing the headdress are depicted in association with bighorn sheep. The authors themselves did not reach a consensus. Munsey was inclined toward perhaps the most common assumption, that the horns are of bighorn sheep. Allen's opinion, based on visual analysis, is that while bison horns were likely intended in some cases, bighorn sheep horns were rarely, if ever, intended. The interpretation as bison horns can be defended if it is concurrently argued that the horns were removed from the sides of the animal's head and reconfigured to achieve the vertical deployment seen in the horns of the "classic horned" headdress, as the Northern Plains Indians did with some bison headdresses. It is even more difficult to defend their interpretation as bighorn sheep horns which are centrally placed and splay outwards and then curl downwards and forwards. Allen proposes the horns of the "classic horned" headdress may sometimes have been intended to represent antelope horns. The horns of male antelopes are similarly distantly set, curve in, and achieve the height and verticality depicted in the headdress. When the antelope's head is viewed frontally, the short tines in front scarcely have visual impact, and the abrupt terminal incurve is especially evocative of the horns sometimes represented in the "classic horned" headdress. Based on practices among the historic Ute and Southern Paiute, moreover, much more ceremony and costuming were associated with hunting antelope than hunting deer, elk, and other animals; and one might therefore suspect a particular interest in wearing and depicting antelope costumes among the prehistoric predecessors in the region also: see below in text and Stewart, *Culture Element Distributions*, 241, 244, and 336.

51. Cf. Schaafsma, *Indian Rock Art of the Southwest*, 171–172 and fig. 127 (Classic Vernal Style, Dry Fork Valley, Utah).

52. Griffith, "Kachinas and Masking," 764.

53. Cf. the photos of the Hopi kachina Masawu, whose below the neck costuming consists of a rabbitskin robe extending to mid shin, which would project a columnar or trapezoidal shadow or silhouette: Griffith, ibid., 767, figs. 3–4.

54. Other examples of anthropomorphs apparently wearing animal headdresses deployed in this manner: Schaafsma, *The Rock Art of Utah*, (Fremont, Classic Vernal Style, Ashley-Dry Fork Valleys) 16, fig. 8

(second register, first image from viewer's left; and bottom register, second image from viewer's left); (Fremont, Classic Vernal Style, Ashley-Dry Fork Valleys) 19, pl. 8 (third anthropomorph from viewer's left); (Fremont, Nine Mile Canyon) 30, fig. 25 (anthropomorph with ram headdress?); and, (Fremont, Nine Mile Canyon) 31, fig. 26 (anthropomorph at viewer's left, wearing antler headdress).

55. For reasons to avoid wearing sheep costumes except during the rutting season or when pursuing ewes or lambs alone, see above, p. 105.

56. Several examples from Nine Mile Canyon were published by Schaafsma, *The Rock Art of Utah.* The scene in her fig. 25, p. 30 shows two examples. One is a sheep, probably a ram, given the size of the horns, at the top of the scene: the ram is depicted with its proper left side in foreshortened profile looking away from the viewer such that the back of its head and its horns are seen in three-quarter perspective. The other is the second animal from the viewer's right in the middle. It is depicted with its proper right side toward the viewer and its head turned sharply to its left, such that the head itself, shown in three-quarter view, is turned away from the viewer. Schaafsma's pl. 14, p. 34, shows a sheep rising on its hind legs, as though stepping up on the terrain. It has its proper right side to the viewer but looks front in three-quarter view: its body is foreshortened, while the head is frontal. Two bison in the same scene are depicted in three-quarter views, one toward the viewer and one away from the viewer. Schaafsma's fig. 38, p. 38, shows a sheep whose proper right side is portrayed in profile and the head in three-quarter view. Schaafsma's comment in the caption that the frontal perspective is portrayed as incorrect. This is indicated by the shape of the sheep's face, which is not frontal; and by the rendering of the horn on the viewer's left, which dips below that on the right and which appears to be positioned over the neck rather than the head, an artistic device giving the illusion of foreshortening in three-quarter view. There are also numerous examples of sheep with profile bodies and frontal heads at the Cosos Range site, a mixing of perspective sometimes referred to as "twisted perspective:" David Sucec, Barrier Canyon Project, personal communication, July 2001. The dominant "horned" anthropomorph in the Sheep Hunter's House panel, our Figure 36a, is also portrayed in three-quarter view, striding toward and partially turned toward the main action; note the manner in which this anthropomorph's proper right horn and shoulder dip below those of his left, creating the illusion of foreshortened perspective. The fact that his proper left leg is longer than his right indicates he is striding diagonally toward the action, further enabling the rendition of three-quarter perspective. Archaic rock art artists appear to have been experimenting with depth and distance in rock art in the Holy Ghost panel in Barrier Canyon, in which figures are overlapped and rendered in progressively diminishing sizes to make some look farther away than

others: David Sucec, Barrier Canyon Project, personal communication, July, 2001.

57. Other interpretations are possible: Matheny et al., "Animal Ethology," 88, interpreted this element as male genitalia; yet, since probably only men hunted, it would seem redundant on the artist's part to depict the genitalia of hunters, nor does it seem to be the norm to do so.

58. Matheny et al., ibid., 90, also noted the protuberance on this figure's head seems to correspond to the snout of a sheep.

59. For another hunter in sheep costume, cf. Panel NP 26 in Nine Mile Canyon in Schaafsma, *The Rock Art of Utah*, (Fremont, Nine Mile Canyon) 34, pl. 14, where we base identification on the shape of the anthropomorph's face, for the horns are either omitted or not easily discernible.

60. A purview of images of multi-character paintings, narrative bas reliefs, peopled mosaics, etc., in any introduction to art history book will readily reveal this.

61. Polly Schaafsma, "Rock Art," in *Great Basin*, ed. Warren L. D'Azevedo, vol. 11, *Handbook of North American Indians,* ed. W. C. Sturtevant (Washington, D.C.: Smithsonian Institution, 1986), 226. Also quoted in Matheny et al., "Animal Ethology," 84. Gunnerson saw a connection between horned anthropomorphic beings in Fremont rock art and certain Hopi kachinas with horns; between pictographs "in the Fremont area" of a hunchbacked flute player and Hopi Kokopeli; between pictographs of anthropomorphs holding snakes and snake rituals performed by the Hopi, and so on. These visual similarities led him to suspect a correlation in the basic ideology and religious practices of the Fremont and Pueblo kachina societies: see Gunnerson, *The Fremont Culture*, 161.

62. Matheny et al., "Animal Ethology," 87.

63. Ibid., 84, 88–89; cf. also, Polly Schaafsma, *Indian Rock Art of the Southwest*, 179.

64. Stewart, *Culture Element Distributions*, 240: (formal hunt chief) Monache Ute, Southern Ute, San Juan Ute; (informal hunt chief) Moanunt Ute, Pahvant Ute, White River Ute, Kaibab Southern Paiute; (magic) Timpanogos Ute, Northwestern Navajo.

65. For bands practicing the list of culture elements related to antelope hunting, see Stewart, ibid., 241, nos. 63–83. Neither magic and nor references to shamans were listed under other hunted animals, i.e., buffalo, mountain sheep, bear, eagle, waterfowl, although some bands preceded and concluded rabbit hunts with dance.

66. David Hurst Thomas, Lorann S. A., Pendleton, and Stephen C. Cappannari, "Western Shoshone," in *Great Basin*, ed. Warren L. D'Azevedo, vol. 11, *Handbook of North American Indians,* ed. W. C.

Sturtevant (Washington, D.C.: Smithsonian Institution, 1986), 267–268.

67. Stewart, *Culture Element Distributions*, 240, nos. 36–37. But, cf. Donald Callawy, Joel Janetski, and Omer C. Stewart, "Ute," in *Great Basin*, ed. Warren L. D'Azevedo, vol. 11, *Handbook of North American Indians,* ed. W. C. Sturtevant (Washington, D.C.: Smithsonian Institution, 1986), 341, who state "no Ute hunter used charms in hunting antelope."

68. D'Azevedo, "Washoe," 477–478.

69. Cf. Griffith, "Kachinas and Masking," 766, who says specifically of Pueblos who have kachinas: "It is the placement of the mask upon the head of the individual that completes the transformation from man into something much greater, removed from the specific time and space of the village and in touch with the truths and powers of the cosmos."

70. Ruth L. Bunzel, *Zuni Ceremonialism* (Albuquerque: University of New Mexico Press, 1992), 491–493. Cf. also, M. Jane Young, *Signs from the Ancestors: Zuni Cultural Symbolism and Perceptions of Rock Art* (Albuquerque: University of New Mexico Press, 1998), 160, whose summary of Bunzel's compulsive magic is particularly succinct. Perhaps somewhat similar to Bunzel's compulsive magic is "imitative" or "sympathetic magic:" cf. William A. Haviland, *Cultural Anthropology* (10th ed., Orlando, Fla: Harcourt College Publishers, 2002), 378.

71. Young, *Signs from the Ancestors*, ibid., 160.

72. Ibid., 160–161.

73. Ibid., 160, 163.

74. Brody, *Pueblo Indian Painting*

75. Ibid., 19–21, cf. figs. 11–12 and pl. 5.

76. Ibid., 18.

77. Ibid., 18.

78. While this paper examined parallels for the headdress in Fremont rock art, a broader examination that includes Anasazi rock art would no doubt bring further support to the thesis but was beyond the scope of research delimited by the project.

IN SEARCH OF INSIGHTS: BASKETRY IN THE PECTOL-LEE COLLECTION

Leslie-lynne Sinkey

Basketry presents a gold mine of information for the attentive archaeologist. Because of the virtually infinite number of ways in which baskets can be constructed, shaped, and decorated, they are extremely sensitive indicators of ethnicity, aesthetic variability, and cultural interaction.[1] The Pectol-Lee collection features a diverse assemblage of coiled, twined, and plaited baskets, all said to have come from the Capitol Reef area of southern Utah and all worthy of close study. Inhabited by Paleoindian and Archaic hunters in the distant past, this region was more recently home to three distinct cultures, that is, the Fremont, Anasazi, and Numic-speaking groups. Paleoindians are not known to have made basketry; however, Archaic hunters and gatherers, Fremont and Anasazi farmers, and the later Numic ancestors of the modern Ute and Paiute are all known to have made and used baskets. Ideally, the Pectol-Lee baskets—many of which are very well preserved and therefore conducive to close analysis—should be examined in light of the basketry traditions of all these cultures. Such a study might yield more information about dating and cultural affiliation and provide insights into technical variability within these basketry traditions.

This article, however, has a narrower focus: it tackles what can be discerned through more traditional analyses of basketry construction techniques and form. Notably, it will not address Archaic basketry traditions. In fact, it is difficult to say at present whether the Pectol-Lee collection is representative of Archaic times. Some of the twined artifacts, for example, could potentially date as far back as 8500 or 9000 BC (cf. cat. nos. 53–60),[2] since the technique itself has such a deep history in the archaeological record of the Southwest. Although the Pectol-Lee examples are very well preserved and seem unlikely to be of such deep antiquity, radiocarbon dating would be necessary to determine this definitively, an undertaking regrettably not feasible within the budget of the present research project. Coiling, plaiting, and certain distinctive twining techniques, on the other hand, tend to be more visually diagnostic, and among these types of baskets in the collection are Fremont, Anasazi, and Numic examples, with the bulk being Fremont. Again, because cultures tend to have distinct basketry traditions—even people living within close geographic proximity—careful study holds promise for identification on the basis of construction and form.

This paper examines a select group of Fremont baskets in the collection. By and large, most of the Fremont as well as the recognizably Anasazi (cat. no. 48–49) and Numic (cat. no. 51) baskets in the collection are typical of their respective cultures, and they will therefore not receive special treatment here. A small number of Fremont baskets in the collection, on the other hand, diverge sharply from what archaeologists currently consider "typically Fremont." These are several unparalleled, decorated trays (cat. nos. 28–31), several fine, decorated bowls (cat. nos. 35, 43, 44); an unusual jar (cat. no. 38) and a possible fragment of another (cat. no. 39); and, notably, the Pectol-Lee cradle board and several analogous fragments exhibiting highly decorative twining (cat. nos. 61–64). This paper focuses on just these articles, for they attest the Fremont basketry repertoire had more variety than previously thought and therefore contribute significantly to our understanding of Fremont basketry. As this paper will show, they may also have implications regarding current notions of cultural interaction in the Capitol Reef area during prehistory.

TECHNIQUES OF BASKET CONSTRUCTION AND DECORATION

It will be beneficial to preface a discussion of the unusual Fremont baskets in the Pectol-Lee collection with a brief introduction to techniques of basketry construction and decoration. Basketry making is an intricate and exacting craft. Just describing structure, for example, requires an understanding of how various distinct elements—warps, wefts, stitches, rods, bundles—must converge through precise manipulation—twisting, interlocking, wrapping, piercing, bunching—in order to yield a basket. Structure and decoration, moreover, are often related and need to be understood in association with each other. All this, in turn, requires special terminology. Only after one grasps the principles of construction and decoration and gains familiarity with the terminology, can one appreciate the features that distinguish this group of unusual Fremont baskets from its more usual counterparts.

Basketry construction techniques are divided into three general categories, coiling, twining, and plaiting, and all are represented in the Pectol-Lee collection.[3] Each, in turn, has a wide spectrum of variations.

Because the thirteen baskets that form the focus of the present article are all either coiled or twined, this section will describe only these two types of basketry.

Basket-making materials are also important to note in this section. The choice of materials is influenced to some extent by cultural traditions and individual preference, although it is limited by what is available in the local environment. For example, the prevalence of dogbane as a bundle material in the Pectol-Lee baskets may simply represent its abundance in the area. But other factors of selectivity may also be at work. For example, in an area where dogbane is limited but yucca abounds, an individual basket maker might still seek out dogbane, for it is easier to strip dogbane from its stalk than separate coarse yucca strands from their sharp parent leaves. In other instances, choice of material does seem to be culturally determined. For example, although they inhabited the same territory, Numic groups made extensive use of squawbush (*Rhus sp.*) for the foundation rods in their coiled baskets, whereas the Fremont used willow (*Salix sp.*) almost exclusively.[4]

Twining

Although the majority of baskets in the Pectol-Lee collection are coiled, some of the most significant pieces, including the cradle board, are twined. Twining is considered the oldest basket-making technique in the Great Basin and American Southwest culture regions,[5] with the earliest examples dating from as early as approximately 9000 BC according to Adovasio.[6] Twining has a large number of variations that enable its use in a range of applications from flexible bags to rigid cradle boards. It is accomplished through several variations on a basic theme: two flexible "wefts" pass on either side of a "warp," with the wefts crossing over one another before passing around the next warp (Figure 37). Wefts twisted clockwise are referred to as "z-twined," whereas a counter-clockwise weft twist is referred to as "s-twined." The use of a minimum of two wefts is required, but the use of multiples beyond two is possible. Either flexible or rigid warps may be used. Successive rows of twining may be closely spaced, resulting in close twining, or separated by a space, resulting in open twining. Work may progress in rows, or spiral outward from a central point. Construction of an unusual variation called close wrapped twining (Figure 38) was accomplished by laying a rigid weft element perpendicular across the top of a series of rigid warp elements and lashing it into place with a second, flexible weft element, which in turned passed around each intersection of warp and weft.

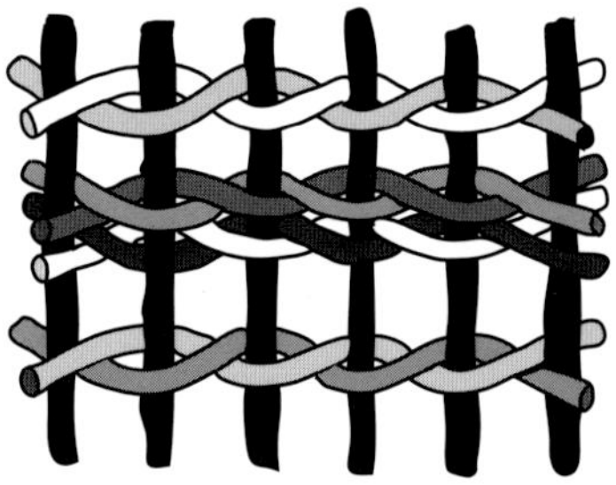

Figure 37. Open and close simple twining. Top and bottom rows are s-twined, middle two rows are z-twined. Adapted from James Adovasio, *Basketry Technology* (Aldine: Chicago, 1977), 18, with permission of Taraxacum.

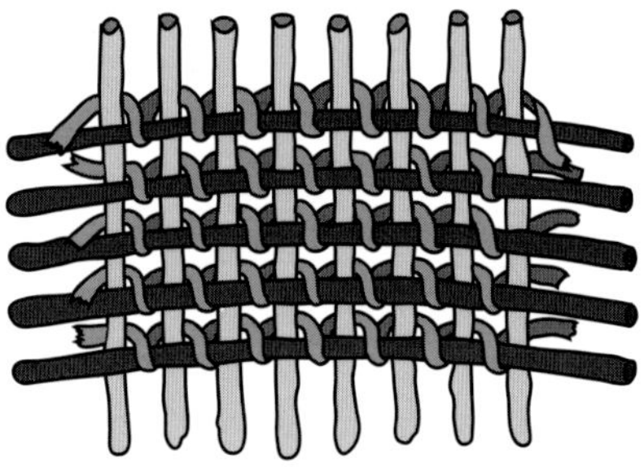

Figure 38. Close wrapped twining, showing the vertical warp elements and horizontal rigid and flexible weft elements. The flexible wefts engage both the warps and rigid wefts. Adapted from James Adovasio, *Basketry Technology* (Aldine: Chicago, 1977), 19, with permission of Taraxacum.

Coiling

Coiling was the most common basketry technique used in both the prehistoric Great Basin and Southwest, going back to at least Archaic times, with the technique largely superceding twining by approximately 2500 BC.[7] Of all of the basketry techniques, coiling perhaps lends itself

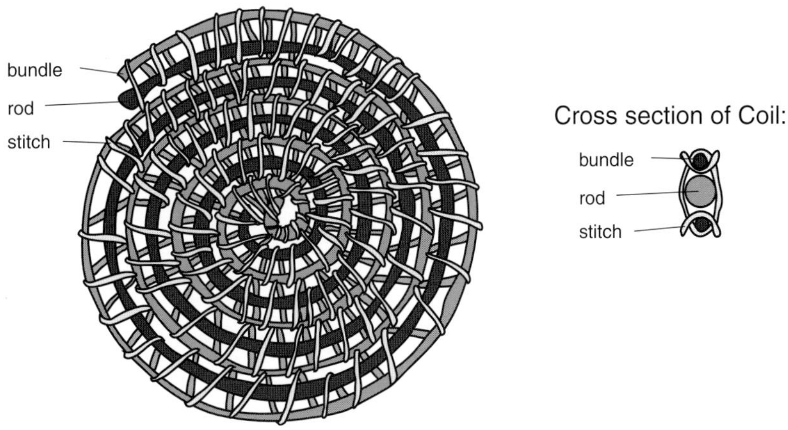

Figure 39. Construction of a coiled basket, illustrating the spiral originating in the center. Adapted from James Adovasio, *Basketry Technology* (Aldine: Chicago, 1977), 58, with permission of Taraxacum.

best to a wide range of decorative variations. In coiling, the basket is built outward in a spiral from the center (Figure 39), resulting in a basket generally round in form, although oblong shapes do occur. The coil itself may consist of a foundation made of a single element or "rod," such as a wooden stick; or it may, instead, be a "bundle" of shorter, fibrous elements such as grass or pine-needles. Differences in the materials used for these elements and the manner of combination are important to observe because, as will be seen below, such variations were frequently culturally determined. For example, one culture might favor bunching or stacking multiple rods on top of the other to form a foundation; while another culture might show proclivity to use both a rod and a bundle, in which case the basket maker would stack or bunch the two elements or enclose the rod within the bundle. Whatever the choice of foundation, the coils had to be stitched into place.

Stitching introduces yet another spectrum of variation. The stitches may pierce the foundation or encircle it, split the stitches made on the row below, or interlock with them (Figure 40). Subsequent rows of stitches may be arranged vertically above each other, or may form other patterns such as a spiral springing from the center of the basket. Additionally, if the rows of coiling abut each other, the basket is referred to as "close-coiled," whereas if they are separated by an open space it is referred to as "open-coiled."

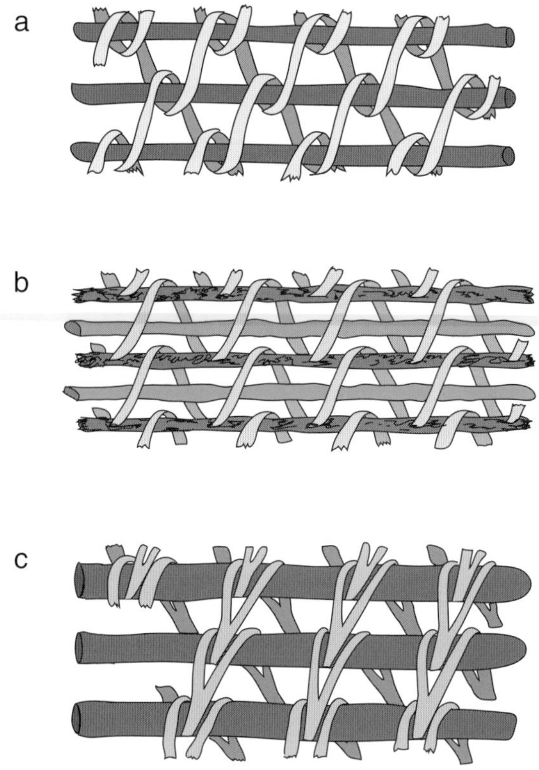

Figure 40. Various stitch treatments used in coiled basketry: a) interlocking stitches; b) non-interlocking stitches; c) split stitches. Adapted from James Adovasio, *Basketry Technology* (Aldine: Chicago, 1977), 66–67, with permission of Taraxacum.

Decoration

There are two main techniques of basket decoration, "non-structural" and "structural," and either could be used for coiled and twined baskets. Non-structural decoration is applied after the basket is finished, such as the addition of feathers or paint. It is referred to as non-structural decoration because it is not integrated into the actual structure of the basket. Structural decoration, on the other hand, is a result of the technique of manufacture; for example, the basket maker may use different colors of stitching material or vary the patterns of stitches during construction. Both structural and non-structural techniques of decoration are evident in the baskets in the Pectol-Lee collection.

THE BASKETRY TRADITIONS OF CAPITOL REEF

The basketry traditions of the Capitol Reef area are nearly as diverse as the landscape itself. This section briefly describes the regional basketry traditions contemporary with and subsequent to the Fremont culture. Fremont, Anasazi, and Numic peoples all lived in the Capitol Reef region and used variations upon some of the same basic construction and decoration techniques. Unless one is aware of the idiosyncracies in the ways construction details such as rods and bundles were employed within a given culture, a potential exists for misattributing unprovenienced baskets. It is, therefore, necessary to clarify what archaeologists currently consider to be characteristic of Fremont, Anasazi, and Numic basket making. A definition of the features distinguishing these basketry traditions from each other will not only enable discussion of why the unusual baskets in the Pectol-Lee collection are probably Fremont as opposed to Anasazi or Numic, but will also clarify how these thirteen baskets alter our perceptions of the Fremont tradition.

The Fremont and Anasazi occupied the Capitol Reef region roughly contemporaneously, with the appearance of the Fremont culture in the region dating around AD 400 and the abandonment of the area by all agricultural groups around approximately AD 1300. Although in-depth research into the question has not yet been undertaken, it is likely this nine hundred year co-existence in the area had impact upon basketry traditions of both cultures. While the general lifestyles of these two groups were similar, their basketry styles—particularly in the way they coiled baskets—were distinctive. Fremont and Anasazi basketry traditions also differ from those of later Numic groups.

Fremont Basketry

The Fremont generally made their coiled baskets using variations upon the single-rod or single-rod-and-bundle construction techniques that had persisted since the Archaic period. Nearly flat, shallow trays and shallow to deep, wide-mouthed, globular bowls were the most typical basketry forms. The Fremont most commonly used split-rod-and-bundle foundations, with both non-interlocking and interlocking stitches employed to secure the foundation.[8] Willow (*Salix sp.*) was used almost exclusively for the foundation rods and stitches, with dogbane (*Apocynum cannabinum*) and milkweed (*Asclepias sp.*) being more common for bundles. The Fremont also occasionally used juniper bark (*Juniperus sp.*) and yucca (*Yucca sp.*) for bundles.[9]

In addition to coiling, the Fremont employed seven different twining techniques, although twining was less frequently used.[10] The most common twining method was open diagonal twining worked over two warp elements. Wefts were always paired, never tripled or quadrupled. Most Fremont twining was used for either semi-rigid mats or flexible bags.

Anasazi Basketry

Coiled baskets generally took a wider variety of forms among the Anasazi than among the Fremont. Like the Fremont, the Anasazi manufactured trays, although these were notably deeper than was typical among the Fremont. They made wide-mouthed bowls, as well as globular baskets with constricted mouths and a variety of jar forms.[11] They also made straight-sided bowls, hour-glass shaped baskets, and split-based ritual baskets. With a few exceptions, such as open-coiled, intricate-stitch baskets, the Anasazi generally used multiple-rod foundations, building upon a phenomenon that arose as early as 6000–5500 BC.[12] Multiple rods were often employed in combination with a bundle, and close-coiling was the norm,[13] although open-coiling was also used.[14] Decoration on Anasazi baskets could be elaborate and included geometric and zoomorphic forms.[15] Willow (*Salix sp.*) was generally employed for both the foundation rods and the stitches.[16]

Twining reached a high degree of sophistication among the Anasazi, although like among their Fremont neighbors, it was replaced over time as coiled baskets gained popularity.[17] However, the Anasazi continued to use twining in their distinctive woven sandals as well as for making mats and bags.[18]

Numic Basketry

Following the abandonment of the region by agricultural groups, Numic-speaking peoples ancestral to the modern Ute and Paiute occupied the region. Like the Anasazi and their Puebloan descendants to the south, the Ute and Southern Paiute used multiple-rod foundations in their coiled basketry, and two- and three-rod variations predominated, although some Ute tribes occasionally used single-rod foundations.[19] Round-bottomed water-jug baskets, which were frequently pitched to make them watertight, were common in Numic coiled basketry. Other shapes favored by the Numic were square-shouldered, bottle-neck baskets, bowls, conical burden baskets, circular trays, winnowing trays (see cat. no. 50), and hats, some of which were commonly twined.[20]

In contrast to their Anasazi and Fremont predecessors, Numic peoples made a rich variety of twined baskets. They used both open and close twining, normally pairing the wefts. They also practiced diagonal twining which found a wide variety of expression in its details. Unlike the Fremont and Anasazi, who tended to confine twining to the production of flat mats and flexible bags, Numic peoples used twining to create numerous three-dimensional forms. These included circular and oval shapes such as winnowing baskets, conical burden baskets, water jugs, and bowls.[21]

THE PECTOL-LEE DECORATED BASKETS

It has long been held that the most notable difference between Fremont and Anasazi basketry is the prevalence of decoration in Anasazi basketry and its virtual absence in Fremont baskets. However, the Pectol-Lee collection features a number of baskets that bring this maxim into question. At least seven baskets in the collection appear to be a melding of these two traditions, that is, the single-rod variation baskets, known to be favored by the Fremont, but exhibiting abundant decoration long assumed to be indicative of Anasazi workmanship. Likewise, two baskets feature rod-in-bundle foundations, a technique not generally considered to be part of the repertoire of either group, nor of their Numic successors. Additionally, there are four pieces in the collection—including the cradle board—that exhibit a twining technique not previously known to have been practiced by any of these groups. This next section will describe the pertinent features of the thirteen baskets so that the subsequent section may consider Fremont affiliation in light of these features.

Decorated Single-Rod Baskets (cat. nos. 28–31, 35, 43, 44)

The Pectol-Lee collection features two types of decorated baskets, shallow trays and wide-mouthed bowls. The four large, shallow, close-coiled, split-rod-and-bundle trays preserve traces of a reddish-purple pigment (Color Plate 18), and three wide-mouth bowls exhibit geometric designs in black or dark gray on a pale background (Color Plate 19).

The four decorated trays (cat. nos. 28–31) are all large, that is, between 42 and 50 centimeters in diameter. In each case the foundation rod of willow (*Salix sp.*) was split lengthwise and paired with a small bundle of plant fiber, with the split side down. The stitches encircle the rod, but pass through the bundle. The bundle material varies from basket to basket, with one of yucca (*Yucca sp.*) and three of dogbane or milkweed (*Apocynum cannabinum* or *Asclepius sp.*). Both the foundation rods and stitches are decorticated, that is, have had the bark removed. In each instance the stitches are non-interlocking. In all cases the concave, interior surface of the basket was the working surface, that is, the side which would have faced the craftsperson while the basket was under construction.

All four baskets preserve traces of reddish-purple pigment and appear to have been richly decorated at one time (Color Plate 18). In the two best-preserved examples (cat. nos. 28–29) there is a perceptible pattern in the distribution of this pigment, indicating the staining was a form of decoration as opposed to a food residue or damage resulting from circumstances of burial. The decoration on one of the trays (cat. no. 28) consists of four, regularly spaced, concentric black rings extending out from the center and deployed on the reddish-purple background. On the other tray (cat. no. 29), a black stripe bisects the center and joins a hemispherical black line around the perimeter, all on a reddish-purple field (Figure 41). Due to the passage of time, there is some uncertainty regarding the original color of the background, which grades from a rich, reddish-purple to a rusty brown.[22] However, there can be no question regarding the existence of decoration on these baskets and the patterns described.

Unfortunately, the original design is not distinguishable on the two remaining baskets (cat. nos. 30–31) owing to their poor preservation, although the better preserved of the two (cat. no. 30) appears to include a large, dark circle in the center of the basket. The decoration on these baskets is more difficult to discern, in part because it has been wholly obliterated in places. The fact that the reddish-purple pigment has proved extremely attractive to insects suggests it may have been derived from a berry juice or other organic substance. The rich reddish-purple hue is suggestive of the color of a berry juice. The baskets in question show massive destruction in the bundle portions of the foundation, i.e., the permeable portions that absorbed the greatest proportion of the pigment;[23] whereas the foundation rods and, in some cases, the stitches are largely intact. Consumption of the bundle follows the curve of the coil, resulting in a peculiar spiral pattern of destruction, rather than patchy destruction interspersed with relatively untouched areas, as one would normally expect. This spiral pattern of damage can clearly be seen in the photographs in the catalogue section. Significantly, this pattern of damage is only evident in the trays with the reddish-purple coloring.

In contrast to the homogeneity of technique seen in the trays above, the three decorated bowls in the Pectol-Lee collection vary slightly in construction technique and materials (Color Plate 19), both of which are ultimately important for establishing cultural attribution. One bowl (cat.

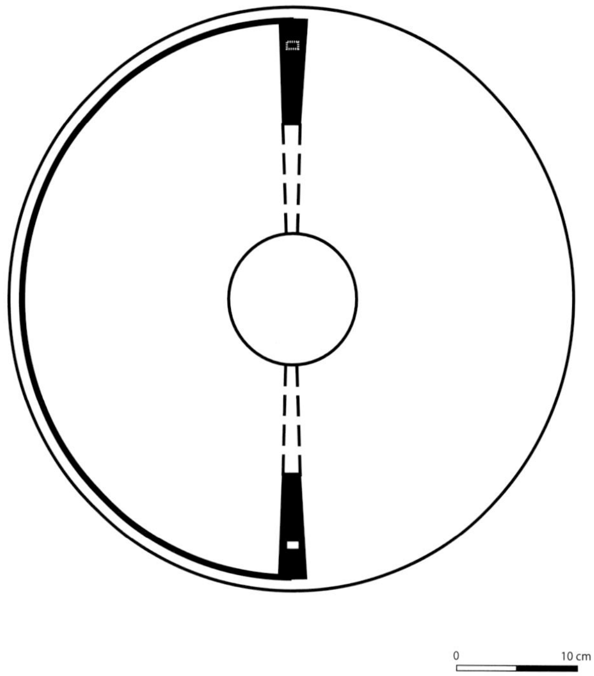

Figure 41. Diagram of decoration on cat. no. 29. Drawing by Debbie Silversmith, 2001.

no. 35) was constructed using a split-rod-and-bundle foundation similar to that seen in the decorated trays. The stitches are willow(*Salix sp.*). Willow was likewise used for the split rods, while the bundle is of yucca (*Yucca sp.*). The other two bowls (cat. nos. 43–44) were constructed using a whole-rod foundation with no bundle. The stitches are also of willow (*Salix sp.*) but are worked around a rabbitbrush (*Chrysothamnus sp.*) foundation.

The most notable feature of these bowls is the elaborate patterns worked in contrasting dark stitches on a pale background. This decoration is structural in nature and is, therefore, mirrored on both the inside and outside of the bowls. The split-rod-and-bundle bowl (cat. no. 35) preserves faint traces of a geometric design consisting of narrow, stepped lines radiating from the center of the bowl (Figure 42). A fugitive black pigment was used for the lines. Over time these lines have become so faded that they are barely visible against the pale background of the basket.

Both whole-rod baskets (cat. nos. 43–44) exhibit geometric designs of varying complexity. In both cases the decoration on the exterior surfaces of the bowls is somewhat faded, whereas on the interior it is still evident.

Figure 42. Diagram of decoration on cat. no. 35. Drawing by Debbie Silversmith, 2001.

The larger specimen (cat no. 44) is simply decorated with a single, dark band a short distance below the rim. The smaller bowl (cat. no. 43), by contrast, is decorated with four, dark zig-zags or "lightning bolts" which spiral outwards from a dark circle in the bottom of the basket to meet a dark line near the rim.

Rod-In-Bundle Baskets (cat. nos. 38–39)

The two bulrush baskets in the collection are of interest because neither the shape nor the construction technique are known to have been commonly employed by the Fremont, the Anasazi, or Numic groups (Color Plate 20). The first of these baskets (cat. no. 38) is a very large, globular jar, nearly spherical in shape, with a small upright neck. The other (cat. no. 39) is a tray, or perhaps more likely, the base of a basket similar to the jar. The top portion of this basket has perished entirely, or perhaps was never completed. The two baskets exhibit strong similarities in size, construction technique, and wall angle, suggesting the fragment either was, or was meant to be, a jar like the complete specimen.

Figure 43. Wrapped twined basketry from the Pectol-Lee collection. Clockwise from cradle board: cat. nos. 61, 63, 64, 62. Photo by Leslie-lynne Sinkey, 2001.

Both baskets were constructed of a large foundation bundle consisting of a split wooden rod enclosed in a bundle of mixed marshland rushes, including cattail (*Typha sp.*) and three-corner grass (*Scirpus olneyi*), secured with haphazardly arranged, interlocking, undecorticated willow (*Salix sp.*) stitches. In contrast to the careful construction of the other baskets in the collection, construction of both of these baskets appears to have been somewhat expedient.

Close Wrapped Twined Basketry (cat. nos. 61–64)

Four artifacts in the Pectol-Lee collection were made using close wrapped twining, a basketry technique not previously documented among Southwestern cultures (Figure 43). This includes the cradle board (cat. no. 61) and three other basketry fragments (cat. nos. 62–64). In the cradle board close wrapped twining was employed in construction of both the back of the cradle board and the sun shade. The back was worked in two colors of flexible weft in a checkerboard pattern similar to that used on two of the fragments (cat. nos. 62–63, see description below).[24] Willow (*Salix sp.*) was employed for both the warps and rigid and flexible wefts; while on the two larger fragments, yucca (*Yucca sp.*) cordage was used along the selvage.

The decoration employed on two of the smaller fragments (cat. nos. 62–63) is similar in appearance and construction to that of the cradle board, the checkerboard pattern having been created by sections of lashing interspersed with unworked portions. Although these two fragments are remarkably similar, they represent portions of two different artifacts. The curvature of these two fragments, their general size, and the treatment of their warp selvages are all very similar to the sunshade on the Pectol-Lee cradle board, and the possibility exists they may be fragments of cradle boards as well. However, since the Pectol-Lee collection is the first recorded instance of this type of basketry in the Four Corners area, the range of artifacts for which this technique may have been employed remains unknown.

The third fragment of this type (cat. no. 64) is extremely small and consists of just a few rows, but it appears unlikely to have been a part of either of the other two wrapped twined fragments.

CULTURAL AFFILIATION

As stated in the introduction to this paper and as will be demonstrated in this section, the baskets discussed above all appear to be Fremont despite the decorative features archaeologists currently consider to be rare or unusual in Fremont basketry. Indeed, in the absence of the Pectol-Lee decorated baskets, this assumption would seem well founded for, to the author's knowledge, only two decorated Fremont baskets have been documented to date. One is a tray fragment with a single circuit of stitches dyed red, and the other is a bowl fragment with feathers sewn to it.[25]

Trays (cat. nos. 28–31)

The trays in the Pectol-Lee collection (Color Plate 18) can be firmly assigned to the Fremont culture on the basis of several characteristics. The shallow tray form, the split-rod-and-bundle foundation, the use of non-interlocking stitches, and the location of the working surface are all consistent with Fremont basketry. The materials used, that is, willow for the foundation and stitches, and dogbane, milkweed, or yucca for bundles, are also in keeping with the Fremont basketry tradition. As previously noted, both Anasazi and Numic groups preferred multiple-rod foundations, and the trays made by both Anasazi and Numic peoples tended to be deeper than those fashioned by the Fremont. Although Numic groups were known to periodically make use of single-rod foundations, they did not employ the single-rod-and-bundle combination. Moreover, Numic basket makers used squawbush (*Rhus sp.*) as well as willow (*Salix sp.*) for their foundation rods and are not known to have used willow for stitches.[26]

Thus, based on construction technique, the trays appear to be Fremont. Assuming the trays do, indeed, all hail from the same region as claimed, the possibility exists that the decoration represents a localized aesthetic, rather than a broader cultural phenomenon.[27] Although this possibility should not be dismissed, the other decorated baskets in the collection suggest decorating was, indeed, a more consistent phenomenon than previously assumed.

Bowls (cat. nos. 35, 43, 44)

Like the decorated trays above, the rod-and-bundle bowl (cat. no. 35) can be firmly assigned to the Fremont based on its construction technique, and no further discussion seems necessary for attribution. However, the two, single-rod foundation bowls (cat. nos. 43–44) are not as straightforward. Adovasio reports that single-rod, interlocking-stitch baskets such as these are rare among the Fremont and are generally confined to the period AD 300–800,[28] although the popularity of this technique continued among Fremont groups living in the Parowan Valley and Uinta Basin.[29]

Single-rod coiling was not entirely limited to the Fremont, however. It is also present among Virgin Anasazi groups living well to the west and south of Capitol Reef.[30] The possibility exists, therefore, that these baskets were obtained from external sources by trade, or brought by immigrants to the area when the Virgin region was abruptly abandoned in the twelfth century AD.[31] Adovasio notes that single-rod foundations tend to occur later in the Anasazi area than in the Great Basin,[32] suggesting radiocarbon dating of these materials might help elucidate cultural affiliation.

Nevertheless, a Fremont attribution seems likely. The single-rod foundation, the use of willow stitches and rabbitbrush foundation rods, and the wide-mouthed bowl forms are all typically Fremont. Not only is the construction Fremont, but the geometric motifs employed in the decoration find parallels in decorated Fremont pottery (see Figure 44). In particular, numerous motifs on the Pectol-Lee baskets, notably, the zig-zag lines, the division of the pattern into four distinct quadrants, and the blank, undecorated circular field in the center of the bowl, are all

Figure 44. Fremont pottery decorations. From Joel C. Janetski, Richard K. Talbot, Deborah E. Newman, Lane D. Richens, James D. Wilde, Shane A. Baker, and Scott A. Billat, *Clear Creek Canyon Archaeological Project Volume Five: Results and Synthesis*, Museum of Peoples and Cultures Technical Series 95-9 (Provo: Brigham Young University, 1997), 72–73.

characteristics of decorated Fremont pottery.[33] Admittedly, this statement is made without the benefit of a thorough art historical analysis of how Fremont styles of pottery and basketry decoration compare (or contrast) to Anasazi styles.

Jars (cat. nos. 38, 39)

The two rod-in-bundle bulrush baskets (Color Plate 20 and cat. nos. 38–39) present a problem in cultural attribution, because they are unlike "typical" baskets of the Fremont, the Anasazi, or Numic groups, both in construction and form. While rod-in-bundle construction has no parallels among Anasazi or Numic basketry traditions,[34] it has at least been noted as a rare component of the Fremont basketry repertoire.[35] Therefore, there is some basis for attributing these baskets to the Fremont culture on the basis of construction alone.

The globular shape of the Pectol-Lee baskets may be unusual but still finds parallels within the Fremont repertoire. While the large, globular jar form is not typical of any of the Capitol Reef groups, two similar jars likely to be Fremont are known from the Uintah Basin area of Utah. One is a basketry jar from Blytho's Spring virtually identical in shape and construction to that in the Pectol-Lee collection.[36] Although the Blytho's Spring basket has not been dated, both its provenience and the fact that maize and other domesticates were among its contents suggest it is Fremont, for later Numic groups occupying that area did not raise maize. The other example is a partial, spherical grass basket recovered in Steinaker Draw, not far from Blytho's Spring. The upper portion has perished, but based on its spherical shape, it was likely a jar in its original state. Significantly, this basket also exhibits the unusual rod-in-bundle construction seen in the Capitol Reef bulrush baskets.[37] The presence of such similar baskets so far north of the Anasazi region suggests the Capitol Reef bulrush baskets are not Anasazi but rather Numic or Fremont. Radiocarbon dating would be helpful in weighing this question.

For other examples of rod-in-bundle baskets, one must look far south of the Capitol Reef region, where the technique was extensively used by the Hohokam of southern Arizona and the Mogollon of southern New Mexico.[38] Given the rather expedient construction of the Pectol-Lee specimens, it seems unlikely such a basket would be traded in; more likely, the idea itself of rod-in-bundle construction would have traveled north. Perhaps the rod-*in*-bundle technique arose as a natural elaboration of the rod-*and*-bundle technique so prevalent in Fremont baskets.[39] Considerable research outside the scope of the present inquiry would be necessary to investigate this question, however. In the absence of that research, and without the benefit of a radiocarbon date, the preponderance of the evidence suggests Fremont affiliation for the Pectol-Lee globular jars, and that rod-in-bundle construction is a heretofore largely unrecognized component of the Fremont basketry tradition.

Cradle boards (cat. nos. 61–64)

The examples of wrapped twined basketry in the Pectol-Lee collection (Figure 44 and cat. nos. 61–64) are unparalleled in the eastern Great Basin and Four Corners area. Fortunately, however, the cradle board can be attributed independently of the basketry construction technique itself due to the presence of a distinctively Fremont figurine bound to it (see Allen and Munsey, pp. 56–58, this volume). This attribution is further strengthened by radiocarbon dating of the basketry component, which resulted in a calibrated date of AD 910–1030.[40] It is entirely reasonable to attribute the cradle board—if not the three, close wrapped twined fragments in the collection—to that culture. Thus, although not previously documented as part of the Fremont tradition, the close wrapped twining technique of construction appears to number among the basketry techniques practiced by the Fremont.

CONCLUSIONS

The unusual features of some of the baskets in the Pectol-Lee collection provide new insights into the Fremont basketry tradition and, perhaps, into the nature of cultural interaction in the Capitol Reef area in prehistory. The thirteen baskets examined in this paper indicate Fremont basket makers were both more versatile and more inclined to decorate their products than previously believed. Whereas experts have long believed decoration to be virtually absent in Fremont basketry, several of the Fremont baskets in the Pectol-Lee collection were not only highly decorated but done so with a bold color heretofore undocumented in the Fremont repertoire.[41] The extent to which this reddish-purple decoration on the trays was commonly known or was a localized aberration cannot be established at this time. However, these trays, along with several baskets in the Pectol-Lee collection with black geometric decorations, significantly expand the corpus of decorated Fremont baskets which formerly consisted of only two documented examples. Further examination of extant collections of Fremont basketry and careful consideration of assemblages excavated in the future are warranted, if we are to determine the extent to which Fremont basketry was decorated.

The Pectol-Lee collection also expands our understanding of the range of basketry techniques and forms used by the Fremont. The rod-*in*-bundle technique, previously noted as rare in Fremont basketry, finds further Fremont representation in the Pectol-Lee collection; and, for the first time, there seems to be evidence that the Fremont tradition also included a highly decorative form of twining, that is, close wrapped twining. It further appears necessary to add another shape to the Fremont basketry repertoire, the large, globular jar.

These discoveries are significant for refining currently held perceptions of Fremont basketry. They may also have important implications regarding the extent to which people inhabiting the Capitol Reef area interacted among themselves and with cultures further afield. The use of decoration on the rod-and-bundle and single-rod trays and bowls may reflect close interaction between the Anasazi and Fremont cultures in the Capitol Reef region. Although this paper has not addressed what constitutes "typically Anasazi" decorations in baskets, it is commonly recognized that the Anasazi did employ decorations in their basketry, indeed, to the extent that, when technique of construction is unclear but decoration is present, researchers tend to attribute baskets from the Four Corners region to the Anasazi. For example, a decorated basketry tray from the Lang-Lyman collection now at the Museum of Peoples and Cultures was attributed to the Anasazi on the basis of its provenience (San Juan County) and its style of decoration, since the construction technique was "indeterminable;"[42] yet, based on the author's examination of the basket, the construction technique is rod-and-bundle, and therefore the basket is Fremont.

Indeed, it would seem prudent to re-evaluate the attribution of decorated baskets of unspecified construction currently attributed to the Anasazi. For example, Mason provides photographs of a number of shallow basketry trays found in southeastern Utah exhibiting geometric patterns, particularly involving combinations of rings and zig-zags. Mason attributed them to the "cliff-dwellers," as the Anasazi were then known, but unfortunately provided no information regarding the construction techniques of these baskets. His 1904 publication, moreover, pre-dates the definition of the Fremont as a culture separate from the Anasazi.[43]

The decoration that makes the baskets in the Pectol-Lee collection so distinct may reflect a unique combination of circumstances arising from close contact between two cultures with very different approaches to basket construction. Certainly, the sharing of ideas, including tastes in artistic forms and decoration, would seem a natural consequence of two peoples living similar lifeways in close proximity to one another. Additional research—especially in the realm of comparative art historical analysis—is needed to address whether there was indeed any cross-influence between Fremont and Anasazi basket makers.

The presence of rod-in-bundle globular jars in the Fremont repertoire may also have implications regarding the Fremont sphere of interaction with other cultures. Although it seems reasonable to suppose the Fremont developed this technique *in situ* as an outgrowth of the rod-and-bundle technique, the possibility remains they borrowed it from elsewhere. If so, the nearest source would appear to be far to the south among the Hohokam and Mogollon, who are known to have used the technique extensively.

While the potential for such far-reaching exchange of basketry techniques may seem improbable, the possibility that basketry technology was exchanged over large distances is strengthened now that close wrapped twining appears to be part of the Fremont repertoire. No previous occurrence of close wrapped twining has been documented for the eastern Great Basin in any period, nor does it form a part of the Southwestern twining repertoire.[44] The only previously recorded instance of this technique anywhere in the Great Basin is in the northern and western regions, that is, Nevada, where close wrapped twining occurs coupled with the use of a variety of weft colors as a decorative technique.[45] This is the same type of elaboration seen on close wrapped twined basketry in the Pectol-Lee collection. Wrapped twining is a significant departure from other twining techniques; the likelihood that the same variation, including the use of multiple weft colors, should arise independently on opposite sides of the Great Basin seems slight.

The range and variety of basketry styles and techniques in the Pectol-Lee collection provide new insights into the nature of Fremont basketry which appears to be far more colorful, decorative, and diverse than previously believed. By extension, these discoveries raise new and tantalizing questions regarding the nature and extent of intercultural contact and exchange in the Capitol Reef region, particularly regarding the possibility of close interaction between Fremont and Anasazi basket makers in the Capitol Reef area, as well as Fremont connections further afield. What was perhaps most unexpected about the Pectol-Lee collection is the fact that so much of importance could be gleaned through the study of unprovenienced basketry. These findings hint of the vast task that lies ahead in re-evaluating other baskets languishing for research in museums and private collections.

1. James Adovasio, "Artifacts and Ethnicity: Basketry as an Indicator of Territoriality and Population Movements in the Prehistoric Great Basin," in *Anthropology of the Desert West: Essays in Honor of Jesse D. Jennings* edited by Carol J. Condie and Don D. Fowler (Salt Lake City: University of Utah Press, 1986), 45. The works of James Adovasio are relied upon heavily throughout this article, in part because of his significant contribution to the standardization of basketry technology, and in part because much of his early work involved extensive, pioneering studies in the basketry of Great Basin cultures. Basketry terminology used throughout is that used by Adovasio in his numerous publications, although it is acknowledged that alternative terminologies exist and are equally appropriate.

2. James Adovasio, "Prehistoric Basketry," in *Great Basin*, ed. Warren L. D'Azevedo, vol. 11, *Handbook of North American Indians,* ed. W. C. Sturtevant (Washington, D.C.: Smithsonian Institution, 1986), 202.

3. In total, the Pectol-Lee collection includes baskets or basket fragments made with the following techniques: (Fremont) rod and bundle, split-rod-and-bundle, single-rod, rod-in-bundle, and intricate stitch coiling, and wrapped twining; (Anasazi) twill plaiting; (Numic) diagonal twining; and open simple twining and close simple twining, which by their presence in all three cultures precludes attribution of those baskets without a thorough search for comparanda in the literature and/or radiocarbon dating.

4. Adovasio, "Artifacts and Ethnicity," 62; Adovasio, "Fremont Basketry," *Tebiwa* 17:2(1975): 69.

5. Adovasio, "Artifacts and Ethnicity,"48.

6. Adovasio, "Prehistoric Basketry," 202.

7. Ibid.

8. Adovasio, "Fremont Basketry," 68.

9. Ibid., 69.

10. Ibid.

11. Otis Tufton Mason, *American Indian Basketry* (New York: Dover, 1988), 444–447.

12. The Virgin Anasazi did adopt single-rod coiling in the later prehistoric period: see James Adovasio, "Prehistoric North American Basketry" in *Nevada State Museum Anthropological Papers Number 16* Collected Paper No. 5 (Carson City, Nev.: Nevada State Museum, 1974), 119; and James Adovasio, "Origin, Development, and Distribution of Western Archaic Textiles," *Tebiwa* 13:2 (1970), 12.

13. Adovasio, "Prehistoric North American Basketry," 120.

14. Ibid., 121.

15. James Adovasio, *Basketry Technology* (Chicago: Aldine, 1977), 144–145; Mason, *American Indian Basketry*, 444, 448.

16. Mason, ibid., 443.

17. Adovasio, "Origin, Development, and Distribution of Western Archaic Textiles," 18.

18. Adovasio, *Basketry Technology*, 135–138.

19. Specifically, the Moanunts, Taviwatsiu, and Mowatci Ute were known to use single- or split-rod foundations: see Adovasio "Artifacts and Ethnicity," 61.

20. Adovasio, "Artifacts and Ethnicity," 70; Mason, *American Indian Basketry*, 434–440.

21. Adovasio, ibid., 58, 64.

22. While this may be the result of oxidation or UV exposure of the pigment, resulting in fading and discoloration, Pamela Miller, Curator of Archaeology, College of Eastern Utah Prehistoric Museum, Price, Utah, cautions that the original background may have been the rusty brown, whereas the purple may represent staining from a food residue. However, she concurs that the baskets were decorated. While more muted colors are the norm in archaeological collections, this may in part be a function of the passage of time. It should be noted that the reddish-purple pigment used to decorate these trays appears on a few other artifacts in the Pectol-Lee collection (e.g., cat. no. 114), although in these cases it is more akin to a patchy accretion rather than applied in well defined zones as here.

23. Adovasio notes Fremont rod-and-bundle baskets were watertight, as upon exposure to liquid the bundle would absorb moisture and expand, thus sealing gaps and preventing leakage: Adovasio, "Origin, Development, and Distribution of Western Archaic Textiles," 10. Whether the concentration of pigment in the bundles represents pigment applied after the construction of the baskets, which then soaked into the bundle, or the "bleeding" of the pigment into the bundle when the baskets became damp, is unknown.

24. Both wefts appear to be the same material, suggesting the darker weft was dyed.

25. See Adovasio, "Fremont Basketry," 69; and, James Adovasio, "Comment by Adovasio" *American Antiquity* 44:4 (1979), 724.

26. Adovasio, "Artifacts and Ethnicity," 62.

27. That the trays may represent a localized aesthetic, even that they were made by one hand, was suggested by Pamela Miller, Curator of Archaeology, College of Eastern Utah Museum, Price, Utah. Miller discerned analogous patterns of wear, damage, and staining on these trays, suggesting the trays not only shared the same burial situation but were stacked one inside the other. If made by one hand, the trays could be expressions of individual taste and not culturally representative of the Fremont. [Editor's note: Subsequent to Sinkey's submission of this article, the editor discovered a curious statement among Ephraim Pectol's

papers indicating that some of the baskets in the collection were found stacked: "Next comes baskets, eight in number nested together when found . . . . Their coloring is natural, they are of a very fine woven texture of cedar bark, and designed in brown and black . . . ." See E. P. Pectol, "Wayne County: Wayne Wonderland and Its Ancient Culture" (unpublished manuscript in possession of Neal Busk, Richfield, Utah, 1947), 5. If Pectol was accurate in his description of the stacked baskets, it is unlikely this statement refers to any of the decorated trays currently in the collection.]

28. Adovasio, "Origin, Development, and Distribution of Western Archaic Textiles," 12.

29. Adovasio, "Fremont Basketry," 70; Adovasio, "Comment by Adovasio," 728.

30. Adovasio, "Origin, Development, and Distribution of Western Archaic Textiles," 12; Margaret Lyneis, "Virgin Anasazi, Far Western Puebloans" *Journal of World Prehistory* 9:2 (1995), 200.

31. Lyneis, "Virgin Anasazi, Far Western Puebloans," 232.

32. Adovasio, "Origin, Development, and Distribution of Western Archaic Textiles," 12.

33. Cf. the illustrations in Joel C. Janetski, Richard K. Talbot, Deborah E. Newman, Lane D. Richens, James D. Wilde, Shane A. Baker, and Scott A. Billat, *Clear Creek Canyon Archaeological Project Volume Five: Results and Synthesis*, Museum of Peoples and Cultures Technical Series 95-9 (Provo: Brigham Young University, 1997), 72–73; and R. E. Madsen, *Prehistoric Ceramics of the Fremont,* Ceramic Series No. 6 (Flagstaff: Museum of Northern Arizona, 1977). Regarding visual correspondence between the motifs in the Pectol-Lee decorated baskets and motifs on decorated Fremont pottery: Lane Richens, staff archaeologist, Office of Public Archaeology, Brigham Young University, personal communication, 2001, and Grant Smith, graduate student, Department of Anthropology, Brigham Young University, personal communications, 2001.

34. Adovasio, "Prehistoric North American Basketry," 120; Adovasio, "Artifacts and Ethnicity," 61.

35. Sharyl Kinnear-Ferris, "An Analysis of Canyonlands Region Woven Perishables and a Comparison with those of Surrounding Regions" (unpublished M.A. thesis, Regis University (1999), 74.

36. Lawrence De Ved and Rhoda De Ved, "Prehistoric Baskets from the Leo C. Thorne Collection, Part 1," *Utah Archaeology 1994* 7:1 (1994), 120.

37. Lawrence De Ved and Rhoda De Ved, "Prehistoric Baskets from the Leo C. Thorne Collection, Part 1," 124; Lawrence De Ved, personal communication, 2001.

38. See Adovasio, "Prehistoric North American Basketry," 120.

39. Ibid., 115, 119–120.

40. Beta 154227, AMS date (plant material), 1040 +/- 40 BP. Calibrated dates (two sigma range) AD 910–920 and AD 960–1030.

41. Color previously undocumented: Pamela Miller, Curator of Archaeology, College of Eastern Utah Prehistoric Museum, personal communication, April 2001.

42. Marti Lu Allen and Shane A. Baker, eds., *Of Earth, Stone, and Corn: The Anasazi and their Puebloan Descendants*, Museum of Peoples and Cultures Popular Series 2 (Provo: Brigham Young University, 2000), 147, cat. no. 23. That the tray is in such good condition makes it difficult to discern the construction. A thorough comparative study of style in Fremont pottery and Anasazi basketry and pottery motifs is warranted.

43. Mason, "American Indian Basketry," pl. 205, 207, and 208.

44. Adovasio, "Prehistoric North American Basketry," 119–121.

45. Adovasio, "Prehistoric Basketry," 195, 197; Charles E. Rozaire, "Analysis of Woven Materials from Seven Caves in the Lake Winnemucca Area, Pershing County, Nevada," in *Nevada State Museum Anthropological Papers Number 16*, Collected Paper No. 4 (Carson City, Nev.: Nevada State Museum, 1974), 67, 71.

Color Plate 1. Pectol-Lee model cradle board (cat. no. 61), obverse. Fremont, ca. AD 1000. Photo by David Hawkinson, 2001.

Color Plate 2. Pectol-Lee model cradle board (cat. no. 61), detail of figurine. Photo by David Hawkinson, 2001.

Color Plate 3. Pectol-Lee model cradle board (cat. no. 61), reverse. Photo by David Hawkinson, 2001.

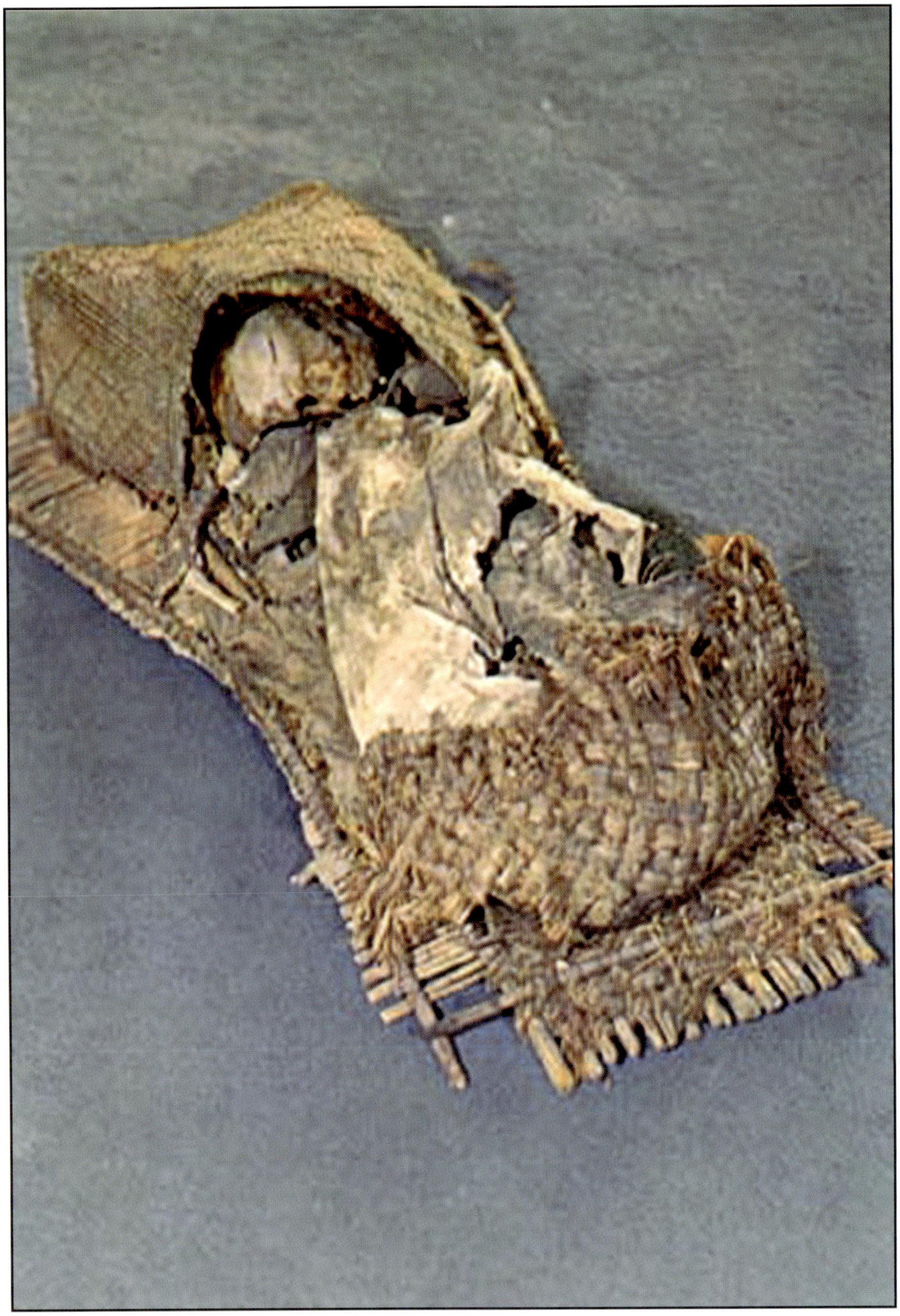

Color Plate 4. Full-size cradle board said to be from Nine Mile Canyon, obverse. Fremont? Formerly in College of Eastern Utah Prehistoric Museum, Price, Utah. Post card of unknown manufacture. Photo taken ca. 1960–1965.

Color Plate 5. Pectol-Lee model cradle board (cat. no. 61), detail of feet. Photo by David Hawkinson, 2001.

Color Plate 6. Pectol-Lee deer headdress (cat. no. 71), obverse. Late Prehistoric. Note the stitched eye, propped ear, traces of yellow pigment to the viewer's right of the ear, and hide stitches along the "nape." Photo by David Hawkinson, 2001.

Color Plate 7. Pectol-Lee deer headdress (cat. no. 71), reverse. Late Prehistoric. Photo by David Hawkinson, 2001.

Color Plate 8. Pectol-Lee deer headdress (cat. no. 71), detail of ear. Late Prehistoric. Photo by David Hawkinson, 2001.

Color Plate 9. Pectol-Lee deer headdress (cat. no. 71), detail of dorsal sinew stitching. Late Prehistoric. Photo by David Hawkinson, 2001.

Color Plate 10. Deer headdress from Mantle's Cave, Castle Park, Colorado. Obverse. Fremont, before ca. AD 900. University of Colorado Museum (6102), Boulder, Colorado. Photo by Christopher D. DiCicco, 2001.

Color Plate 11. Deer headdress from Mantle's Cave, Castle Park, Colorado. Reverse. Fremont, before ca. AD 900. University of Colorado Museum (6102), Boulder, Colorado. Photo by Christopher D. DiCicco, 2001.

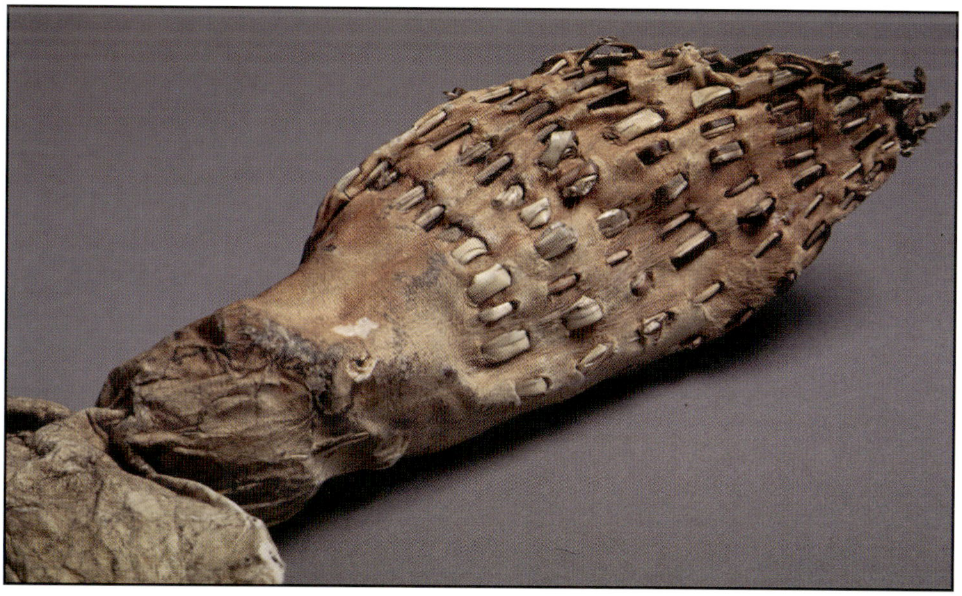

Color Plate 12. Deer headdress from Mantle's Cave, Castle Park, Colorado. Detail of proper left ear. Fremont, before ca. AD 900. University of Colorado Museum (6102), Boulder, Colorado. Photo by Christopher D. DiCicco, 2001.

Color Plate 13. Deer headdress from Mantle's Cave, Castle Park, Colorado. Detail of stitched slit. Fremont, before ca. AD 900. University of Colorado Museum (6102), Boulder, Colorado. Photo by Christopher D. DiCicco, 2001.

Color Plate 14. Bighorn sheep headdress with olivella shell pendants, College of Eastern Utah Prehistoric Museum, Price, Utah (CEUM 9462). Fremont (AD 400–1300)/Agricultural Period (AD 1–1300). Photo courtesy College of Eastern Utah Prehistoric Museum, Price, Utah.

Color Plate 15. Bison mask. Plains Indian, ca. 1860. From Madan, Fort Berthold Indian Reservation, North Dakota. Photo courtesy Buffalo Bill Historical Center, Cody, Wyoming (NA.203,359), Chandler-Pohrt Collection. Photo by Lucille Warters.

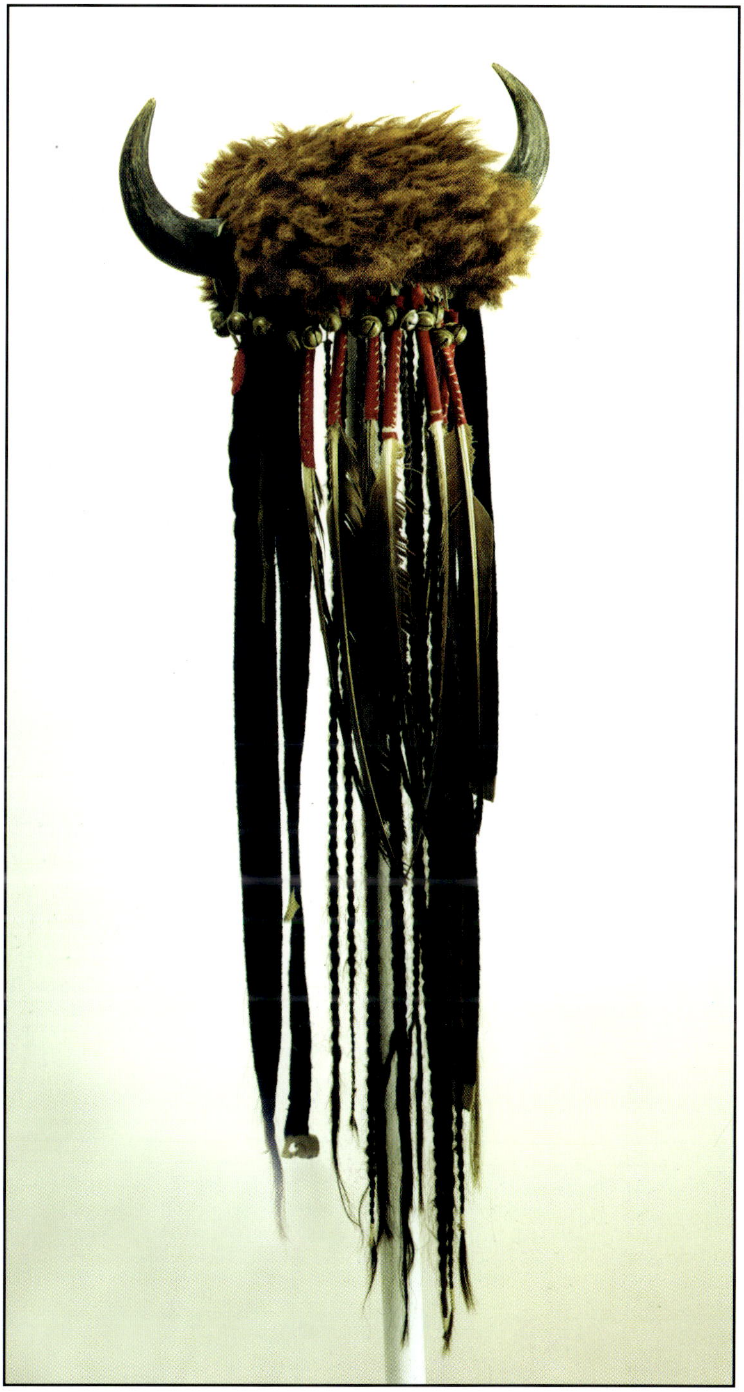

Color Plate 16. Bison headdress ("buffalo horn bonnet"). Gros Ventre Tribe, ca. 1880, Northern Plains. Buffalo Bill Historical Center, Cody, Wyoming (NA.203.136). Gift of Mr. and Mrs. Larry Larom. Photo by Devendra Shrikhande.

17a

17b

17c

Color Plate 17. Watercolor painting of Zia Buffalo Dance (untitled) by Velion Shije Herrera, Ma-Pe-Wi, Zia Pueblo, ca. 1918. Characters salient to discussion in text have been excerpted as 17a, 17b, and 17c. Note the antlers, the propped ears, the cape attachment, and the faces of the wearer showing beneath the headdresses. Photo courtesy Museum of Indian Arts and Culture/Laboratory of Anthropology, Museum of New Mexico, Santa Fe, New Mexico (14220/13). Photo by Blair Clark.

Color Plate 18. Decorated basketry trays from the Pectol-Lee collection. Clockwise from top left: cat. nos. 29, 28, 31, 30. Photo by Leslie-lynne Sinkey, 2001.

Color Plate 19. Decorated basketry bowls from the Pectol-Lee collection. Left to right: cat. nos. 44, 35, 43. Photo by Leslie-lynne Sinkey, 2001.

Color Plate 20. Rod-in-bundle bulrush baskets from the Pectol-Lee collection. Left to right: cat. nos. 39, 38. Photo by Leslie-lynne Sinkey, 2001.

CATALOGUE

PREFACE

The students completed detailed condition reports for each object according to the MPC's standards for incoming and outgoing loans, which are liability-oriented. In the interest of space, these reports were shortened for publication in this catalogue, but are available in full to interested parties through the Museum. The following standard was used for shortening the condition reports:

Included:

Statement addressing overall assessment of condition—e.g., very good, fair, poor.

Statement addressing degree of intactness—e.g., intact, partially intact, reconstructed from fragments, in fragments.

Statement addressing degree of completeness—e.g., complete, largely complete, partially complete, fragmentary.

Report of modern repairs or restorations.

Description of damage, significant accretions, or other condition resulting during the life of the object or from burial, except dirt and abrasions—e.g., handle missing, efflorescence, desiccation, pungent odor, delamination.

Description of potentially significant damage, accretions, or other condition, when post-burial or of unknown origin—e.g., cracks, abrasions, fly specks, particulation, charring.

Summary of non-specific or presumably non-significant accretions—e.g., "various accretions," rather than "dark brown stain on handle, three small patches of fibrous-looking black accretions near the middle, white specks, and powdery orange accretions."

Statement addressing stability—e.g., stable, weak, unstable.

Excluded (unless there were compelling reasons to include):

Structural damage of clearly modern origin—e.g., nail holes.

Accretions of clearly modern origin—e.g., pencil marks, paint spatters, permanent accession numbers, cotton fibers adhering.

Minor abrasions, dirt accretions, and general soiling resulting from burial situation.

Minor weathering.

Signs of infestations that have clearly been arrested—e.g., insect carcasses, moth frass, spider webs.

Manufacturing anomalies—e.g., fire clouds, scars from inclusions in pottery, and inherent defects such as knot holes.

Remarks about ancient repairs and use wear are included with the object description rather than the condition report—e.g., polish from use, wear on work edges, grime from handling, charring from cooking, food accreted to interior.

The basketry classification terminology employed here and throughout the catalogue is that used by James Adovasio, *Basketry Technology* (Chicago: Aldine, 1977).

Measurements provided in the catalogue represent maximum dimensions. Abbreviations used for dimensions are as follows:

H	Height
W	Width
D	Depth
L	Length
Diam	Diameter
Circum	Circumference
cm	centimeters

RAW MATERIALS AND MATERIAL STORES

1 YELLOW OCHRE SPECIMEN

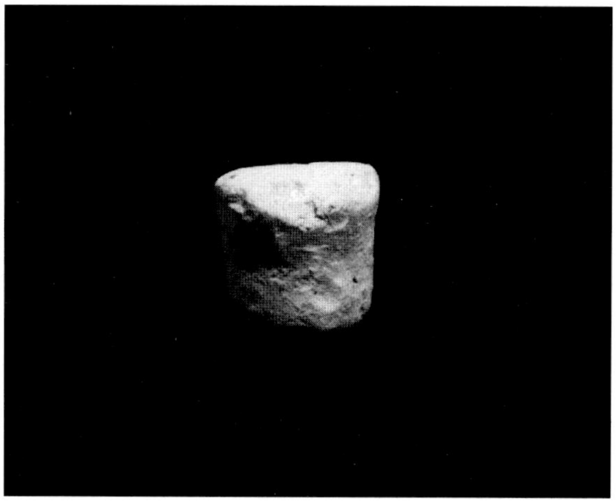

Prehistoric/Historic (before ca. AD 1900)?
Lent to Capitol Reef National Park
(On display at Visitor Center)
CARE 1621

L: 4.1 cm
W: 4.3 cm
D: 3.5 cm

Roughly shaped cube of yellow ochre; small white and brown inclusions.

Good condition; intact but weak. Particulating. Slight cracks. Numerous scattered pits. Reverse abraded.

2 RESIN SLAB

Prehistoric/Historic (before ca. AD 1900)
Lent to MPC, 2000–2005
CARE 197

L: 14.7 cm
W: 10.6 cm
D: 2.7 cm

A rectangular slab of tightly compacted resin preserving a groove or channel extending the entire width of one face (near the accession number) and a few partial grooves, possibly impressions from a cord or the edge of a paddle used to shape and compress the mass. Various botanical inclusions preserved in resin. Coloration varies from dark purple to shades of brown and red.

Good condition; intact and complete. Stable.

Comments:
The rectangular shape of this resin slab suggests it was deliberately compacted as a store for future use. Collected as sap from trees, sticky resin had many uses in prehistoric times. It was used by both the Fremont and Anasazi as a kind of "glue" for repairing pottery and bonding elements of composite artifacts. Because it was impervious to water, the Ute and other peoples sometimes used it to waterproof baskets.

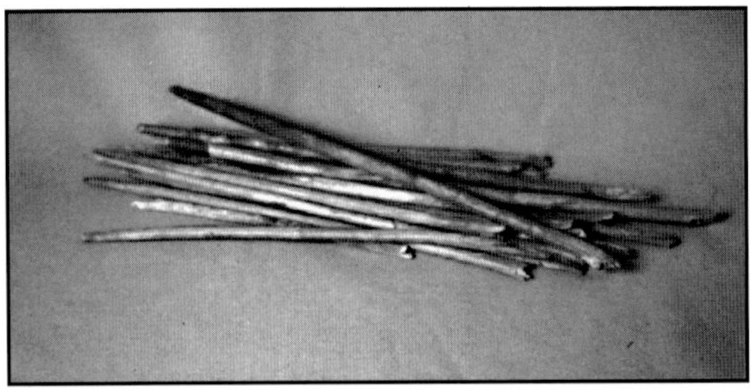

3 MATERIALS FOR ARROW FORESHAFTS?

Willow?
Agricultural Period
(Anasazi or Fremont, AD 1–1300)?
Lent to MPC, 2000–2005
CARE 20

L: 14.0 cm–36.4 cm
D: 0.5 cm–0.9 cm

Group of 23 medium-thick wood rods, 10 of which are significantly shorter than the rest. Rods apparently associated, given the fact they are in similar states of preparation: they have been pruned and straightened, and many are sharpened at one end and exhibit snap breaks at the other.

Good condition; intact. Some charred on ends. Scattered resin accretions; various other accretions. Stable.

Comments:
These wood rods may be part of a materials store that also included multipurpose sticks (cat. no. 4), composite arrow shafts (cat. no. 90), and basketry wefts (cat. no. 52). All four lots were given the same accession number, a fact possibly reflecting the collectors' knowledge, now lost, of an original contextual association. A similar store from Hogup Cave consisted of sticks for arrows.[1] Still another anciently bundled group of composite arrow shafts and partially worked rods, recovered from San Juan County, Utah, is now in the Museum of Peoples and Cultures.[2]

4 MULTIPURPOSE STICKS

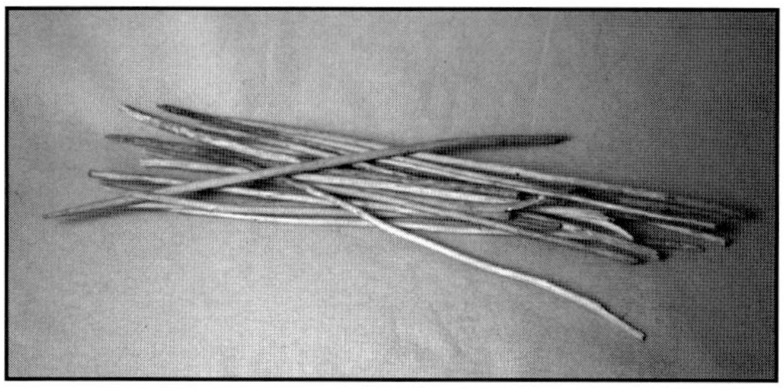

Willow?
Agricultural Period
(Anasazi or Fremont, AD 1–1300)?
Lent to MPC, 2000–2005
CARE 20

L: 20.8 cm–34.7 cm
D: 0.4 cm–0.5 cm

Group of 16 thin, unbound sticks which have been pruned, straightened, and sharpened at one end and snap-broken at the other with associated splitting. One preserves a notch on the tapered end, but this notch would not be suitable as a bowstring grip.

Good condition; intact. Two are slightly charred. Scattered resin accretions; fly spots. Stable.

Comments:
These wood rods may been part of the store described in the previous entry, but they are too thin to have been intended for arrows. They are, however, the appropriate size to be made into snares.

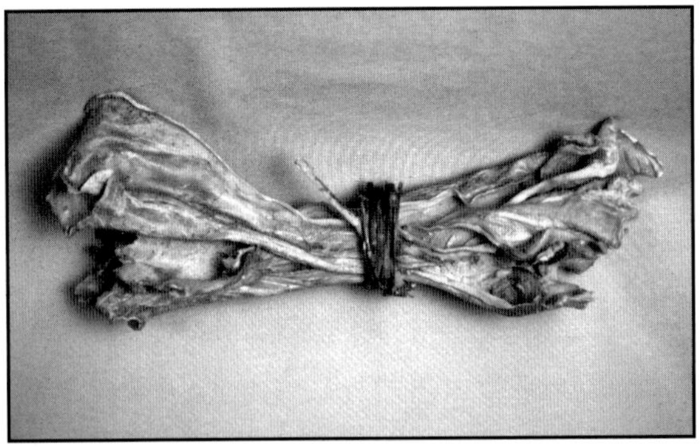

5 **HOCK BUNDLE**

Bighorn sheep, willow(?)
Fremont (AD 400–1300)?
Lent to MPC, 2000–2005
CARE 155, 156, 157, 158

Average measurements of individual hocks:
L: 33.0 cm
W: 15.0 cm

Four rawhide bighorn sheep hocks in a state of partial preparation and bundled together at the midpoints with a willow(?) twig.

Poor condition; intact and complete. Dew claws largely deteriorated. Desiccated. Stable.

Comments:
The Fremont used deer hocks to make a very distinctive kind of moccasin,[3] and it seems reasonable to suspect hocks from bighorn sheep could have served the same purpose.

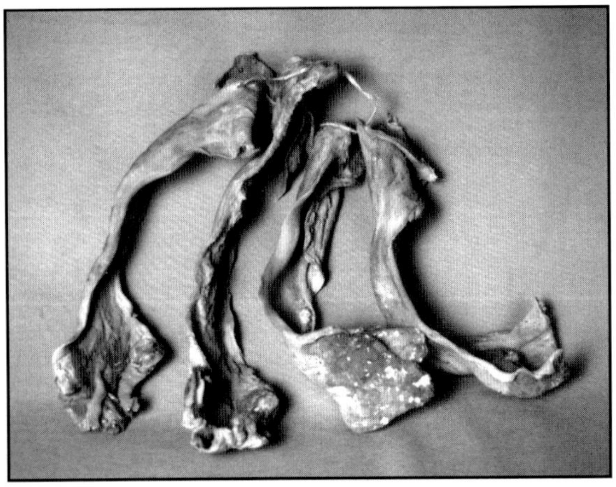

6 **HOCK BUNDLE**

Bighorn sheep
Fremont (AD 400–1300)?
Lent to MPC, 2000–2005
CARE 76

L: 27.0 cm
W: 23.8 cm

Four rawhide bighorn sheep(?) hocks in a state of partial preparation and tied together with sinew thread through a slit in each hock at the proximal end. Two hocks cut anteriorly, two posteriorly.

Poor condition; intact and complete. Dew claws largely deteriorated. Patches of hair remaining. Desiccated. Fly spots and large quantities of bird excrement(?). Weak (hair slipping).

7 **HOCK**

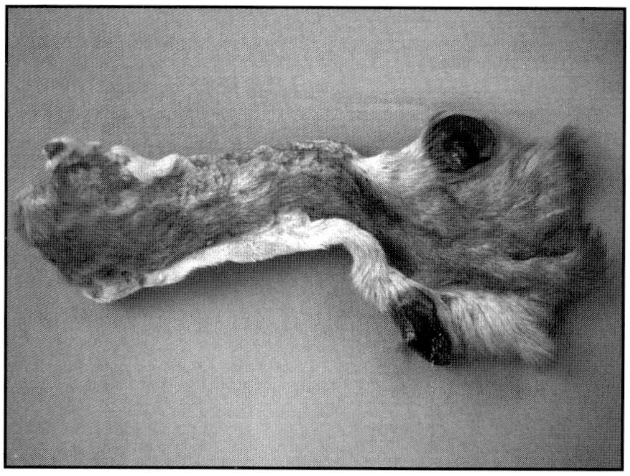

Bighorn sheep
Fremont (AD 400–1300)?
Lent to MPC, 2000–2005
CARE 62

L: 18.5 cm
W: 8.2 cm

A single bighorn sheep hock cut posteriorly with dew claws intact.

Fair condition; intact and complete. Desiccated, resulting in cockling; scattered hair loss. Various accretions. Stable.

8 **HOCK**

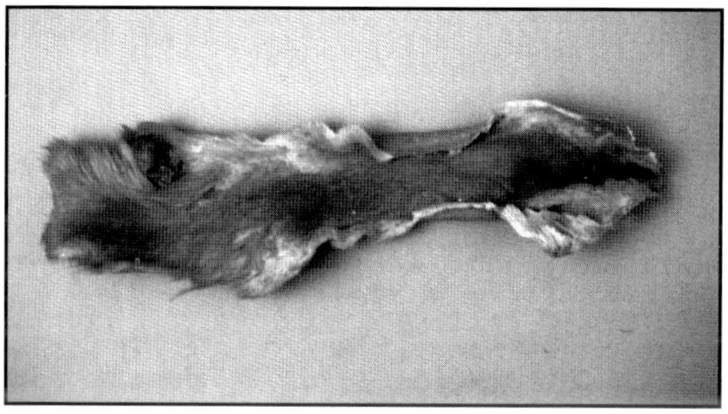

Bighorn sheep
Fremont (AD 400–1300)?
Lent to MPC, 2000–2005
CARE 61

L: 22.3 cm
W: 5.5 cm

A single rawhide bighorn sheep hock partially defleshed on inner face, one dew claw and hair largely intact.

Fair condition; intact and largely complete. One dew claw missing. Desiccated; cockling; scattered hair loss. Fly spots. Various accretions. Stable.

9 **HOCK**

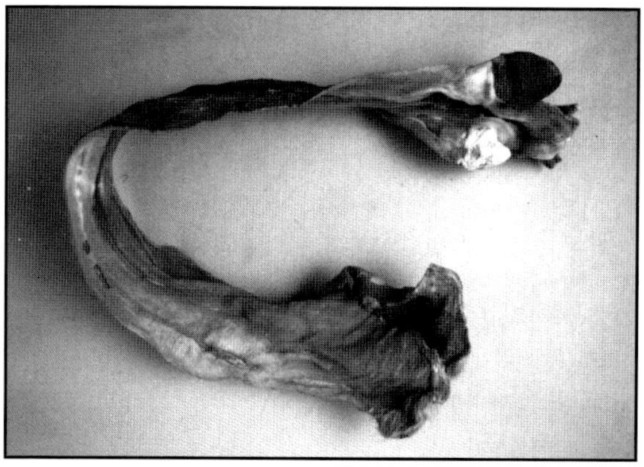

Deer
Fremont (AD 400–1300)?
Lent to MPC, 2000–2005
CARE 72

L: 37.8 cm
W: 6.5 cm

A single rawhide deer hock cut posteriorly with small patches of hair remaining and one dew claw intact.

Poor condition; intact and largely complete. One dew claw missing. Insect damage resulting in small lacunae. Dessicated; cockling. Fly spots. Stable.

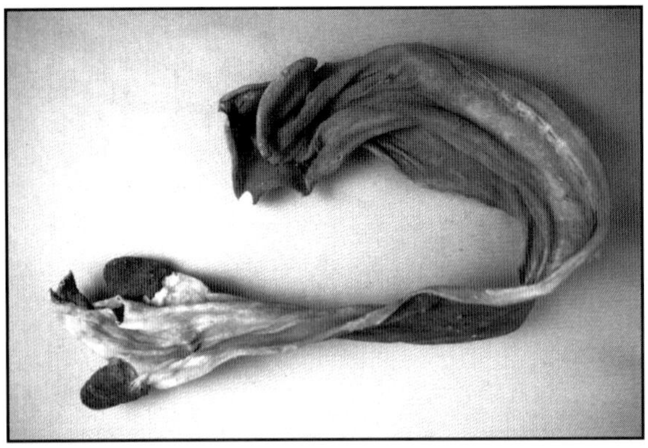

10 HOCK

Deer
Fremont (AD 400–1300)?
Lent to MPC, 2000–2005
CARE 74

L: 34.4 cm
W: 6.5 cm

A single rawhide deer hock cut posteriorly with small patches of hair remaining and dew claws intact.

Poor condition; intact and complete. Desiccated, cockling. Fly spots. Stable.

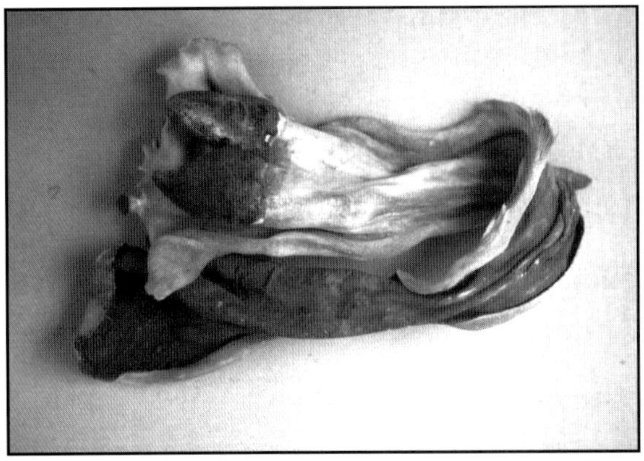

11 HOCK

Deer
Fremont (AD 400–1300)?
Lent to MPC, 2000–2005
CARE 73

L: 27.0 cm
W: 6.5 cm

A single rawhide deer hock cut anteriorly with small patches of hair remaining and dew claws intact.

Poor condition; intact and complete. Desiccated, cockling. Fly spots. Stable.

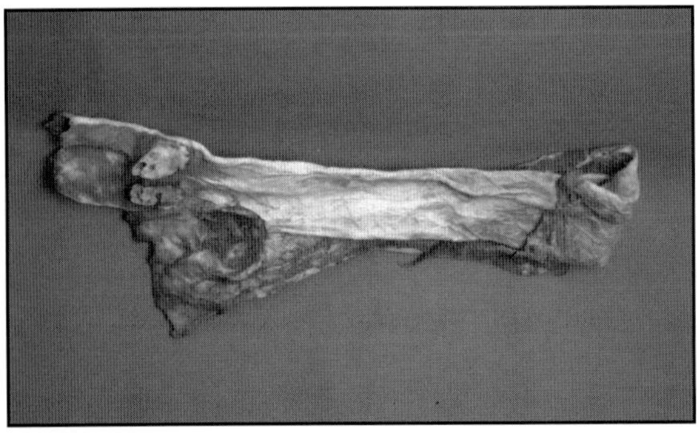

12 HOCKS

Deer or bighorn sheep
Fremont (AD 400–1300)?
CARE 75

L: 17.0 cm
W: 11.0 cm

Two tanned ungulate hocks cut anteriorly and sewn together at anterior ends to form one long piece in which dew claws are at opposite ends. S-spun, z-twisted sinew stitches. Ancient(?) crease near sewn area.

Poor condition; intact and complete. Dew claws largely deteriorated. Insect damage resulting in losses. Desiccated. Discoloration near sinew stitches. Fly spots. Stable.

13 FIBER BUNDLE

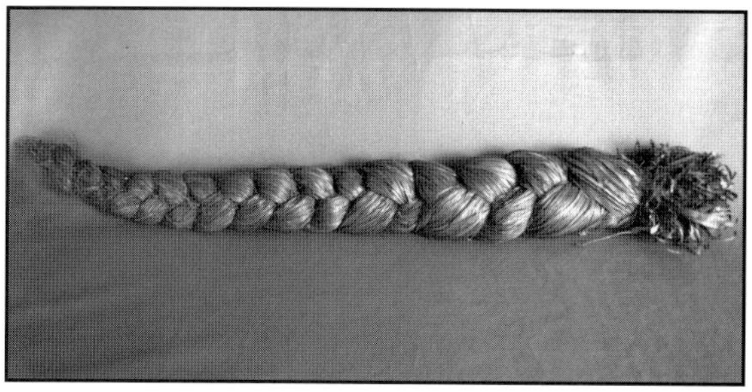

Dogbane
Agricultural Period
(Anasazi or Fremont, AD 1–1300)?
Lent to MPC, 2000–2005
CARE 209

L: 76.0 cm
W: 11.0 cm
D: 7.0 cm

Mass of dogbane bark strands groomed into an attenuated, three-strand braid terminating in a single overhand knot. Braid consists of several hundred strands of partially decorticated dogbane fiber, bound at the top with a piece of two-ply, z-spun, s-twisted dogbane cordage. The cordage is wrapped three times around the top of the hank and tied in a reef knot. One end of the cordage is knotted to prevent unraveling; the other is not tied and is unraveling.

Very good condition; intact and complete. Exfoliation and particulation. Numerous fly spots. Fragile but stable and still somewhat pliant.

14 FIBER BUNDLE

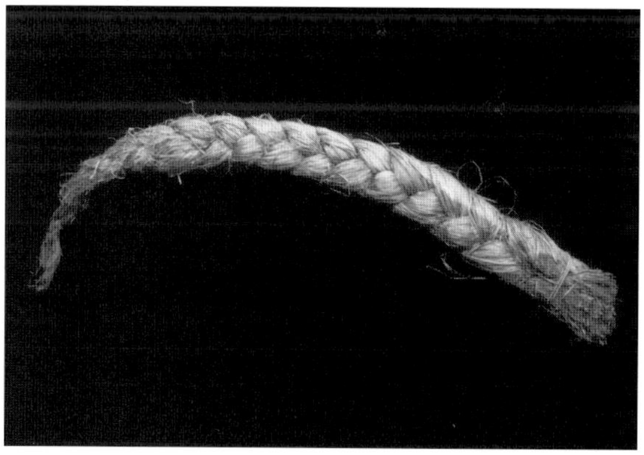

Dogbane
Agricultural Period
(Anasazi or Fremont, AD 1–1300)?
Lent to Capitol Reef National Park
(On display at Visitor Center)
CARE 196

L: 68.8 cm
W: 6.0 cm
D: 3.5 cm

Mass of light yellowish-tan dogbane bark strands groomed into a three-strand braid. Braid consists of several hundred strands of partially decorticated dogbane fiber secured at the larger end by two passes of a piece of z-spun, s-twisted dogbane cordage and a double overhand knot. Decortication may be incidental to removal from stalk and/or handling and passage of time. Overall cordage length ca. 43 cm. Smaller end is unsecured.

Very good; intact and complete. Fraying and particulation. One end of cordage is frayed and unraveling. Badly faded. Fly spots. Stable.

15 FIBER BUNDLE

Dogbane
Agricultural Period
(Anasazi or Fremont, AD 1–1300)?
Lent to MPC, 2000–2005
CARE 13

L: 47.5 cm
W: 11.0 cm
D: 5.0 cm

Elongated fiber bundle consisting of more than 100 strands; loosely s-twisted and tied with a single overhand knot. Longer end of the bundle is doubled back on itself and the end tucked into the knot. Overall strand length ca. 100 cm; maximum width of individual fibers is 0.5 cm.

Very good condition; intact and largely complete. Some particulation and exfoliation. Nominal embrittlement; some fiber ends have split. Fragile but stable.

16 FIBER BUNDLE

Dogbane
Agricultural Period
(Anasazi or Fremont, AD 1–1300)?
Lent to MPC, 2000–2005
CARE 132

L: 52.0 cm
W: 37.5 cm
D: 11.5 cm

Long roll of several hundred strands of partially decorticated dogbane fiber with a few traces of cortex remaining. Roll consists of two bundles, loosely s-spun and then z-twisted together. Bundle attenuates sharply at one end to ca. 0.5 cm in diameter. Fiber at this point is over-spun, resulting in fibers kinking and doubling back on themselves. This end terminates with the ends of the two bundles being tied in a single overhand knot.

Very good condition; intact and largely complete. Some particulation and exfoliation. Some embrittlement due to desiccation. Fragile but stable.

17 FIBER BUNDLE

Dogbane
Agricultural Period
(Anasazi or Fremont, AD 1–1300)?
Lent to MPC, 2000–2005
CARE 206

L: 18.6 cm
W: 5.2 cm
D: 4.2 cm

Tightly bound bundle of largely decorticated dogbane fiber. Several hundred strands, tightly s-spun. Bundle is then doubled back on itself, and longer end is wrapped in a tight spiral around the shorter end.

Very good condition; intact and complete. Particulation and some fraying. Fly spots on upper surface. Strong odor of fumigant. Stable.

18 FIBER BUNDLE

Yucca
Agricultural Period
(Anasazi or Fremont, AD 1–1300)?
Lent to MPC, 2000–2005
CARE 14

L: 82.0 cm
W: 13.0 cm
D: 8.8 cm

Large, loose bundle of thousands of strands of decorticated yucca fiber, loosely z-spun and tied in a single overhand knot. Shorter end is bent back under the bundle, and longer end is loosely z-spun into eleven separate strands.

Very good condition; intact and largely complete. Extensive exfoliation and some fraying. Strong odor of fumigant. Fly spots. Stable.

19 FIBER MASS

Grass
Agricultural Period
(Anasazi or Fremont, AD 1–1300)?
Lent to MPC, 2000–2005
CARE 1659

L: 25.0 cm
W: 18.5 cm
D: 3.5 cm

Compressed, flattened mass of grass fiber.

Very good condition; intact and complete. Some particulation. Brown discoloration of one corner. Scattered black particles. Desiccation and embrittlement. Fragile but stable.

CORDAGE AND ROPE

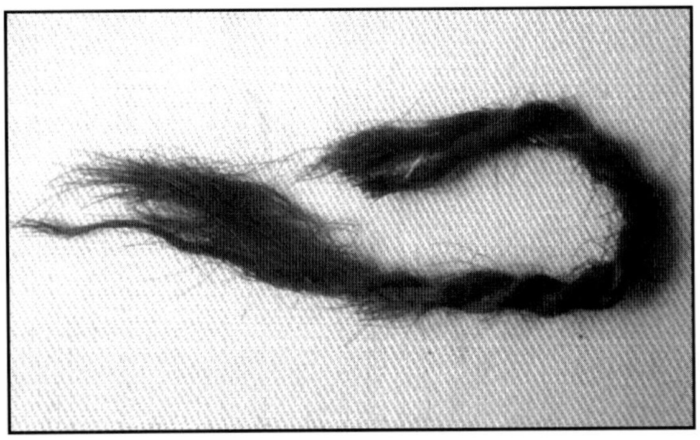

20 CORDAGE

Human hair
Late Prehistoric/Historic (ca. AD 1250–1900)?
Lent to MPC, 2000–2005
CARE 1661

L: 13.5 cm
W: 0.5 cm
D: 0.5 cm

Fragment of human hair cordage, z-spun and s-twisted. Dark brown, although original color may have been black.

Excellent condition; intact but fragmentary. Fragments of plant fiber (probably grass) caught in singles while being spun. Fragile but stable.

Comments:
This fragment of hair cordage matches that on a child's sandal (cat. no. 131), which exhibits an analogous length of hair cordage. It may be detached from this sandal or its possible mate (cat. no. 130), hence our dating of this hair specimen.

21 CORDAGE BUNDLE

Dogbane
Anasazi, Fremont, or Numic (ca. AD 1–1880)
Lent to MPC, 2000–2005
CARE 205

L: 216.0 cm
W: 7.0 cm
D: 4.8 cm

Cordage bundle consisting of 62 pieces of two-strand dogbane fiber cordage tied in a single overhand knot near center. Z-spun, s-twisted. Tips of some strands have been tied in a single overhand knot at the end to prevent unraveling. Thirteen strands have been tied together in an additional loose single overhand knot. Cordage diameter varies from 1.4–2.4 mm.

Excellent condition; intact and complete. Particulation, some ends unraveling. Stable.

22 ROPE

Dogbane
Agricultural Period
(Anasazi or Fremont, AD 1–1300)?
Lent to MPC, 2000–2005
CARE 208

Circum (circle): 66.0 cm
Diam (rope): 1.2 cm

Three pieces of cordage tied together to form a circle. Z-spun and s-twisted. Two pieces are joined with a double overhand knot. One join is made with a reef knot, while the other joining knot (closest to the double overhand knot) is of undetermined type. Section of rope between the double overhand knot and the undetermined knot consists of two finer z-spun singles that were s-twisted and then s-twisted again with a z-spun single approximately twice the diameter of the others. Rope ends at double overhand knot are cut close to the knot and not readily visible. Attenuated portions of three of the exposed rope ends have been z-spun and s-twisted, perhaps to reduce fraying. The fourth end shows no modification.

Good condition; intact and incomplete. Badly frayed, both at rope ends and all along length of strand. Minor particulation. Desiccation and embrittlement. Fragile but stable.

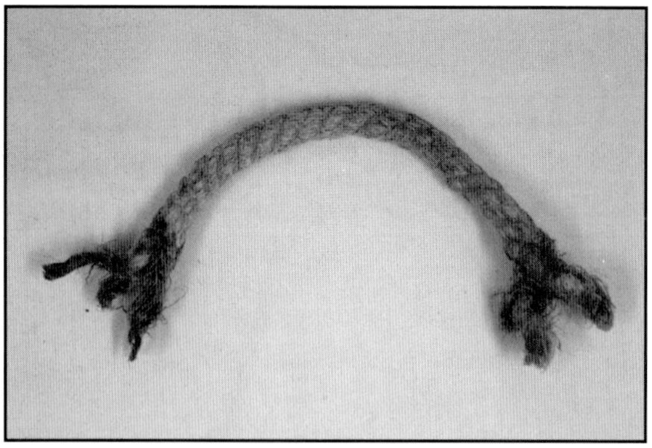

23 ROPE FRAGMENT

Yucca
Historic (AD 1750–1900) or earlier
Lent to MPC, 2000–2005
CARE 207

L: 33.7 cm
Diam: 1.6 cm

Small stretch of three-strand rope, z-spun and s-twisted. Both ends unraveling a length of about 5 cm. Rope is heavily abraded (use?).

Good condition; intact and incomplete. Particulation. Ends discolored to a dark brown. Red stain near midpoint, possibly from iron oxide. Strong odor of fumigant. Stable.

Comments:
This stretch of rope is almost identical in material and construction to the ensuing specimen (cat. no. 24) and was accessioned with it under the same number. The two may originally have been part of the same strand despite the fact that they are not physically connected.

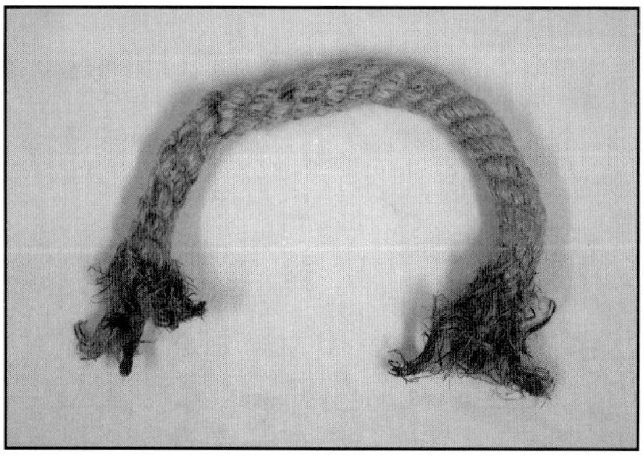

24 ROPE FRAGMENT

Yucca
Historic (AD 1750–1900) or earlier
Lent to MPC, 2000–2005
CARE 207

L: 31.6 cm
Diam: 1.6 cm

Stretch of three-strand rope, z-spun and s-twisted. Both ends unraveling for a length of about 5 cm. Heavily abraded (use?).

Good condition; intact and incomplete. One ply cut through 11.0 cm from the end. Small black discolored patch, possibly a mildew stain, 10.0 cm from end. Ends discolored to a dark brown. Particulation. Strong odor of fumigant. Stable.

Comments:
This rope fragment may originally have been part of the same strand as the preceding specimen (cat. no. 23).

25 CORDAGE AND MAKESHIFT "SPOOL"

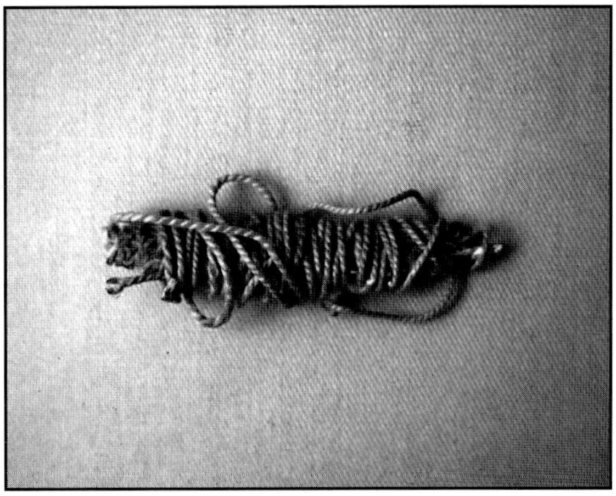

Basketry fragment wrapped in cordage
Willow and dogbane or milkweed, yucca
Fremont (AD 400–1300)?
Lent to MPC, 2000–2005
CARE 203

L: 5.2 cm
W: 6.8 cm
D: 0.8 cm

Two coils of a close-coiled, split-rod-and-bundle basketry fragment, wrapped with dogbane or milkweed fiber cordage. Basketry foundation rods and stitches are decorticated. Bundle appears to be yucca fiber. Basketry is worked right to left, stitches are split. Coil diameter 6.0 mm. Fragment is not from rim of basket. Cordage is z-spun, s-twisted and wrapped more than 30 times around the basketry fragment. Cordage is irregularly stained with red ochre, indicating that staining occurred prior to wrapping. One end of cordage is unknotted and raveling, opposite end is tied in two overlapping overhand knots.

Very good condition; intact and incomplete. Yellowish discoloration on sections of cordage. Polyester fiberfill caught in cordage and adhering to ends of basketry fragment; in addition, considerable dirt accretions on basketry fragment, but not on cordage, suggesting cordage was wrapped or re-wrapped around fragment in modern times. Fragile but stable.

Comments:
The basketry fragment may be identified as Fremont due to the construction technique, and it is possible the cordage is contemporary with the basket fragment. However, since modern cotton fibers adhere the entire length of the cordage, we cannot rule out the possibility that this is a pastiche, that is, conjoined artifacts disparate in origin and possibly even date.

FIBER AND BASKETRY CIRCLETS

26 BASKETRY CIRCLET (OLLA RING?)

Sagebrush
Agricultural Period
(Anasazi or Fremont, AD 1–1300)?
Lent to Capitol Reef National Park
(On display at Visitor Center)
CARE 243

Diam: 15.0 cm
Circum: 19.0 cm
D: 3.9 cm

Slightly D-shaped circlet, perhaps an olla ring, consisting of partially decorticated sagebrush fiber wrapped repeatedly around a core of an unknown nature, perhaps an olla ring.

Fair condition, intact and complete. Considerable particulation and exfoliation. Two small patches of mineral crystal formation on outer edge. Unstable.

27 BASKETRY CIRCLET

Willow
Anasazi, perhaps Pueblo III (AD 1100–1300)
Lent to MPC, 2000–2005
CARE 29

Diam: 22.2 cm
Width (wrapped rods): 3.4 cm

One intact basketry circlet and two fragmentary pieces. Intact circlet consists of partially decorticated twig bent into a rough circle. Twig makes two 360 degree passes before ends are joined, forming one crossover at the point of joining. Circle is then wrapped in a figure eight pattern around the two foundation rods with pieces of slender, undecorticated, flexible twig. Splices are bound under. Each of the two fragmentary pieces (9.5 cm and 11.0 cm long) consist of two curved twigs, wrapped with additional, smaller diameter twigs in a figure eight as above. Raw ends are broken, not cut. End of one foundation rod is bent at a 90 degree angle. Construction of these pieces appears to have been the same as the intact circlet noted above.

Very good condition; intact, one largely complete, two incomplete. Some delamination and loss of cortex. One weft twig on intact circlet is broken and prone to detachment. Some wefts loose and prone to displacement along frame. Some particulation. Embrittlement. Fragile but stable.

Comments:
A similar example was recovered from Antelope House, Canyon de Chelley, in northeastern Arizona, a site dated to the Pueblo III period, i.e., AD 1100–1300.[4]

COILED BASKETS

Close-coiled, single-, split-rod-and-bundle

See also Color Plate 18.

28 BASKETRY TRAY

Willow stitches and foundation, dogbane or milkweed bundle
Fremont (AD 400–1300)
Lent to MPC, 2000–2005
CARE 249

H: 5.9 cm
Diam: 48.0 cm

Large, decorated, close-coiled, single-, split-rod-and-bundle basketry tray. Foundation rods split, split side down. Rods and stitches both decorticated. Vertically arranged, noninterlocking stitches pierce bundle. Worked right to left. Coil diameter 7.8 mm. Stitches 2.1 mm wide. Four stitches and two rows per centimeter. One in 20 accidentally split stitches in 5 cm on working side; three in 10 in 5 cm on nonworking side. Stitch splices bound under and clipped. Decoration consists of four concentric black circles, each four rows wide, extending out from the center of the basket, on a reddish-purple background.[5]

Fair condition; intact and largely complete. Rim and center missing. Loss of stitch material, especially toward center. Insect gnawing. Particulation. Interior has large patches of dark purplish stain overlying all other accretions. Localized dark brown accretions near outer edge and ca. 7 cm from the center. Patch of powdery white accretions near outer edge. Mineral crystal encrustation. Two patches of whitish encrustation resembling bird guano. Fragment of cordage (z-spun, s-twisted) near outer edge. Reverse has extensive dirt accretions, patches of white mineral crystal formation, and extensive occurrence of small powdery white patches, especially between coils. Small oily black patch. Fragile, somewhat unstable.

29 BASKETRY TRAY

Willow stitches and foundation, dogbane or milkweed bundle
Fremont (AD 400–1300)
Lent to MPC, 2000–2005
CARE 218

H: 6.0 cm
Diam: 46.5 cm

See also Color Plate 18 and Figure 41.

Large, decorated, close-coiled, single-, split-rod-and-bundle basketry tray. Remaining decoration consists of a dark purple field with a black band 2.6 cm wide bisecting the basket and terminating two coils short of rim (see Figure 41). Black line connects at a 90 degree angle to another black line a single coil wide which follows the circumference of the rim in a clockwise direction, at least one-quarter of the way around the perimeter. The wide black radial line is interrupted 5.5 cm from the rim by a dark purple rectangle (9.5 x 5.5 mm) in the middle of the band. Although the radial band pattern is bilateral, the perimeter band is not.

Foundation rods are split, with the split side down. The rods and stitches are both decorticated. Worked right to left. Noninterlocking, vertically arranged stitches pierce bundle. Coil diameter 7.1 mm. Stitches 1.5 mm wide, no gap. 5.5 stitches and two rows per centimeter. No accidentally split stitches on the working side; six in 23 within 5 cm on the nonworking side. Stitch splices bound under. Self rim.

Fair condition; intact and largely complete. Loss of center and portions of rim. Large patches of stitch loss, especially toward the middle. Insect bore holes. Extensive stitch abrasion throughout. Particulation. Several dark brown, oily-looking stains on obverse side. Numerous fly spots throughout. Two thin strips of brown paper have been glued to the foundation rods near the middle on reverse. Various accretions. Fragile but stable.

See also Color Plate 18.

30 BASKETRY TRAY

Willow stitches and foundation, dogbane or milkweed bundle
Fremont (AD 400–1300)
Lent to MPC, 2000–2005
CARE 215

H: 6.0 cm
Diam: 50.8 cm

Large, close-coiled, single-, split-rod-and-bundle basketry tray. Foundation rods halved, split side down. Both foundation rods and stitches decorticated. Worked right to left. Noninterlocking, vertically arranged stitches pierce bundle. Coil diameter 8.3 mm. Stitch width 1.8 mm; five stitches and two rows per centimeter. No accidentally split stitches on working side; one in two within 5 cm on nonworking side. Stitch splices bound under and close clipped. Self rim and normal center. Two fragments of cordage (z-spun, s-twisted) pass between the coils of the basket and are visible as loops on the back side. One loop spans two coils, and the other spans three coils. The free ends of these loops are visible as ends on the interior, and one end is knotted. Extensive dark purple staining may be remnant of decoration.

Poor condition; intact and largely complete. Loss of both foundation rods and stitching in four areas, partial loss of rim and outer coils. Large patches of extensive stitch loss, especially near the outer edge and center. Occasional stitch loss throughout. Extensive insect gnawing. Evidence of massive past infestation. Extensive particulation. Large patches of accretion on interior. Fly specks. Mildew. Small patches of black accretions. Small patch of white paint from accession number near the center. Patches of glue-like accretions between some foundation rods and joining the broken ends of some rods. Glue has become brittle over time, and some joints have separated. Fly specks. Stable.

31 BASKETRY TRAY FRAGMENT

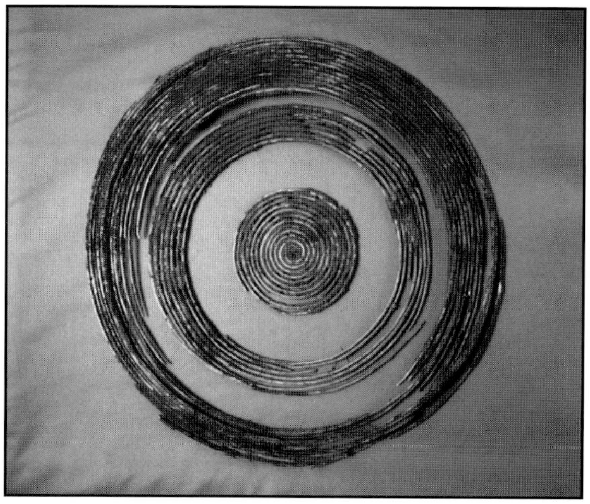

See also Color Plate 18.

Willow stitches and foundation, yucca bundle
Fremont (AD 400–1300)
Lent to MPC, 2000–2005
CARE 213

H: 1.0 cm
Diam: 42.5 cm

Fragmentary remains of a close-coiled, single-, split-rod-and-bundle basketry tray, surviving as three disarticulated sections. Foundation rods are split, split side down. Foundation rods and stitches are decorticated. Bundle is minimal. Coil diameter 6.8 to 5.1 mm. Two coils and five stitches per centimeter. Worked right to left. Noninterlocking, vertically aligned stitches, unsplit on working surface; ca. one in three accidentally split stitches within 5 cm on nonworking surface. Bundle is pierced by stitches. Stitches 1.4 mm wide. Splices bound under. Normal center. Traces of dark purple stains may be remnants of decoration.

Very poor condition; not intact; incomplete. Middle portion disarticulated from two outer rings. Sections of coils completely detached. Fragmentary. Extensive particulation. Coils separating, extensive loss of stitch material. Considerable insect gnawing of foundation rods and evidence of massive past infestation. Some foundation rods broken. Considerable abrasion throughout. Broken and loose stitches, prone to detachment. Desiccation and embrittlement. Strong odor. Mildew on obverse, heavy mineral crystal formation on underside. Middle ring virtually denuded of stitching. Nominal mineral crystal formation. Outer ring exhibits heavy dirt accretions over all. Obverse has various accretions and heavy localized mineral crystal formation. Mildew damage. Unstable.

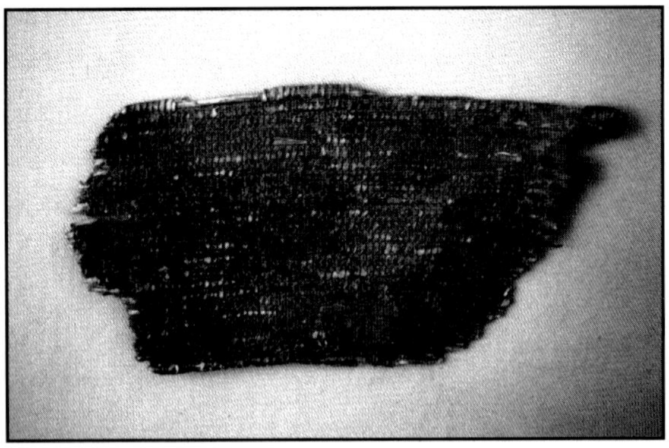

32 FRAGMENT OF BASKETRY TRAY

Willow stitches and foundation, yucca bundle
Fremont (AD 400–1300)
Lent to MPC, 2000–2005
CARE 64

L: 12.7 cm
W: 3.6 cm

Single-, split-rod-and-bundle, close-coiled basketry fragment. Noninterlocking, vertical stitches. Foundation rods split, flat side down. Coil diameter 5.0 mm. Four stitches and three rows per centimeter. Stitches 1.4 mm across. Worked right to left. No split stitches on working surface; one in 10 accidentally split stitches within 5 cm on nonworking surface. Stitch pierces coil. Ends of stitches bound under and close-clipped.

Good condition; intact and incomplete. Some stitches broken or missing, sheen from abrasion throughout. Warping of fragment. Stable.

33 FRAGMENT OF BASKET TRAY

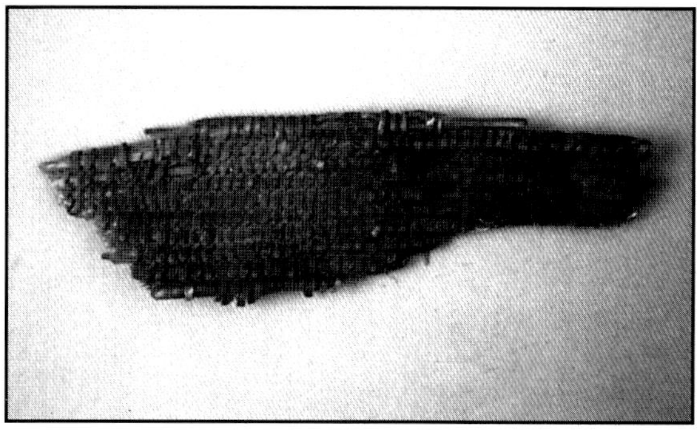

Willow stitches and foundation, yucca bundle
Fremont (AD 400–1300)
Lent to MPC, 2000–2005
CARE 64

L: 17.8 cm
W: 8.6 cm

Fragment of undecorated, close-coiled, single-, split-rod-and-bundle basket. Foundation rods split, split side down. Foundation rods and stitches decorticated. Noninterlocking, vertically arranged stitches pierce bundle. Yucca bundle only partially decorticated. Worked right to left. Coil diameter 5.1 mm. Stitch width 1.8 mm. Five stitches and three rows per centimeter. Stitch gap ca. 0.5 mm. Stitch splices bound under. One in 24 split stitches in 5 cm on working side; one in 12 within 5 cm on nonworking side.

Good condition; intact, but fragmentary. Some warping of fragment. Loss of stitches on top and bottom edges and along sides of fragment. Patchy loss of stitches on both obverse and reverse. Obverse has post-depositional polish on stitch surfaces. Large, shiny, brown accretion in upper right-hand corner of obverse side (may be pitch). Shiny accretion between coils in upper left-hand corner. On the reverse, there are various accretions in an area of heavy loss of stitching material. Stable.

34 BASE OF BASKETRY TRAY OR BOWL

Willow stitches and foundation, yucca bundle
Fremont (AD 400–1300)
Lent to MPC, 2000–2005
CARE 10

H: 2.9 cm
Diam: 15.8 cm

Small, undecorated, close-coiled, single-, split-rod-and-bundle basketry tray or bowl base. Foundation rods split, split side down. Both rods and stitches decorticated. Worked right to left. Noninterlocking, vertically arranged stitches pierce bundle. Coil diameter 5.3 mm. Stitch width 2.6 mm, 0.5 mm gap. Three stitches and two rows per centimeter. Two in 15 accidentally split stitches in 5 cm on working side; eight in 15 within 5 cm on nonworking side. Stitch splices concealed under bulging stitch. Normal center.

Very good condition; intact and partially complete. Loss of rim and portions of foundation rods and stitches of subsequent coils and upper edge. Loss of stitches on exterior due to abrasion, in some areas exposing extensive portions of foundation rods. Various accretions, especially powdery white. Stable.

35 BASKETRY BOWL

Willow stitches and foundation, yucca bundle
Fremont (AD 400–1300)
Lent to MPC, 2000–2005
CARE 219

H: 8.8 cm
Diam: 22.8 cm

Small, decorated, close-coiled, split-rod-and-bundle basketry bowl. Geometric decoration consists of stepped lines, radiating from the bottom of the bowl (Figure 42). Foundation rods split, split side down. Both rods and stitches decorticated. Worked right to left. Noninterlocking, vertically-arranged stitches pierce bundle. Coil diameter 5.5 mm. Stitch width 2 mm, no gap. Five stitches and 2.5 rows per cm. One in 25 accidentally split stitches on working side; four in 25 on nonworking side within 5 cm. Stitch splices bound under and close clipped. Normal center, self rim.

Excellent condition; intact and largely complete. Loss of portions of top two courses of coils. Small patch of stitch loss on interior near upper edge. Insect bore holes. Some localized abrasion and polish of stitches. Decoration faded. Various accretions, including powdery white and orange. Polish and dark discoloration of rim. Fly specks. Fragile but stable.

See also Color Plate 19 and Figure 42.

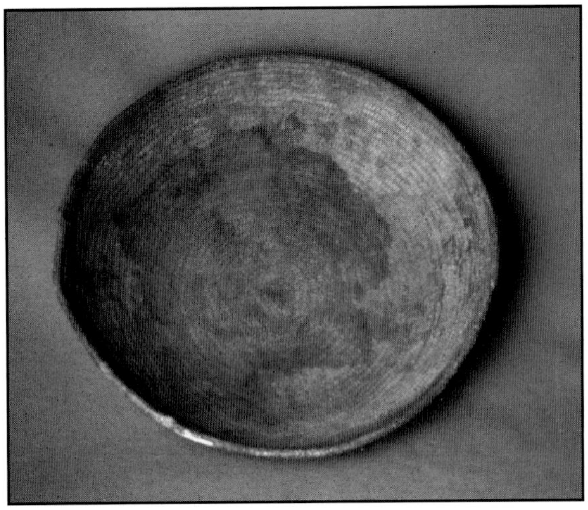

36 BASKETRY BOWL

Willow stitches and foundation, yucca bundle
Fremont (AD 400–1300)
Lent to MPC, 2000–2005
CARE 220

H: 7.4 cm
Diam: 25.0 cm

Undecorated, close-coiled, single-, split-rod-and-bundle, flat-bottomed, wide-mouthed bowl. Foundation rods split, split side down. Both rods and stitches decorticated. Worked right to left. Interlocking, vertically arranged stitches pierce bundle. Coil diameter 6.2 mm. Stitch width 1.2 mm, no gap. Five stitches and 2.5 rows per centimeter. One in five accidentally split stitches in 5 cm on working side; one in four within 5 cm on nonworking side. Stitch splices bound under. Normal center.

Very good condition; intact and largely complete. Rim missing, put uppermost row shows polishing, suggesting substantial handling or use after loss of rim. Two sections of stitch loss exposing foundation rods on interior and exterior. Multiple insect bore holes on exterior. Extensive particulation (dirt and some fiber particles). Interior has large brown stain encompassing bottom and part of walls. Various accretions, including powdery white and orange.

Exterior exhibits dark grayish-brown stain near upper edge, corresponding to a similar stain on the interior, and powdery white accretions. Stable.

37 FRAGMENT OF BASKETRY BOWL OR JAR

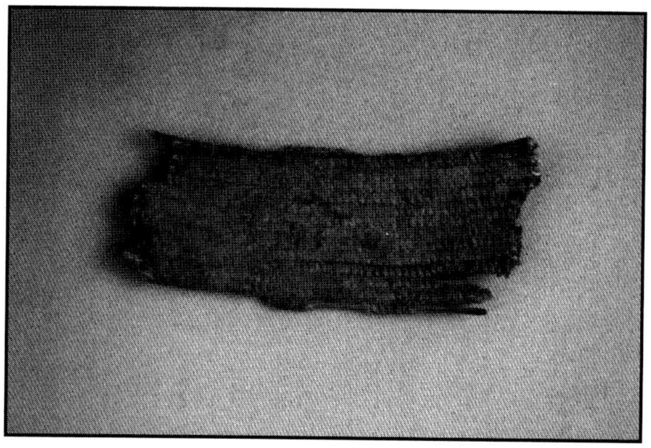

Materials unidentified
Fremont (AD 400–1300)
Lent to MPC, 2000–2005
CARE 64

L: 10.6 cm
W: 4.1 cm

Undecorated, single-, split-rod-and-bundle, close-coiled basketry fragment from the wall of an upright vessel (bowl or jar). Original diameter of basket ca. 25 cm. Foundation rods split, flat side up. Foundation rods and stitches decorticated. Noninterlocking, vertically arranged stitches pierce bundle. Worked left to right. Coil diameter 5.4 mm. Stitches 1.8 mm wide. 4.5 stitches and 3.5 rows per centimeter. Stitch gap 0.5 mm. Stitch splices bound under. One in 26 accidentally split stitches in 5 cm on working side, three in 26 within 5 cm on nonworking side.

Good condition; intact, but fragmentary. Stitches are missing entirely from a 5.2 cm long section of one foundation rod on exterior surface. Stitches missing along top and bottom edges and side of fragment. Exterior exhibits some polish (post-depositional). Occasional fly spots. Stable.

See also Color Plate 20.

38 BASKETRY JAR

Bulrush bundle, willow stitches, wood
Fremont (AD 400–1300)
Lent to MPC, 2000–2005
CARE 16

H: 35.0 cm
Diam (body): 36.0 cm
Diam (mouth): 9.5 cm

Large, spherical, close-coiled, single-, split-rod-and-bundle basketry jar with straight neck and restricted mouth. Foundation rods split, split side down. Foundation rods decorticated, stitches undecorticated. Bulrush bundle pierced by interlocking stitches. Coil diameter 1.3–2.0 cm, stitch width 3.7–4.7 mm. Stitch splices bound under, in some instances wrapped around other stitches and tucked under. Worked right to left. Normal center and self rim. Piece of two-ply z-spun s-twisted cordage has been employed in a crude attempt to secure areas of stitch loss near the orifice; whether or not this represents a prehistoric repair is uncertain.

Excellent condition; intact and largely complete. Some delamination and loss of cortex on stitches. Loss of stitches near neck. Particulation. Minor abrasions throughout, particularly on base. Exterior base has large patch of powdery white accretions. Fly spots throughout. Additional stabilization of exterior base has been achieved by the use of strips of heavy brown craft paper, which mimics the appearance and arrangement of the original stitches. Stable.

39 BASE OF BASKETRY TRAY OR VESSEL BASE

See also Color Plate 20.

Bulrush bundle, willow stitches, willow(?) rod
Fremont (AD 400–1300)
Lent to MPC, 2000–2005
CARE 246

H: 5.6 cm
Diam: 41.0 cm

Large, close-coiled, single-, split-rod-and-bundle basketry tray or basket base. Foundation rods split, flat side varies. Foundation rods decorticated, stitches undecorticated. Bulrush bundle pierced by interlocking stitches. Coil diameter 0.9 cm, stitch width 3.5–5.0 mm. Stitch splices bound under. Worked right to left. Normal center. Some accidentally split stitches.

Good condition; intact and incomplete. Extensive loss of rim or sides. Large area of loss near edge of base. Exfoliation. Some delamination and loss of cortex on stitches. Interior and exterior base exhibit abrasion. Several heavy dark brown accretions on interior. Extensive fly spots throughout. Exterior base exhibits profuse, widely scattered minute white specks. Area near loss has been stabilized by the use of strips of heavy brown craft paper, which mimics the appearance and arrangement of the original stitches. Stable.

Close-coiled, single-, split-rod, no bundle

40 BASKETRY TRAY

Willow
Fremont (AD 400–1300)
Lent to MPC, 2000–2005
CARE 221

H: 6.3 cm
Diam: 26.7 cm

Close-coiled, single-, split-rod, shallow undecorated basketry tray with self rim. Foundation and stitches both decorticated. Foundation rods split, flat side down. Coil diameter 6.4 mm, three stitches and five rows per centimeter. Worked right to left. Interlocking, vertically arranged stitches encircle foundation rod. No split stitches on working surface; one in 10 accidentally split stitches within 5 cm on non-work surface. Stitch width 3.0 mm, no gaps. Stitch splices are bound under and clipped off, both fag and moving ends. One moving end folded back and tucked under. Normal center. Small nub of fiber, possibly from a handle, near rim. Base exhibits high proportion of pierced coils. Exhibits a well camouflaged prehistoric mend 4.6 cm long, 4.5 cm from the rim, accomplished by addition of new stitches to existing foundation.

Very good condition; intact and largely complete. Loss of more than half the rim, in some areas loss of up to six additional rows. Various scuffs and abrasions, some polish, especially on the bottom exterior. Some missing stitches. Interior has one large area and three smaller areas where stitches have abraded away. Exterior has a large patch adjacent to the rim where stitches and a portion of the foundation rods have abraded away. Broken stitches in this area prone to detachment. Center has been damaged, possibly by passage of a large screw (stitches and foundation rod are worn). One blackened area, possibly localized charring, on interior. Insect bore-hole near charring. Large amorphous brown stains on interior. Small, powdery white accretions near heavily abraded portion of rim, and one near the center. Exterior has one large dark brown oily stain. Heavy coating of red ochre over ca. one-quarter of the exterior surface. Stable.

41 FRAGMENT OF BASKETRY TRAY OR BOWL

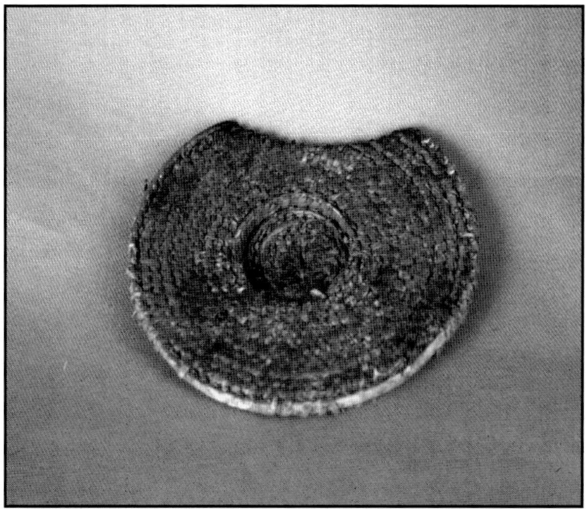

Materials unidentified
Fremont (AD 400–1300)
Lent to MPC, 2000–2005
CARE 212

D: 4.0 mm
Diam: 10.6 cm

Small, undecorated, close-coiled, single-, split-rod circular fragment (center) of basketry tray or bowl. Foundation rods and stitches both decorticated. Interlocking, vertically arranged stitches encircle foundation rod. Foundation rods halved, flat side down. Coil diameter 4.0 mm. Stitch width 1.6 mm. Three stitches and 2.5 rows per centimeter. Stitch gap 1.8 mm. Worked right to left. One in 15 accidentally split stitches in 5 cm on working side (reverse); one in five within 5 cm on nonworking side (obverse). Stitch splices bound under. Reinforced normal center.

Good condition; intact and incomplete. Outer portion of basket (rim and/or sides) missing. Large crescent-shaped area of loss bordered by charring. Stitches in middle have been lost, causing central coils to come loose, connected to rest of fragment only by foundation rod. This central portion protrudes above the rest of the fragment. Extensive abrasion and loss of stitches, especially on reverse. Outer edge largely denuded of stitching. Reverse has several lightly charred areas. Stable.

Close-coiled, single-rod, no bundle

42 BASKETRY BOWL

Willow and rabbitbrush
Fremont (AD 400–1300)
Lent to Capitol Reef National Park
(On display at Visitor Center)
CARE 224

H: 8.3 cm
Diam: 24.3 cm

Medium-sized, undecorated, close-coiled, single-rod basketry bowl. Interlocking stitches encircle foundation rod. Foundation rods and stitches both decorticated. 4.5 rows and 3.5 stitches per centimeter. Coil diameter 4.8 mm. Worked right to left. One accidentally split stitch per 5 centimeters, both interior and exterior. Normal center, rim in stitch and wrap technique. Stitch splices bound under. Prehistoric repair 8.4 cm long accomplished with willow in the bottom of the basket.

Basket is pierced 6.4 mm below the rim for passage of s-spun z-twisted sinew cordage ca. 16 cm long. Cordage is looped through the basket and tied in a double overhand knot, followed by a space of 1.0 cm and a reef knot. Ends of cordage are each tied in a single overhand knot. Rim opposite is pierced 6.9 cm below the rim for the passage of a small piece of vegetal cordage, visible only as a nub on the inner and outer surfaces.

Very good condition; intact and complete. Loss of section of stitches along rim. Occasional stitch loss and patches of extensive stitch loss and abrasion of exposed foundation rods throughout. Extensive stitch abrasion throughout, especially on interior bottom, perhaps representing use wear. Insect bore holes throughout.

43 BASKETRY BOWL

See also Color Plate 19.

Willow stitches, rabbitbrush foundation
Fremont (AD 400–1300)?
Lent to MPC, 2000–2005
CARE 222

H: 6.7 cm
Diam: 14.6 cm

Small, decorated, close-coiled, single-rod basketry bowl. Foundation rods and stitches both decorticated. Noninterlocking, vertically arranged stitches encircle foundation rods. Coil diameter 4.6 mm. Worked left to right. Stitch width 1.4 mm. Four stitches and four rows per centimeter. Stitch gap 1.3 mm. One in six accidentally split stitches in 5 cm on working side (exterior); none on interior. Stitch splices bound under and clipped close. Normal center. Rim in stitch and wrap technique. Decoration is structural, consisting of a dark circle encompassing the bottom of the basket, with four evenly-spaced zigzag elements stepping upwards clockwise towards the rim. Zigzag elements terminate in a dark band 6.2 mm wide 6.0 mm from the rim. In some sections, the appearance of a multiple-rod foundation is created by the addition of new foundation rods along side exhausted ones. Larger, irregularly arranged stitches made with original stitch material are indicative of a prehistoric attempt to repair break in rim.

Very good condition; intact and largely complete. Basket shape is distorted and warped, as a result of manufacture. A break extends downward 13.1 mm from the rim. One large insect bore hole 2.5 mm wide, 8.5 mm from the rim. Extensive patches of stitch abrasion and loss exposing foundation rods, especially on exterior. Particulation (largely dirt). White accretions in space created by break in rim (may be glue). Interior bottom exhibits several small shiny patches, either sheen from abrasion or transparent accretions. Stable.

See also Color Plate 19.

44 BASKETRY BOWL

Willow stitches, rabbitbrush foundation
Fremont (AD 400-1300)?
Lent to MPC, 2000-2005
CARE 245

H: 8.3 cm
Diam: 17.7 cm

Small, decorated, close-coiled, single-rod basketry bowl with slightly constricted orifice. Foundation rods and stitches both decorticated. Noninterlocking, vertically arranged stitches encircle foundation rods. Coil diameter 4.7 mm. Stitch width 1.5-1.8 mm. Three stitches per centimeter, stitch gap 1.5 mm. Worked right to left. No accidentally split stitches on work surface (exterior); none on non-work surface. Stitch splices bound under and close clipped. Unreinforced, slightly oval center. Rim in stitch and wrap technique. Structural decoration consists of a single dark band of stitches 19.5 mm below the rim, which completely encircles the basket. On one side, a piece of s-spun, z-twisted dogbane or milkweed cordage pierces the basket 7.4 mm from the rim, with a single overhand knot tied on the interior, the exterior portion surviving only as a nub. On the opposite side, a piece of s-spun, z-twisted sinew cordage pierces the basket 8.1 mm below the rim, and is tied in a reef knot on the exterior, with one end of the cordage extending 13.2 mm beyond the knot.

Very good condition; intact and largely complete. Patches of stitch loss exposing individual foundation rods, especially on the interior. Extensive insect bore holes in stitches, foundation rods largely unaffected. Patches of abrasion of stitches, especially on exterior bottom. Interior bottom has small spots of shiny transparent accretions, particularly in one localized section, and primarily between stitches. Large amorphous powdery white patch on exterior bottom. Exterior has darkened in coloration, largely obscuring decorative line. Numerous fly spots throughout. Stable.

45 BASKETRY TRAY

Willow
Fremont (AD 400-1300)
Lent to MPC, 2000-2005
CARE 244

H: 2.8 cm
Diam: 30.8 cm
Diam (hole): 9.9 cm

Close-coiled, undecorated, single-rod basketry bowl, center and rim missing. Rods and stitches both decorticated. Interlocking stitches encircle foundation rod; 3.5 stitches per centimeter, worked right to left. No accidentally split stitches per 5 cm. Stitch slices bound under. Coil diameter 5.8-6.8 mm.

Good condition; largely intact and incomplete. Center missing. Irregular break running from outer edge and extending 8.2 cm toward center. Some areas of loss within this break. Basket slightly warped at the base of this break. Opposite the larger crack another crack extends 3.2 cm from the outer edge. Where this crack terminates the coils are separated for 9.8 cm. Another crack extends 2.4 cm from the outer edge. Portions of stitches abraded away, some particulation. Large brown stain extending from center to outer edge. Various other accretions. Fragile but stable.

Close-coiled, single-, split-rod, no bundle, intricate stitch

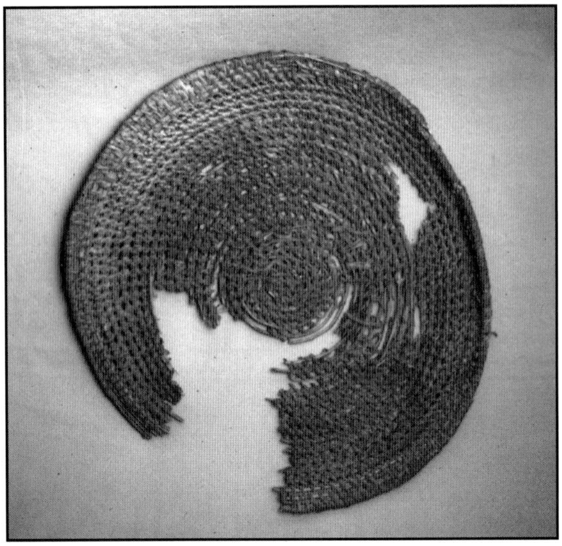

46 BASKETRY TRAY

Willow
Agricultural Period
(Anasazi or Fremont, AD 1–1300)
Lent to MPC, 2000–2005
CARE 30

H: 3.5 cm
Diam: 38.0 cm

Large, undecorated, single-, split-rod, intricate-stitch, shallow basketry tray with close-coiled rim. Foundation rods and stitches both decorticated. Foundation rods halved, split side down. Coil diameter 7.7 mm. 1.25 stitches and 1.5 rows per centimeter. Worked left to right. Intricate stitch encircles foundation rod.[6] Rim consists of three rows worked in close-coiled stitch-and-wrap technique to reinforce it. Stitch width 3.2 mm. Normal center. Ancient repair: the area of most extensive stitch loss was partially stabilized by wrapping with a single strand of sagebrush bark and tying it in a single half hitch. A small bundle of sagebrush fiber was tied to this area on the reverse with a piece of z-spun, s-twisted vegetal cordage with a double overhand knot on exterior.

Good condition; intact and partially complete. Large section of side missing, with another area of loss opposite. One large patch and several smaller areas of stitch loss. Light abrasion of stitches on reverse. Particulation. Cordage is heavily abraded and frayed. Reverse exhibits large, dark brown stain near the largest loss. Small powdery white accretion also near this loss. Six pieces of light-weight paper, ca. 4–6 cm long and 3.5 mm wide adhere (apparently glued) to basket in areas of greatest stitch loss (likely a modern attempt at stabilization). Stable.

47 BASKETRY TRAY

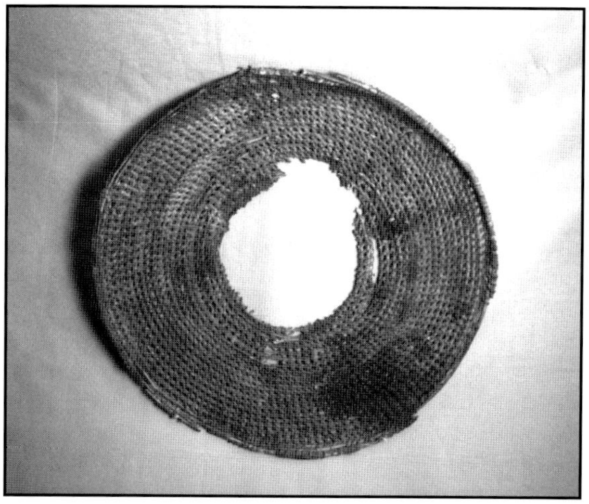

Willow
Agricultural Period
(Anasazi or Fremont, AD 1–1300)
Lent to MPC, 2000–2005
CARE 217

H: 4.5 cm
Diam: 40.5 cm

Large, undecorated, split-rod, intricate-stitch, shallow basketry tray with close-coiled rim. Foundation rods and stitches both decorticated. Foundation rods halved, split side down. Coil diameter 8.5 mm. 1.25 stitches and 1.5 rows per centimeter. Worked right to left. Intricate stitch encircles foundation rod. Rim consists of three rows worked in close-coiled stitch and wrap technique. Stitch width 3.0 mm. Stitch splices concealed under bulging stitch and close clipped on reverse. Ancient repairs: large patch of shiny dark brown accretion (pitch) near outer edge, which may conceal some charring; additional, large, shiny reddish accretion at the outer edge (also pitch), which has fragments of conifer needles, rocks, and detritus embedded in it.

Good condition; intact and partially complete. Center and portion of rim are missing. Intermittent patches of stitch loss, especially toward the middle. Some stitch abrasion on underside. Particulation. One small char mark 3.3 cm from the rim, with resulting partial loss of stitches. Several other small black patches may represent charring. Dark area near middle represents partial penetration of pitch from exterior. Encrustations of pitch on interior on exterior with dirt, vegetable matter, and detritus adhering. Large, shiny, dark stain extending from middle almost to the rim (may be pitch residue), likewise a similar smaller stain opposite, near rim. Stable.

PLAITED

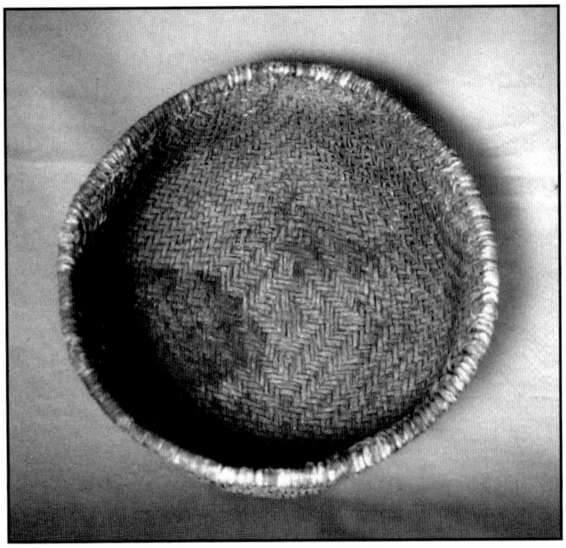

48 BASKETRY BOWL

Yucca and wood
Anasazi, Basketmaker III–Pueblo II (AD 400–1100)
Lent to MPC, 2000–2005
CARE 225

H: 9.3 cm
Diam: 28.8 cm

Flat-bottomed, straight-sided, semi-flexible, plaited basketry bowl in 2/2 twill pattern. Complex shifts in bottom of basket, resulting in a single large diamond pattern 15 x 17 cm. Elements cross at a 90 degree angle. New elements laid in. Element width 4.2 cm. Rigid rim consisting of a single 180 degree self-selvage over an undecorticated twig 7.4 mm in diameter. Folded elements are individually secured in place over the rim by a single row of s-twined yucca cordage, with two elements acting as a unit.

Very good condition; intact and complete. Abrasion of wefts along rim, resulting in total loss of portions of three elements. Loss of cortex on several elements near center of interior. Abrasion and delamination of elements on bottom, resulting in the complete loss of portions of some elements. Desiccation and embrittlement. Large amorphous brown stain on interior bottom is less noticeable on exterior. Small black char marks also within this stain, resulting in delamination and partial loss of cortex on some elements. Powdery white accretions inside and out. Stable.

Comments:
An Anasazi twill plaited ring basket from Cottonwood Wash, Utah, now in the Utah Museum of Natural History, is smaller but provides a close parallel to this example in technique, shape, and state of preservation.[7] It has been dated to Basketmaker III–Pueblo II (AD 400–1100).

49 PLAITED MAT

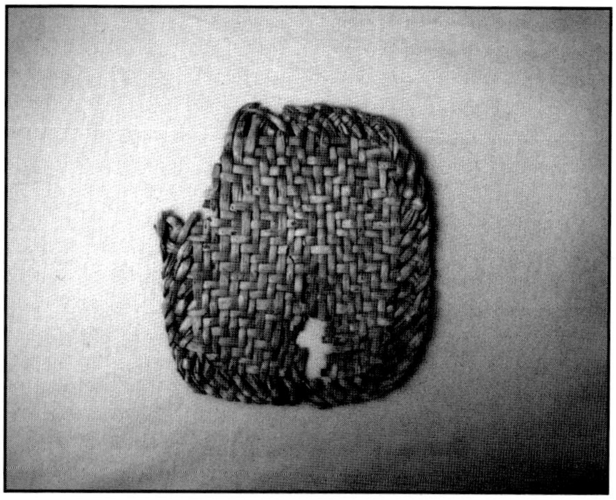

Tule
Anasazi (Basketmaker II–III, AD 1–700)
Lent to MPC, 2000–2005
CARE 211

L: 16.5 cm
W: 15.3 cm
D: 0.7 cm

Small, undecorated 2/2 twill plaited mat with selvage. One accidental shift 2/3/2 with the adjacent element shifting 2/1/2. Elements consist of a single flattened strip ca. 5 mm wide, crossing at a 90 degree angle. Small size of artifact obviates the need for splices. Ninety degree self-selvage with shifts encompasses all four sides, in a pattern of 2/1/1/1 apex fold 1/1/1 clipped. Ends are clipped at a 45 degree angle.

Very good condition; intact and largely complete. Loss of one corner and additional small patch of loss near selvage. Fly spots throughout. Stable.

TWINING

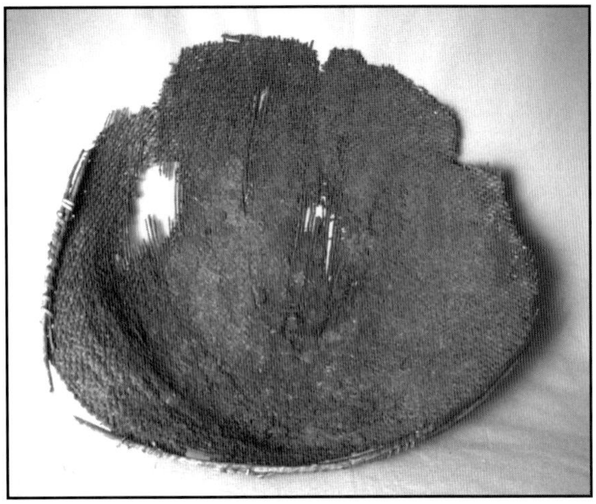

50 WINNOWING TRAY

Willow and unidentified Rosaceae twigs
Numic, AD 1640–1810
Lent to MPC, 2000–2005
CARE 216

H: 10.5 cm
L: 59.0 cm
W: 53.0 cm

Large, close-, diagonally twined, clam-shaped winnowing tray. Willow or Roseaceae warps are undecorticated, 2.0–3.5 mm in diameter, two warp elements worked as a unit. Wefts are split willow, decorticated, 3.0–4.0 mm across with the split side down. S-twined, two weft rows per centimeter. New warps inserted into pre-existing weft crossings. Weft splices laid in under exhausted weft.

Construction was initiated by securing eight long willow warps together in the middle with four rows of twining. These warps were then curved to form an arc, and four additional warps were abutted perpendicular to the already established twined section and twined into place. Work then proceeded in an arc pattern, through the eight original warps on one side, across the four additional warps, and through the eight original warps on the other side, before doubling back and repeating the pattern. New warps were inserted into the existing weft crossings as necessary to expand the basket outward. Work proceeded in this manner for an additional 16.0 cm, where one decorative row of diagonal twining worked across four warps (rather than two) was inserted. Twining over two warps continued for another 13.0 cm, where a second similar decorative row was added. A third such row was added another 13.0 cm beyond the second. The final termination of this work cannot be determined, as that portion of the edge is missing.

The rim consists of decorticated double willow rods ca. 8 mm in diameter which have been added to the outermost course of warps with willow stitches, in order to provide some additional rigidity to the structure. Large crude prehistoric repair at bottom edge, and two more in the middle of the basket. Thick residue lines most of interior.

Fair condition; intact and largely complete. Loss of sections of rim, two other large and two small areas of loss. Rim broken in two places, loss of one course of double rim for a large section. Abrasion and loss of stitches throughout. Desiccation, embrittlement and cracking of warps, splitting of wefts throughout. Loss of warp cortex. Particulation and exfoliation. Reverse has large, amorphous, oily-looking black stain near one edge and other accretions. Fly spots throughout. Modern stabilization attempted by gluing four pieces of tissue-thin paper to basket near loss on viewer's right, three more near edge on viewer's left. Structurally weak.

Comments:
This basket is entirely typical of Numic winnowing trays and radiocarbon dated AD 1640–1810.[8] Analysis of basketry elements indicate the materials used to construct the basket were willow (*Salix*) and perhaps an undetermined member of the Roseceae family.

The surface residue on the interior of the tray—one sample from the interstitial areas between the basketry elements and one from the deepest part of the center—were examined macroscopically (70x) and proved to be uncharred Chenopodium (goosefoot) seeds, suggesting the basket was used to parch goosefoot seeds. The purpose of parching would have been to dry the seeds to make them easier to grind.[9] Parched seeds could be ground into meal for cakes or mush. Chenopodium leaves are rich in vitamin C and have medicinal qualities. No pollen or starches were identified in the specimens. Two phytoliths were identified but noted as possibly a rogue occurrence.

51 CENTER OF UNFINISHED BASKET

Unidentified wood
Prehistoric, as early as ca. 3000–2000 BC
Lent to MPC, 2000–2005
CARE 210

H: 2.7 cm
Diam: 31.5 cm

Twelve-spoke, close-twined basket center of woody plant material. Both warps and wefts rigid and decorticated. Z-twined wefts, weft width unequal, 3.0–6.8 mm. Two warp elements operate as a unit. New wefts are abutted to exhausted ones. Center is formed of two single pieces of wood laid perpendicular to one another and bound with a split piece of weft. Each end of the perpendicular units was then split into three weft spokes. Warp ends are cut, not broken. Construction is rough, suggesting an expedient function. Wefts are occasionally left untwined between warps, and several wefts have split at apex of path over warp, while material was still green

Very good condition; intact and incomplete. Extensive splitting of both warps and wefts, probably during manufacture. Some abrasion of wefts on obverse. One spoke is loose and prone to detachment. Fly spots throughout. Mineral encrustation on obverse and underside. Small patch of encrustation resembling guano on underside. Stable.

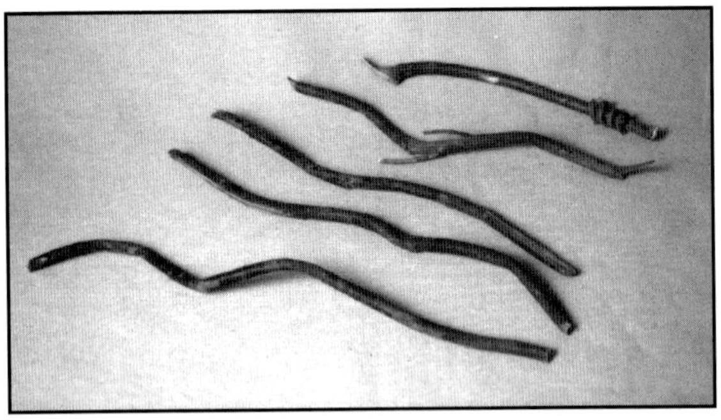

52 BASKETRY WEFT FRAGMENTS

Willow?
Agricultural Period
Anasazi or Fremont (AD 1–1300)?
Lent to MPC, 2000–2005
CARE 20

L (average): ca. 20 cm

Five undecorticated sticks purposefully bent while green. One has a willow(?) twig wrapped around one end four times.

Fair condition; intact but embrittled. Crackling of bark with associated exfoliation. Stable.

Comments:
These weft fragments were given the same accession number as a group of composite arrow shafts (cat. no. 90) that also included rods of analogous size probably destined to be made into arrow shafts (cat. no. 3) and numerous thinner rods probably being prepared as net or snare elements (cat. no. 4). All the sticks may have comprised a single materials store despite the different purposes for which they were intended.

Twined Bags and Mats

53 TWINED BAG

Sagebrush
Prehistoric, as early as 8500 BC,
but likely more recent
Lent to MPC, 2000–2005
CARE 15

L: 69.0 cm
W: 57.5 cm

Large, flexible, roughly conical open simple-twined sagebrush bag. Bundles of partially decorticated sagebrush bark 0.8–1.0 cm in diameter form the warp. Z-spun sagebrush singles 0.4–0.6 cm in diameter are z-twined around the warps. Gap between weft rows 2.3–2.8 cm. Numerous missed warp elements, two elements twined together, etc.

Good condition; intact and partially complete. Loss of top, bottom, and most of one side of bag. Desiccation and embrittlement. Particulation and exfoliation. Abrasion and polish of some stitches, particularly on the reverse. Fly spots throughout. Fragile but stable.

<u>Comments</u>:
In the Southwest the technique of twining goes back centuries, at least as early as 8500 BC and some would say 9000 BC.[10] The state of preservation in all the twined mat fragments in this collection, however, is far too good for such an early dating, nor have any examples from such an early period been recovered from this region. A much more recent date seems more reasonable. Clothing of twined sagebrush bark was still being made by the Northern Ute in the late nineteenth century, as we know from some examples in the Museum's own Dillman collection, as well as among the Western Shoshone in the early twentieth century.[11] In the absence of radiocarbon dating or any firmly dated comparanda, the date of these bags and mats will remain in question.

54 TWINED BAG FRAGMENT

Sagebrush
Prehistoric, as early as 8500 BC
Lent to Capitol Reef National Park
(On display at Visitor Center)
CARE 248

L: 27.0 cm
W: 16.5 cm
D: 0.4 cm

Flexible, tubular, open, simple-twined bag fragment. Bundles of partially decorticated sagebrush bark ca. 1.5 cm in diameter form the warp. Z-spun, s-twisted, partially decorticated sagebrush bark form the s-twined weft. Weft diameter 4.4–6.2 mm. Continuous weft.

Very good condition; intact and incomplete. Desiccation and embrittlement, some exfoliation and particulation. Some fraying, particularly of warp elements. Fragile but stable.

55 MAT FRAGMENT

Tule and milkweed or dogbane, yucca
Prehistoric, as early as 8500 BC
Lent to MPC, 2000–2005
CARE 194; also numbered 247

L: 22.6 cm
W: 21.8 cm
D: 1.4 cm

Large fragment of open, simple-twined tule mat. Two warp elements act as a unit. Warp elements 4.0–5.0 mm across. Z-twined with z-spun s-twisted dogbane or milkweed cordage, twining rows 1.2–2.0 cm apart. Cordage diameter ca. 1–2 mm. Two weft elements act as a unit. Upper selvage is created by folding warp units 180 degrees around a piece of z-spun, s-twisted yucca cordage ca. 3–4 mm in diameter. (These single pieces of tule, doubled back on themselves, form the double warp.) First row of twining is directly below this header cord. Side selvages (both are present) are continuous weft, simple-twined selvages, with wefts being twined around each other four or five times before beginning of subsequent weft row. Last warp pair at each selvage edge is z-spun around itself to provide stability. No warp splices are evident. Weft splices are accomplished by tying a knot and clipping it close.

Good condition; intact and largely complete. Extensive loss of warp, especially in two large patches near selvages. Extensive abrasion of warp throughout. Some abrasion and fraying of weft. Weft is unraveling in sections. Particulation and exfoliation throughout. Fly spots throughout. Staining and discoloration of warp in patches on obverse. Rodent feces adhering. Stable.

Comments:
Twining was the earliest basketry technique represented at Danger Cave, and Jesse D. Jennings pictured an example, very close to this one, recovered from level D III (7800 BC).[12]

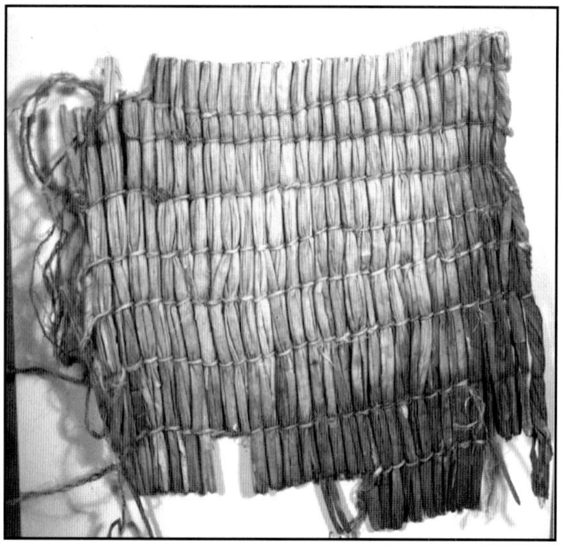

56 FRAGMENT OF MATTING

Tule warp and yucca weft
Prehistoric, as early as 8500 BC
Lent to Capitol Reef National Park
(On display at Visitor Center)
CARE 247

L: 28.5 cm
W: 28.3 cm
D: 0.6 cm

Fragment of open, simple-twined tule matting. Four warp elements act as a unit, two weft elements as a unit. Warp elements 11.2–11.9 mm across, weft rows 1.7–2.4 mm in diameter, 2.6–4.4 cm apart. Weft of z-spun yucca singles. Continuous weft, simple twined selvage. Selvage warp is the same as the others, but is s-twisted to provide stability. One warp strand from adjacent warp is twisted into the selvage at one point. Weft splices tied to exhausted weft.

Very good condition; intact and incomplete. Loss of cortex on sections of warps due to abrasion. Fraying and unraveling of wefts on side opposite selvage, sporadic fraying of wefts elsewhere. Staining and discoloration near selvage on obverse side. Desiccation and embrittlement. Fly spots. Fragile but stable.

Comments:
This technique of doubling the warp over a piece of cordage to form an upper selvage was commonly used in matting (cf. also next three catalogue entries).[13] Jennings pictured a similarly selvaged mat fragment recovered from level V of Danger Cave (4000 BC–AD 20).[14]

57 FRAGMENT OF MATTING

Tule and milkweed or dogbane, yucca
Prehistoric, as early as 8500 BC
Lent to MPC, 2000–2005
CARE 194

L: 12.8 cm
W: 12.2 cm
D: 0.8 cm

Selvage fragment from open, simple-twined mat. Mat had a two-ply warp. Two warp elements act as a unit. Warp elements 5.0–8.0 mm across. Z-twined with s-spun yucca and dogbane blend singles. Weft rows 3.8–4.2 cm apart. Variation on a simple-twined selvage formed by separating the two layers of weft elements, folding them inward at a 90 degree angle, and securing them with the next twining stitch but skipping one, resulting in a selvage that resembles a three-strand braid when viewed edge-on. In other words, the two units of warp element 1 are folded outward around the elements of warp unit 2, then inward and down between the elements of warp unit 3, and bound in place between them with the weft stitch for that unit. The two elements of warp unit 2 are then folded outward to pass around the elements of warp unit 3, and then curved inward and down to be secured between the elements of warp unit 4 with the weft stitch for that unit, and so on.

Good condition; intact and incomplete. Abrasion and loss of cortex on warps throughout. Abrasion, fraying and raveling of wefts throughout. Particulation. Oily-looking black accretions on obverse. Discoloration of one warp element near selvage may be due to charring. Fly spots throughout. Fragile but stable.

Comments:
This mat fragment, along with two others (cat. nos. 58–59), may all derive from the same artifact.

58 MAT FRAGMENT

Tule and milkweed or dogbane, yucca
Prehistoric, as early as 8500 BC
Lent to MPC, 2000–2005
CARE 194

L: 8.9 cm
W: 5.0 cm
D: 0.8 cm

Selvage fragment from open, simple-twined mat. Mat had a two-ply warp. Two warp elements act as a unit. Warp elements 5.0–8.0 mm across. Z-twined with s-spun yucca and dogbane blend singles. Variation on a simple-twined selvage formed by separating the two layers of weft elements and folding them inward at a 90 degree angle, and securing them with the next twining stitch skipping one, resulting in a selvage that resembles a three-strand braid when viewed edge-on (cf. preceding entry).

Very good condition; intact and incomplete. Abrasion, polish, and loss of cortex on warps throughout, especially on the reverse. Abrasion and fraying of stitches, cordage ends unraveling. Fragile but stable.

59 MAT FRAGMENT

Tule and milkweed or dogbane, yucca
Prehistoric, as early as 8500 BC
Lent to MPC, 2000–2005
CARE 194

L: 8.6 cm
W: 5.7 cm
D: 0.8 cm

Selvage fragment from open, simple-twined mat. Mat had a two-ply warp. Two warp elements act as a unit. Warp elements 5.0–8.0 mm across. Z-twined with s-spun yucca and dogbane blend singles. Variation on a simple-twined selvage formed by separating the two layers of weft elements, folding them inward at a 90 degree angle, and securing them with the next twining stitch skipping one, resulting in a selvage that resembles a three-strand braid when viewed edge-on (cf. cat. no. 57).

Good condition; intact and incomplete. Abrasion, polish, and loss of cortex on warps throughout, especially on the reverse. Abrasion and fraying of stitches, cordage ends unraveling. Warp elements loose and prone to detachment. Fragile but stable.

60 MAT FRAGMENT

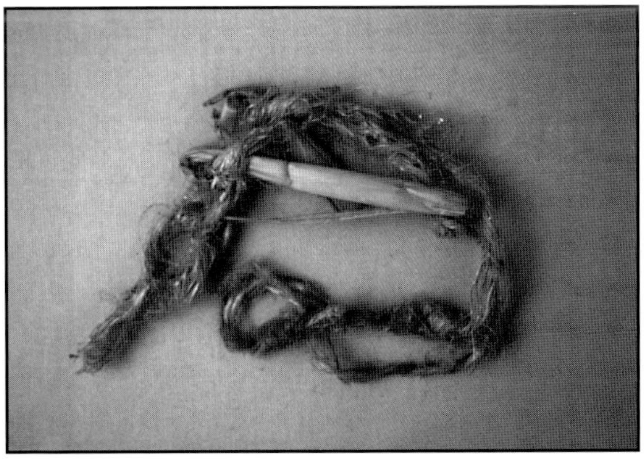

Tule and milkweed or dogbane, yucca
Prehistoric, as early as 8500 BC
Lent to MPC, 2000–2005
CARE 194

L: 23.0 cm
W: 4.6 cm
D: 1.4 cm

Fragment of s-spun yucca and dogbane blend single, z-twisted around two fragments of tule and knotted in two places.

Fair condition; intact. Extensive abrasion, raveling and fraying of cordage. Abrasion and loss of cortex on warps. Particulation and exfoliation. Warp elements loose and prone to detachment. Stable.

EXOTICS

Cradle Boards

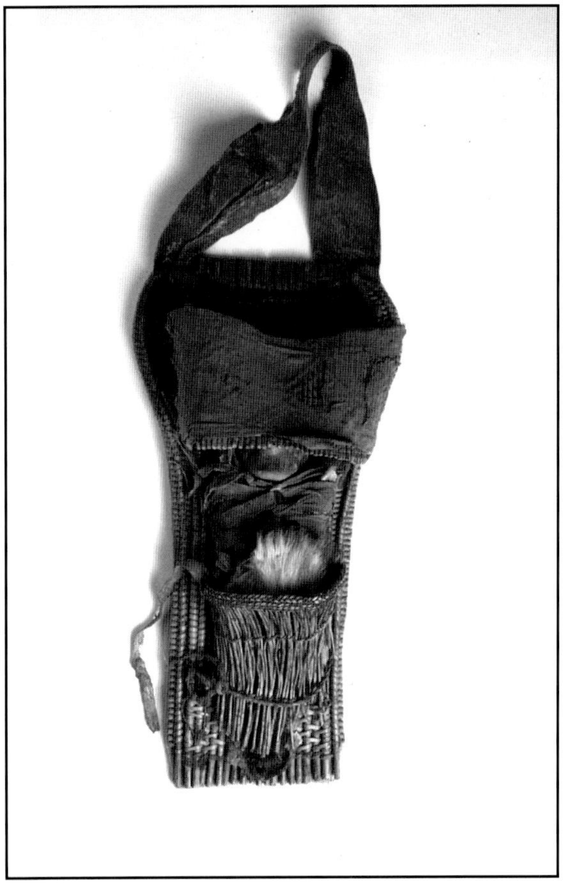

See also Color Plates 1, 2, 3, and 5, and Figures 12, 14, 15, and 16.

61 CRADLE BOARD WITH FIGURINE

Willow and rabbitbrush, cotton, animal pelts, clay, yucca
Fremont, ca. AD 1000
Lent to MPC, 2000–2005
CARE 192

Figurine:	Cradle Board:
H: ca. 16.0 cm	H: 11.3 cm
W: 10.4 cm	L: 41.8 cm
D: 0.7 cm	W: 22.4 cm

One-half life-size, wrapped twined basketry cradle board of willow and rabbitbrush bearing a Fremont clay figurine swaddled in cotton textile and furs. The cradle board has two basketry components affixed to it: the bassinette with the figurine and a hide-covered sunshade. A carrying strap of tanned, bighorn sheep hide is secured to the top of the cradle board back. It attaches at each end to rigid wefts of the cradle board back. It preserves several phases of red ochre coloring and heavy grime accreted from use.

Figurine:
The figurine is of the large, elaborate variety of Fremont figurines, although modest by the usual standard in trappings. It consists of a round-shouldered, flat-chested, trapezoidal body with a flat, circular face and two tubular protuberances at its base, perhaps legs or feet. It presents the following diagnostic features: dorsal head concavity; pinched nose; "coffee bean" appliqué eyes with painted black pigment on the lids and red in the inner corners; one tier of alternating red and white ticks vertically deployed along lower half of face; and a chin that is disengaged or separated from the neck. Tool marks apparent at points where the surface of the face was smoothed. Body below chin is completely obscured by wrappings, but x-rays reveal no jewelry or other adornment nor indication of gender. Light reddish brown (Munsell 2.5YR6/4), sun-baked.[15]

The figurine is tightly wrapped in a brown cotton textile worked in a balanced plain weave, ca. 40 ends per inch and 40 threads per inch in both warp and weft directions, using z-spun singles. On the viewer's right a rolled hem has been created and stitched with z-spun, s-twisted red cotton yarn ca. 1.5 mm, stitched in a running stitch. The complete or nearly complete pelt of an unidentified rodent drapes over the textile-clad figurine, preserving hind legs, face, and whiskers, and oriented with the head toward the figurine's legs and the hind legs under the face of figurine. Overlaying the figurine is a "travois" constructed of a stick A-frame with hide lacing. The travois is secured at the viewer's right with a line of sinew stitches and loosely affixed to the cradle board frame at viewer's left with cordage tied in slip knots. The uppermost layer of swaddling clothes is a swatch of tanned deer fawn or, possibly, bighorn sheep hide, with bright red-ochre pigment covering the flesh side. It is folded under and tucked under the bassinette. Underlying the swaddled figurine and laying directly on the surface of the cradle board back is a swatch from an unidentified animal pelt. On top of this pelt and corresponding to a "diaper" (see Allen and Munsey, p. 65) is a pad of shredded juniper bark. This is positioned under the buttocks and legs of the figurine.

Basketry components:
On the front of the cradle board, the lower, curved "bassinette" is composed of rabbitbrush. The top is a composite selvage consisting of one row of a variation on a simple-twined selvage with both warp ends left unclipped, resulting in a double layer of warp. Immediately below this, the outermost warps created by the selvage are then worked in three successive rows by twisting each warp unit counterclockwise 180 degrees around the warp unit immediately to its right. (Thus, 1 and 2 are twisted, then 2 and 3, then 3 and 4, etc., across the entire width of the piece.) This is then repeated, starting at the left-hand side.

Two rows of simple s-twining are then worked across the bassinette, securing the warps in bundles of four to five with s-spun, z-twisted yucca cordage ca. 1.4 mm in diameter. The first course of simple twining is ca. 3 cm below the bottom of the selvage rows, the second course ca. 5 cm below the first course. The side selvages of the simple twining are tied with a double overhand knot.

The bassinette is secured to the cradle board back with two pieces of two-ply, s-spun, z-twisted yucca cordage ca. 2 mm in diameter. The cordage is knotted on the reverse of the cradle board, then passed through the spaces between the second and third lateral warps and the rigid wefts, ca. 10 cm from the bottom. On the obverse these two strands are tied across the front of the bassinette in a slip knot on the viewer's left. The cursory manner in which the bassinette is secured, combined with the hasty workmanship of the simple-twined cordage and the marked difference between this and the rest of the cradle board, suggest the bassinette was the last to be constructed. It may be only partially complete—possibly, the bassinette was going to be completed in the same manner as the three rows immediately below the selvage.

The sunshade bends across the upper portion of the cradle board. It is composed of s- and z- close wrapped twining worked in a diamond pattern. One

Detail of cradle board, side view.

warp acts as a unit, with warp diameter being between 1.5 and 3.8 mm. The warp units are undecorticated. The rigid weft unit diameter ranges between 3.0 and 3.8 mm, and the flexible wefts range between 2.0 and 2.3 mm across. Both rigid and flexible wefts are decorticated. The small size of the piece precluded the use of warp splices, and no weft splices are visible due to the hide overlay. Adjacent to the selvage on the viewer's left, the light brown flexible wefts in one row are worked all the way across the warps. The remainder of the piece is worked in dark brown flexible wefts. A simple-twined selvage is formed by bending the warp ends 180 degrees from the reverse to the obverse around a decorticated stick at each selvage. The warp units are then bound back upon themselves in groups of two with two-ply, s-spun, z-twisted yucca cordage (1.2 mm diameter) on the right hand side, which is s-twined around the warps and secured with a reef knot. The left-hand selvage is treated in the same manner, but z-twined. Rigid weft elements terminate 5.0 mm beyond the end of the last warp element.

The sunshade is secured to the cradle board at the top and bottom of the sunshade selvages with s-spun, z-twisted yucca cordage (ca. 1 mm diameter). The top center portion of the sunshade is anchored to the cradle board by looping a piece of s-spun, z-twisted yucca cordage (ca. 3 mm diameter) around three warp units on the cradle board and three rigid weft elements on the sunshade, then securing with two large knots of undetermined type.
A very thin, close-fitting, tanned hide panel

extends across the basketry shade and drapes over the gap at the top. Outlines of weft elements and stitching of shade are visible through the hide in several places. Tears or cuts in the leather panel were stitched anciently with sinew.

The cradle-board back itself consists of an elongated, lyre-shaped, close wrapped, basketry frame, s- and z-twined in a checkerboard pattern. Two colors of flexible wefts are used—light and dark brown. One rigid warp element acts as a unit, with warp diameter being between 4.1 and 6.8 mm, although at the bottom portion of the cradle board two warps occasionally act as a unit. Both warp and wefts are decorticated. Both warps and rigid wefts are unsplit. Rigid wefts are 3.0–4.2 mm in diameter; dark brown flexible wefts are 1.8–3.3 mm wide, whereas the light brown flexible wefts are 2.0–3.4 mm wide. Flexible weft splices are bound under and close clipped. Ends of warps extend beyond final weft row; ends of rigid wefts extend 5.0 mm beyond final warp row and have been trimmed to shape after twining was completed.

Viewed from the reverse (the working side), the bottom eight rigid weft rows are twined all the way across the bottom, alternating s- with z-twining and are worked in light brown weft. Subsequent rows are generally worked in a six row by five stitch checkerboard pattern. However, the top row of checkerboards consists of five rows by five stitches, and the square in the lower right hand corner of the cradle board has some rows consisting of six stitches. The first checkerboard rows from the bottom are bordered by two stitches of dark brown weft, but in subsequent rows this pattern is continued in light brown weft, although the border on the lower left has an extra row of light weft. There are 12 rows of checkerboard in total. The top two rows of wefts are z-twined all the way across, with the lower z-twined row being worked on the viewer's right in dark brown and, on the viewer's left, in light brown flexible wefts. The top row, or frame piece, is z-twined in dark brown flexible wefts all the way across. The top row is occasionally worked with two warps acting as a unit.

The left and right margins of the cradle board are secured with s-twining on the viewer's right and z-twining on the viewer's left, forming a curvilinear pattern that follows the lyre-shaped outline of the cradle board and corresponds to the shape of the single lateral warp on either edge. These warps are then bent and passed in front of the central parallel warps to become the top row of rigid weft. The angle of truncation on the warps is 90 degrees, while on the rigid weft elements it is 60–90 degrees, accommodating the overall lyre shape of the cradle-board back.

The base of the cradle board has been s-twined with one row of s-spun, z-twisted yucca cordage exhibiting reddish staining (ochre?).

Mainly excellent condition; intact and complete. Bridge of nose of figurine appears to have been broken and repaired. Hide parts desiccated, with cracking and delamination in areas; pelt parts exhibit hair slippage and damage from a prior infestation. Rodent pelt shows advanced, active hair slippage. The textile is fraying and unraveling. Cordage abraded, fraying, and unraveling throughout. The bassinette exhibits abrasion, particularly of the selvage and three succeeding rows. Lowest course of twining loose and separating from warps. Loss of some warp elements or portions thereof, particularly on the viewer's right. Some warp elements broken, loose, and prone to detachment. Loss of warp and weft elements on lower viewer's left edge of sunshade. A 4.0 cm stretch of the cordage securing the sunshade to the reverse on viewer's left is nearly severed from the rest of the cordage and is prone to detachment. Basketry parts exhibit abrasion throughout, particularly of flexible weft elements, and embrittlement. Splitting and crazing of some flexible weft elements on cradle board back and sunshade. Loss of some flexible weft elements on obverse of cradle board at viewer's upper left. Liberal flyspecks throughout, especially on basketry parts. Stable except for hair slippage in pelt parts.

Comments:
A sample of the basketry taken from the reverse of the cradle board radiocarbon dated AD 910–1030.[16] The cradle board is the subject of an article in the text (see Allen and Munsey, p. 55, this volume).

See also Figure 43.

62 CRADLE BOARD FRAGMENT?

Willow
Probably Fremont, ca. AD 1000
Lent to MPC, 2000–2005
CARE 1660

L: 24.9 cm
W: 12.5 cm

Close wrapped twined basketry fragment with z- and s-twist wefts in a checkerboard pattern, perhaps a section from a cradle-board back. Checkerboard is created by blocks of wrapped twining, four rows by 10 stitches each. Two weft elements function as a unit. Flexible wefts are 2.1–3.1 mm wide and are split with the flat side down. Rigid wefts are whole, 3.5–3.8 mm in diameter. Warps are undecorticated; wefts (both rigid and flexible) are decorticated. One whole rigid warp element functions as a unit. Warp diameter 3.1–4.7 mm. Two warp rows and two weft rows per centimeter. Flexible weft splices are bound under.

Viewed with the convex side up and the selvage toward the viewer, a simple-twined selvage is formed by bending warp ends 180 degrees around an undecorticated stick from reverse to obverse and binding them to themselves with two-ply z-spun, s-twisted yucca cordage. Cordage is twined around the warp elements in groups of two or three, with twining switching from s- to z- at random and tied at the viewer's left side in a double overhand knot. On one side of knot, cordage extends 4.4 cm beyond the knot, and the other end extends 5.7 cm beyond the knot. Thicker warp elements are split in half at the selvage in order to facilitate passage around the stick, and the flat sides of these elements are down. Ends of rigid wefts and selvage stick have been cut, whereas non-selvage warp ends are broken. These warp ends curve slightly toward the reverse prior to termination. One piece of darker s-spun, z-twisted yucca cordage ca. 12 cm long is looped around three warp elements near the selvage on the viewer's left and tied into a reef knot on the reverse of the artifact. One end of this cordage extends 3.5 cm beyond the knot.

Good condition; largely intact but incomplete. Cortex of warp elements is delaminating. Some loss of cortex. Cut marks along the surface of the warps on obverse have accelerated this process. Extensive loss of cortex at selvage. Selvage stick is embrittled and has split longitudinally for a distance of 5.6 cm. Some warp elements broken, loose, and prone to detachment. Embrittlement and cracking of flexible wefts. Particulation. Sporadic specks of white accretions and fly spots throughout. Shorter end of cordage twining the selvage is unraveling and frayed. Stable.

See also Figure 43.

63 CRADLE BOARD FRAGMENT?

Willow
Fremont, ca. AD 1000
Lent to MPC, 2000-2005
CARE 1660

L: 18.9 cm
W: 17.5 cm

Close wrapped twined basketry fragment with z- and s-twisted wefts in a checkerboard pattern. Checkerboard is formed by blocks of wrapped twining, six rows by 13 stitches in the middle blocks and six rows by 10 stitches on the sides. Four rows of light-colored s-twined wefts create a border near the selvage. Warps are undecorticated, wefts (both rigid and flexible) are decorticated. Two weft elements function as a unit. Light brown flexible wefts are 1.7–4.4 mm wide and split with the flat side down. Dark brown flexible wefts are 1.9–2.8 mm wide and are halved with the flat side down. Rigid wefts are whole, 3.8–4.5 mm in diameter. One whole rigid warp element functions as a unit. Warp diameter 1.8–5.7 mm. Two warp and two weft rows per centimeter. Flexible weft splices bound under.

Viewed with the convex side up and the selvage toward the viewer, a simple-twined selvage is formed by bending warp ends 180 degrees around an undecorticated stick from reverse to obverse and binding them to themselves with two-ply, z-spun, s-twisted yucca cordage. Cordage is s-twined around the warp elements in groups of two or three. One piece of z-spun, s-twisted yucca cordage ca. 11 cm long is looped around the selvage stick near midpoint and tied in a double overhand knot. Fragment of sinew is tied around last warp element on viewer's left (visible only on reverse), tied in a double overhand knot, and one loose end is tied again in a single overhand knot.

Very good condition; intact but incomplete. Delamination of warp cortex throughout, especially at the selvage. Some delamination of selvage stick. Particulation. Loss of part of selvage stick and warps in one corner, angular breakage of warps and wefts along opposite edge. Embrittlement and splitting of flexible warps. Abrasion and loss of rigid warp ends, some abrasion of flexible wefts. Fly spots. Stable.

Comments:
This may be part of a sunshade of a full-size cradle board similar to the Pectol-Lee model cradle board (cat. no. 61).

64 CRADLE BOARD FRAGMENT?

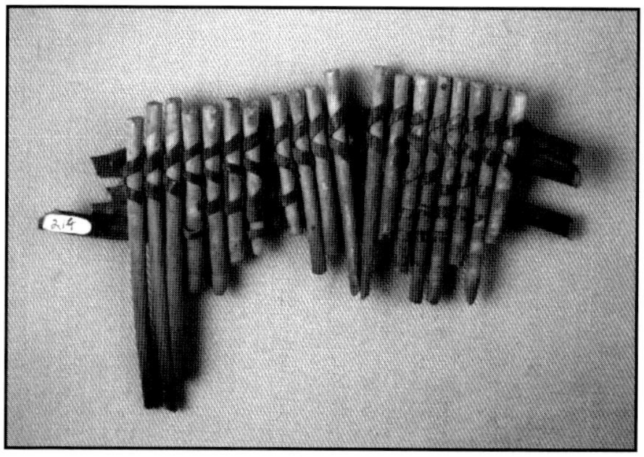

See also Figure 43.

Willow
Fremont, ca. AD 1000
Lent to MPC, 2000–2005
CARE 214

L: 12.5 cm
W: 7.4 cm
D: 2.0 cm

Close wrapped twined basketry fragment, s- and z-twined, perhaps a section of a cradle-board back. One warp acts as a unit. Warp diameter 2.3–4.5 mm in diameter. Warps undecorticated, both rigid and flexible wefts decorticated. Rigid wefts are whole, 3.5–4.2 mm in diameter. Flexible wefts 2.0–2.8 mm wide. Flexible weft splices bound under and close clipped. Rigid wefts truncated beyond last warp row and trimmed after completion.

Good condition; intact but incomplete. Loss of portions of the flexible wefts. One portion broken, loose, and prone to detachment. Embrittlement and splitting of flexible wefts. Abrasion and polish of stitches throughout, especially on the reverse. Fly spots and dirt accretions throughout. Stable.

Clay Figurines

65 FIGURINE

Sun-baked clay
Fremont (AD 400–1300)
Lent to MPC, 2000–2005
CARE 506

L: 4.5 cm
W: 1.5 cm

Small, complete, anthropomorphic figurine with flat dorsal side, terminating in handle shape ("handle terminus" type).[17] Roughly modeled body with no limbs. Facial features indeterminate. Light red (Munsell 2.5YR6/6) tempered with sand and mica particles and sun-baked. A few shrinkage marks.

Good condition; intact and complete. Blind hairline crack on top of head. Numerous dents incurred before baked. Gouges in location of face. Small dark oily stains. Stable.

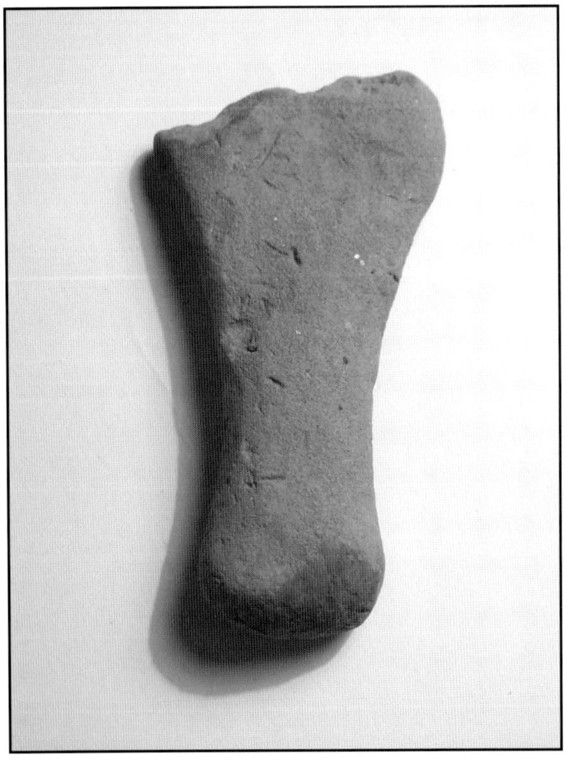

66 FIGURINE

Sun-baked clay
Fremont (400–1300)
Lent to MPC, 2000–2005
CARE 502

L: 5.5 cm
W: 3.5 cm

Nearly complete anthropomorphic figurine with trapezoidal body and half of head broken off; flattened dorsal side; terminates in handle terminus. Body rendered summarily with no indication of limbs. Pale red (Munsell 10R6/3) tempered with sand and mica particles and sun-baked.

Good condition; intact and largely complete. Several large dents incurred before baked. Oily stains on both ends. Fragile but stable.

67 HEAD OF FIGURINE

Sun-baked clay
Fremont (AD 400–1300)
Lent to MPC, 2000–2005
CARE 505

L: 3.6 cm
W: 2.9 cm
D: 2.5 cm

Head broken off an anthropomorphic figurine. Angle of chin in relation to surviving portion of neck indicates the figure originally held its head high and appeared to be looking up. No forehead or crown: flattened brow ridge suffices as top of head. Summarily rendered facial features: eyes rendered by means of holes poked into clay; "eyelids" (intact on proper right only) carefully executed in appliqué clay encircling the eye hole. Long pinched nose, largely unarticulated from cheeks, such that the cheeks descend from the nose ridge in flat planes. Nose ridge has a modelled nub at its base (chin?) with a shallow gash just above it (mouth?). Holes have been pricked into the perimeter of head: two at approximate ear level on each side and two on side of neck area, perhaps evidence of attachments such as plant material representing a headdress. Reverse of head is flat. Traces of red paint on cheeks. Light reddish brown (Munsell 2.5YR6/4), sand-tempered(?), sun-baked.

Good condition; intact and partially complete. Broken off at neck; chip on proper left eyebrow near root of nose; chips along proper right perimeter of face. Scattered surface pocks in association with sand temper. Stable.

68 HEAD OF FIGURINE

Sun-baked clay
Fremont (AD 400–1300)
Lent to MPC, 2000–2005
CARE 507

L: 3.9 cm
W: 3.6 cm
D: 1.9 cm

Fragment of an anthropomorphic figurine preserving proper right side of face and lower portion of proper left side. Summarily rendered facial features: proper left eye rendered by means of hole poked into clay, traces of now missing appliquéd "eyelid" just discernible; lower half of long pinched nose, largely unarticulated from cheeks, such that the cheeks descend from the nose ridge in sloping planes. Flat on reverse side of head. Weak red (Munsell 10R5/3), sun-baked. Plant inclusions on proper right of face.

Good condition; intact and largely incomplete. Stable.

69 FIGURINE FRAGMENT

Sun-baked clay
Fremont (AD 400–1300)
Lent to MPC, 2000–2005
CARE 504

L: 4.5 cm
W: 3.9 cm
D: 1.7 cm

Fragment of clay figurine, preserving a flattened mass with portions of two appendages. Reverse has been pressed against a hard flat surface; obverse preserves a central thumb-sized depression. Possible interpretations: a head with horns or antennae-like protuberances; a body fragment (torso) with portions of legs surviving. Weak red (Munsell 10R5/4), micaceous, sun-baked. Several shrinkage cracks along perimeter between appendages.

Good condition; intact and partially complete. One appendage broken off near origin point. A few inclusion pocks. Dark oily stain accretions. Stable.

70 FIGURINE FRAGMENT

Sun-baked clay
Fremont (AD 400–1300)
Lent to MPC, 2000–2005
CARE 503

L: 3.4 cm
W: 2.7 cm

Fragment of shaped clay, possibly the head of a horned animal, preserving cursorily modeled peak on obverse (face, muzzle?) and portions of two appendages broken off at the point of origin (horns?). Possible interpretations: a head with horns or ears and torso broken off, or large-bellied torso with legs and head broken off. Reverse uneven. Weak red (Munsell 10R5/3), sun-baked. Partial fingerprints on obverse and reverse. Black inclusions discernible on reverse.

Poor condition; intact and largely incomplete. Impact damage on proper right "cheek" with associated open cracks and surface loss, a source of particulation. Hairline crack under accession number. Stable except for minor particulation.

Ceremonial Items

See also Color Plates 6–9.

71 DEER HEADDRESS

Deer hide
Late Prehistoric, AD 1470–1660
Lent to MPC, 2000–2005
CARE 79

L: 38.0 cm
W: 29.6 cm
H: 13.5 cm

Upper portion of proper right side of the face of a deer (white tail or mule deer) preserving portion of one antler and patch of hair near antler. Eye is sewn shut with sinew. The ear has been modified by inserting a curved twig that follows contour of ear, probably to maintain life-like shape and keep it erect. End of twig is wrapped with thin hide strips tinted with red ochre. The ear is filled with grass and "quilted" with sinew stitches to hold elements in place. It appears the purpose of some stitches was to close the incision where the ear had been skinned. Sinew stitching (s-spun, z-twisted) along top of head probably closed a dorsal skinning cut. Head piece was attached at nape to another component (complete hide of deer?) by hide lacing stained with red ochre. Traces of yellow ochre(?) on exterior suggest it may have been painted. Cut marks visible on flesh side; partially defleshed.

Fair condition; intact and partially complete. Delamination near antler. Desiccation resulting in stiffness. Small lacunae near eye. Insect damage on bottom half of face. White powdery accretion on flesh side. Scattered fly spots. Stable.

Comments:
This headdress was once part of a deer costume that was probably used as a hunting disguise. There are both prehistoric and historic precedents for wearing animal costumes (see Allen and Munsey, p. 99, this volume). This headdress is Late Prehistoric, having yielded a radiocarbon date of AD 1470–1660, or ca. AD 1500.[18]

72 BURDEN STRAP

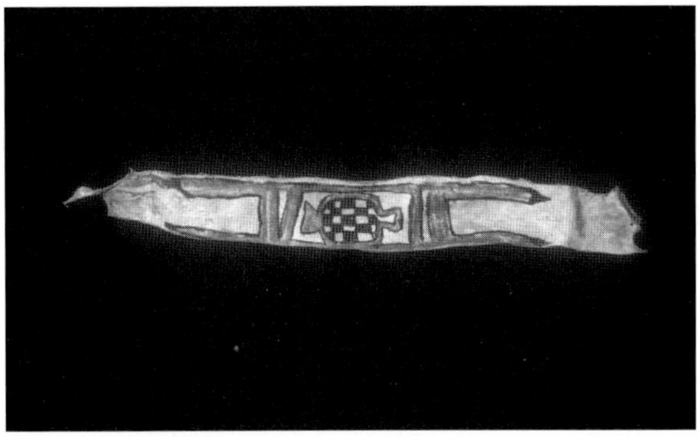

Elk hide? Mineral paints
Apache or Comanche, 14th–15th century AD?[19]
Lent to Capitol Reef National Park
(On display at Visitor Center)
CARE 227

L: 65.0 cm
W: 6.7 cm

Rawhide burden strap with decorations in black, orange, and green mineral paints and remains of stake holes (for stretching and drying) on each end. Decorations consist of fish or turtle motif enclosed within a rectangle drawn in reserve. This rectangle is, in turn, flanked on each side by the closed end of an open-ended rectangle or C-shaped motif, both also drawn in reserve. Fish or turtle motif is filled in with black checkers. The borders delineating the reserve rectangle and C-shaped motifs are outlined in black and infilled with brown and green lines. Reverse partially defleshed with pronounced chatter marks.

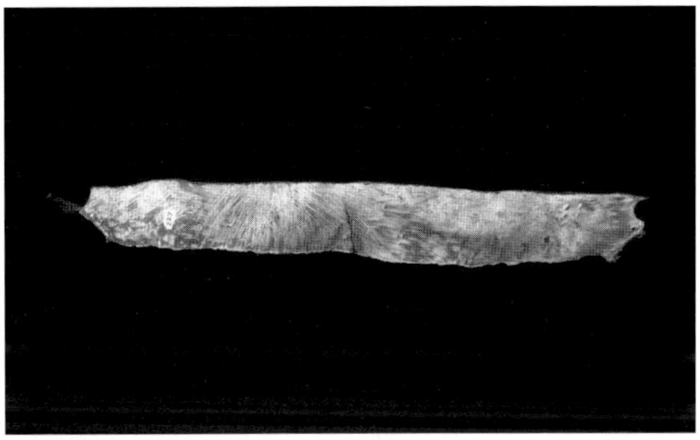

Reverse.

Good condition; intact and largely complete. Stiff and embrittled. Small, yellow ochre(?) accretions on reverse near nail hole. Stable.

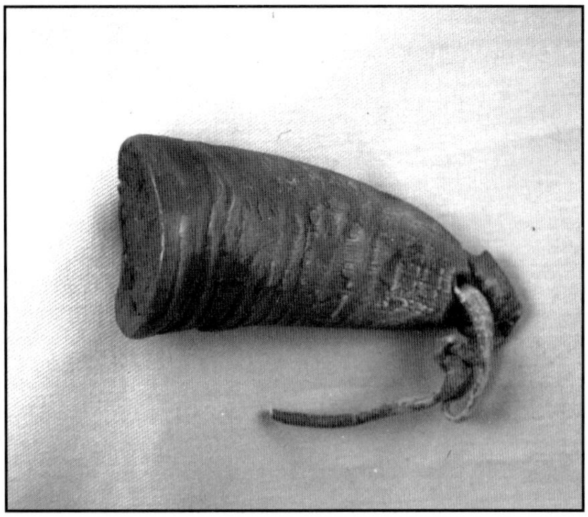

Detail of interior with contents.

73 PAINT CONTAINER

Bighorn sheep horn
Late Prehistoric/Historic, ca. AD 1250–1800
Lent to MPC, 2000–2005
CARE 195

L: 9.9 cm
W: 4.6 cm
D: 3.7 cm

Tip of horn from bighorn sheep ewe adapted to store paint. Biconically drilled hole in distal end with tied leather strips for suspending. Red substance is very fine grained, dense, and hard packed and appears to be red ochre mixed with a binder. Significant polish on outer surfaces of horn from use.

Good condition; intact and complete. Cracks along the grain; some delamination; scattered scratches. Black accretion on horn and strap (polish, pitch, dirt, grime from handling?). Scattered fly spots. Stable.

<u>Comments</u>:
This is one of two horn paint containers in the collection (see also cat. no. 74).

A close parallel for the Pectol-Lee paint containers is a bison horn containing compacted, powdered, red hematite, which was recovered from an unknown stratum at Hogup Cave.[20] Like the Pectol-Lee paint horn, it has hide carrying thongs.

Based on the excellent state of preservation of the Pectol-Lee paint container and considering the progressive decimation of bighorn sheep populations in the Capitol Reef area, it seems likely this container could date as early as Late Prehistoric but probably not after about AD 1800.[21]

74 PAINT CONTAINER

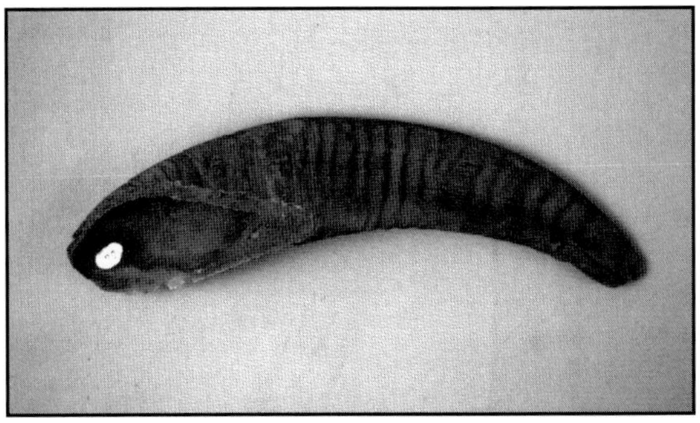

Bighorn sheep horn
Late Prehistoric/Historic, ca. AD 1250–1800
Lent to MPC, 2000–2005
CARE 70

L: 25.0 cm
W: 4.5 cm
D: 2.5 cm

Tip of horn from bighorn sheep ewe adapted to store paint. An elliptical section was cut away at the proximal end, enabling greater access to contents. Paint is dense and compacted and appears to be red ochre with a binder. Polish and abrasions from use throughout surface.

Fair condition; intact and complete. Thorough open crack emanating from distal end. Scattered charring with associated discoloration. Scattered blind hairline cracks and delamination. Stable.

Comments:
This is the second of two paint horns in the collection (see cat. no. 73).

Items of Leisure and Adornment

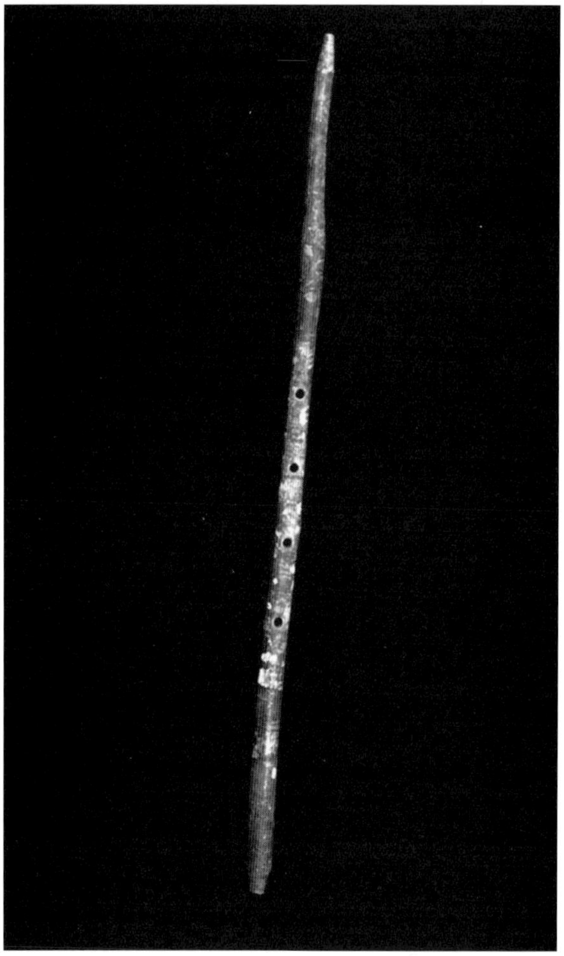

75 FLUTE

Unidentified wood
Agricultural Period
(Anasazi or Fremont, AD 1–1300)?
Lent to Capitol Reef National Park
(On display at Visitor Center)
CARE 236

L: 61.0 cm
Diam: 2.0 cm

Long, wooden flute with tapered mouthpiece and four round, evenly spaced holes, all on one face. May originally have been bound with tanned hide strips, as suggested by numerous concentric bands of pitch-like residue extending around the circumference and remains of one small strip of leather on distal end.

Fair condition; intact and complete. Numerous scattered chips. Salting? Thick resin accretion on distal end. Stable.

76 NECKLACE

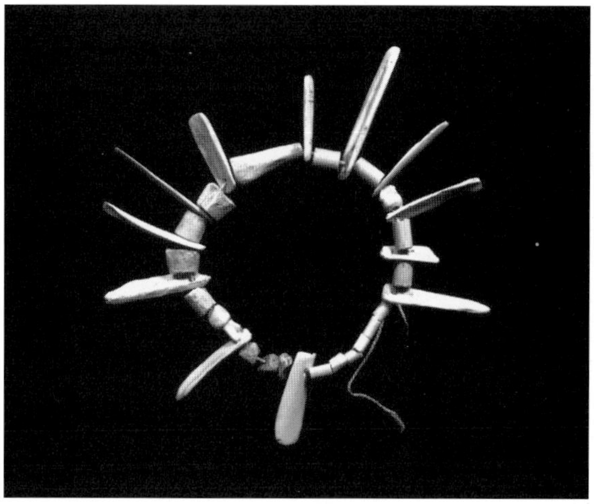

Bone and reed
Agricultural Period
(Anasazi or Fremont, AD 1–1300)?
Lent to Capitol Reef National Park
(On display at Visitor Center)
CARE 237

Circum: 37.5 cm

L (longest bone): 7.3 cm
W (longest bone): 0.4 cm

L (smallest bone): 4.1 cm
W (smallest bone): 1.6 cm

Necklace composed of thirty-three pieces of shaped bone and reed sections strung on z-spun, s-twisted cordage (dogbane or milkweed?). Bones consist of eleven large mammal diaphysis metatarsal midshafts; three distal metatarsals from small artiodactal; two medium-sized mammal long bones; phalanx of large mammal; the distal third of diaphysis metatarsal midshaft; and one of each of the following: distal ephisal humerous of small mammal; metacarpal artiodactal. Reed consists of four phragmites (*communis*?) sections. Stringing holes worn; tool marks from shaping

Very good condition; intact and complete. Outer surface loss of phragmites pieces. One cortical bone exhibits rodent gnawing on edges. Stable.

77 UNFINISHED TINKLERS OR GAMING PIECES?

Bone
Prehistoric/Historic (before 17th century AD)
Lent to MPC, 2000–2005
CARE 52, 53, 54, 56, 57

L (average): 5.5 cm

Five bone articles in the shape of truncated cones, possibly unfinished tinklers or gaming pieces. Fashioned from the first phalanges of deer or bighorn sheep. Joints have been ground down and preserve tool marks on remainder of bone shaft.

Excellent condition; intact and complete. Stable.

Comments:
These conical tubes resemble tinklers recovered from the uppermost layer (D-V) of Danger Cave in Nevada which had already been removed before Jesse D. Jennings began his excavations there and was therefore not dated,[22] although a later report by Jennings assigns the broad date of 4000 BC–AD 20 to level V.[23] These bone items also resemble artifacts thought to be Fremont gaming pieces.[24]

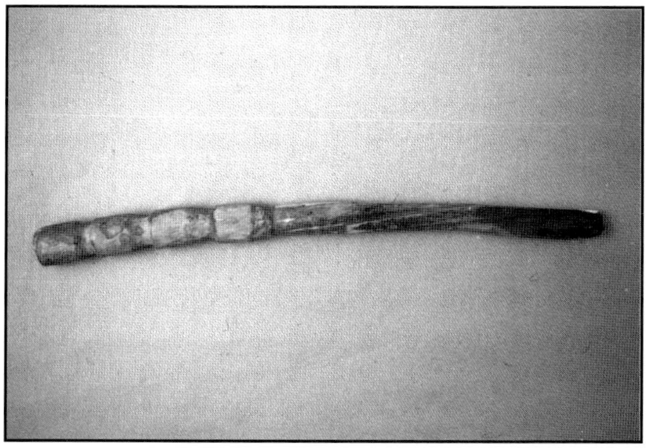

78 GAMING STICK
Unidentified wood
Historic Shoshone? Probably 19th century
Lent to MPC, 2000–2005
CARE 148

L: 20.4 cm
W: 1.3 cm
D: 1.3 cm

A carved wood stick with decorative "handle" and charred distal end. Handle has been circumferentially notched (whittled) to resemble four stacked, tubular knobs, each tapered on the end leading to the next. This work is reminiscent of lathe work but appears to be turn-carved by hand. At point where handle terminates, the shaft is slightly z-twisted—this was accomplished when the stick was green and may be incidental to turn-carving the handle. Four short grooves and traces of more are present on the extant surface of the shaft, all cut perpendicular to the grain. These have a less deliberate character than the handle decorations. Grime in some of the recesses between the knobs, and the flat surface area of the knobs exhibit polish but are fairly free of soiling except in a few concentrated areas—these surface anomalies might be consistent with use as a gaming stick with hide caps protecting the knobs (see comments below).

Fair to good condition; intact and partially complete. Charred on unfinished end. Scattered hairline cracks. Open blind cracks along grain throughout and on the shaft surface loss along the grain. Dark, resin-like accretion on shaft. Liquid stains on knobs. Fly spots. Stable.

Comments:
This stick looks very much like a pair of sticks collected on the Wind River Reservation, Wyoming, from the Eastern Shoshone in 1901.[25] The Shoshone examples, of uncertain length but decorated with three nearly identical knobs, are complete with hide caps over each knob and hide thongs dangling from the unfinished end. In the Shoshone examples the wood knobs are painted (top to bottom) red, yellow, and red, while their hide caps and thongs are painted red on one example and yellow on the other. They were part of the set of paraphernalia used in a game known as the ring game.

Eastern Shoshone territory is considerably north of Capitol Reef, but this people traveled widely in bands and had a wide pattern of annual movement, especially during the period 1825–1880. For example, they were encountered on the Little Colorado in Navajo country in 1826 by James O. Pattie.[26]

POTTERY

79 BOTTLE

Pottery
Fremont (AD 400–1300)
Lent to Capitol Reef National Park
(On display at Visitor Center)
CARE 21

H: 20.0 cm
Diam: 16.0 cm

Bi-globular bottle with one handle, a constricted neck and direct rim, and red painted decoration. Structurally the bottle consists of a small, globular, single-handed jug ca. 8 cm in height surmounting a jar-shaped element ca. 12 cm in height. Decorations consist of vertical red lines running from lip of vessel to point of constriction/juncture of the two bulbous elements. A red line also runs the entire circumference of the juncture.

Good condition structurally, but paint badly faded and barely discernible. Intact and complete. Chips in rim. A few minor scratches. Calcareous inclusions erupting on surface with associated pocks (very minor). Small area of efflorescence. Paint faded and blistered with associated paint loss. On one side, large area and many small areas of mineral deposits. Black accretion on rim (pitch?). Structurally stable.

80 JAR

Pottery
Fremont (AD 400–1300)
Lent to Capitol Reef National Park
(On display at Visitor Center)
CARE 263

H: 26.1 cm
Diam: 25.0 cm

Medium-sized, coiled, gray ware jar with slightly restricted neck and everted rim. Extensive charring.

Poor condition; intact and largely complete. Small loss on rim. Thorough hairline cracks along base. Powdery white substance: salting? Charred material flaking off outer surface. Stable.

81 JAR

Pottery
Fremont (AD 400–1300)
Lent to Capitol Reef National Park
(On display at Visitor Center)
CARE 228

H: 15.0 cm
Diam: 13.5 cm

Small, one-handled jar with restricted neck and direct rim. Mottled surface—mostly black with patches of isolated pale gray. Rather crude manufacture: coils cursorily smoothed (especially apparent in the contour), and insufficient attention given to bonding the coils, as indicated by separation of coils; uppermost coil on rim still partly intact. Fire clouds; uneven firing; gritty matrix and temper pocks.

Fair condition; intact and largely complete. Loss (chip) on lip; deep abrasions on shoulder. Blind open cracks with associated minor losses. Surface crack along coil (separation or poor smoothing over of coils). Inclusions erupting on surface with associated pocks. Efflorescence; powdery white substance in low areas and interior (salting). White discoloration on handle (as though bleach dripped down it). Structurally weak.

82 JAR

Pottery
Fremont (AD 400–1300)
Lent to MPC, 2000–2005
CARE 28

H: 20.5 cm
Diam: 29.6 cm

Rather large, Sevier gray ware jar with one handle, restricted neck, and direct rim. Heavy charring on outside; thick, flaking, brown incrustations (food residue?) on inside. Dark brown (Munsell 7.5YR3/2), sand-tempered.

Fair condition; intact and largely complete. Loss of 2/3 of rim including small portion of shoulder and small circular lacuna in body. Hairline crack emanating from loss on shoulder; blind hairline cracks along base. Scattered temper pocks. Scattered accretions of powdery efflorescence, heavy in areas, including some salting. Hard, thick incrustations of dirt(?) on body, including an area on lower body that seems to be permeated with an oily substance. Stable.

83 JAR

Corrugated pottery
Numic (ca. 1400–1850)
Lent to MPC, 2000–2005
CARE 38

H: 25.0 cm
Diam: 10.8 cm

Medium, wide-mouthed, corrugated jar, slightly conical bottom, restricted neck, and direct rim. Black (Munsell 7.5R2/) with sand temper and calcareous inclusions on the surface and associated pocks; occasional straw(?) impression on surface. Pronounced scrape marks visible on interior. Crusty accretions lining interior appear to be charred food remnants.

Poor condition; largely intact and largely complete. Hairline cracks along the line of coil construction at lower body and descending from loss at the neck. Loss of 3/4 of neck—fourteen rim fragments are detached. Accretions on interior prone to detachment and some pieces are loose on the jar bottom. Odor (rodent urine?). Structurally weak.

Comments:
Analysis of surface scrapings on the interior of the pot yielded no clear evidence of organic residues.[27] If corn had been cooked in the vessel, phytoliths from the glumes at the base of the kernels would have been expected, but none were observed. A variety of plant cells might represent seed coats, but would likely need 400x magnification for identification.

84 DECORATED POT FRAGMENT

Mancos Black-on-white pottery
Kayenta Anasazi (AD 1100–1300)
Lent to MPC, 2000–2005
CARE H 4897

L: 4.6 cm
W: 0.3 cm

Bichrome pottery sherd with alternating black and gray filled checkerboards. Very pale brown (Munsell 10YR7/3), slipped light gray (Munsell 2.5YN6/0).

Good condition; intact. Stable.

85 DECORATED POT FRAGMENT

Sosi Black-on-white pottery
Mesa Verde Anasazi (AD 1100–1300)
Lent to MPC, 2000–2005
CARE H 4898

L: 4.0 cm
W: 0.2 cm

Bichrome pottery sherd with black parallel lines. Light gray (Munsell 10YR7/1).

Fair condition; intact. Crackling. Scattered chips and scratches. Stable.

86 POT FRAGMENT

Tusayan Style Corrugated pottery
Kayenta Anasazi (AD 1100–1300)
Lent to MPC, 2000–2005
CARE H 4899

L: 3.6 cm
W: 0.3 cm

Red corrugated pottery sherd. Light reddish brown (Munsell 5YR6/4).

Good condition; intact and stable.

87 BOWL

Pottery
Santo Domingo, 1928 or earlier
Lent to MPC, 2000–2005
CARE 17

H: 9.5 cm
Diam: 7.6 cm

Small, polychrome, pottery bowl with direct rim. Decorations consist of two main zones, the upper of which has vegetal decorations in black and the lower of which is solid red. The upper, decorated zone consists of a rectangular tan frieze that terminates, just short of being complete, in two vertical parallel lines, forming what might be a "spirit break." A double, scalloped garland painted in black loops across the frieze. Light red, sand-tempered matrix (Munsell 10YR6/6) slipped pinkish gray (Munsell 7.5R7/2). "Santo Domingo N. Mexico 1928" in ball point pen.

Fair condition; intact and largely complete. Reconstructed from three large fragments with glue. Lacuna in center. Scattered crackling on inner and outer surfaces. Inner surface: hairline crack emanating from rim. Blind hairline crack with associated chip. Scattered scratches. Water(?) spots; brown lines emanating from rim; patches of discoloration in center. Outer surface: a few calcareous(?) inclusions. Numerous scattered scratches, nicks, and gouges. Stable.

WORKED WOOD

Hunting Implements

88 ARROW SHAFT

Wood
Agricultural Period,
Anasazi or Fremont, AD 400–1300
Lent to MPC, 2000–2005
CARE 251

L: 40.0 cm
W: 0.4 cm

Painted wood arrow shaft preserving bow string slot (nock) on one end and the sinew thread wrapped around it; other end broken. Quill pieces remaining from fletching under two separate sinew ties. Painted decoration: two bands of red ochre near sinew wrappings. Use wear: nock smoothed and polished from contact with bow string; stains and soiling consistent with use.

Fair condition; intact and largely complete. Snap break at end with associated splitting. Scattered nicks and chips. Abrasions resulting in loss of surface in areas. Stable.

Comments:
The bow and arrow first came into use in the Southwest about AD 400 or possibly as early as the second or third century AD (see Talbot, p. 8–9, this volume).

89 COMPOSITE ARROW SHAFT

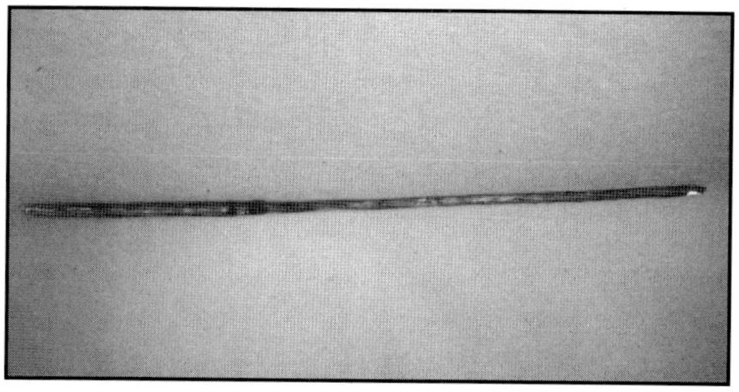

Willow?
Agricultural Period, Fremont or Anasazi,
AD 400–1300
Lent to MPC, 2000–2005
CARE 150

L(foreshaft): 48.6 cm
L (shaft): 17.5 cm

Long composite arrow with phragmites reed shaft still attached. Preserves sinew lacing in two areas of the foreshaft shaft. Foreshaft (antriplex) has been sharpened on one side at the end.

Poor condition; intact and largely complete. Phragmites reed shattered and splitting for half of length. Discoloration on sharpened end of antriplex. Scattered fly spots. Stable.

90 COMPOSITE ARROW FRAGMENTS

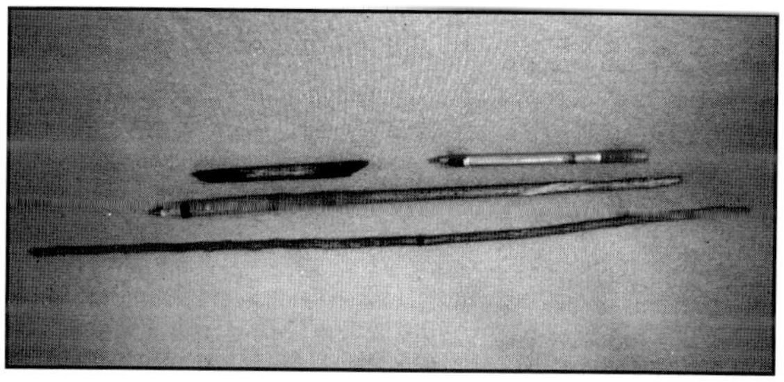

Willow?
Agricultural Period, Anasazi or Fremont,
AD 400–1300
Lent to MPC, 2000–2005
CARE 20

L (foreshafts): 43.0 cm, 31.0 cm
L (shafts): 12.2 cm, 10.0 cm

Four fragments of composite arrows. Two of the fragments are foreshafts (antriplexes). One of the foreshafts preserves a phragmites reed shaft (L: 6.3 cm) attached with sinew thread; its other end is twisted, presumably while green. The other two fragments are of phragmites reed, corresponding to shafts, the longest of which has sinew lacing in two areas where it is attached to the foreshaft, the shorter of which is charred.

Good condition; intact. Stable.

Comments:
These composite arrow fragments, along with some partially prepared rods (cat. nos. 3–4) and some basketry wefts (cat. no. 52), may all have been part of a single materials store.

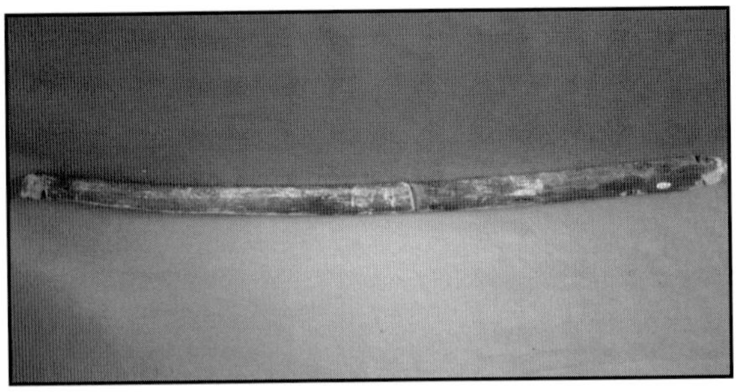

91 MODEL BOW

Wood
Prehistoric/Historic, AD 400–1900
Lent to MPC, 2000–2005
CARE 250

L: 50.0 cm
W: 2.5 cm

Small wood bow with bilateral side notches on both ends for stringing. Slight curvature corresponding to requirements of use; soiling and wear on side notches consistent with use.

Fair condition; reconstructed from two fragments but complete. Slight delamination on one end. Several scattered chips and gouges. Numerous abrasions resulting in loss of surface; scattered scratches. Fly spots. Stable.

92 SCISSORS SNARE

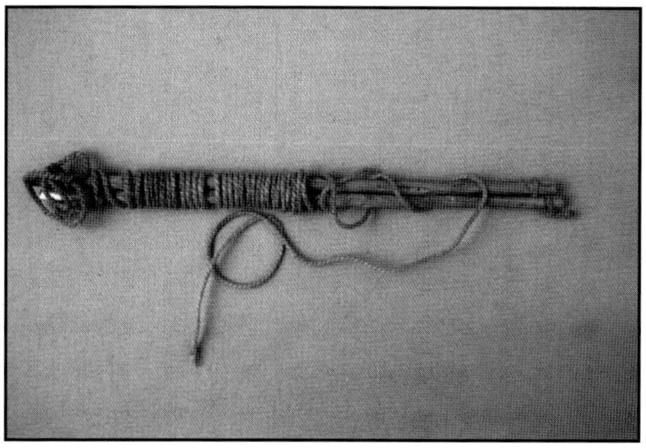

Greasewood, dogbane or milkweed cordage, sinew
Probably Agricultural Period
(Anasazi or Fremont, AD 1–1300)
Lent to MPC, 2000–2005
CARE 201

L: 18.3 cm
W: 1.9 cm
D: 0.8 cm

Two straight greasewood twigs, tied with dogbane or milkweed fiber cordage. Twigs are decorticated and incised circumferentially ca. 4 mm from the proximal end, and each is tied with a slip knot to opposite ends of the same piece of cordage. Free ends of cordage are tied in a single overhand knot to prevent slippage and fraying. Distal end of one stick has a short length of cordage (ca. 1.5 cm) bound to it with a band of sinew to form a loop. Distal end of the other stick is incised with five cross-wise grooves, two groups of two grooves lying in the same mathematical planes, and one isolated groove. This end is looped with a slip knot, again with the free end tied to prevent slippage and fraying. Overall length of this cord is ca. 140 cm. Cordage extends ca. 17 cm before passing through the sinew-secured loop on the other twig and then is wrapped around both sticks together. Free end of this cord is not fastened or tied, and some raveling has started to occur. Cordage diameter varies from 1.0 to 1.8 mm. Ends of both twigs are cut through, not broken.

Excellent condition; intact and complete. Some cracking along the grain, particularly adjacent to knot-holes in twig. Some discoloration of cordage. A few fly spots. Stable.

93 SCISSORS SNARE

Greasewood, dogbane or milkweed cordage, sinew
Probably Agricultural Period
(Anasazi or Fremont, AD 1–1300)
Lent to MPC, 2000–2005
CARE 198

L: 19.1 cm
W: 1.4 cm
D: 1.0 cm

Two straight greasewood twigs, tied with dogbane or milkweed fiber cordage. Twigs are decorticated and incised circumferentially ca. 6 mm from the proximal end, and each is tied with a slip knot to opposite ends of the same piece of cordage. Free ends of cordage are tied in a single overhand knot to prevent slippage and fraying. Distal end of one stick has a short length of cordage (ca. 1.5 cm) bound to it with a band of sinew to form a loop. Distal end of the other stick is wrapped four times and tied with a double overhand knot. Overall length of this cord is ca. 100 cm. Cordage extends ca. 1 cm before passing through the sinew-secured loop on the other twig then is wrapped around both sticks together. Free end of this cord is tied with a single overhand knot to prevent raveling. Cordage diameter varies from 1.0 to 1.8 mm. Cordage consists of two pieces tied together with a reef knot. One section of cordage has a single overhand knot tied partway down its length. Ends of both twigs are cut through, not broken.

Excellent condition; intact and complete. Some discoloration of cordage. Stable.

94 SCISSORS SNARE

Greasewood, dogbane or milkweed cordage, sinew
Agricultural Period
(Anasazi or Fremont, AD 1–1300)?
Lent to Capitol Reef National Park
(On display at Visitor Center)
CARE 231

L: 19.0 cm
W: 1.4 cm
D: 1.1 cm

Two straight greasewood twigs, tied with dogbane or milkweed fiber cordage. Twigs are decorticated and incised circumferentially ca. 4 mm from the proximal end, and each is tied with a slip knot to opposite ends of the same piece of cordage, separated by a gap ca. 1 cm wide. Free ends of cordage are tied in a single overhand knot, probably to prevent slippage and fraying. Distal end of one stick has a short length of cordage (ca. 1.5 cm) bound to it with a band of sinew to form a loop 2.0 cm from the end. Distal end of other stick is looped with cordage and secured with a slip knot, again with the free end tied, probably to prevent slippage and fraying. Cordage is wrapped around the sticks 43 times. Overall length of this piece of cordage is ca. 120 cm long.

Very good condition; intact and complete. Sporadic staining and discoloration of cordage. White paint from accession number is tacky and transfers easily. Stable.

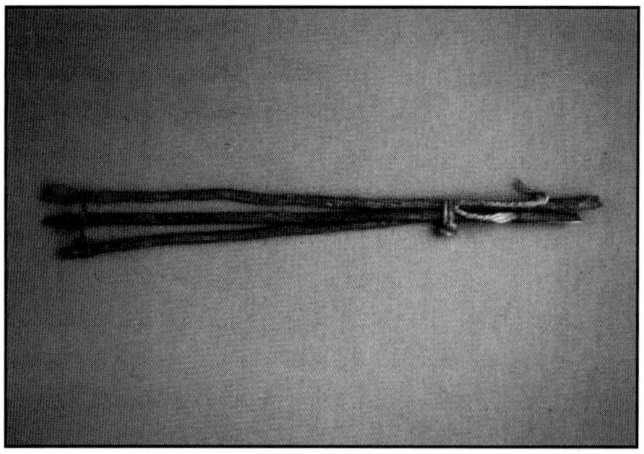

95 SCISSORS SNARE

Greasewood twigs and dogbane or milkweed cordage
Agricultural Period
(Anasazi or Fremont, AD 1–1300)?
Lent to MPC, 2000–2005
CARE 200

L: 18.4 cm
W: 0.8 cm
D: 0.7 cm

Bundle of three straight greasewood sticks incised circumferentially ca. 7 to 8 mm from one end and tied with a slipknot of dogbane or milkweed cordage (z-spun and s-twisted). All three sticks are decorticated. Two of the sticks are bound with slip knots to opposite ends of the same cord. The third stick is tied with a slipknot, but the end of the cord is cut off at the knot. In all three cases the free end of the cordage was tied in a single overhand knot to prevent slippage or fraying. All proximal stick ends are cut, as are the distal ends of two of the sticks, but the distal end of the third is broken and split. All three are wrapped twice and tied with modern commercial cotton string near one end.

Excellent condition; intact and complete. Some cracking along the grain, particularly adjacent to knot-holes in twig. Proximal end of one stick and associated cordage show dark discoloration. Soiling of modern string, the ends of which are frayed. Stable.

96 PART OF SNARE

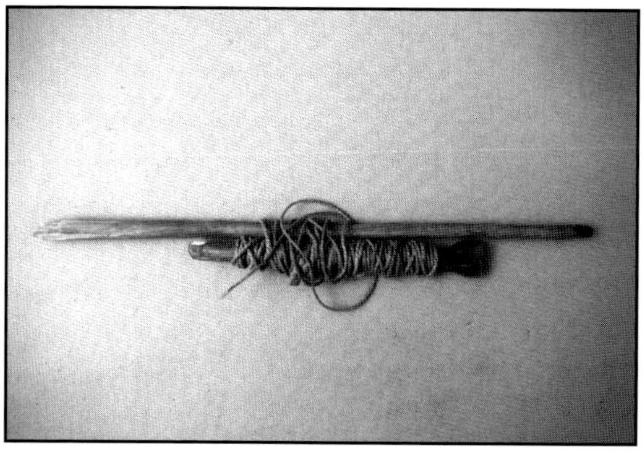

Wood and dogbane or milkweed cordage
Agricultural Period
(Anasazi or Fremont, AD 1–1300)?
Lent to MPC, 2000–2005
CARE 199

L: 22.5 cm
W: 2.0 cm
D: 3.9 cm

Two sticks, one with squared head tightly wrapped with fiber cordage, the other, longer one largely unmodified and loosely bound to the shorter one. Longer stick is decorticated and has one snap-broken and splintered end, while the opposite end is tapered and burned. Traces of red ochre (possibly transferred from the cord) near the midpoint. Shorter stick features a worked head which is flattened and squared off, and which tapers to a rounded shaft. Opposite end is slightly tapered. Shaft of this stick is wrapped in excess of 60 times with dogbane or milkweed cordage. Cordage loops loosely over the longer stick only eight or nine times. Cordage is z-spun and s-twisted and exhibits irregular staining with red ochre in a manner indicating it was stained before the cord was wrapped. Cordage consists of two lengths joined with a reef knot. Both free ends of the cordage at this knot are tied in a double-overhand knot, probably to prevent fraying. Squared-off end of shorter stick has use wear in the form of polish and considerable accretions of oily-looking dirt.

Excellent condition; intact and complete. Traces of white lint (likely polyester fiberfill) are caught in the cordage. Stable.

Comments:
This could be an innocent pastiche: the stick with the squared head that appears to be a component of a snare was probably alone associated with the cordage, while the stick loosely held within the cordage loops may be an interpolation.

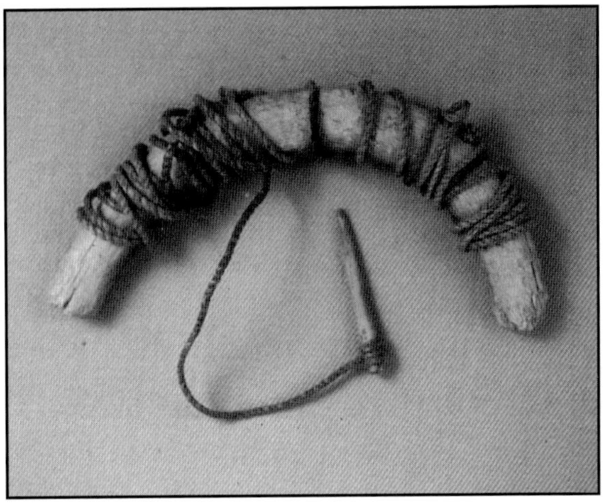

97 PART OF SNARE ASSEMBLAGE

Cottonwood, greasewood, and yucca
Agricultural Period
(Anasazi or Fremont, AD 1–1300)?
Lent to MPC, 2000–2005
CARE 202

L: 10.9 cm
W: 5.4 cm
D: 1.6 cm

Curved cottonwood stick wrapped 29 times with a piece of yucca cordage. Overall cordage length ca. 115 cm. Cordage consists of two separate lengths joined with a reef knot. One end of cordage is kinked and tucked under. The other end terminates in a knot tied around the blunt end of a sharpened piece of greasewood twig.

Excellent condition; intact and complete. Some cracking and splitting of cottonwood along grain. Dark gray stain on cottonwood near middle of arc. Staining and discoloration of cordage. Pattern of staining indicates it occurred before cordage was wrapped around stick. Flyspecks. Stable.

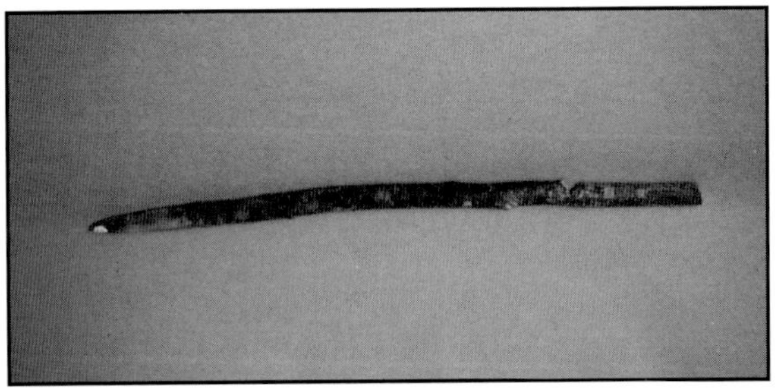

98 PART OF SNARE ASSEMBLAGE?

Unidentified wood
Historic (AD 1750–1900)?
Lent to MPC, 2000–2005
CARE 151

L: 38.3 cm
W: 1.6 cm
D: 1.2 cm

Slightly modified stick of unidentified wood, tapered on distal end and having deep notch and surface gouge near proximal end. Tapered end is peeled and exhibits use wear on tip. Proximal end, gouge, and notch appear to have been cut when tree was still alive as evidenced by partial healing.

Fair condition; intact and largely complete. Deep distal gouge and debarked portions may be damage by animal or insect. Shallow hairline cracks along grain in distal end. Scattered scratches, dark stains, and powdery light brown accretions (dirt, efflorescence?) on distal end. Bark intact over most of stick but lifting and prone to detachment in some areas. Weak, but stable.

99 FISH HOOKS AND LINE

Yucca, mammal long bone, wood, dogbane
Agricultural Period
(Anasazi or Fremont, AD 1–1300)?
Lent to Capitol Reef National Park
(On display at Visitor Center)
CARE 1662

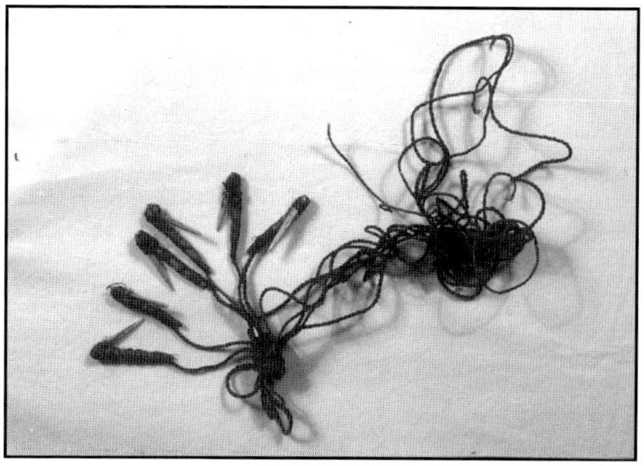

L: 17.0 cm
W: 10.5 cm
D: 1.4 cm

Six composite fish hooks and attached fishing line. Tangs of fish hooks are composed of small or medium-sized mammal long bone, bound with dogbane fiber to a twig, and the distal end is wrapped with yucca cordage. Cordage is fine (ca. 1.0–1.5 mm), z-spun and s-twisted. Total length of cordage ca. 60 cm. The six strands of cordage are tied together in a slip knot.

Excellent condition; intact and complete. One ply of cordage has frayed through near knot; companion strand is somewhat frayed. Ends of cordage are unraveling and frayed. Dogbane hafting has loosened and frayed in places. Fragile but stable.

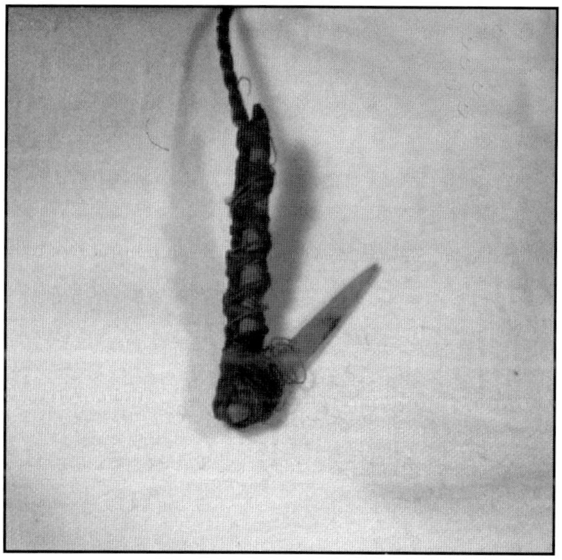

Detail.

Scooping Implements

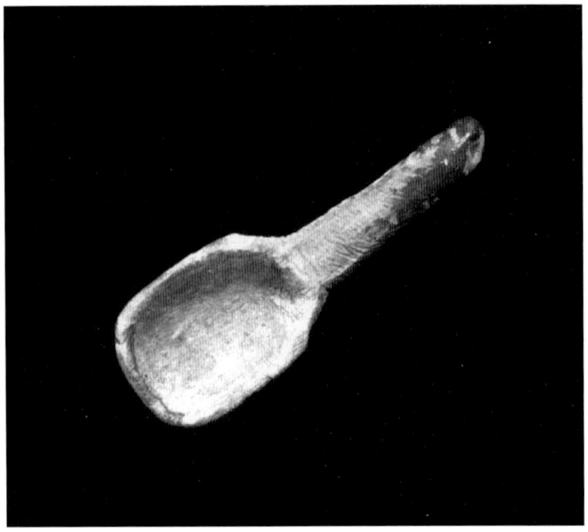

100 SPOON

Unidentified wood
Agricultural Period
(Anasazi or Fremont, AD 1–1300)?
Lent to Capitol Reef National Park
(On display at Visitor Center)
CARE 239

L: 12.5 cm
W: 4.5 cm
D: 2.0 cm

Wood spoon with square bowl and extended handle. Edges toward tip of bowl rounded, while edges toward handle more cursorily worked. Grooves run diagonally across handle and on sides of scoop near handle (tool marks, decoration?). Polish on handle from use.

Good condition; intact and complete. Obverse: loss on end of handle. Dirt accretion on inside of scoop. Scattered abrasions. Large stain (water?) in bowl that continues onto reverse. Reverse: cracks along corner of scoop; hairline cracks along grain. Stable.

101 BLADE OF COMPOSITE SHOVEL

Juniper?
Fremont, ca. AD 1050–1150
Lent to MPC, 2000–2005
CARE 36

L: 22.5 cm
W: 20.0 cm
D: 1.4 cm

Trapezoidal wood shovel with short handle. Scooping edge exhibits extensive bifacial wear. Traces of red tint on back of handle. Substantial soiling resembling dirt or clay on both faces and on handle (use wear?). Grooves on the handle may indicate point of attachment to the missing longer handle.

Poor condition; intact and partially complete (missing long handle). Obverse: open, thorough cracks on scooping edge and face due to use and/or weathering; numerous partial cracks, some blind, on front along the grain. Losses on viewer's right edge, edges of handle, and top edges (weathering and handling?). Charring. Reverse: significant delamination, insect(?) burrow holes, and water(?) stains. Chalky yellow and white accretions on front and back. Structurally stable but surface powdery.

Comments:
A composite shovel is one in which a long, separately made handle attaches to the shorter handle of the blade or pan. What survives here is only the lowest element of a shovel that, when attached to the long handle, could have been used while standing up. Separated from the long handle, it could have been used as a scoop.

A similar example of a composite shovel with a broken handle was recovered from the Scottsdale Site (42Em1769) in the San Rafael Swell area along with some digging sticks, net sticks, a phragmites bundle, and a fire drill. One of the sticks radiocarbon dated to ca. AD 1050–1150.[28]

Gunnerson reports that three cottonwood composite shovels and their long handles were recovered near a rock shelter about 200 feet above Minnie Maud Creek in Nine Mile Canyon, which he attributed to the Fremont.[29] He also reported a fourth composite shovel, much smaller but with a longer handle, derived from the fill of the Alvey Site (42Ka172), a rock shelter on a tributary of the Escalante River about 160 miles south of Nine Mile Canyon, which he attributed to the Anasazi, suggesting that "the Nine Mile shovels represent a Fremont elaboration upon such two-piece digging sticks."[30] All four shovels were surface finds.

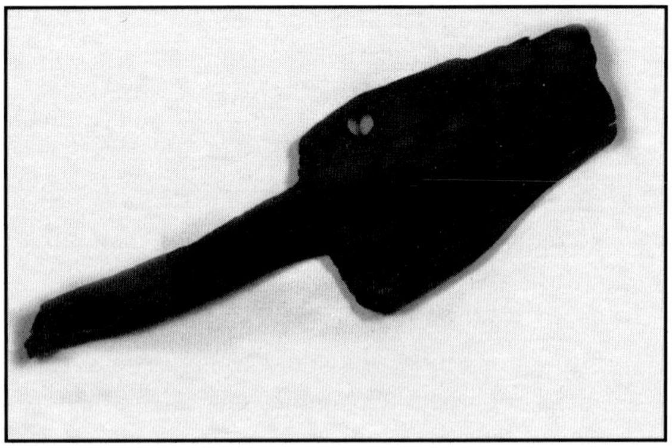

102 BLADE OF COMPOSITE SHOVEL?

Unidentified wood
Fremont, AD 1050–1150
Lent to Capitol Reef National Park
(On display at Visitor Center)
CARE 232

L: 55.0 cm
W: 17.0 cm
D: 3.0 cm

Paddle-shaped, wood shovel with rectangular "head" and short handle with broken tip, probably from a composite shovel. Quarter-sized hole drilled into upper portion of "head." Use wear along all edges.

Poor condition; intact and partially complete. Open, thorough cracks emanating from scooping edge along grain; numerous open, some blind, cracks along grain; scattered patches of crackling; scattered dents and scratches; insect furrows on reverse. Desiccated with significant delamination. Scattered chips on reverse of handle; scattered dark stains and dark spots (charring?). Stable.

103 FRAGMENT OF COMPOSITE SHOVEL?

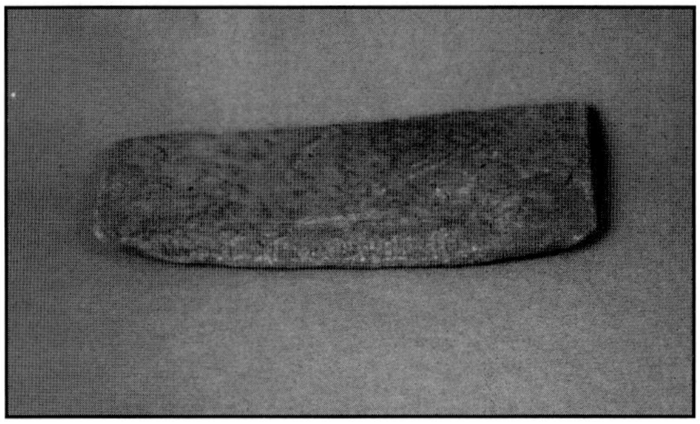

Cottonwood
Fremont, ca. AD 1050–1150
Lent to MPC, 2000–2005
CARE 41

L: 18.5 cm
W: 7.7cm
D: 1.0 cm

Flattened, rectangular section of a wooden implement preserving three intact edges with use wear, possibly a fragment of a composite shovel. One long edge (distal) exhibits the most wear, the other a clean break.

Poor condition; intact and partially complete. Clean break along proximal edge. Shallow cracks against grain on distal edge; losses along grain, especially on numbered side. Significant insect furrows and holes throughout. Scattered fly spots; water(?) staining. Stable.

Comments:
In material, curvature, thickness, and wear, this implement is very reminiscent of the small, square, cottonwood composite shovels found in Nine Mile Canyon and currently on exhibit at the College of Eastern Utah Prehistoric Museum. They were found embedded in the rock and interior sections of a collapsed Fremont cliff granary and possibly were used to mix and apply clay to the granary during construction.[31]

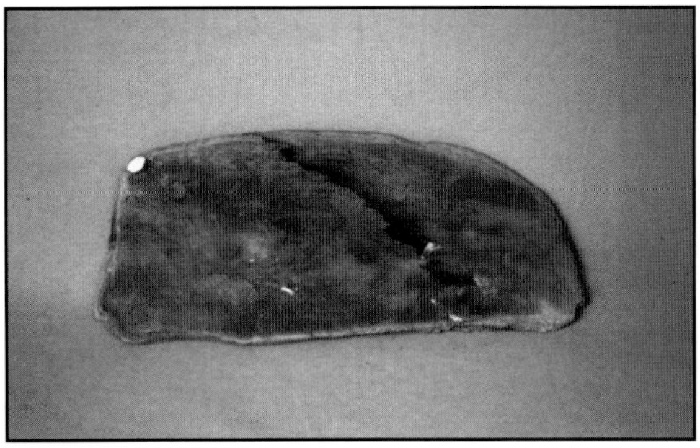

104 PADDLE OR SCOOP?

Pinyon or Juniper?
Anasazi (AD 500–1300)
Lent to MPC, 2000–2005
CARE 40

L: 22.4 cm
W: 10.8 cm
D: 1.0 cm

Rectangular section of flat wooden implement preserving three finished edges.

Good condition; intact and partially complete. Obverse: losses on edge; various accretions, insect burrow holes, and scattered fly spots. Reverse: delamination; scattered scratches and long dents (impact scars); resin-like accretion. Stable.

Comments:
Although this implement is fragmentary, it resembles the wooden platters from West Water Ruin in San Juan County.[32] The function of those platters is unknown, but they could have been used as paddles or scoops.

Digging Implements

105 DIGGING STICK

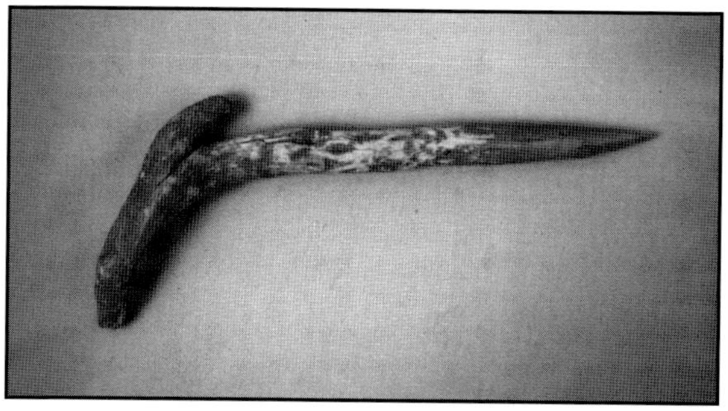

Greasewood?
Agricultural Period
(Anasazi or Fremont, AD 1–1300)?
Lent to MPC, 2000–2005
CARE 226

L: 37.7 cm
W: 12.5 cm
D: 2.3 cm

Wooden digging stick with "T"-shaped handle and attenuated point. Significant polishing (a stretch ca. 15 cm long) and stains on point and handle, apparently from use.

Good condition; intact and complete. Scattered hairline cracks along grain emanating from the knots; blind cracks on handle; scattered blind hairline cracks. Scattered losses of bark and cortex; exfoliation on both ends of handle and on digging point. Ancient loss (indicated by polish superimposing it) with associated cracks on digging point. Stable.

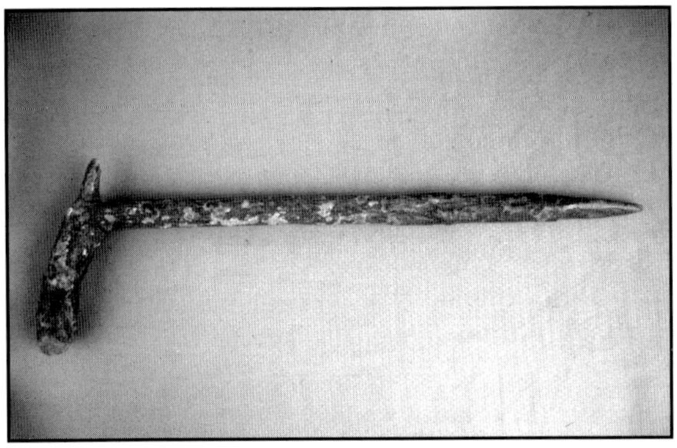

106 DIGGING STICK

Greasewood?
Agricultural Period
(Anasazi or Fremont, AD 1–1300)?
Lent to MPC, 2000–2005
CARE 8

L: 25.7 cm
W: 10.2 cm
D: 2.1 cm

Wooden digging stick with "T"-shaped handle and attenuated point. Significant use wear on point and handle resulting in smooth, heavy polish and associated soiling. Purplish stains generally over surface.

Fair condition; intact and nearly complete. Tip of point broken off. Wide, open, thorough cracks at the point and handle; numerous blind, hairline, and open cracks throughout shaft and handle; open blind cracks on handle—all also along grain. Delamination on tips of handle and on shaft just below the handle. Various accretions. Stable.

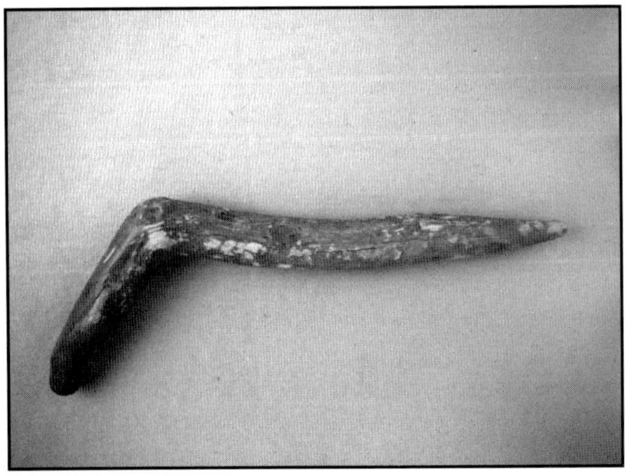

107 DIGGING STICK

Unidentified wood
Agricultural Period
(Anasazi or Fremont, AD 1–1300)
Lent to MPC, 2000–2005
CARE 9

L: 25.4 cm
W: 10.3 cm
D: 2.5 cm

Digging stick of cane-like wood with attenuated point. Considerable polish on handle, point worn smooth (use wear).

Fair condition; intact and complete. Numerous blind and some open cracks along grain; delamination on handle and shaft. Crackling on shaft; charring on handle and point; desiccation indicated by light weight and crackling. Losses on point and shaft. Crystalline efflorescence in bend of handle. Scattered peeling of bark. Resin-like accretion on shaft. Scattered fly spots. Stable.

108 DIGGING STICK

Unidentified wood
Agricultural Period
(Anasazi or Fremont, AD 1–1300)
Lent to Capitol Reef National Park
(On display at Visitor Center)
CARE 7

L: 46.5 cm
W: 10.0 cm
D: 3.0 cm

Long, wood digging stick with "T"-shaped handle and an attenuated tip. Significant polishing and soiling from use.

Good condition; intact and complete. Tip and handle particulating. Several open and some blind cracks along grain. Delamination on tips of handle. Scattered chips. Deep furrow on reverse. Black resin-like accretion. Stable.

Weaving Implements

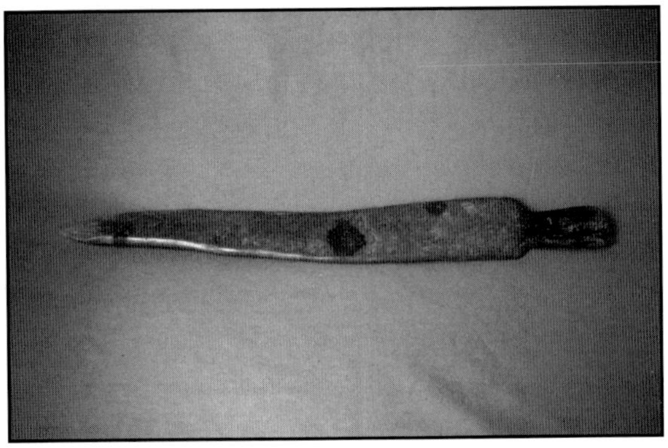

109 WEAVER'S BATTEN

Wood
Puebloan, Late Prehistoric/Early Historic
(AD 1300–1750)?
Lent to MPC, 2000–2005
CARE 233

L: 52.5 cm
W: 7.2 cm
D: 1.2 cm

Sword-shaped wood implement, probably a batten sword, with attenuated tip and extended, articulated grip. Extensive polish on blade and grip (use wear).

Good condition; intact and complete. Numerous hairline and open cracks along the grain and emanating from loss along grain. Splinters lifting along grain on handle and tip. Surface loss on end of blade not consistent with use wear (weathering?). Dents—some scattered, others concentrated in areas. Scratches along use edge, a few scattered fresh scratches near painted accession number. Shiny brown, resin-like accretion on blade. Water(?) stains on blade. Abundant fly spots. Stable.

Comments:
Mason published some Pueblo III examples of weaving swords resembling this one, although this one is probably not so early.[33] Battens were used to open the shed through which the weft is passed, to select warps needed to create the design, and to beat down the weft.

110 WEAVER'S TOOL?

Unidentified wood
Anasazi or Puebloan, AD 1000 or later
Lent to MPC, 2000–2005
CARE 42

L: 23.0 cm
W: 7.2 cm
D: 1.3 cm

Small, oblong, flattened wood plank with slight curvature (or warp?) preserving portions of four work edges. Traces of red pigment, especially concentrated on one long edge where original finish may have survived mostly intact. Use wear on all edges, but especially on reverse near number, where weathering has also caused loss.

Very poor condition; intact and nearly complete. On obverse, open blind cracks perpendicular to grain. On reverse, loss along grain: this is a long gouge or furrow down the center with lifting splinters prone to detachment. Thorough open cracks along grain on one end. Surface loss on both shorter ends with associated delamination and insect damage; scattered dents. Insect burrows(?). Water(?) stains on both faces. Weak.

<u>Comments</u>:
The size of this implement and the wear on all four work surfaces suggest it might have been a batten for a backstrap loom. There is no evidence of looms before AD 1000.[34]

Reverse.

Miscellaneous Wood

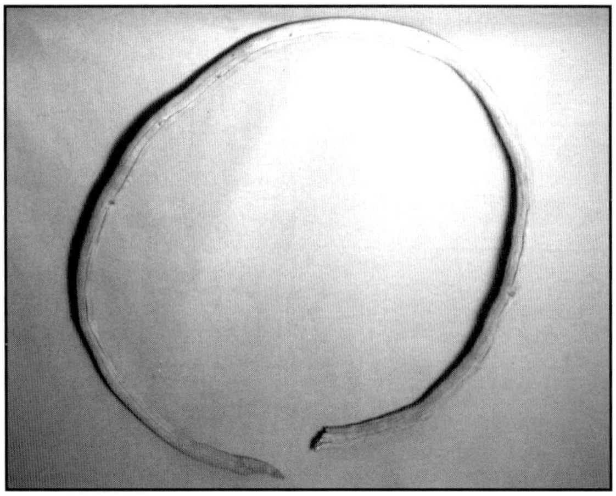

111 HOOP FRAME

Unidentified wood
Prehistoric (Basketmaker or Pueblo III, AD 1–1300) or Historic (AD1750–1850)
Lent to MPC, 2000–2005
CARE 69

L: 133.0 cm
Diam (when ring closed): 47.0 cm
D: 1.8 cm

Decorticated wood stick bent through heating or steaming into a ring shape. The ends terminate in breaks, but the configuration of these breaks suggests they could easily have been overlapped and bound to create a good join. The tension in the hoop does not preclude that it could have been joined in precisely this way.

Good condition; intact but incomplete. Numerous open, some blind, cracks following grain; significant delamination with associated splintering; deep crackling with black dirt accretions on inner side at midpoint. Differential coloring possibly due to differential exposure to light or dirt; near continuous line of dark discoloration running along inside. Scattered chalky white accretions on lighter side. Darker side: some cracks against the grain near opening (impact marks?); shiny resin-like spots. Fly spots and possibly other excrement (bat? rodent?) with associated stains on outside at midpoint. Stable.

Comments:
This desiccated wood ring may look like a plain, unmodified stick, yet it is decorticated—possibly as a result of use—and, in order to attain such a dramatic bend, heating or steaming had to be used. It is likely the ends were once joined to form a frame for a more complex artifact. The complete denudement of cortex and the powdery surface of the ring would be consistent wear if the ring had indeed been bound closed to support a network of warps and wefts or a lattice construction in its center.

There are several possibilities for its original function. Possibly it was the frame of a soft-back cradle board of Basketmaker type that lost its "spring" when the warps and wefts that supported the baby were lost. If so, it would date AD 1–700. Examples of such cradle boards are held in the collections of the Museum of Peoples and Cultures, one of which is lyre-shaped and the other elliptical.[35]

Because the shape of the Pectol-Lee ring is closer to a true circle, however, it more closely resembles two hoops, published by James Adovasio, from Antelope House, a predominantly Pueblo III-period site in Canyon De Chelley, northeastern Arizona.[36] These two hoops support an open weave, yucca and willow lattice-work center, and one, in particular, is closely analogous in size, shape, and in the manner the two ends are overlapped and bound. If the Pectol-Lee hoop is an example of such an artifact, it would probably date AD 1100–1300.

Adovasio suggested the latticed hoops from Antelope House may have been the "bottoms of some variety of collapsible containers."[37] In form and construction, however, they bear a striking resemblance to a pair of Eastern Shoshone model child's snowshoes with a *leather* lattice work collected on the Wind River Reservation in 1900, a type Shimkin reports the Ute also wore in Historic times, although usually in areas north of Capitol Reef.[38] Considering the Ute presence at Capitol Reef, however, it seems an Historic dating is also possible.

112 REWORKED IMPLEMENT

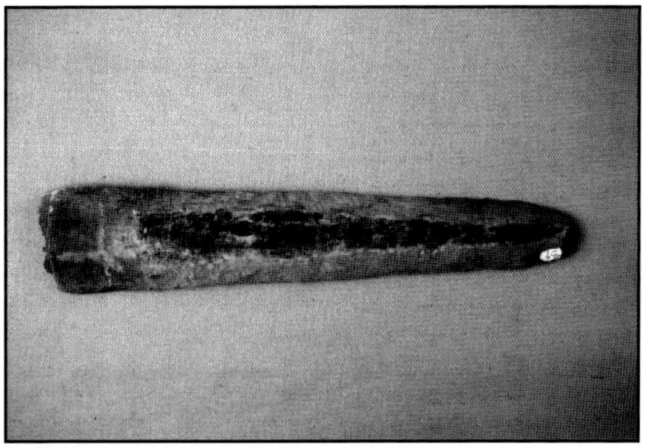

Unidentified wood
Historic (AD 1750–1900)?
Lent to MPC, 2000–2005
CARE 39

L: 18.5 cm
W: 3.6 cm
D: 1.4 cm

Crudely worked object resembling a modern toy sword or one end of a modern toy bow, made by laterally splitting a cylindrical object and reworking (beveling) the edges. Tool marks visible on beveled edges. Only a strip of original surface with natural knot hole survives—this strip, extending down the middle of the shaft, appears to be carbonized, and red pigment is discernible under the carbonized layer. At widest end, adjacent to a snap break and perpendicular to the grain, is a carved channel 2.0 cm wide, perhaps made contemporaneously with the beveling. Both this channel and the tip are soiled and slightly polished, as though through use.

Fair condition; intact and partially complete. Hairline crack along grain; cracks on reverse, splintering and losses along grain in association with the cut that laterally split the object. Resin-like accretion near channel on reverse and several stains. Yellow, powdery accretion near center on reverse; dark discoloration. Stable.

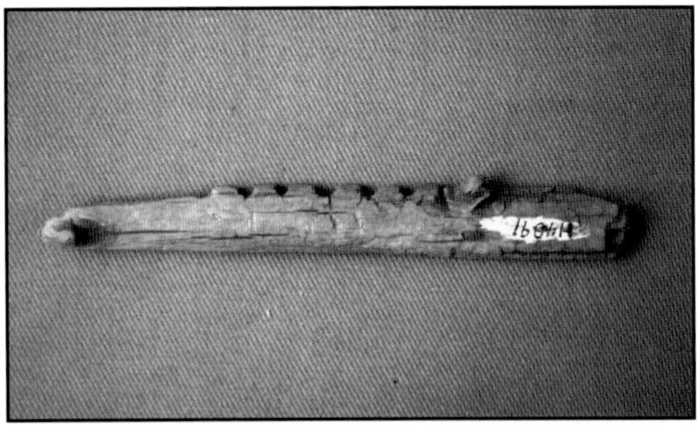

113 NOTCHED STICK

Unidentified wood
Late Prehistoric/Historic (ca. AD 1250–1900)?
Lent to MPC, 2000–2005
CARE H4891

L: 10.6 cm
W: 1.2 cm
D: 0.7 cm

Small wood artifact reminiscent of a rasp, laterally split with six complete and several partial notches.

Very poor condition; intact and partially complete. Open cracks along grain, sometimes with associated loss; numerous tiny cracks perpendicular to grain; crackling in recessed areas on split side; shallow indentations perpendicular to grain. Severely desiccated. Structurally weak.

114 STICK WITH GRASS PADDING

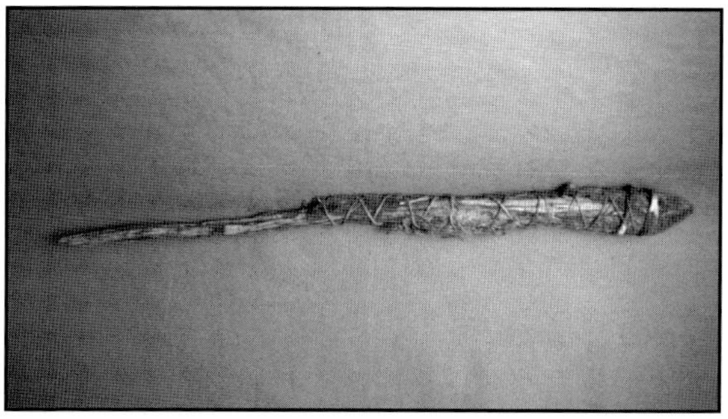

Sagebrush wood, grass, dogbane, willow
Anasazi, perhaps before ca. AD 500?
Lent to MPC, 2000–2005
CARE 238

L: 52.5 cm
Diam: 4.3 cm

A sagebrush stick, partially decorticated (or rubbed off) and irregularly covered for two thirds its length with dried grass. Near the wrapped end undecorticated willow twigs (one whole and one split) are cursorily wrapped around the stick; and, about two thirds the way down the stick, there is a third willow twig. The grass and twig mass is secured with dogbane cordage (z-spun, s-twisted; diameter ca. 1–2 mm) wrapped in a criss-cross pattern around the fiber. Cordage consists of three different lengths which have been joined with reef (square) knots. The free ends of the cordage have not been tied, but have been tucked back underneath the cordage where it passes around the stick. One end of the cordage has been tied with an overhand knot, probably to prevent raveling.

Good condition; intact and largely complete. Stick is abraded, embrittled, cracked, and checking. Cracking and cortex exfoliation on willow twig, polish from abrasion. Fiber exfoliating. Fraying and raveling of cordage. Reddish-purple stain, similar to that on some of the decorated baskets in the collection (cat. nos. 28–31), occurs spottily the entire length of the stick and in a few places on the cordage, but not on the grass. Cordage is frayed and broken at one point where the staining is evident. Dirt and fly spots throughout. One piece of z-spun cotton single is caught under the cord. Unstable (cordage prone to detachment).

Comments:
This padded stick resembles several artifacts from Cowboy Cave, an Anasazi site in southeast Utah. Dubbed "problematical objects,"[39] they are lengths of *phragmites* reeds, the longest of which is 27.5 cm. They are wrapped at one end with fibrous wads, and several have fibrous bark or thin strips of split wood spiraling some distance up the reed. They were found in the layers designated IV (ca. 1740–1300 BC) and V (ca. AD 5–515).

WORKED HORN

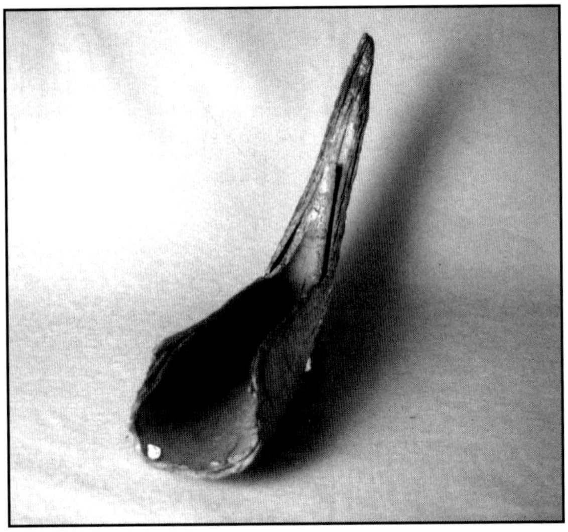

115 SCOOP OR LADLE

Bighorn sheep horn
Agricultural Period
(Anasazi or Fremont, AD 1–1300)?
Lent to MPC, 2000–2005
CARE 190

L: 27.5 cm
W: 7.4 cm
D: 6.9 cm

Horn sheath roughly shaped to form a crude scoop with a handle. The tip of the horn has been adapted for the handle, while the base of the horn serves as the scoop (bowl). The horn's base was left intact to give the bowl high walls and maximum capacity. Tool marks visible especially where the underside of the bowl was thinned and shaped. One deep groove in bowl near scooping edge may be a tool mark, possibly unintentional. Discoloration along scooping edge and also on handle (use wear?)

Poor condition; intact and complete. Significant delamination due to weathering. Open cracks along grain in upper area of inner bowl area, crackling on interior of bowl. Scattered fly spots. Stable.

116 FLAKER

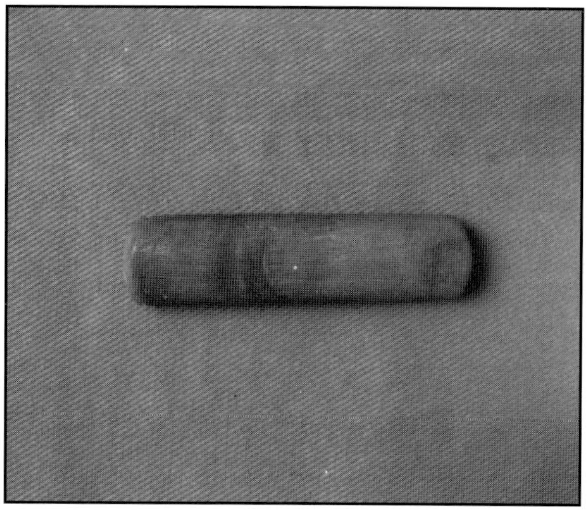

Bighorn sheep horn
Probably Agricultural Period
(Anasazi or Fremont, AD 1–1300)
Lent to MPC, 2000–2005
CARE H4894

L: 6.0 cm
W: 1.5 cm
D: 1.1 cm

Small horn flaker fashioned from bighorn sheep horn. Polished surface, rounded edges, and slightly worn end with accompanying scratches (use wear?).

Very good condition; intact and complete. Numerous scratches (some long) especially concentrated on non-flaking face. Stable.

Comments:
Scholars know that the Anasazi used horn pressure flakers, but new information seems to indicate the Fremont did as well. According to Phil Geib,[40] a small cave on the Kaiparowits Plateau preserved both a horn pressure flaker and Fremont pottery. An AMS ^{14}C on collagen extracted from a tiny sample of the horn flaker radiocarbon dated to AD 960–1040 (1030 +/- 40 BP, calibrated two-sigma range)—well within the time of Fremont occupancy for the plateau and before Anasazi occupation.

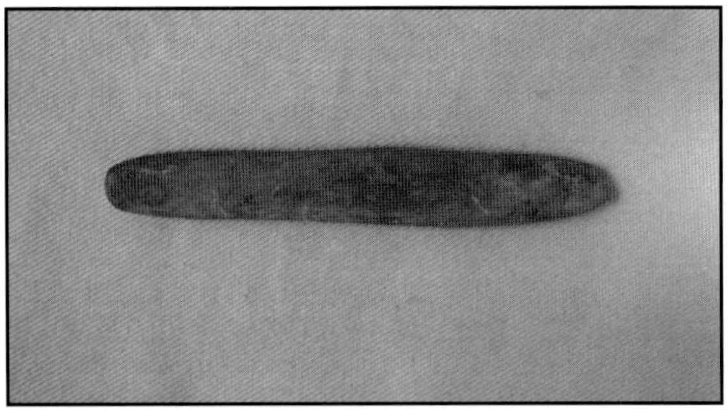

117 FLAKER[41]

Bighorn sheep horn
Probably Basketmaker II (100 BC–AD 500)
Lent to MPC, 2000–2005
CARE 48

L: 9.7 cm
W: 1.4 cm
D: 0.8 cm
Weight: 8.9 g

Small pressure flaking tool of bighorn sheep horn cut and abraded to shape. Original horn exterior evident on one face. Horn exterior polished and slightly discolored; ends also somewhat polished except where disrupted by pits and grooves from use of the tool in stone working. Other use wear may include warping, slight discoloration, and indentations possibly corresponding to placement of thumb and fingertips during flaking act.

Fair condition; intact and complete. Several cracks against grain; few scattered chips; several scratches. Dark reddish stain on non-worked face; resin-like accretion on reverse. Stable.

Comments:
This artifact is similar in size and form to tools Phil Geib has identified as horn pressure flakers from Basketmaker II contexts of northeast Arizona and southeast Utah. In contrast to the specimens previously examined by Geib, the ends of this specimen exhibit only a slight amount of use wear, and the wear is concentrated towards the center of the ends rather than their margins. Silica fragments might be embedded in one end, but a magnification higher than 60x is needed to verify this.

118 MULTIPURPOSE IMPLEMENT

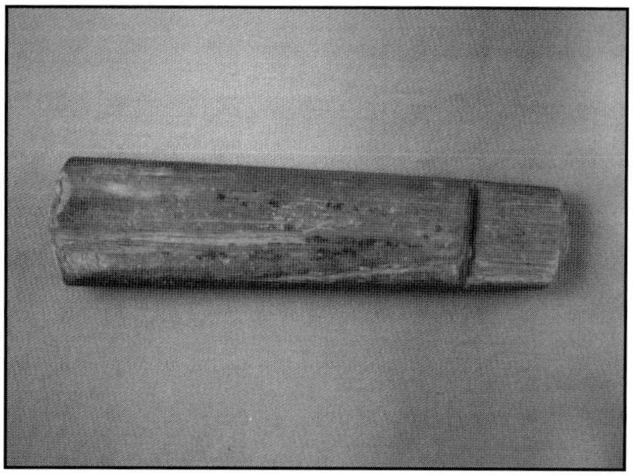

Bighorn sheep horn
Agricultural Period
(Anasazi or Fremont, AD 1–1300)?
Lent to MPC, 2000–2005
CARE 43

L: 16.1 cm
W: 3.6 cm
D: 1.8 cm
Weight: 112.3 g

Long rectangular section of a bighorn sheep horn used as a tool and probable 'core' for creating smaller horn artifacts. Widest end of the tool exhibits heavy compressional deformation and crushing of the horn along with pitting and incised linear grooves along the grain most of the length. Several silica fragments, both orangish and colorless, are embedded into the tool end as determined by 60x magnification. One square piece of horn has been chiseled or spalled out, and a chert fragment occurs in this gouge.

Fair condition; intact and complete. Badly weathered as indicated by delamination and numerous cracks along and against the grain on outer surface. Two corners chipped; scattered scratches. On the reverse are scattered accretions of pine pitch, especially in two channels. Small black and white accretions on sides. Stable.

Comments:
One of the principal functions of the tool was as a percussion flaker in stone tool reduction, as evidenced by the compressional deformation and related use wear. The horn easily has sufficient weight to have functioned as a billet for percussion flaking of stone bifaces, especially if using heat-treated materials. The incised linear grooves may reflect use for sharpening wood or bone implements or a cursory attempt to further sub-divide the horn lengthwise. The carefully spalled area suggests deliberate removal of one or more rectangular slivers for use in making other implements.

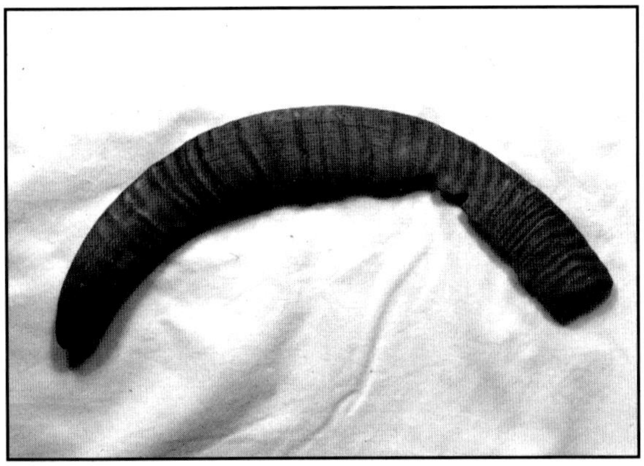

119 IMPLEMENT

Bighorn sheep horn
Agricultural Period
(Anasazi or Fremont, AD 1–1300)?
Lent to Capitol Reef National Park
(On display at Visitor Center)
CARE 256

L: 29.5 cm
W: 4.2 cm
D: 1.3 cm

Split, sickle-shaped, bighorn sheep horn with hole drilled in distal end. An indentation may be compression damage caused by hand during use. Significant polish and soiling from use particularly along edges.

Good condition; intact and complete. Numerous hairline cracks along grain. Serious delamination on reverse and distal end. Stable.

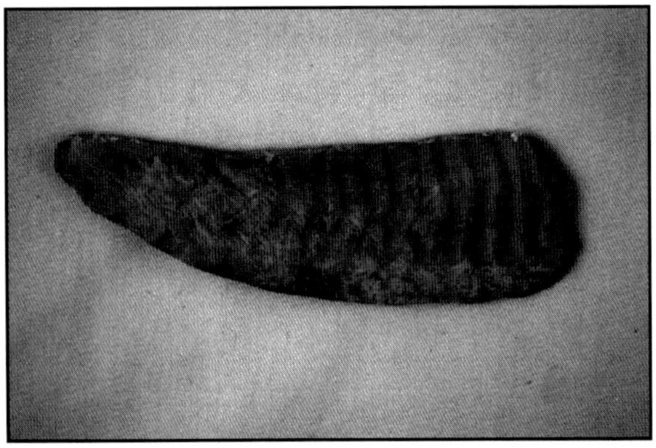

120 IMPLEMENT

Bighorn sheep horn
Agricultural Period
(Anasazi or Fremont, AD 1–1300)?
Lent to MPC, 2000–2005
CARE 71

L: 15.2 cm
W: 4.9 cm

Portion of one surface of a horn of a female bighorn sheep. Tool marks. Yellow and red-orange accretions on ridged side may be ochre. Dorsal side abraded from use resulting in slight beveling of edge. Polish on proximal end (use?).

Fair condition; intact and complete(?). Small hairline cracks emanating from ventral edge. Slight delamination on distal end. Charring with associated checking on inside surface. Stable.

WORKED ANTLER

121 SCOOP?

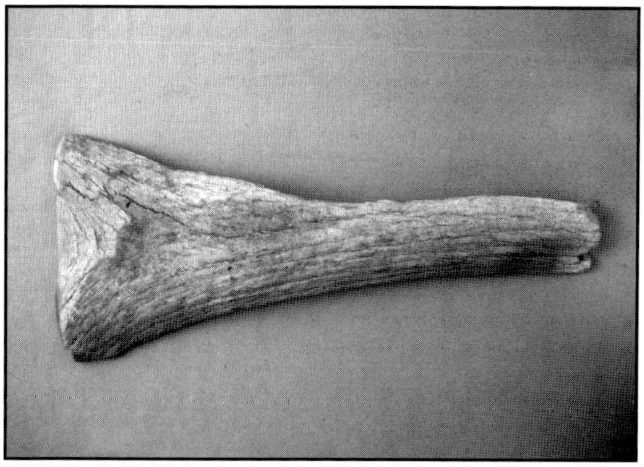

Elk antler
Agricultural Period
(Anasazi or Fremont, AD 1–1300)?
Lent to MPC, 2000–2005
CARE 259

L: 27.7 cm
W: 11.2 cm
D: 1.4 cm

A halved elk antler modified for use as a scoop or small shovel. Fourth point tine split off at fork of tine, with juncture of tines corresponding to bowl of the implement. Abundant polish and scratches on the lateral edges and distal end (use).

Fair condition; intact and complete. Severely weathered with numerous cracks running along grain. A few areas of localized crystalline efflorescence on both faces. Scattered fly spots. Stable.

122 DIGGING STICK

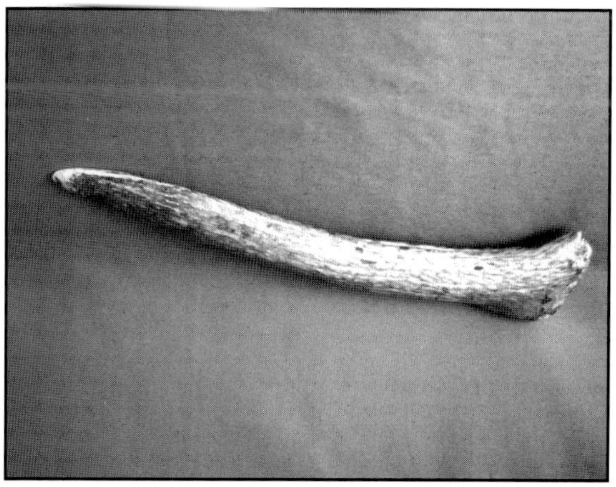

Elk antler
Agricultural Period
(Anasazi or Fremont, AD 1–1300)?
Lent to MPC, 2000–2005
CARE 258

L: 37.6 cm
W: 9.4 cm
D: 4.0 cm

Tine of elk antler with multiple tiny scratches and significant polishing from use, particularly on distal end.

Good condition; intact and complete. Cracks along the grain and charring on proximal end. Shiny yellow resin on distal end. Stable.

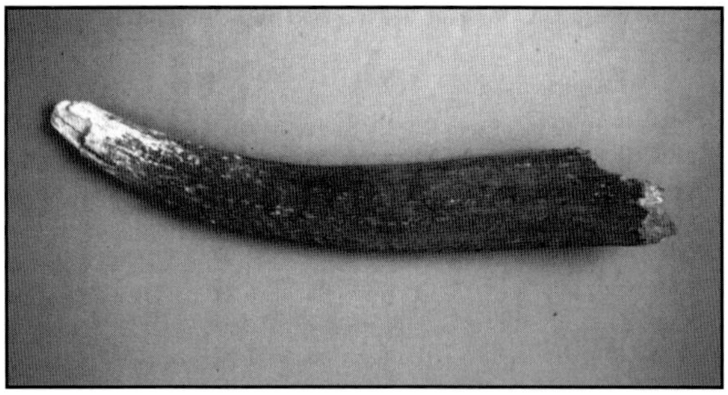

123 IMPLEMENT (DIGGING STICK?)

Elk antler
Agricultural Period
(Anasazi or Fremont, AD 1–1300)
Lent to MPC, 2000–2005
CARE 99

L: 26.0 cm
W: 4.2 cm
D: 3.3 cm

Elk antler tine with weathered distal end. Polish on shaft, possibly from handling.

Fair condition; intact and largely complete. Open and hairline cracks along and against grain on distal end. Losses on point at distal end; scattered abrasions. Shiny yellow and black accretions on distal end. Scattered fly spots. Stable.

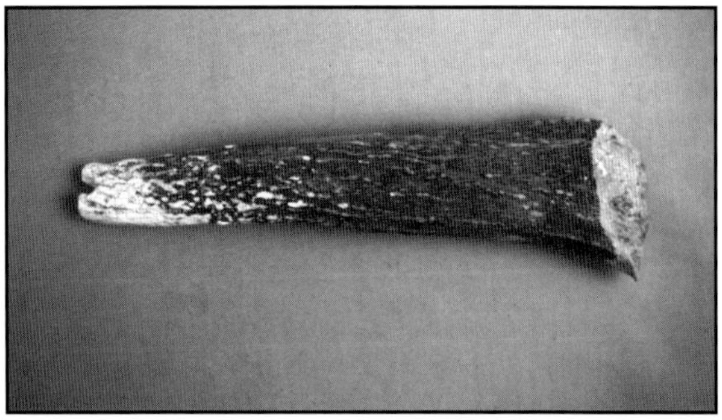

124 IMPLEMENT (DIGGING STICK?)

Elk antler
Agricultural Period
(Anasazi or Fremont, AD 1–1300)?
Lent to MPC, 2000–2005
CARE 98

L: 22.5 cm
W: 6.1 cm
D: 3.0 cm

Elk antler tine with distal end missing, exposing antler core. Polish on natural protuberances (use wear?). Scratches (tool marks?) on proximal end.

Fair condition; intact and largely complete. Scattered thorough and hairline cracks. Significant weathering on distal end. Stable.

125 MULTIPURPOSE IMPLEMENT

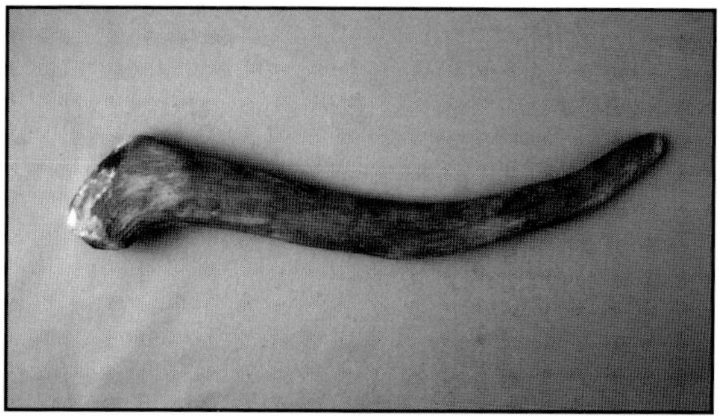

Elk antler
Agricultural Period
(Anasazi or Fremont, AD 1–1300)?
Lent to MPC, 2000–2005
CARE 257

L: 35.2 cm
W: 6.6 cm
D: 3.8 cm

Tine of elk antler with considerable polish, scratches, and impact dents. Discoloration on one side perhaps due to handling.

Fair condition; intact and complete. Blind hairline cracks along grain near distal end and along grain of shaft. Proximal end shows charring. Scattered fly spots. Stable.

Comments:
The wear on this implement is consistent with use as a digging stick, club, and fire tender. The pointed tip is highly polished indicating use as a digging stick. Use wear on the shaft of the antler indicates it was gripped in the manner of a club and this seems confirmed by the multiple impact marks on the proximal end. Localized charring on the proximal end suggests it had controlled contact with coals.

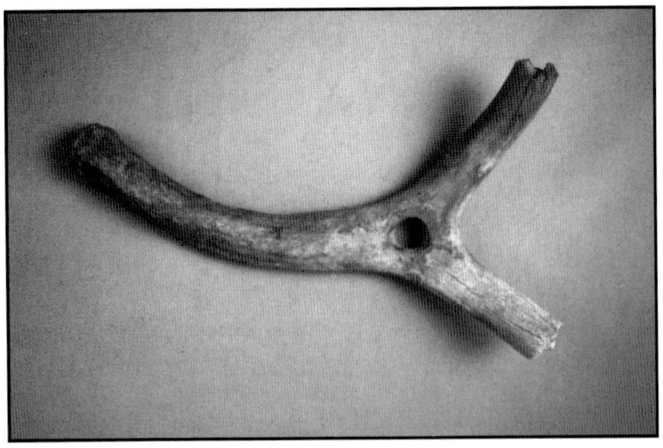

126 SHAFT STRAIGHTENER

Deer antler?
Late Prehistoric, ca. 16th century AD?
Lent to MPC, 2000–2005
CARE 31

L: 21.4 cm
W: 1.3 cm
D: 2.9 cm

Mule deer(?) antler preserving two tines with hole drilled just below fork of tines. Wear and polish in hole consistent with use as a shaft straightener; polish on handle from use.

Good condition; intact and complete. One tine bleached and weathered with associated blind hairline cracks along grain. Hairline cracks emanating from distal end of other tine; scattered chips on both tines. Scratches on ventral side near hole. Water(?) stains on tines. Stable.

Comments:
A good parallel for this is a shaft straightener in the Gordon Creek bundle at the College of Eastern Utah Prehistoric Museum in Price, Utah, which radiocarbon dated to AD 1551.[42]

127 SCRAPER?

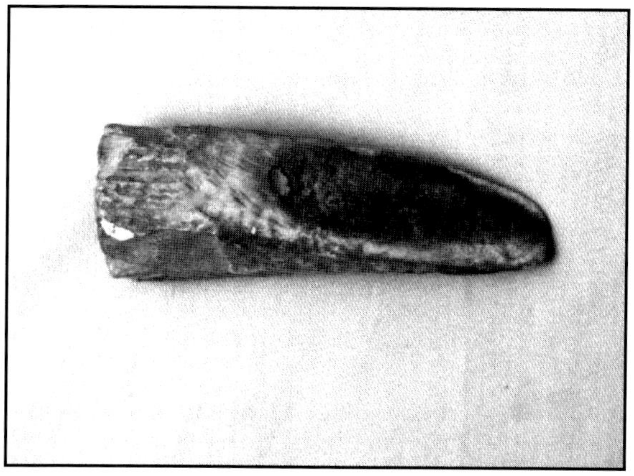

Elk antler
Late Prehistoric, ca. 16th century AD?
Lent to MPC, 2000–2005
CARE 44

L: 12.2 cm
W: 4.5 cm
D: 4.5 cm

Wedge-shaped portion of an elk antler with channels cut out bilaterally, suggesting previous hafting. Significant bi-facial use wear consistent with grating (de-fleshing?). Top abraded from use resulting in polish. Tool marks present on underside.

Good condition; intact and complete. Sun-bleached and weathered. Charring near edge of top and on abraded area on underside. Stable.

Comments:
The end of this scraper is highly reminiscent of an antler adze scraper in the Gordon Creek bundle at the College of Eastern Utah Prehistoric Museum in Price, Utah. The bundle radiocarbon dated to the 16th century (AD 1551).[43]

128 IMPLEMENT

Antler
Agricultural Period
(Anasazi or Fremont, AD 1–1300)?
Lent to MPC, 2000–2005
CARE 32

L: 6.7 cm
D: 2.8 cm

Section of antler broken at one end and resulting in two peaks surrounding a partially hollow core; other end abraded, resulting in wedge-shape.

Very poor condition; intact. Severe weathering resulting in numerous cracks (some open) along the grain, bleaching of surface, and particulation. Rodent gnawing. Unstable.

WORKED HIDE

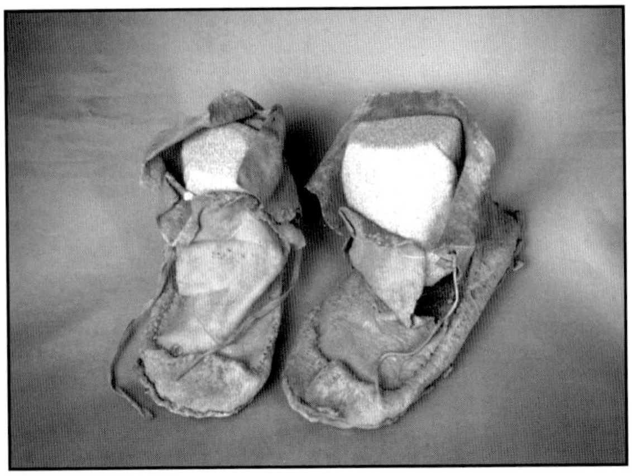

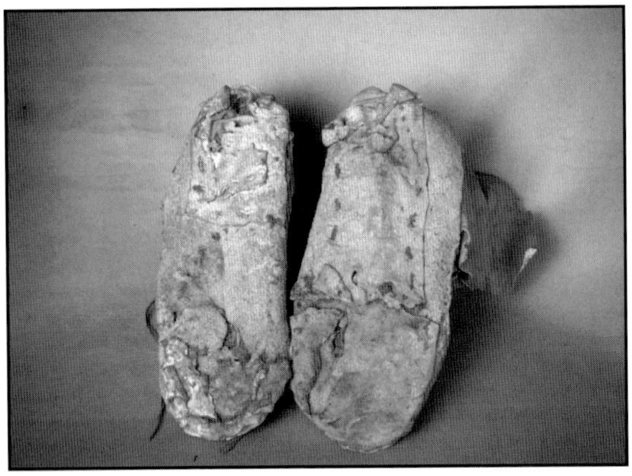

Underside.

129 MOCCASINS

Tanned hide
Fremont? Ca. AD 1100
CARE 193

L: 25.0 cm
W: 10.3 cm

Pair of moccasins constructed of three pieces of tanned hide: one thick piece for entire sole that also cups up to cover the toe, one thinner piece comprising the upper panel, and another thin piece comprising the back of the heel. These sections are sewn together with sinew cordage. Both moccasins were originally laced by means of a leather lace anchored to each side of the ankle. On the proper right moccasin, both laces survive, and each preserve their sinew stitch "anchors." On the other moccasin, only the proper right survives, and it is anchored by means of a knot. Ancient alterations: one small leather patch (L: 2.5 cm) stitched on, apparently to expand the width of the toe area; repairs consisting of four patches sewn with sinew cordage on the sole of the right foot and three on the sole of the left foot. Several large pieces of leather are stained with red ochre(?). Grass padding inside moccasins. Soiling and stains consistent with use.

Fair condition; intact and largely complete. Scattered small lacunae. Significant fraying resulting from abrasions on soles. Creasing. Scattered black accretions (pitch?). Stable.

<u>Comments</u>:
This style of moccasin would not be considered typical of either the Fremont or the Anasazi, but a sample taken from one of the moccasins radiocarbon dated to ca. AD 1100,[44] suggesting range in prehistoric footwear could be more variable than previously expected. The grass that pads the inside of the mocassins is reminiscent of an isolated mass of grass (cat. no. 19) also included in the collection.

130 CHILD'S SANDAL

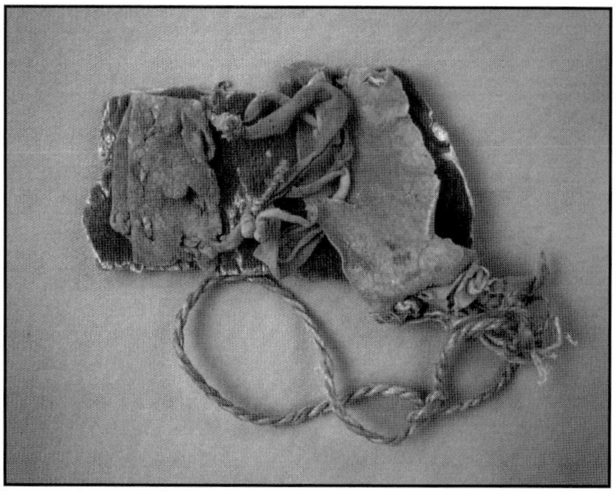

Bighorn sheep, bison or bear, juniper
Late Prehistoric/Historic (ca. AD 1250–1900)?
Lent to MPC, 2000–2005
CARE 242

L: 14.8 cm
W: 8.0 cm
D: 0.6 cm

Juvenile, open toed, left foot sandal with bison hide, fur side-up and bighorn sheep hide straps, possibly mate to ensuing entry. Preserves hide toe strap; two or three thin, hide ankle straps; and an additional s-spun, z-twisted juniper cordage ankle strap. These straps are attached to the sandal by sinew. There are two ancient repairs consisting of hide patches attached with s-spun, z-twisted sinew, one to heel of sole and the other along outside edge of heel.

Fair condition; intact and complete. Badly embrittled, desiccated. Black accretions on bottom of sole and top of toe strap; scattered red stains on toe and ankle straps. Stable.

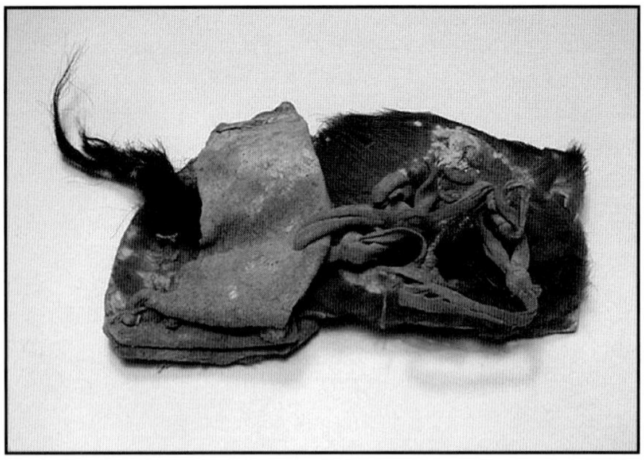

131 CHILD'S SANDAL

Bighorn sheep, bison or bear, human hair
Late Prehistoric/Historic (ca. AD 1250–1900)?
Lent to MPC, 2000–2005
CARE 241

L: 14.8 cm
W: 7.5 cm

Juvenile, open-toed, right foot of sandal with bison or bear hide, fur side up, as sole of sandal, and bighorn sheep hide straps, possibly mate to preceding. Preserves wide, leather toe strap with thin circular ankle strap attached to it by a knot. Human hair cordage (z-spun, s-twisted) extends out from under the toe strap. Straps attached to sole by s-spun, z-twisted sinew cordage stitching. Warping resulting in convex shape of sandal due to use(?). Ancient repair consisting of hide patch sewn to underside of ball of foot with sinew cordage stitches. Hair rubbed off from use in toe and arch of foot area. Grime accretions and incrustations on superior of sole (use).

Fair condition; intact and largely complete. Badly embrittled, desiccated; delamination; fraying and raveling of human hair cordage. White chalk-like accretions on interior of sole (efflorescence?). Unstable (hair slipping).

Comments:
A length of human hair cordage catalogued above (cat. no. 20) may be an extension of the hair cordage of this sandal.

132 SOLE OF SANDAL

Bison hide?
Late Prehistoric/Historic (ca. AD 1250–1900)?
Lent to MPC, 2000–2005
CARE 196

L: 15.5 cm
W: 9.4 cm
D: 1.6 cm

A roughly rectangular slab of thick, cardboard-like hide, perhaps bison, probably the heel and ball parts of a sandal sole. Preserves s-spun, z-twisted sinew stitching throughout. Ancient repairs consisting of three patches on underside of sole. Significant soiling from wear, particularly on heel and ball of foot, with associated compression damage and delamination.

Poor condition; intact and partially complete. Losses throughout due to insect damage; significant fraying resulting in erosion of surface on underside. Resin accretion on upper side in viewer's left toe area. Weathering with associated embrittlement. Stable.

Comments:
The fibrous texture of this and the ensuing hide fragment, along with the felting and severe delamination observed, are consistent with wear patterns of bison hide.[45]

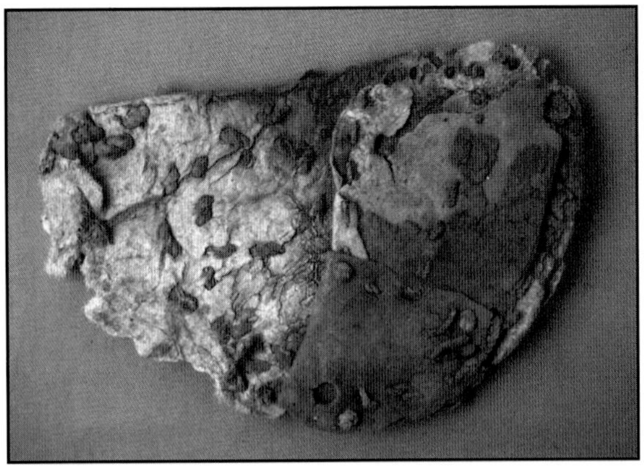

133 SOLE OF SANDAL

Bison hide?
Late Prehistoric/Historic (ca. AD 1250–1900)?
Lent to MPC, 2000–2005
CARE 261

L: 17.5 cm
W: 11.5 cm

A roughly rectangular slab of thick, cardboard-like hide, perhaps bison, preserving toe cover for right foot sandal, possibly mate to preceding. S-spun, z-twisted sinew cordage stitching woven throughout sandal. Ancient repairs consisting of several patches to bottom of sole. Significant use wear: soiling and grime, compression damage, and delamination.

Poor condition; intact and partially complete. Weathering with associated embrittlement and fraying and loss of fibers of leather. Significant insect damage. White, chalk-like accretions (efflorescence?) on superior of sole. Stable but weak (fibers exfoliating).

134 LEATHER PANEL

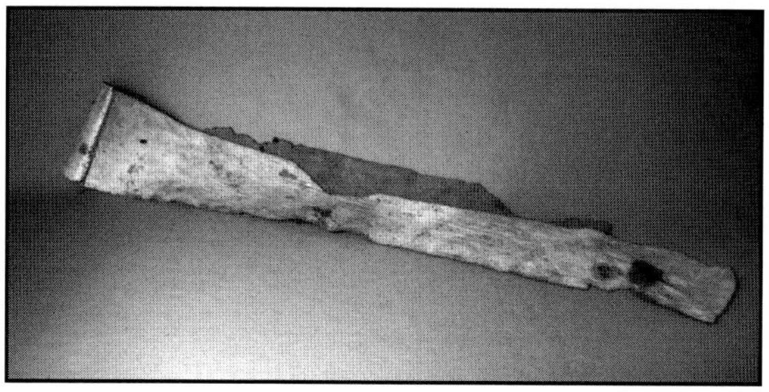

Bighorn sheep or deer hide?
Late Historic, 19th century AD
Lent to MPC, 2000–2005
CARE 143

L: 138.0 cm
W: 11.0 cm

Two tanned leather strips stitched together at ends with s-spun, z-twisted sinew cordage to form one long piece.

Fair to good condition; intact and complete. Insect damage resulting in scattered losses. Various scattered dark stains on both sides. Soiling on hair side. Resin stains on flesh side. Stable.

Comments:
In width, length, and size this leather article and the three that follow roughly correspond to the type of bandolier Native Americans have sometimes included with ceremonial wear. Late Historical bandoliers are sometimes highly decorated with beads.[46]

This excerpt from a typed draft of a history of Wayne County, written by Ephraim Pectol sometime after 1926, records an anecdotal comment about a bundle of hides in the collection, although it is not known which hides he was referencing:

> Next comes the interesting roll of burial robes made of tanned elk hide, sheep skin, and antelop [sic]. Near these was the grave of a small child, bons [sic] not intact . . . . These skins are the property of Earl F. Behunin and E. P. Pectol, and they, the skins, along with the shields are preserved in the L. D. S. Church Museum in Salt Lake City, Utah, only as a loan.[47]

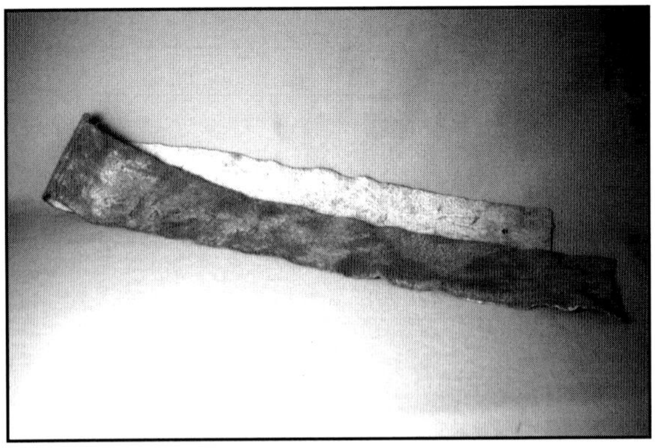

135 LEATHER PANEL

Elk or bison?
Historic (AD 1750–1900)?
Lent to MPC, 2000–2005
CARE 144

L: 138.0 cm
W: 12.0 cm
D: 2.0–2.5 cm

Two thick, tanned leather strips (one is ca. 4 cm wider than the other) stitched together at ends with s-spun, z-twisted sinew cordage to form one long piece.

Fair condition; intact and complete. Loss of epidermal layer in scattered areas. Scattered abrasions with associated soiling. Yellowish stains on hair side. Stable.

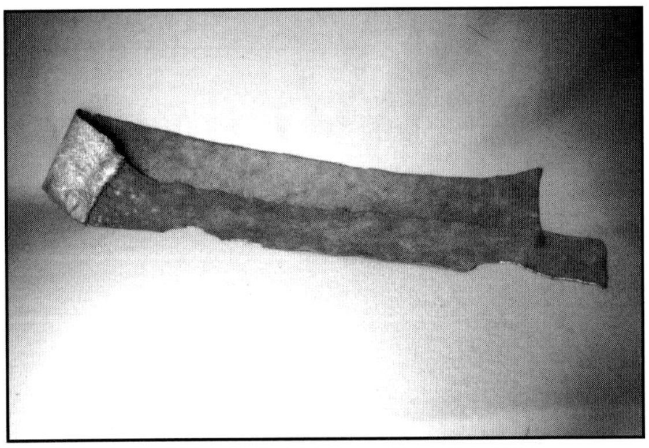

136 LEATHER PANEL

Bighorn sheep or deer?
Historic (AD 1750–1900)?
Lent to MPC, 2000–2005
CARE 145

L: 138.0 cm
W: 11.0 cm

Two tanned leather strips sewn together to form one long piece. The flesh side of one is sewn to the hair side of the other. S-spun, z-twisted sinew stitches. Traces of red-orange accretions (ochre?).

Poor condition; intact and complete. Insect damage resulting in losses on edges. Scattered losses in epidermal layer. Strong (tanning?) smell. Stable.

137 LEATHER PANEL

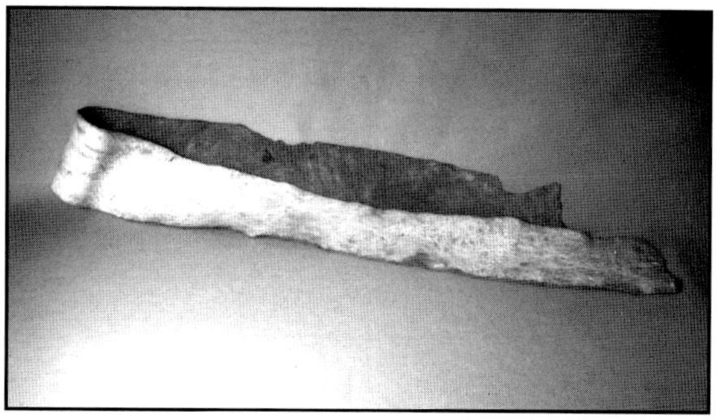

Bighorn sheep or deer?
Late Prehistoric/Historic, 17th century AD or later?
Lent to MPC, 2000–2005
CARE 1602

L: 147.0 cm
W: 10.0 cm

Single long piece of tanned hide with scattered patches of dark red and orange pigment.

Fair condition; intact and complete. Insect damage resulting in losses on edges. Abrasions with associated soiling stains. Scattered dark stains. Strong smell. Stable.

138 REWORKED GARMENT

Bighorn sheep
Original garment: Historic (AD 1750–1900)
Probably reworked in modern times
Lent to MPC, 2000–2005
CARE 142

L: 47.0 cm
W: 36.0 cm

Proper left yoke of an adult garment fashioned from an older, well tanned, hide shirt. At least two phases of work are evident. Belonging to original phase of work: seam scars along the center where a decorative placket was originally located; two holes at the head of the opening, apparently for lacing thongs to close the opening. Faint black and white decorations on red ochre background may be contemporaneous with the original phase. Belonging to next phase(s) of work: line of the shoulder; arm hole trimmed for a set-in sleeve; curved neckline; current center front opening; an irregular hole in pectoral area to viewer's right; modern pin holes. The edges associated with the later phase(s) of work are embrittled and have a dark gray sheen. The edge of the hole in the pectoral area has the same characteristics. Intact patches of white and tan hair, including guard hair remaining of original hide.

Fair condition; intact but incomplete. Insect damage resulting in lacunae, losses. Soiling. Stable.

Comments:
This yoke was probably cut in modern times from a genuine, late Historical leather shirt and deliberately made to look like a fragment of an old garment, as in a ruse. It was cut down from a larger, heavily used garment, possibly an old, leather "mountain man" shirt. The original garment had sleeves and a center front opening decorated with a placket and closed with a lacing thong. Not only was the "new," recut garment patterned from a piece of leather of insufficient size to complete the yoke, but it was never worn nor attached to any other part of clothing, as is indicated by the lack of any trace of stitching or lacing holes along the shoulder, arm hole, or side. The dark sheen and embrittlement of the edges of the garment's perimeter and of the pectoral hole are contemporaneous but anomalous—they cannot be explained through normal patterns of cutting, weathering, handling, or wear. The dark sheen on these edges may result from a soft, charcoal lead pencil such as that sometimes used to trace the outline of a garment from a pattern. Or, they may result from an unusual method of cutting the garment (possibly involving burning?), or from an oil or other substance rubbed into the edges for unknown purpose (seal the edges? give freshly cut edges an aged look?). The modern pin holes could have resulted from pinning the article to a surface for display or, perhaps, served as an aid for reworking in modern times.

139 HIDE FRAGMENT

Bighorn sheep
Late Prehistoric, 16th–17th century AD?
Lent to MPC, 2000–2005
CARE 34

L: 13.9 cm
W: 9.8 cm

Small, tanned hide fragment with patches of fur remaining. Reverse is felt-like and stained with dark red ochre(?). One side preserves an elongated, trapezoidal compression in the felt-like surface, possibly a decoration achieved by rubbing white pigment into the skin with a bone or wood implement.

Fair condition; intact but incomplete. Small lacunae and frayed edges (insect damage?). Abrasion resulting in loss of felt on flesh side. Scattered white accretions. Stable.

Comments:
This hide fragment and the one following have features resembling two nearly complete decorated bison robes from Nine Mile Canyon and a third bison robe from Gordon Creek, all now in the College of Eastern Utah Prehistoric Museum.[48] These larger hides were also thoroughly tanned, treated with ochre, exhibit comparable stitching, and are in a similar state of preservation. The two robes from Nine Mile Canyon radiocarbon dated to AD 1634 and 1656. The Gordon Creek bundle radiocarbon dated to AD 1551.

140 HIDE FRAGMENT

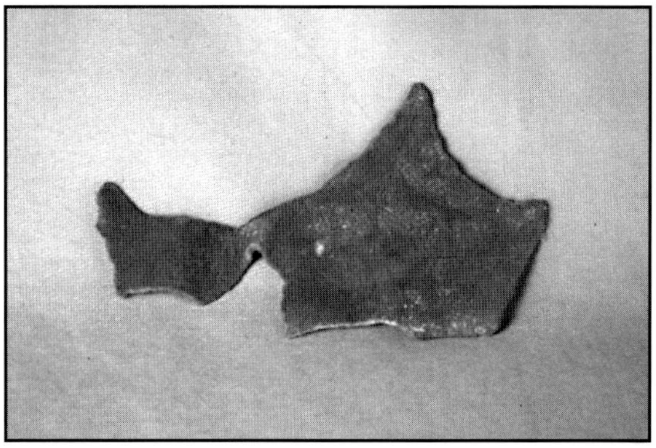

Bighorn sheep
Prehistoric/Historic, probably before ca. AD 1850
Lent to MPC, 2000–2005
CARE 33

L: 18.5 cm
W: 9.8 cm

Fragment of tanned hide. Both faces are felt-like and stained with dark red ochre(?).

Good condition; intact but incomplete. Areas of dark discoloration (soiling?). Stable.

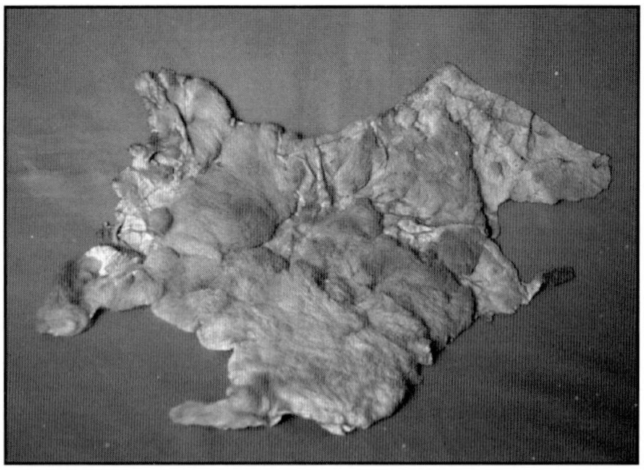

141 PELT FRAGMENT

Bighorn sheep
Prehistoric/Historic, probably before AD 1850
Lent to MPC, 2000–2005
CARE 1601

L: 60.4 cm
W: 39.8 cm

Fragment of tanned bighorn sheep hide preserving majority of hair, including the guard hair. Reverse stained with red ochre(?). Several ancient(?) sinew stitches; several modern threads remain, presumably from hanging.

Fair condition, intact but fragmentary. Scattered tears and lacunae. Insect damage on some edges. Creasing and folding. Scattered soiling; resin-like accretions on reverse. Unstable (hair slipping).

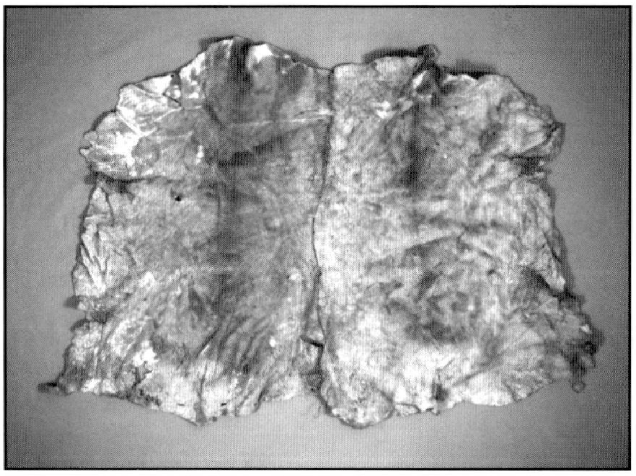

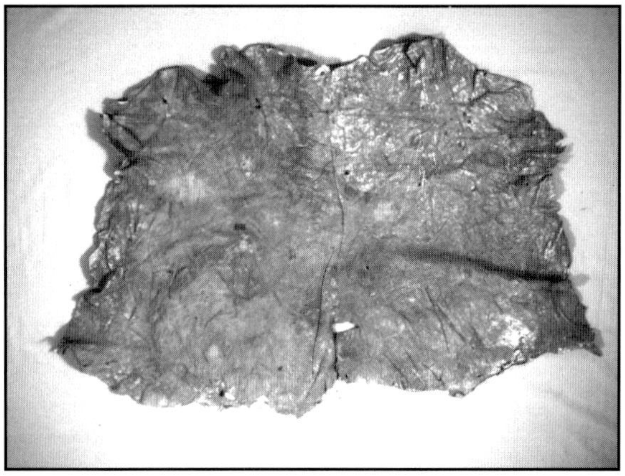

Underside.

142 PELT ARTICLE

Bighorn sheep
Prehistoric/Historic, probably before ca. AD 1850
Lent to MPC, 2000–2005
CARE 1602

L: 126.2 cm
W: 83.5 cm

Hide article consisting of two bighorn sheep pelts, apparently the spring hides of adolescent females, sewn together with sinew and stained with ochre over entire underside. Partially defleshed, chatter marks. Two holes repaired anciently with s-spun, z-twisted sinew thread. Under-hair has red ochre stains in localized areas (edges).

Fair condition; intact and largely complete. One end of hide has pulled away from stitching with associated tear. Some delamination on outside edges. Scattered insect damage resulting in quarter-sized holes in two locations. On hair side, black accretion on viewer's lower left, scattered black, gummy accretions (pitch?). On flesh side, bluish accretion on viewer's lower left and upper right (mold, bloom?). Scattered hair loss. Stable except for hair slippage.

143 PELT

Bighorn sheep
Prehistoric/Historic, probably before ca. AD 1850
Lent to MPC, 2000–2005
CARE 140

L: 132.3 cm
W: 90.1 cm

Tanned bighorn sheep hide, apparently the winter coat of a male, partially defleshed. Red accretions, some globular, on flesh side may be ochre.

Poor condition; intact and largely complete. Considerable hair loss and exfoliating of under-fur. Scattered large lacunae. Considerable insect damage. Black gummy accretion associated with discoloration on edge of flesh side. Scattered discoloration on hair side; dark globular accretion on hind end (rodent feces?). Unstable (hair slipping).

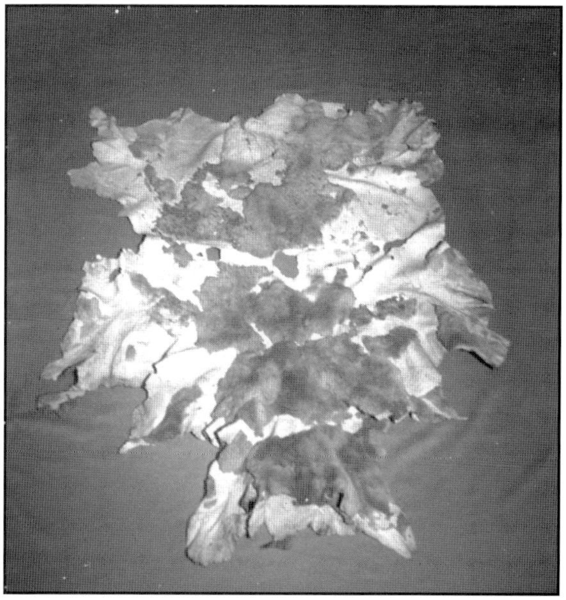

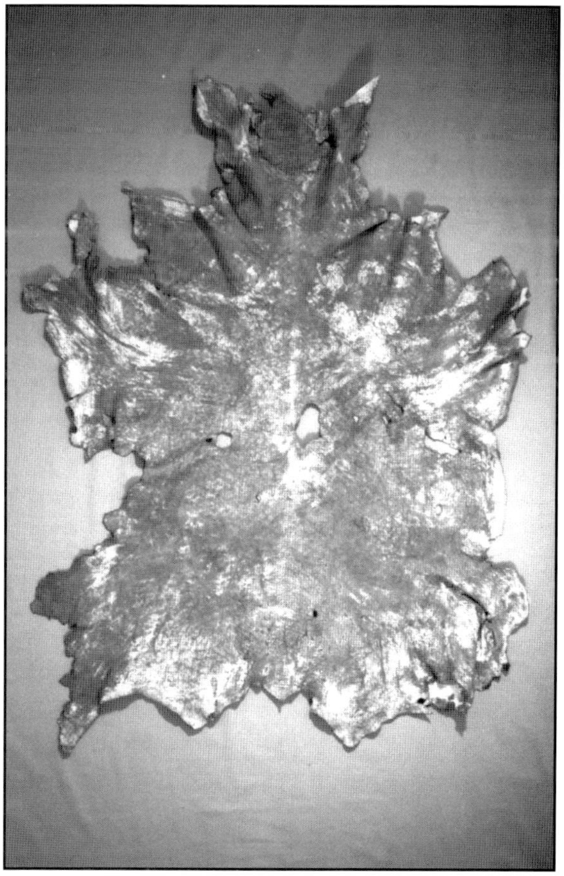

Underside.

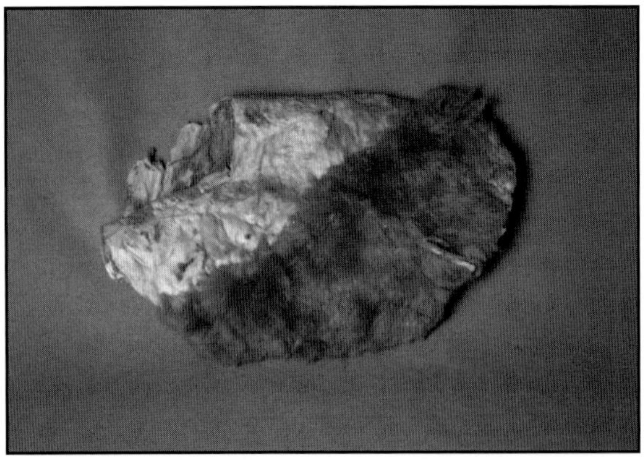

144 PELT FRAGMENT

Beaver?
Prehistoric/Historic (before ca. 1900)?
CARE 204

L: 27.0 cm
W: 23.0 cm

Fragment of poorly tanned hide with considerable amount of tan fur and guard hair remaining. Scattered red ochre(?) patches, some large.

Fair condition; intact. Insect damage resulting in lacunae, losses, and fraying on edges. Desiccated. Creased. Stable.

145 FRINGED ARTICLE

Tanned hide
Probably Historic (AD 1750–1900)
Lent to MPC, 2000–2005
CARE 230

L: 40.0 cm
W: 27.0 cm

Large piece of suede-like, tanned hide folded in half and then cut about eighty percent of its length to form 45 strips of fringe. Strips are then s-spun. A horizontal line of red-orange pigment (ochre) runs entire length of the object. Two puncture holes, presumably for suspension, at either ends. Thirty-two strips broken off at the midpoint may suggest heavy wear there.

Poor condition; intact and partially complete. Desiccated. Scattered lacunae (insect/rodent damage?). Abrasions on end of fringe resulting in loss of epidermal layer; scattered loss of epidermal layer on inside of fold. Scattered dirt and grime particularly on fringe; scattered stains (water?). Fly spots. Stable.

Comments:
The function of this section of fringed leather is unknown but, given the puncture holes at the ends and the fact that the carefully twisted fringe would be seen to best advantage during movement, it is likely the article was worn as a ornament, whether by dancers or, perhaps, as equestrian apparel. A somewhat similar article from Santa Ana Pueblo was identified by Strong as a rattle.[49] In that example, pieces of petrified wood were attached to the thongs and the article, attached to a stick, was worn by dancers at the waist. The attachment of noise-makers or tinklers to the fringe on the Pectol-Lee example would readily explain the damage noted in the condition report.

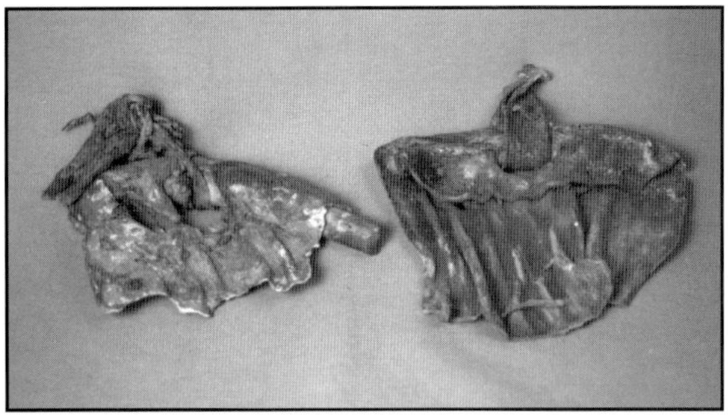

146 EQUESTRINE APPARATUS?

Hide and wood
Probably Historic (AD 1750–1900)
Lent to MPC, 2000–2005
CARE 260

Smaller one:
L: 14.0 cm
W: 17.0 cm

Larger one:
L: 15.0 cm
W: 17.5 cm

Two nearly identical components of a larger artifact of unknown dimension, perhaps saddlery apparatus (saddle bag?). Each one consists of a rawhide panel that folds back over itself after passing over a sturdy, curved wood stick and is then stitched with two rows of hide lacing. A slit in the sewn panel below the curved stick admits the remains of a hide strap used for attaching the object to something else. Soiling and dirt incrustations may be from use.

Poor to fair condition; intact but incomplete. Each piece exhibits a fresh-looking break in its leather carrying or suspension strap. Significant insect damage resulting in losses and lacunae. Severely weathered resulting in cockling, creasing, fraying of ends, delamination, and a scummy accretion on the surface (mold?). Embrittlement. Abrasions resulting in loss of epidermal layer in areas. Scattered accretions and stains including a black, pitch-like substance. Fly spots. Stable.

Comments:
These two articles may originally have been joined together by the hide suspension straps at the points where they show fresh breaks.

147 POUCH WITH CORDAGE

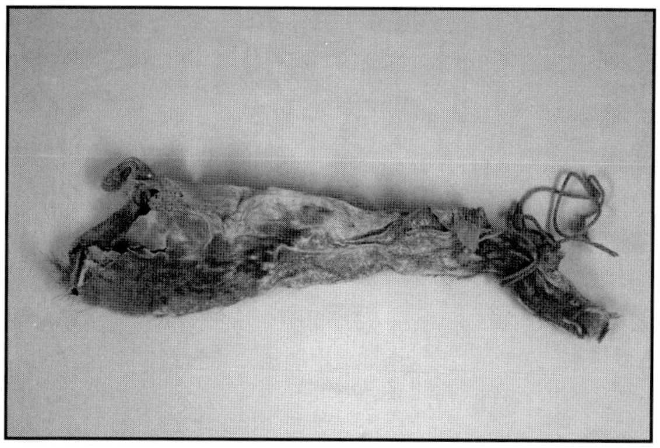

Prairie dog hide, cordage, hair
Fremont, ca. AD 1100
Lent to MPC, 2000–2005
No number

L: 29.5 cm
W: 9.0 cm
D: 4.0 cm

Pouch fashioned from the nearly complete hide of a small mammal, probably a prairie dog. Preserves both front legs, one hind leg, and some hair. Inside pouch is a bundle of z-spun, s-twisted human hair cordage and a mass of unidentified, fibrous vegetal matter (grass? herb?). Proximal opening tied with a double strand of z-spun, s-twisted cordage (milkweed, dogbane, or yucca?).

Poor condition; intact and largely complete. Long tear running most of length of ventral side of body. Cockling and creasing. Considerable insect damage resulting in losses at distal end. Black resin-like accretion. Scattered fly spots. Stable.

Comments:
According to a notation made in April 1961 by a Mr. or Ms. Clark in the catalogue records at Capitol Reef, both this bag and the one following were originally attached to the bandolier with pouch below (cat. no. 149).[50] Also according to the catalogue records, James D. Wilde[51] examined the bandolier in 1986 but made no mention of errors in the catalogue text, suggesting he saw what Clark did. If all three bags were originally attached to the bandolier, that would explain why this and the next pouch have no accession numbers: they were all accessioned as CARE 146.

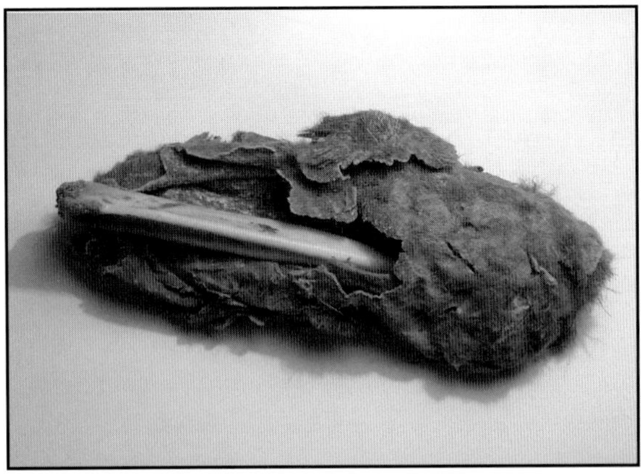

148 POUCH WITH AWL

Unknown rodent hide, bone
Fremont, ca. AD 1100
Lent to MPC, 2000–2005
No number

L: 13.5 cm
W: 5.0 cm
D: 3.2 cm

Small bag fashioned from an unidentified rodent hide and containing a bone awl inside. The bag preserves brown hair on exterior. Bone awl preserves tool marks and polishing from use.

Pouch in poor condition, awl in good condition. Intact and largely complete. Hole for opening enlarged in size due to insect damage. Considerable insect damage on all edges. Embrittlement. White, chalk-like substance accreted on surface of both pouch and awl (efflorescence?). Unstable (hair slipping, hide flaking).

Comments:
Because the bone awl is loose inside the bag, we cannot be certain the two were associated originally; however, this association has been maintained since at least April 1961 when the bag was catalogued at Capitol Reef National Park.

149 BANDOLIER WITH POUCH

Tanned hide
Fremont, ca. AD 1100
Lent to MPC, 2000–2005
CARE 146

<u>Bandolier</u>:
L: 157.0 cm
W: 5.5 cm

<u>Pouch</u>:
L: 16.0 cm
W: 6.2 cm

<u>Awl</u>:
L: 12.5 cm
W: 0.3 cm

Tanned hide bandolier suspending a hide bag with awl inside and preserving patches of red ochre. The bandolier is composed of seven separate pieces of hide stitched together with sinew and repaired several times with milkweed(?) cordage (see detail, at right). It is folded in two along its entire length and so has the appearance of being only half its width. It has four cords attached to it, one of which is z-spun, s-twisted and secures the pouch (see detail, below). A second length of z-spun, s-twisted hide cordage is tied to the bandolier by means of an indistinct knot. The third length of cordage, tied onto the stitching of the bandolier, is a piece of z-spun, s-twisted cordage consisting of two knots which result in three loops. The fourth is a thin leather lace, which is tied onto one of the ends that must have been part of a longer or mended lace, as there is a double overhand ("granny") knot. The tied ends of the bandolier are formed by thinner pieces of hide inserted between another hide piece which has enveloped it and then is stitched with z-spun, s-twisted cordage to secure it (see drawing, p. 316). Heavy soiling and grime, located particularly on ends where bandolier would have been tied together, may be use wear. Cracking on the surface and extensive creasing due to the fold that bisects it.

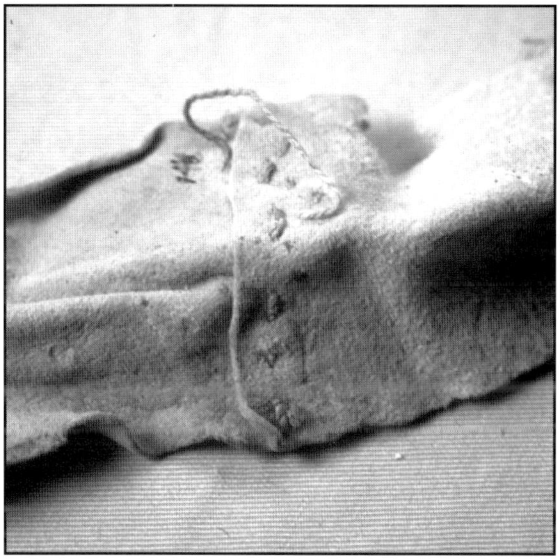

Detail of a seam on bandolier.

The pouch was fashioned from a nearly complete skin of rodent, possibly Golden Mantled Ground Squirrel, that preserves both hair, guard hair, and hind legs. Contains a ball of dogbane(?) cordage with some s-spun and z-twisted fibers and a bone awl that preserves tool marks. Two separate areas

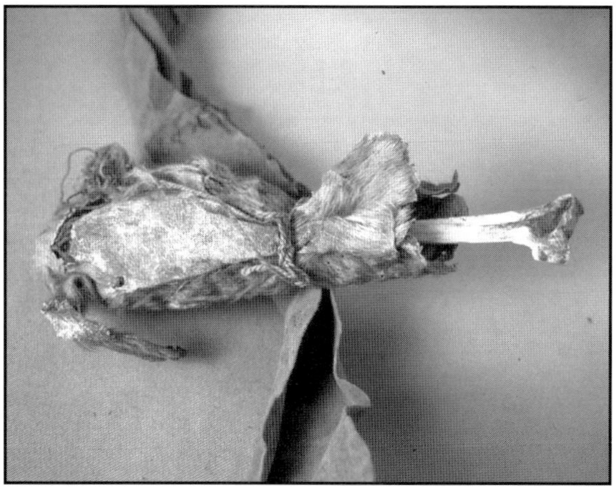

Detail of pouch with awl.

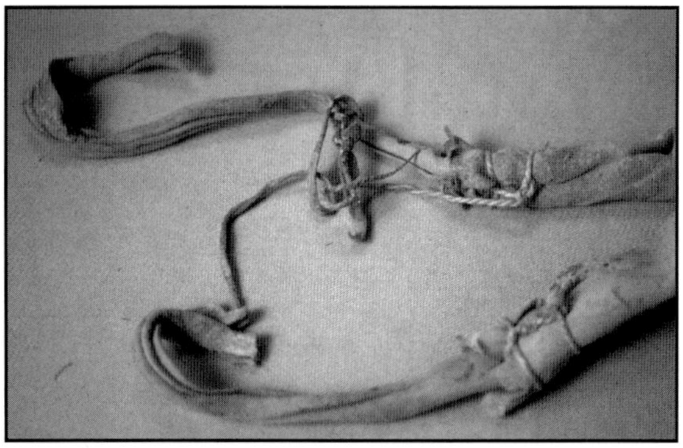

Detail of ends of bandolier.

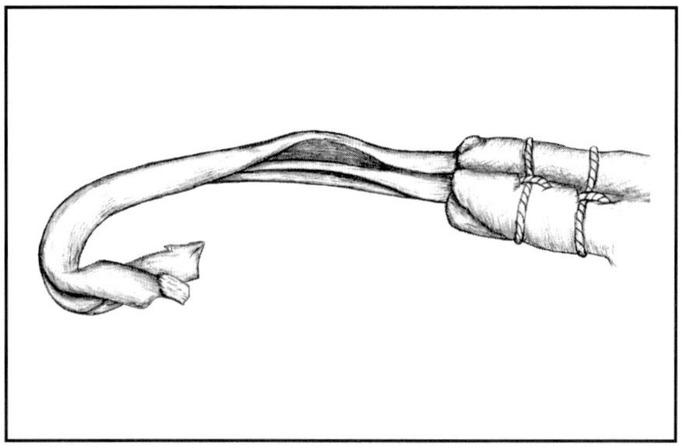

Drawing of end of bandolier by Debbie Silversmith, 2001.

of the bag were stitched: the skinning incision was stitched with sinew; the other was stitched with cordage and may be an ancient repair of a tear. Hair loss on belly appears to be use wear, as caused by rubbing. Red ochre(?) on fur.

Poor condition; intact and largely complete. Bandolier has scattered tears, especially at point of attachment to pouch; possible insect damage resulting in fraying on all edges and loss of epidermis in areas of bandolier and disrupted coloration. Light powdery accretion near pouch (mold?); scattered grime accretions; scattered stains and accretions, including water(?) and resin. Pouch exhibits loss of epidermis and lacunae due to desiccation and insect damage. Awl has blind, hairline cracks along grain and discoloration on one side and end. Pouch unstable (acute embrittlement, hair slippage).

Comments:
According to Capitol Reef National Park records going back to at least 1961, this bandolier originally had two other pouches attached to it whose descriptions match the unnumbered pouches in the two preceding entries (cat. nos. 148–149).

Bandoliers are frequently portrayed in classic Fremont rock art where they are shown crisscrossing the chests of anthropomorphic figures, for example, in Nine Mile Canyon,[52] Ferron Canyon,[53] Salt Creek Canyon,[54] and Capitol Reef National Park.[55] A classic Fremont date (AD 900–1150) is entirely consistent with the radiocarbon date the pouch yielded, i.e., AD 980–1140.[56]

150 PART OF BOILING BAG?

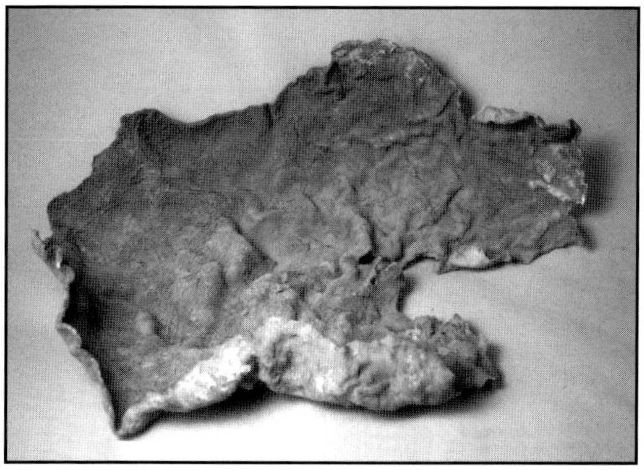

Animal stomach?
Numic or earlier (ca. AD 1250–1880)
Lent to MPC, 2000–2005
CARE 77

L: 55.0 cm
W: 45.0 cm
D: 0.7 cm

Possibly, the lower portion of boiling bag preserving part of hanging hole on one edge. What remains is a large, circular segment of hardened, cockled animal material resembling thick rawhide or an organ, such as stomach, curling around edges. Gray substance on exterior may be ash or charring. Substances accreted on interior wall may be remains of food.

Very poor condition; intact. Loss of top layer in some areas. Cracked surface. Delamination. Desiccation resulting in stiffness, warping, distortion, and severe cockling (or natural organ contours?). White chalk-like accretion (efflorescence?). Scattered discoloration and/or stains. Stable.

Comments:
This artifact may be part of a boiling bag. Boiling bags were used to cook food; one could drop hot rocks into the bag of food or suspend the bag over a fire. A Plains Indian example is gathered along one side and tied to support posts in four places, making the aperture rectangular in shape.[57]

WORKED BONE

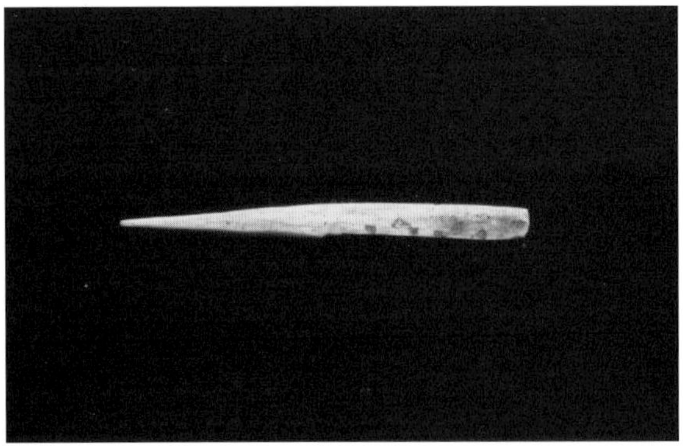

151 AWL

Bone
Agricultural Period
(Anasazi or Fremont, AD 1–1300)?
Lent to Capitol Reef National Park
(On display at Visitor Center)
CARE 153

L: 12.2 cm
W: 1.0 cm
D: 0.3 cm

Medium-sized bone awl with use wear. Tool marks (grooves) on lower end.

Very good condition; intact and complete. Loss along edge of handle and end. Light pitting (chips) on handle. Scattered scrapes. Stable.

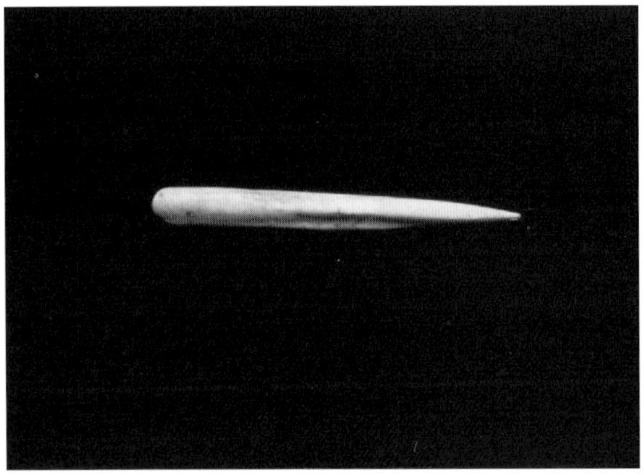

152 AWL

Bone
Agricultural Period
(Anasazi or Fremont, AD 1–1300)?
Lent to Capitol Reef National Park
(On display at Visitor Center)
CARE 154

L: 11.0 cm
W: 1.1 cm
D: 0.6 cm

Medium-sized bone awl with tool marks and polish on both ends from use.

Fair condition; intact and complete. Dull powdery substance over much of surface (efflorescence?). Stable.

153 AWL

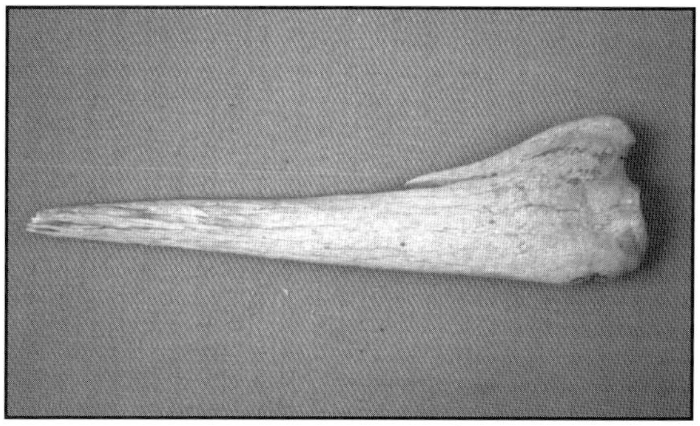

Bone
Agricultural Period
(Anasazi or Fremont, AD 1–1300)?
Lent to MPC, 2000–2005
CARE 51

L: 11.2 cm
D: 0.7 cm

Medium-sized bone awl with polish on the edges from use.

Poor condition; intact and largely complete. Badly weathered; splintering at distal tip with associated hairline cracks along the grain. Stable.

154 AWL

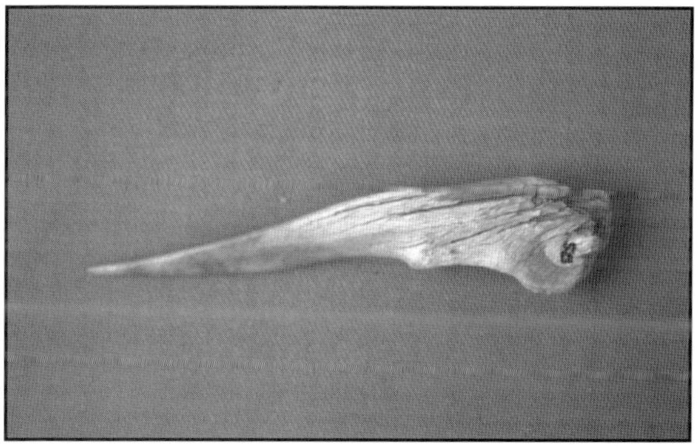

Bone
Agricultural Period
(Anasazi or Fremont, AD 1–1300)?
Lent to MPC, 2000–2005
CARE 50

L: 9.9 cm
D: 1.2 cm

Bone awl fashioned from the medial portion of an ulna bone(?). Polishing on the distal point from use.

Fair condition; intact and complete. Open cracks and thorough hairline cracks along the grain. Slight delamination. Stable.

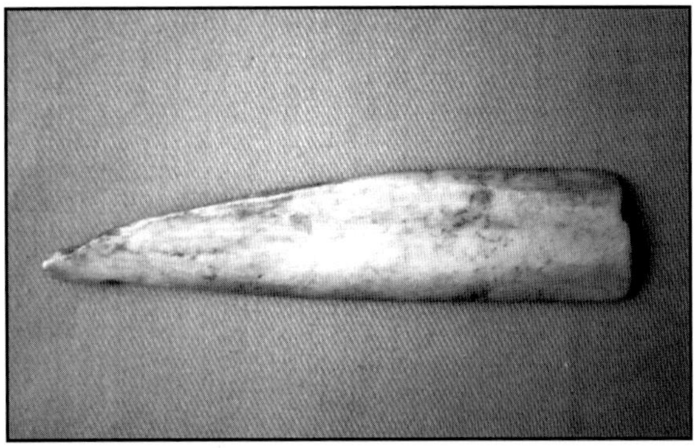

155 AWL?

Bone
Agricultural Period
(Anasazi or Fremont, AD 1–1300)?
Lent to MPC, 2000–2005
CARE 49

L: 10.5 cm
W: 2.5 cm

Large dense piece of long bone which forms a blunt crude point.

Good condition; intact and complete. Stable.

Comments:
According to Capitol Reef records, magnification of the tip revealed several small fractures, leading to the conclusion that this awl was used as a flaking tool.

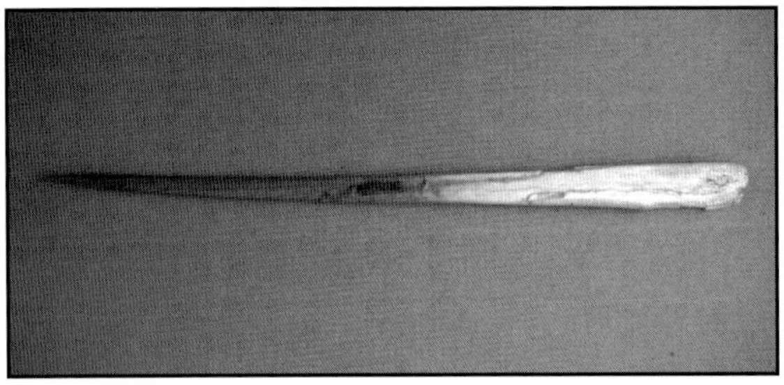

156 AWL OR PIN

Bone
Agricultural Period
(Anasazi or Fremont, AD 1–1300)?
Lent to MPC, 2000–2005
CARE H 4889

L: 20.4 cm
D: 0.6 cm

Long bone shaped similarly to an awl although much longer. Possibly a hair or garment pin.

Fair condition; complete but reconstructed from three fragments. Scattered chips and losses. Discoloration on tip and over one half of shaft. Stable.

CHIPPED STONE

157 HAFTED BIFACE

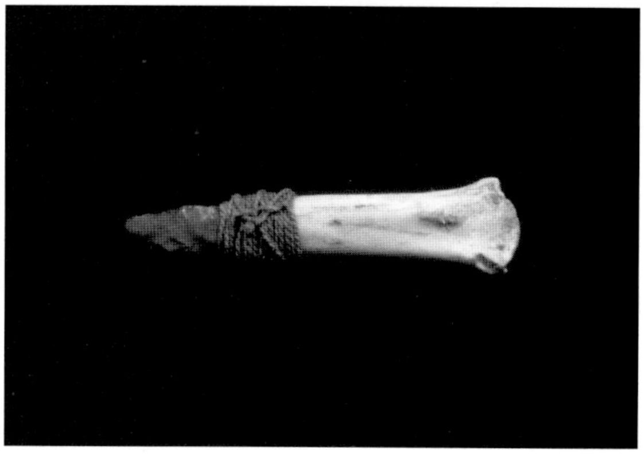

Chert, cordage, bone
Prehistoric (before 17th century AD)
Lent to Capitol Reef National Park
(On display at Visitor Center)
CARE 149

L: 16.1 cm
W: 3.9 cm
D: 1.9 cm

Honey-colored chert biface hafted in diaphysis of ungulate radius with fiber cordage. Biface is not bilaterally symmetric and edges are irregularly flaked. Slightly curved front-to-back. Handle is manufactured from the distal radius of an ungulate. Small bits of soft tissue adhere to articular end. Biface is hafted by wrapping ca. 16 times with s-spun, z-twisted fiber 1.9 mm diameter, likely yucca or dogbane. Estimated total length of cordage is ca. 47 cm, and it is secured with an overhand knot, with free ends tucked back under the wrapping.

Excellent condition; intact and complete. Numerous fine scratches throughout handle. Hairline crack on obverse of handle. Gouges on reverse. Stable.

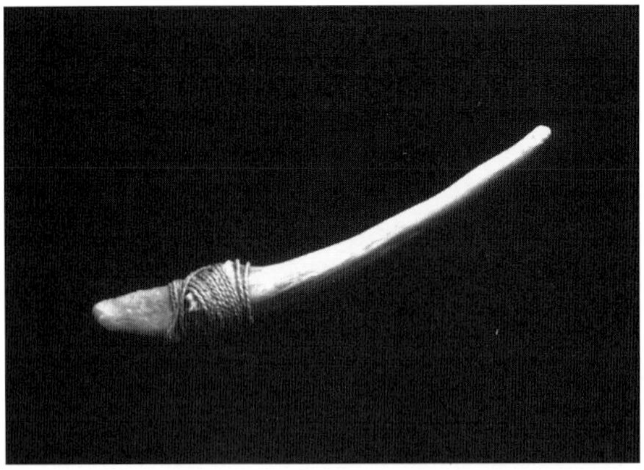

158 HAFTED BIFACE

Antler, chert, dogbane or milkweed
Prehistoric, before 17th century AD
Lent to Capitol Reef National Park
(On display at Visitor Center)
CARE 152

L: 19.8 cm
W: 3.7 cm
D: 2.8 cm

Chert biface hafted to an antler tine with dogbane or milkweed cordage. The biface has a reworked tip and heavy use wear along the edges. Approximately 160 cm of z-spun, s-twisted dogbane or milkweed cordage has been wrapped around the biface and antler 23 times to secure the haft. Polished from handling. Wear on the tip of the tine suggest its possible use as a flaker.

Very good condition; intact and complete. Fraying of cordage. Stable.

159 LARGE PROJECTILE POINT OR KNIFE

Red jasper
Prehistoric (before 17th century AD)
Lent to MPC, 2000–2005
CARE 252

L: 8.7 cm
W: 3.7 cm
D: 0.7 cm

Large corner-notched projectile point or knife of red and yellow chert. Slightly convex base, one notch tends toward side-notched. Slight patination on one side. Corner notches slightly ground.

Excellent condition; intact and complete. Stable.

160 PROJECTILE POINT

Chert
Archaic (8000 BC–AD 1)
Elko Corner-notched
Lent to MPC, 2000–2005
CARE 83

L: 3.9 cm
W: 3.1 cm
D: 0.6 cm

Finely flaked, Elko Corner-notched projectile point.

Good condition; intact and largely complete, but tip and one tang broken off. Stable.

161 PROJECTILE POINT OR KNIFE

Slate?
Prehistoric (before 17th century AD)
Lent to MPC, 2000–2005
CARE 90

L: 6.6 cm
W: 2.5 cm
D: 0.8 cm

Large stemmed projectile point or knife with finely-flaked edge. The proximal end appears to have broken during manufacture. The distal half of this specimen is darker than the proximal with a distinct line of demarcation between them.

Excellent condition; intact and complete. Stable.

162 PROJECTILE POINT

Chert
Archaic (8000 BC–AD 1)
Possible Elko Corner-notched
Lent to Capitol Reef National Park
(On display at Visitor Center)
CARE 253

L: 6.2 cm
W: 3.7 cm
D: 0.9 cm

Large corner-notched projectile point of dark gray chert veined with lighter gray and tan. Tip and margins dulled from use.

Good condition; intact and largely complete. One tang missing, small loss on one side of base and another on remaining tang. Stable.

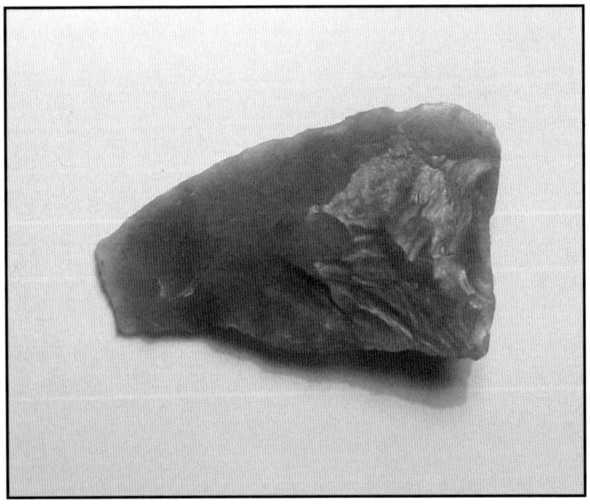

163 PROJECTILE POINT

Chert
Late Prehistoric (ca. AD 1250–1750)
Cottonwood Triangular
Lent to MPC, 2000–2005
CARE 81

L: 2.6 cm
W: 1.7 cm
D: 0.6 cm

This specimen is most likely a Late Prehistoric Cottonwood Triangular projectile point, although it could instead be a point preform from any period. It is crudely shaped and the tip may have broken off in manufacture and subsequently been thinned but not re-tapered.

Excellent condition; intact and complete. Small white accretions, possibly paint transferred from accession number. Stable.

164 PROJECTILE POINT

Chert
Archaic, 2500 BC–AD 500
Gatecliff Contracting Stem
Lent to Capitol Reef National Park
(On display at Visitor Center)
CARE 87

L: 7.1 cm
W: 3.6 cm
D: 0.5 cm

Large contracting stem projectile point of stippled gray chert. Asymmetrical, but finely flaked. Body slightly bowed. One face exhibits little flaking. Some use wear.

Good condition: intact and largely complete. Loss of tip, small losses on one tang and on one face near the tip. Stable.

Comments:
The distribution of contracting stem points seems to be limited to the southern half of the Great Basin and are consistently dated to 2500 BC–AD 500.[58]

165 PROJECTILE POINT

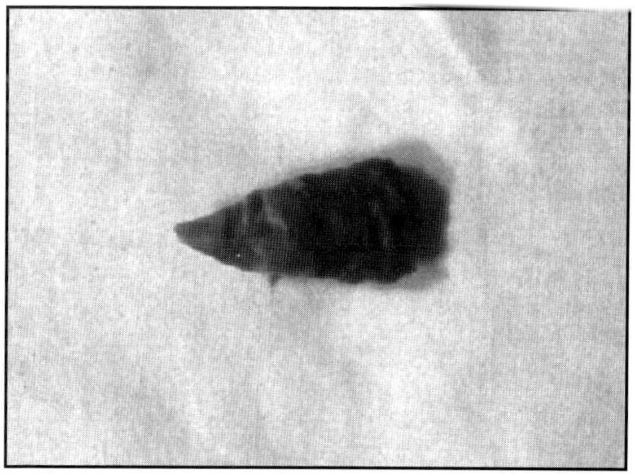

Chert
Possibly Late Prehistoric (ca. AD 1250–1750)
Lent to Capitol Reef National Park
(On display at Visitor Center)
CARE 80

L: 2.8 cm
W: 1.4 cm
D: 0.4 cm

Small triangular projectile point or point preform of brown chert, resembling a Cottonwood Triangular. Symmetrical and fairly thin. All margins appear ground, possibly through manufacture or use.

Good condition; intact and largely complete. Small lateral loss on edge near tip. Stable.

photo not available

166 PROJECTILE POINT

Chert
Prehistoric (before 17th century AD)
Lent to Capitol Reef National Park
(On display at Visitor Center)
CARE 82

L: 5.1 cm
W: 1.8 cm
D: 0.8 cm

Concave-based stemmed point of gray chert. Percussion and pressure-flaked. Exhibits minimal thinning. Basally thinned. Some use wear.

Very good; intact and complete. Stable.

167 PROJECTILE POINT

Chert
Prehistoric (before 17th century AD)
Lent to Capitol Reef National Park
(On display at Visitor Center)
CARE 84

L: 6.5 cm
W: 3.9 cm
D: 0.8 cm

Large side-notched or shouldered projectile point of gray chert. Finely flaked and fairly symmetrical. Broken edge at the base has been retouched/utilized.

Fair condition; intact and partially complete. Loss of base. Small loss at tip. Stable.

168 PROJECTILE POINT OR KNIFE

Chert
Prehistoric (before 17th century AD)
Lent to Capitol Reef National Park
(On display at Visitor Center)
CARE 254

L: 7.4 cm
W: 3.6 cm
D: 1.2 cm

Large side-notched projectile point of gray chert veined with white. Base slightly concave and narrower than body. Fine marginal flaking on one face. Step fracture near tip, resulting from manufacture. Use wear visible as flake scars along one margin.

Excellent condition; intact and complete. Dirt accretions in crevices. Stable.

169 DRILL OR PUNCH

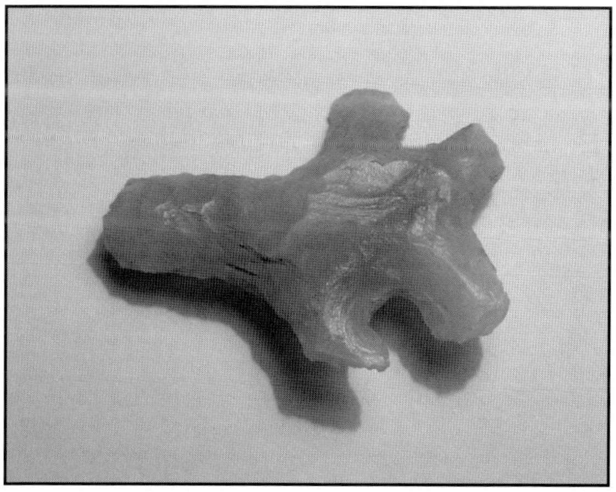

Chalcedony
Prehistoric (before 17th century AD)
Lent to MPC, 2000–2005
CARE 131

L: 2.9 cm
W: 2.2 cm
D: 0.6 cm

Corner- and basally-notched drill or punch, finely flaked and slightly asymmetrical. This specimen appears to be a reworked Elko Eared point.

Good condition; intact; distal tip missing, otherwise complete. Stable.

170 KNIFE FRAGMENT

Red jasper
Unknown Prehistoric
(before 17th century AD)
Lent to MPC, 2000–2005
CARE 86

L: 3.9 cm
W: 1.9 cm
D: 0.6 cm

Distal portion of knife. Finely flaked. Wear on one edge suggests this specimen was used as a knife. Bending fracture suggests it was broken during the process of being reworked.

Good condition; intact and partially complete. Stable.

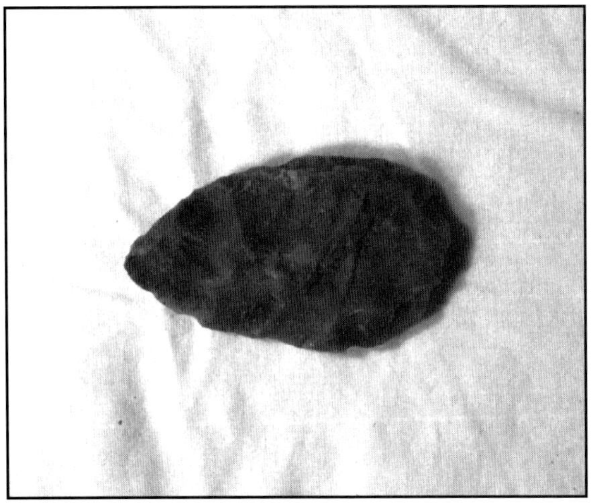

171 BIFACE

Chert
Prehistoric (before 17th century AD)
Lent to Capitol Reef National Park
(On display at Visitor Center)
CARE 92

L: 7.9 cm
W: 4.9 cm
D: 1.4 cm

Tear-drop shaped stage two biface of mottled salmon-colored and white chert. Step fractures on one face and along one margin, resulting from manufacture.

Good condition; intact and complete. Stable.

172 BIFACE

Chert
Prehistoric (before 17th century AD)?
Lent to Capitol Reef National Park
(On display at Visitor Center)
CARE 91

L: 7.9 cm
W: 4.6 cm
D: 1.3 cm

Tear-drop shaped biface of mottled mustard-yellow, white, and salmon-colored chert. Flat on one face, convex on the other. One large step fracture resulting from manufacture on convex face. Pressure flaking along base on flat face. Margins dulled, possibly during manufacture.

Good condition, intact and complete. Stable.

173 PARTIAL BIFACE

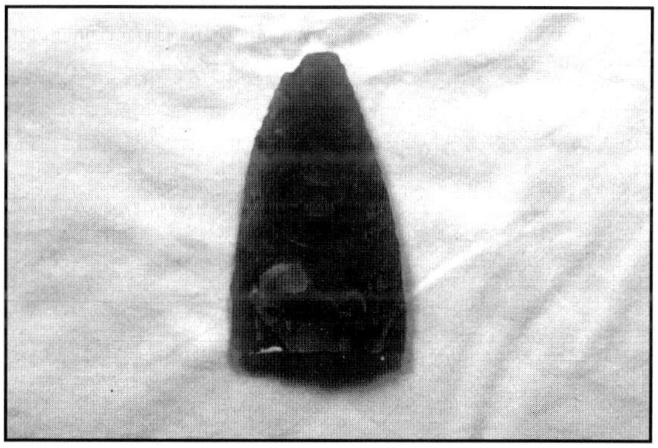

Chert
Unknown Prehistoric (before 17th century AD)
Lent to Capitol Reef National Park
(On display at Visitor Center)
CARE 88

L: 7.4 cm
W: 4.6 cm
D: 1.1 cm

Roughly triangular biface fragment of slightly translucent gray chert. The tip is blunt and appears to be retouched. Symmetrical, with pressure flaking along margins. Large step fracture on one face resulting from manufacture. Margins lightly ground.

Fair condition; intact and partially complete. Base is missing. Stable.

174 PARTIAL BIFACE

Chert
Prehistoric (before 17th century AD)
Lent to Capitol Reef National Park
(On display at Visitor Center)
CARE 95

L: 7.3 cm
W: 5.2 cm
D: 2.4 cm

Fragment of a large, early stage biface of variegated gray chert with crystalline inclusions. The margins exhibit crushed edges and small step fractures.

Fair condition; intact and partially complete.
Stable.

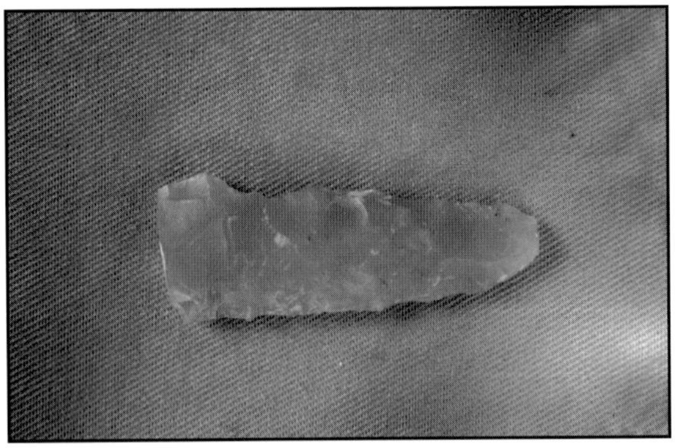

175 PARTIAL BIFACE

Chalcedony
Prehistoric (before 17th century AD)
Lent to MPC, 2000–2005
CARE 85

L: 5.8 cm
W: 2.2 cm
D: 0.7 cm

Roughly flaked biface fragment. Probably a knife or point preform. Bending fractures at the proximal and distal ends suggest the biface was broken during manufacture.

Good condition; intact and partially complete.
Stable.

176 PARTIAL BIFACE

Opal
Prehistoric (before 17th century AD)
Lent to MPC, 2000–2005
CARE 96

L: 5.8 cm
W: 5.1 cm
D: 2.0 cm

Partial biface, roughly hewn, hard-hammer percussion flaking, broken off near midline.

Good condition; intact and partially complete. Extensive yellow accretions along break and less extensively on one face (glue), suggestive of restoration attempt. (Other portion now separated and lost.) Patch of white mineral accretions on one face near break. Stable.

177 END SCRAPER

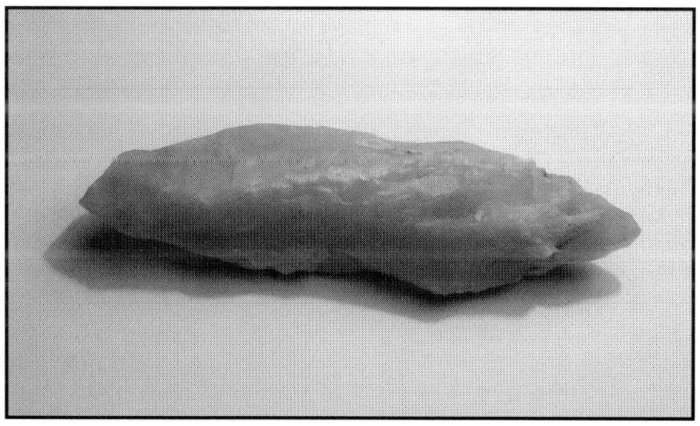

Chalcedony
Prehistoric (before 17th century AD)?
Lent to MPC, 2000–2005
CARE 94

L: 11.1 cm
W: 3.0 cm
D: 2.5 cm

Crude end scraper, roughly flaked and elongate. Hard-hammer percussion flaking. Lateral edges blunted by crushing, perhaps to facilitate handling. Minor use wear on working end.

Excellent condition; intact and complete. Stable.

178 CHOPPER

Quartzite
Prehistoric (before 17th century AD)?
Lent to MPC, 2000–2005
CARE 93

L: 6.9 cm
W: 5.1 cm
D: 3.2 cm

Largely unmodified chert cobble probably used as chopper. Naturally fractured and wedge-shaped with extensive patination. Extensive impact scarring along sharp edge of wedge suggests use as an expedient tool.

Excellent condition; intact and complete. Stable.

GROUNDSTONE

179 AXE HEAD

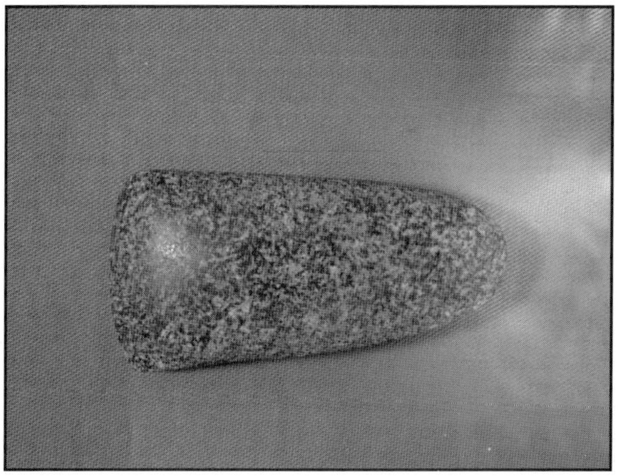

Diorite
Prehistoric/Historic (before AD 1900)
Lent to MPC, 2000–2005
CARE 255

L: 9.4 cm
W: 4.6 cm
D: 2.2 cm

Symmetrical stone axe head, pecked and ground, no evidence of hafting.

Very good condition; intact and complete. Stable.

180 AXE OR ADZE HEAD

Diorite
Prehistoric/Historic (before AD 1900)
Lent to MPC, 2000–2005
CARE 97

L: 8.2 cm
W: 4.4 cm
D: 2.8 cm

Symmetrical axe or adze head, pecked and ground. Small depressions on sides ca. 4.5 cm from blade, possibly to facilitate hafting. Some minor chipping of blade, probably use wear, although remainder of blade preserves a high polish.

Excellent condition; intact and complete. Stable.

181 CLUB OR MACE

Rhyolite head, wooden handle, leather thongs
Pastiche: Late Historic head/Modern handle
Late 19th–early 20th century AD
Lent to MPC, 2000–2005
CARE 229

L: 38.0 cm
L (head): 5.9 cm
Diam (head): 8.1 cm
Diam (handle): 2.5 cm

Club or mace consisting of (composite?) wooden handle socketed into pecked and ground, steeply biconvex stone head with two deep, grooves (industrially?) cut at right angles and intersecting at the top of the head. Top of handle has two perpendicular holes drilled clear through at right angles to accept leather thongs lashing head to handle. Handle is tapered to fit into socket in base of head. Butt end of handle is convex. Lashing consists of a single leather thong passing through the grooves over the head and through and around the handle.

Very good condition; largely intact and complete. Head is chipped on margin and exhibits a few deep scratches, but is in very good condition. Handle is weathered and cracked along grain, but in good condition. Leather thong exhibits some sheen from handling and slight embrittlement, but is otherwise in very good condition, intact, and complete. Stable.

Comments:
This implement may be a pastiche; that is, a work created from separate artifacts, possibly disparate in date. The handle is extraordinarily straight with a dense matrix and has a suspicious resemblance to the handle of an early broom or other historic tool. The leather thong is regularly cut and resembles a boot lace.

Alternatively, this mace may be intrusive to the collection, possibly an acquisition Pectol made in New Zealand while serving a mission there (see Baker, p. 27, this volume).

182 PIERCED DISK (SPINDLE WHORL?)

Green slate
Prehistoric (before 17th century AD)?
Lent to MPC, 2000–2005
CARE 18

Diam: 8.7 cm
Diam (hole): 2.1 cm
D: 1.7 cm

Disk-shaped stone with biconically drilled hole, possibly a spindle whorl for production of rope or heavy cordage. Lightly incised scratches radiating from central hole on one face, unevenly distributed over three quarters of disk face (other quarter is obliterated by surface damage). Similar scratches are absent from the opposite face.

Very good condition; intact and largely complete. Two large areas of surface loss, possibly due to impact; numerous chips along outer margin. Stable.

183 STONE BALL

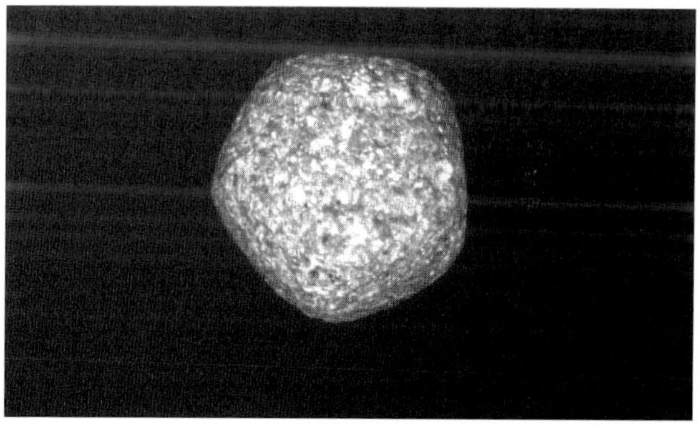

Basalt
Prehistoric (before 17th century AD)?
Lent to Capitol Reef National Park
(On display at Visitor Center)
CARE 1618

L: 5.8 cm
W: 5.4 cm
D: 5.9 cm

Pentagonal stone ball with flat sides and ends. Black basalt with red and white inclusions.

Excellent condition; intact and complete. Stable.

184 STONE BALL

Sandstone
Prehistoric?
Lent to Capitol Reef National Park
(On display at Visitor Center)
CARE 1620

L: 5.4 cm
W: 5.3 cm
D: 5.0 cm

Rounded ball with rough pentagonal shaping, manufactured from pink sandstone with brown and black inclusions.

Excellent condition; intact and complete. Some nicks, possibly incurred during manufacture. Large areas of brown or black discoloration. Dirt accretions throughout. Stable.

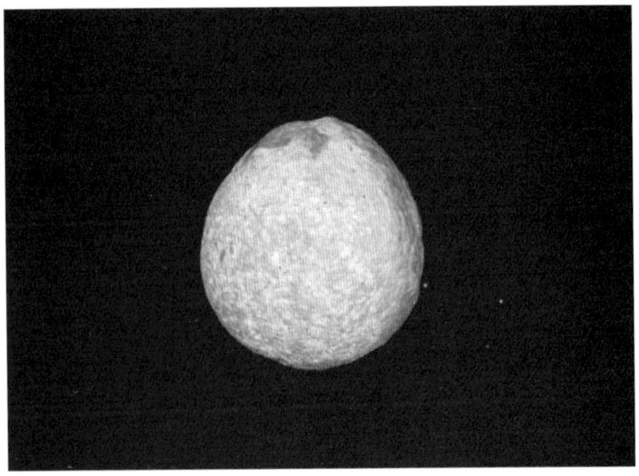

185 STONE BALL

Sandstone
Prehistoric?
Lent to Capitol Reef National Park
(On display at Visitor Center)
CARE 1619

L: 5.3 cm
W: 5.4 cm
D: 5.4 cm

Roughly shaped sandstone ball. One hemisphere is porous brown and white, the other is dark pink and brown and less porous.

Excellent condition; intact and complete. Hairline crack on reverse. Stable.

186 MANO

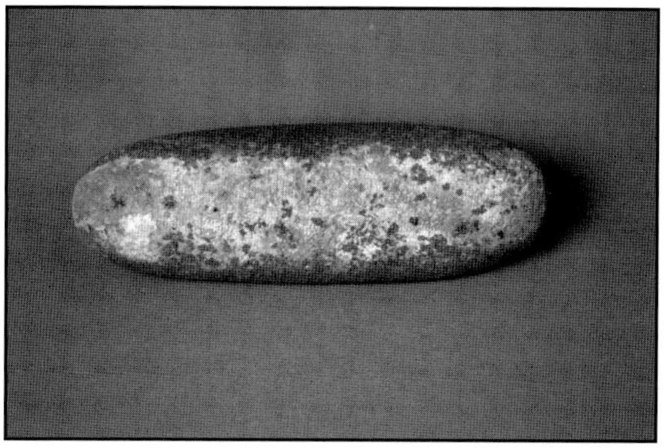

Sandstone
Agricultural Period
(Anasazi or Fremont, AD 1–1300)?
Lent to MPC, 2000–2005
CARE 137

L: 22.5 cm
W: 6.2 cm
D: 6.4 cm

Loaf-shaped, two-handed mano with one grinding surface.

Excellent condition; intact and complete. Extensive, light pink, crusty accretions on grinding surface and extending ca. 1 cm up one side. Dark brown to black accretions (lichen?), one patch of shiny gray-blue accretion resembling graphite, and three specks of red paint, all on the grinding surface and overlying the pinkish accretion. Whitish area of crystalline mineral accretion on grinding surface, also occurring (though less extensively) on the sides and on the top surface. Stable.

187 MANO

Sandstone
Agricultural Period
(Anasazi or Fremont, AD 1–1300)?
Lent to MPC, 2000–2005
CARE 136

L: 15.0 cm
W: 5.9 cm
D: 6.4 cm

Loaf-shaped, heavily pecked, two-handed mano. Two grinding surfaces. Minor post-depositional impact marks and scrapes.

Excellent condition; intact and complete. Shiny gray accretion (possibly graphite) on one side, small patch of shiny dark brown or black accretions on one side. Stable.

188 MANO

Igneous rock
Agricultural Period
(Anasazi or Fremont, AD 1–1300)?
Lent to Capitol Reef National Park
(On display at Visitor Center)
CARE 138

L: 17.0 cm
W: 7.0 cm
H: 4.5 cm

Oblong, two-handed mano of igneous rock. One grinding surface.

Very good condition; intact and complete. Stable.

189 SLAB METATE

Sandstone
Agricultural Period
(Anasazi or Fremont, AD 1–1300)?
Lent to MPC, 2000–2005
CARE 139

Length: 26.8 cm
Width: 23.4 cm
Depth: 3.5 cm

Depth (Trough): 0.8 cm
Width (Trough): 16.0 cm

Half of a slab metate with one grinding surface with poorly defined trough, suggesting limited use of a two-handed mano.

Fair condition; intact and partially complete. Minor impact chips and scrapes. Dark brown accretions on margins of underside and in center of grinding surface. Shiny black accretions in center of grinding surface. Iron oxide accretions on underside, carbon deposits along one side and end. Random fresh scratches on underside. Stable.

AGRICULTURAL ITEMS

190 CORN COB ON STICK

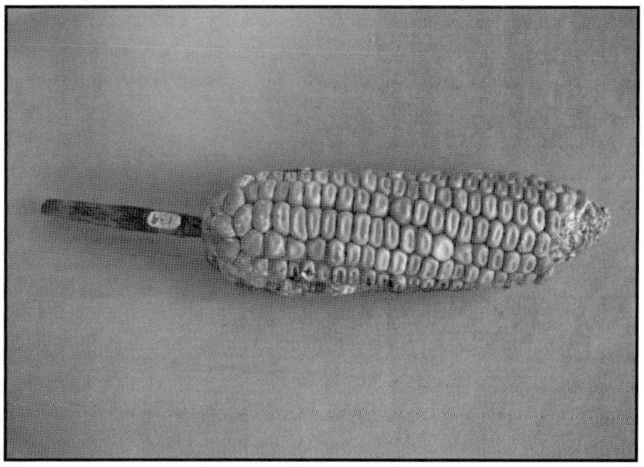

Corn cob and wood
Probably Agricultural Period
(Anasazi or Fremont, AD 1–1300)
Lent to MPC, 2000–2005
CARE 134

L: 18.0 cm
Diam: 3.8 cm

Fourteen-row dent corn cob, some kernels remaining, with slightly tapered stick inserted in stem end of cob.

Excellent condition; intact and complete. Kernels on end and half of base missing. Stick is loose, prone to detachment. Numerous insect bore holes. Underside of cob and stick both exhibit extensive charring. Some kernels in this area have been recently broken. Stable.

191 CORN COB ON STICK

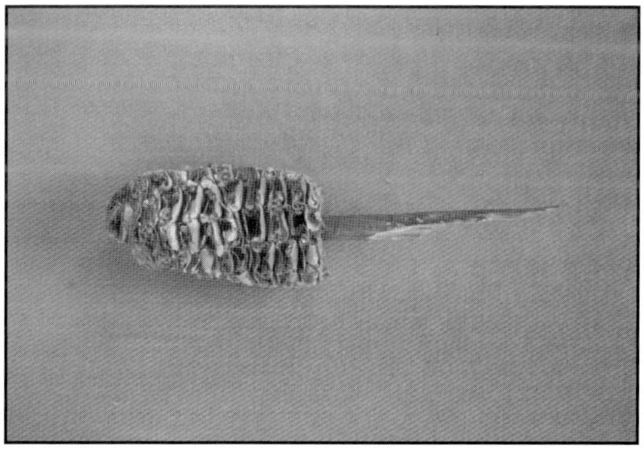

Corn cob and wood
Probably Agricultural Period
(Anasazi or Fremont, AD 1–1300)
Lent to MPC, 2000–2005
CARE 135

L: 8.0 cm
Diam: 2.2 cm

Ten-row corn cob with broken stick inserted in the stem end. Fragments of yellow kernels remain, all kernels removed.

Very good condition, intact and partially complete. Stick split and broken. Stable.

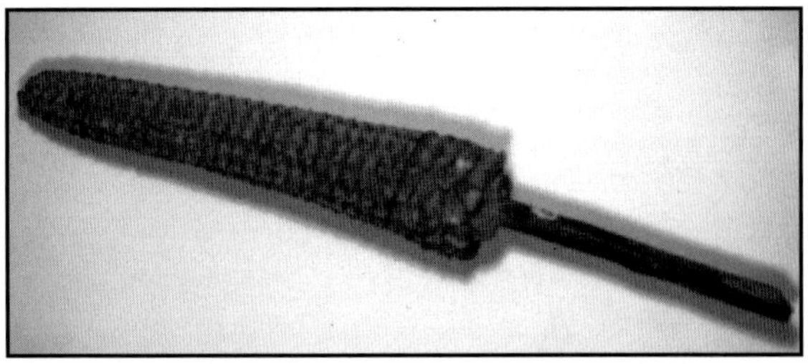

192 CORN COB ON STICK

Corn cob and wood
Agricultural Period
(Anasazi or Fremont, AD 1–1300)?
Lent to Capitol Reef National Park
(On display at Visitor Center)
CARE 24

L: 22.7 cm
Diam: 2.4 cm

Fourteen-row corn cob, no kernels remaining. Stick inserted in stem end.

Very good condition; intact but incomplete. End of stick is splitting. Checking (crackling) and exfoliation of bark on stick. Stable.

photo not available

193 CORN COB ON STICK
Corn cob and wood
Probably Agricultural Period
(Anasazi or Fremont, AD 1–1300)
Lent to Capitol Reef National Park
(On display at Visitor Center)
CARE 25

L: 13.9 cm
Diam: 1.9 cm

Twelve-row corn cob, no kernels remaining. Stick inserted in stem end.

Very good condition; intact but incomplete. End of stick and tip of cob missing. End of stick is splitting; one section is exfoliating. Stable.

194 CORN COB

Corn cob
Probably Agricultural Period
(Anasazi or Fremont, AD 1–1300)
Lent to Capitol Reef National Park
(On display at Visitor Center)
CARE 1616/98

L: 8.0 cm
Diam: 2.8 cm

Twelve-row, yellow dent corn cob with kernels remaining.

Very good condition; intact but incomplete. Tip and stem end of cob missing. Loss of kernels at one end, sporadic kernel loss elsewhere. Insect bore holes. Stable.

195 CORN COB

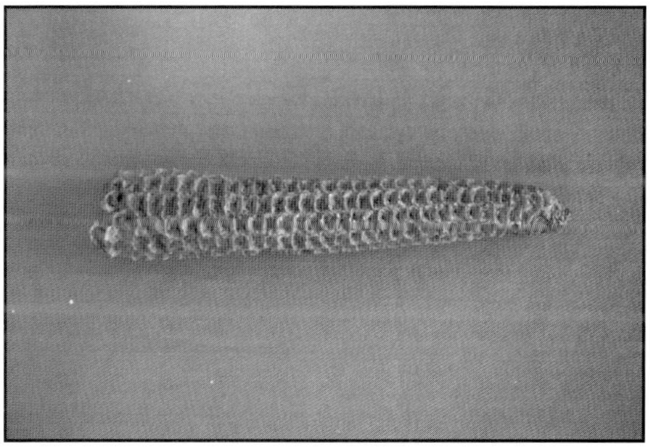

Corn cob
Probably Agricultural Period
(Anasazi or Fremont, AD 1–1300)
Lent to MPC, 2000–2005
CARE 133

L: 14.5 cm
Diam: 2.3 cm

Twelve-row corn cob, all kernels removed.

Excellent condition; intact and complete. Patches of mildew near stem end and near mid-point. Stable.

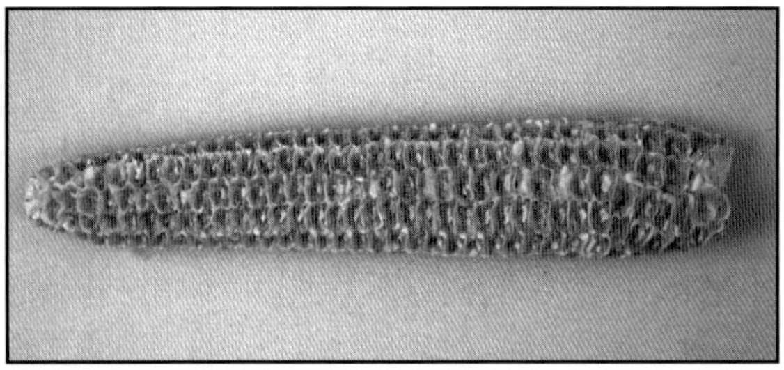

196 CORN COB

Variety unknown
Probably Agricultural Period
(Anasazi or Fremont, AD 1–1300)
Lent to MPC, 2000–2005
CARE 26

L: 6.7 cm
Diam: 2.5 cm

Twelve-row corn cob, all kernels removed. Fragments of red kernel casings remain. Stalk end is somewhat concave.

Excellent condition; intact and complete. Some particulation. Stable.

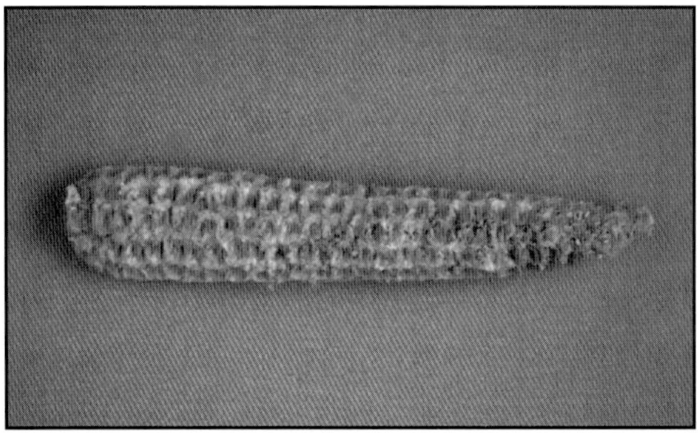

197 CORN COB

Variety unknown
Probably Agricultural Period
(Anasazi or Fremont, AD 1–1300)
Lent to MPC, 2000–2005
CARE 27

L: 17.4 cm
Diam: 1.8 cm

Small, twelve-row corn cob, all kernels removed. Tip of cob indicates insect damage while still growing. Fragments of white or yellow kernels remain.

Excellent condition; intact and complete. Some particulation. Stable.

198 CORN COB

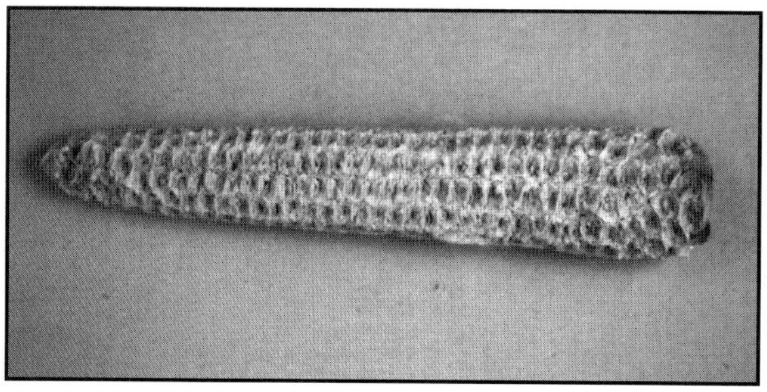

Variety unknown
Probably Agricultural Period
(Anasazi or Fremont, AD 1–1300)
Lent to MPC, 2000–2005
CARE 22

L: 15.2 cm
D: 2.8 cm

Twelve-row corn cob, all kernels removed. Fragments of white or yellow kernels remain. Stalk end is brown, possibly charred.

Excellent condition; intact and complete. Mildew damage on stalk end. Stable.

199 CORN COB

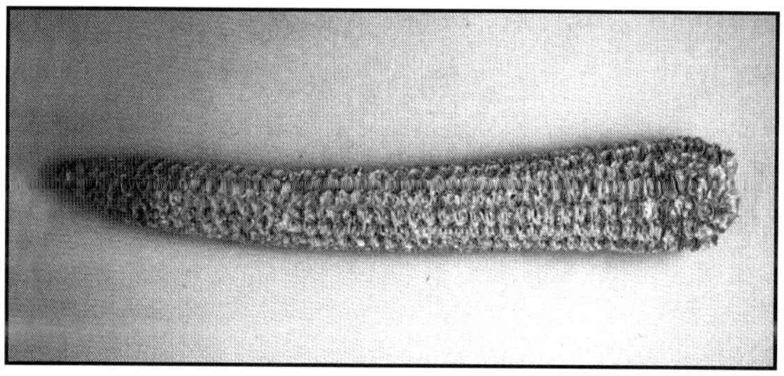

Variety unknown
Probably Agricultural Period
(Anasazi or Fremont, AD 1–1300)
Lent to MPC, 2000–2005
CARE 25

L: 21.2 cm
Diam: 3.2 cm

Sixteen-row corn cob, all kernels removed. Fragments of red kernels remain.

Excellent condition; intact and complete. Impressions (possibly from human fingernail) in stalk end. Mildew damage on stalk end and tip. Stable.

200 CORN KERNELS

Varieties unknown
Probably Agricultural Period
(Anasazi or Fremont, AD 1–1300)
Lent to MPC, 2000–2005
CARE 234

In excess of 150 corn kernels of at least three varieties: red, yellow, and dent corn. One bean and several charcoal fragments.

Excellent condition; intact and largely complete. Some desiccation and shrinkage. Evidence of mildew damage and past infestation. Rodent gnawing of a few kernels. Fly spots. Stable.

201 BEANS AND CORN

Varieties unknown
Probably Agricultural Period
(Anasazi or Fremont, AD 1–1300)
Lent to MPC, 2000–2005
CARE 235

Forty-nine red beans, one white bean, and four corn kernels. Two kernels may be dent corn.

Excellent condition; intact and complete. Skin of some beans is cracked (as are some beans), small surface losses. Some desiccation and shriveling, especially of corn kernels. Some white efflorescence. Stable.

202 GOURD RIND

Variety unknown
Prehistoric (before 17th century AD)
Lent to MPC, 2000–2005
CARE 60

L: 25.0 cm
W: 15.7 cm
D: 12.5 cm

Medium-sized, oblong, hollow gourd rind, charred and blistered from heat exposure.

Very good condition; intact and incomplete. One large area of loss near stem end, four open cracks radiating from it. Largest crack extends to another small area of loss with four thorough cracks and one open crack radiating from the second area of loss. Surface loss where blisters have burst. Numerous scrapes and abrasions. Patches of extensive fly spots. Powdery white accretions on side. Rodent feces. Stable.

Comments:
According to Wills and Huckell, squash was introduced into the Southwest at about the same time as corn, i.e., as early as 1200–1000 BC, while Martin noted remains of squash in Basketmaker coprolites from Glen Canyon (from AD 300).[59]

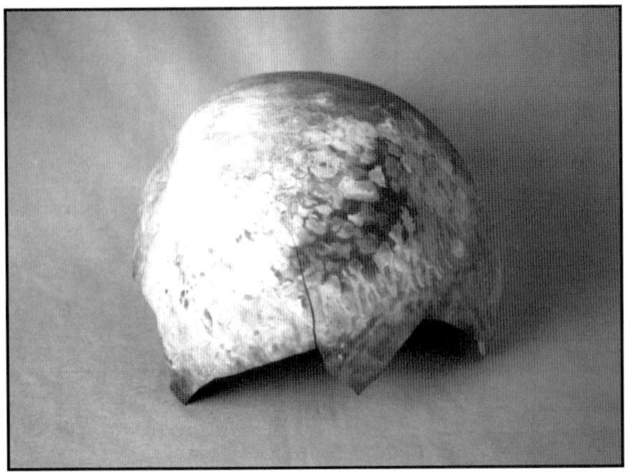

203 GOURD RIND

Variety unknown
Prehistoric (before 17th century AD)
Lent to Capitol Reef National Park
(On display at Visitor Center)
CARE 1617

L: 25.0 cm
W: 25.0 cm
D: 27.5 cm

Roughly spherical, dried gourd rind with hole cut in top.

Fair condition; intact and complete. Cracking throughout, with most cracks radiating from hole in top. Some blind cracks. Charred and darkened surface. Large areas of surface loss, some resembling worm-tracks. Exfoliation of portions of surface. Weak.

204 GOURD RIND

Variety unknown
Prehistoric (before 17th century AD)
Lent to Capitol Reef National Park
(On display at Visitor Center)
CARE 264

L: 53.3 cm
Diam: 15.2 cm

Oblong, dried gourd rind with oval hole cut in upper surface. Surface mottled with a variety of colors.

Good condition; intact and complete. A few deep hairline cracks on sides radiating from end and hole in top. Delamination of outer surface. One large area of surface loss below hole in top. Bottom of interior is stained brown. Possible salting on interior. Discoloration of portions of exterior. Stable.

205 GOURD RIND

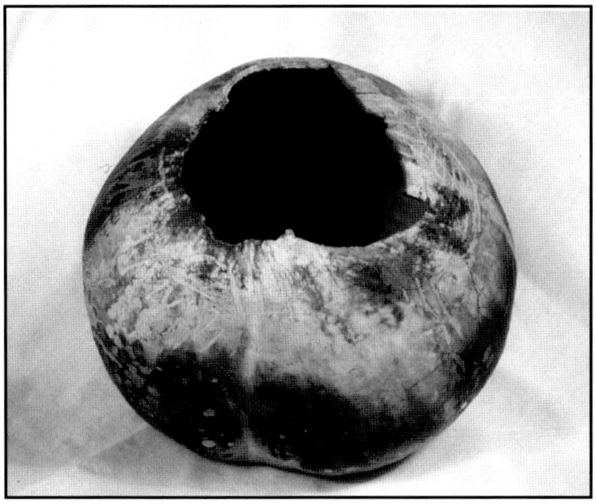

Varieties unknown
Prehistoric (before 17th century AD)
Lent to MPC, 2000–2005
CARE 46

L: 29.8 cm
W: 23.5 cm
D: 20.3 cm

One large oblong gourd rind and 40 fragments (not pictured), including 31 of one variety and nine of second variety. All are charred and blistered from heat exposure.

Good condition; partially intact and incomplete. Largest piece has extensive open cracks and surface loss where blisters have popped. Stem end and large section of the side missing. One large complex crack extending almost to blossom end. Small patches of surface abrasions. Fly spots. Rodent feces. Smaller pieces are charred and blistered, with some surface loss where blisters have burst. Five pieces have extensive mineral crystallization. Evidence of past infestation on various pieces. Powdery white accretions on two pieces. Stable.

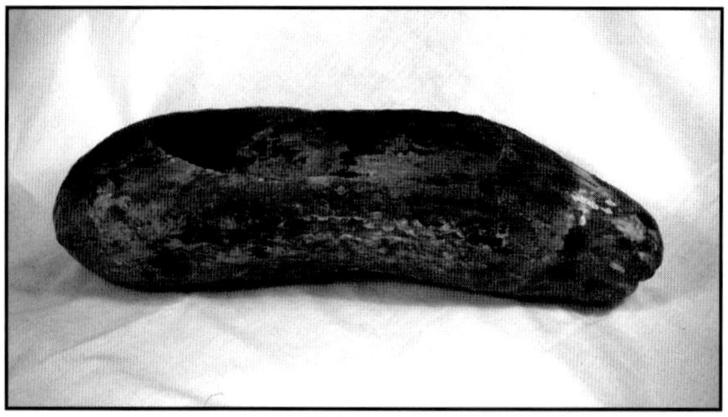

206 GOURD RIND

Variety unknown
Prehistoric (before 17th century AD)
Lent to MPC, 2000–2005
CARE 47

L: 24.5 cm
W: 24.2 cm
D: 15.0 cm

Large, roughly spherical gourd rind. Extensive charring and blistering to outer skin due to heat exposure.

Good condition; broken in three pieces and incomplete. Largest piece has two thorough cracks extending from rim toward base, 10.0 and 7.0 cm in length, respectively. Some warping to side of longer crack. Numerous parallel scratches on outer skin. Medium-sized piece has one small open crack. Minor particulation. Extensive surface loss where blisters have burst. Various scrapes and abrasions on exterior surface. Crusty tan accretions near blossom end may be natural flaws in the gourd's skin. Rodent feces. Fly spots. Evidence of past infestation. Stable.

ARTIFACTUAL FAUNAL ITEMS

207 BUTCHERED RIB FRAGMENT?

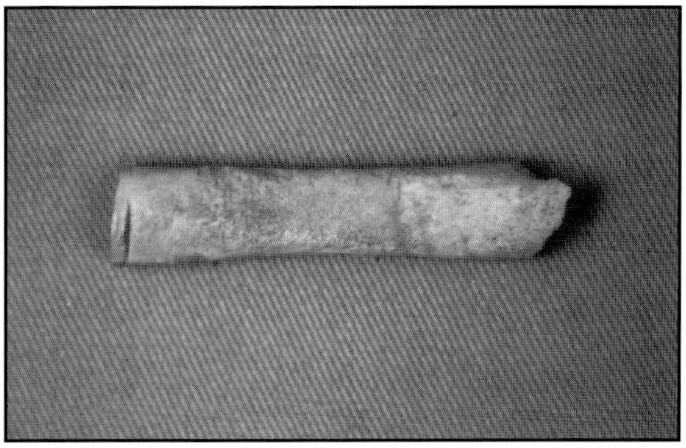

Bone
Agricultural Period
(Anasazi or Fremont, AD 1–1300)?
Lent to MPC, 2000–2005
CARE 55

L: 5.5 cm

Small piece of rib bone preserving a few gnaw marks(?). Two horizontal cut marks creating a jagged edge on one side—the one closest to proximal end was cut one third of the way through and then snapped off.

Good condition; intact and stable.

208 BONES FROM A MEAL?

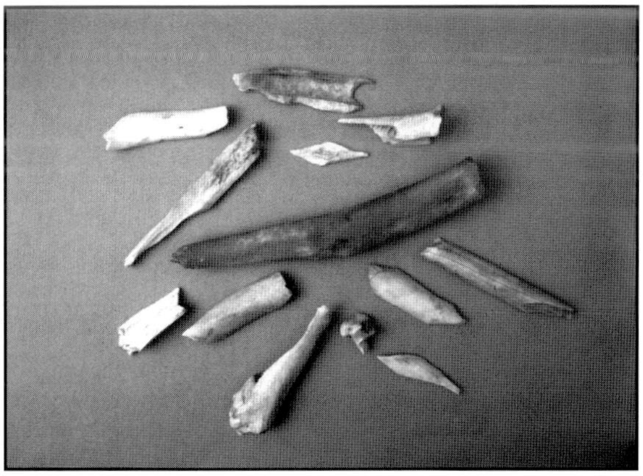

Bone
Prehistoric/Historic (before AD 1900)
Lent to MPC, 2000–2005
CARE H 4903

L: 4.0–6.5 cm

Miscellaneous broken bones with gnaw marks on all of them. Only one shows sign of modification by humans—possible impact scar from breaking to obtain marrow.

Fair condition; intact and stable.

MISCELLANEOUS

Non-Artifactual Faunal Items (not dated or affiliated)

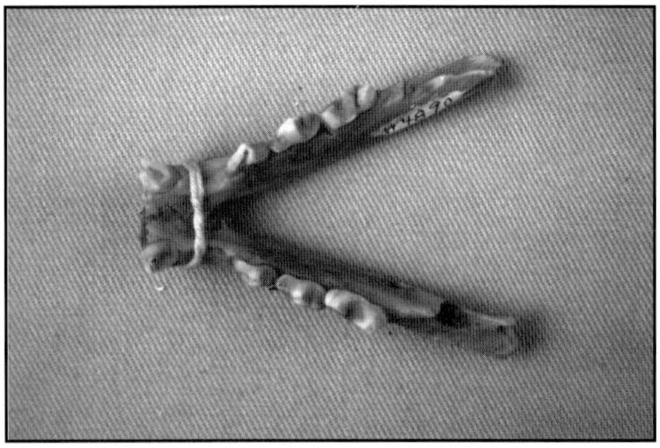

209 MANDIBLE

Bobcat
Lent to MPC, 2000–2005
CARE 4890

L: 6.0 cm
W: 4.5 cm

Mature bobcat mandible preserving all teeth except one lower canine.

Fair condition; reconstructed from two fragments with thread. Largely complete. Structurally unstable (several teeth are loose).

210 VERTEBRA

Bison
Lent to MPC, 2000–2005
CARE H 4902

L: 4.0 cm
W: 5.0 cm

Epiphyseal cap from bison vertebra.

Good condition; intact and complete. Stable.

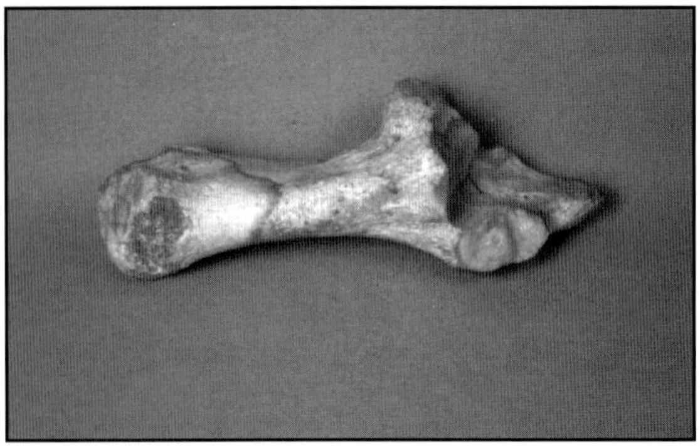

211 HEEL

Bison
Lent to MPC, 2000–2005
CARE 37

L: 19.0 cm
W: 7.5 cm

Bison calcaneus bone.

Fair condition; intact. Sun-bleached? Stable.

212 TAIL SECTION

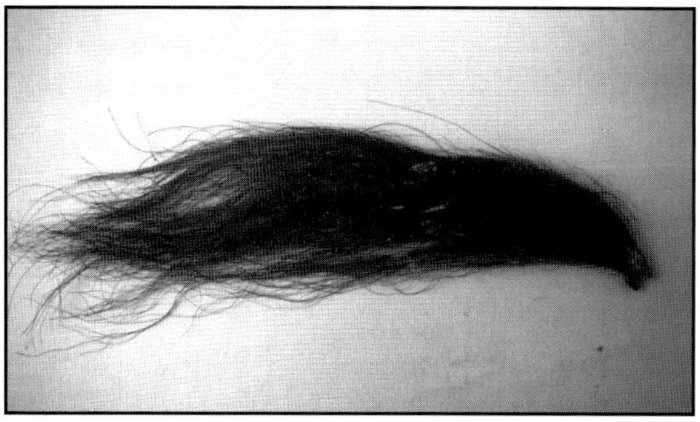

Bison?
Lent to MPC, 2000–2005
CARE 58

L: 30.0 cm

Scalp of animal tail, perhaps of bison, preserving long hair.

Poor condition; intact. Unstable (hair slipping and breaking).

213 SECTION OF MANE OR TAIL

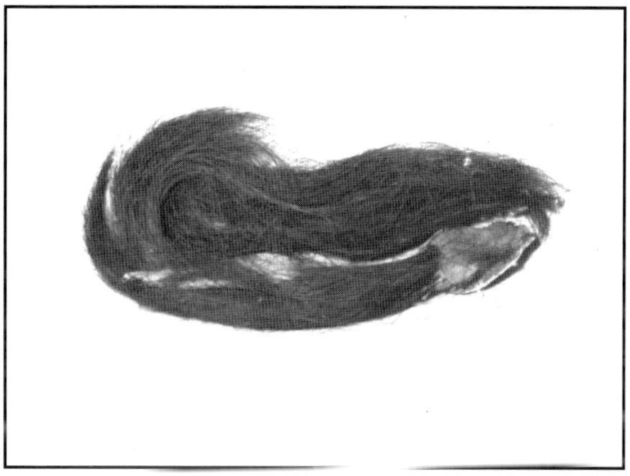

Horse
Lent to MPC, 2000–2005
CARE 159

L: 55.0 cm

Section of rawhide, perhaps of horse, with long hair still attached.

Poor condition; largely intact. Desiccated. Incrustations of dirt. Unstable (hair slipping and breaking).

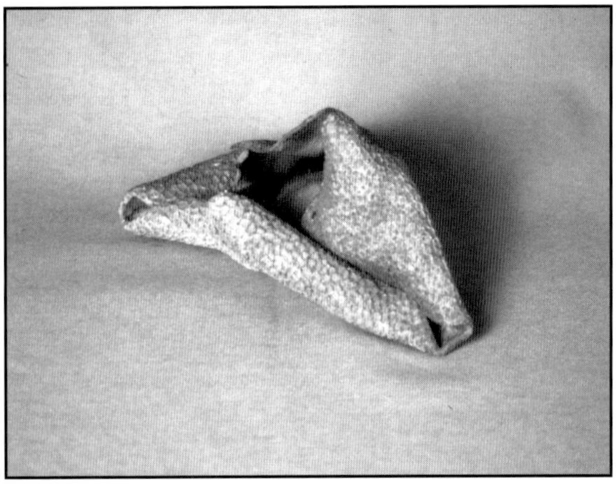

214 SECTION OF HIDE OR ANIMAL ORGAN?

Lent to MPC, 2000–2005
CARE 35

L: 28.0 cm
W: 8.5 cm

Shriveled piece of cut leather or animal organ resembling tripe with a rough cantaloupe-like exterior and smooth interior which is folded over onto itself.

Fair condition; intact. Warped, embrittled. Cloudy white accretions (bloom, mold?). Fly spots. Stable.

215 HORN

Bighorn sheep
Lent to MPC, 2000–2005
CARE 67

L: 33.8 cm
W: 12.5 cm
D: 3.3 cm

Proper right horn from a male bighorn sheep. Yellow pigment (ochre?) on top of horns.

Poor condition; intact and partially complete. Both ends broken off with associated loss and delamination of layers of horn. Missing parts near both ends. Significant damage to ridges of dorsal side, apparently animal gnawing (rodent?). Charring along one side. Pungent odor. Stable.

216 SKULL WITH HORN CORE

Bighorn sheep
Lent to MPC, 2000–2005
CARE 78

L: 35.0 cm
W: 14.5 cm

Upper cranium of a bighorn sheep preserving parietals with base of horn cores and portions of orbitals.

Very poor condition; largely intact but unstable (badly particulating).

217 SKULL WITH HORN CORE

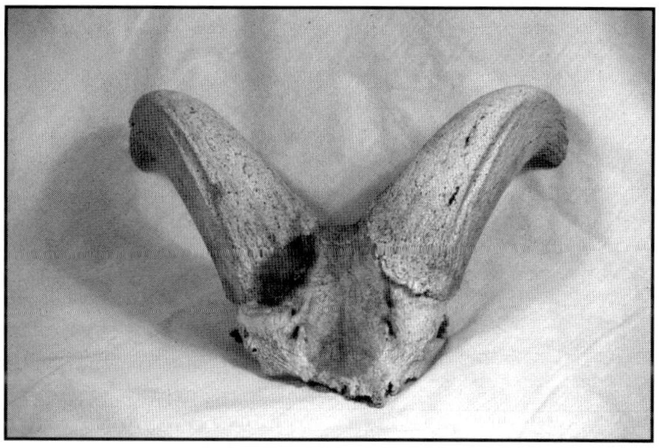

Lent to Capitol Reef National Park
(On display at Visitor Center)
CARE 1612

H: 16.0 cm
W: 39.0 cm
D: 27.0 cm

Bone skull cap and horn core of a bighorn sheep. Remnant of horn attached to proper right horn, large piece on front, and small piece at base of horn on back. Modern cut at base of skull cap. Three holes drilled inside skull cap.

Good condition; intact and complete. Open cracks on distal ends of horn cores; scattered blind cracks along grain. Dessicated. Particulation. Scattered black accretions on horns. Edges of skull cap jagged. Unstable.

218 DEFORMED ANTLER

Deer
Lent to MPC, 2000–2005
CARE 68

L: 68.2 cm
W: 10.0 cm

Unusually formed, four-pointed, deer antler which preserves entire base of antler. Base is partially hollowed out, possibly from infection during life of animal. No evidence of human alteration but may have been saved or collected as a charm or curiosity.

Fair condition, intact. Large dark oily stain on one tine, possibly from handling. Weathering resulting in crackling. Stable.

Ecofact

219 UNMODIFIED COBBLE

Quartz
Lent to MPC, 2000–2005
CARE 45

L: 7.2 cm
W: 4.4 cm
D: 3.2 cm

Unmodified natural cobble resembling an axe. No signs of use—collected as a curiosity?

Excellent condition; intact and complete. Stable.

1. C. Melvin Aikens, *Hogup Cave*, University of Utah Anthropological Papers No. 93 (Salt Lake City: University of Utah Press, 1970), 160–168.

2. Marti L. Allen and Shane A. Baker, eds., *Of Earth, Stone, and Corn: The Anasazi and their Puebloan Descendants*, Museum of Peoples and Cultures Popular Series 2 (Provo, Utah: Brigham Young University, 2000), 151, cat. no. 64.

3. See Robert F. Burgh and Charles Scoggin, *The Archaeology of Castle Park Dinosaur National Monument*, University of Colorado Studies Series in Anthropology, No. 2 (Boulder, Colo.: University of Colorado Press, 1948), 63.

4. James Adovasio, *Basketry Technology* (Chicago: Aldine, 1977), 153, fig. 165.

5. Pamela Miller, Curator of Archaeology at College of Eastern Utah Prehistoric Museum, has cautioned that the intended background color on this and the pursuant decorated trays was reddish brown, and that the reddish-purple coloring may be the result of a subsequent stain. The complex variations in the coloring on these trays makes it difficult to be definitive regarding which shades were intended and which are the result of fading, use, or burial phenomena. Leslie-lynne Sinkey was inclined to interpret the reddish-purple coloring as intended decoration. In her opinion, the dark reddish-purple coloring underlies all accretions, has a discernible patterning that suggests planned application, and was subject to inconsistent fading, which caused the mottled or variegated appearance of the coloration.

6. James Adovasio, *Basketry Technology*, 63, fig. 1a, shows another example of precisely this technique.

7. Allen and Baker, eds., *Of Earth, Stone, and Corn*, 149, cat. no. 29.

8. Beta 152522, AMS date (wood), 150+/-40 BP. Calibrated dates (2 sigma range) AD 1640–1690, AD 1730–1810, and AD 1920–1950.

9. Linda Scott Cummings and Kathryn Puseman, "Pollen, Starch, Phytolith, and Macrofloral Analysis of Residue and Macrofloral Analysis of Basketry Material from the Pectol Collection, Utah," Paleo Research Institute Technical Report 01-43 (unpublished manuscript at Museum of Peoples and Cultures, June 2001).

10. James Adovasio, "Prehistoric Basketry," in *Great Basin*, ed. Warren L. D'Azevedo, vol. 11, *Handbook of North American Indians,* ed. W. C. Sturtevant (Washington, D.C.: Smithsonian Institution, 1986), 202.

11. Cf. David Hurst Thomas, Lorann S. A. Pendleton, and Stephen C. Cappannari, "Western Shoshone," in *Great Basin*, ed. Warren L. D'Azevedo, vol. 11, *Handbook of North American Indians,* ed. W. C. Sturtevant (Washington, D.C.: Smithsonian Institution, 1986), 270, fig. 8.

12. Jesse D. Jennings, *Danger Cave*, University of Utah Anthropological Papers No. 27 (reprint 1970; Salt Lake City: University of Utah Press, 1957), 256; 244, fig. 224c. Jennings assigned dates to Level D III in a later publication: Jesse D. Jennings, *Prehistory of Utah and the Eastern Great Basin*, University of Utah Anthropological Papers No. 98 (Salt Lake City: University of Utah, 1978), 32 and 35, fig. 16.

13. Pamela Miller, Curator of Archaeology, College of Eastern Utah Prehistoric Museum, Price, Utah, personal communication, May 17, 2001.

14. Jennings, *Danger Cave*, 244, fig. 224b.

15. Pottery color readings are from *Munsell Soil Color Charts* (Baltimore: Macbeth Division of Kollmorgen Corporation, 1975).

16. Beta 154227, AMS date (plant material), 1040 +/- 40 BP. Calibrated dates (2 sigma range) AD 910–920 and AD 960–1030.

17. The type terminology followed in these descriptions is based on Jennings, *Prehistory of Utah and the Eastern Great Basin*.

18. Beta 152519, AMS date (animal hide sample), measured age, 230 BP; conventional age, 310 BP; error, +/- 40 BP. Calibrated dates (2 sigma range) AD 1470 to 1660.

19. The Apache attribution was suggested by Benson Lanford and Pamela Miller in "Late Prehistoric Painted Rawhide and Leather Artifacts from Utah, *American Indian Art*, vol. 25, no. 3 (Summer 2000): 38–47.

20. Aikens, *Hogup Cave*, 91 and 94, fig. 56.

21. On the decimation of Desert Bighorn Sheep, see James A. Goss, "Traditional Cosmology, Ecology and Language of the Ute Indians," in *Ute Indian Arts and Culture from Prehistory to the New Millennium*, ed. William Wroth (Colorado Springs: Colorado Springs Fine Arts Center, 2001), 31.

22. Jennings, *Danger Cave*, 200, fig. 182a–b and 201, fig. 184c–d.

23. Jennings, *Prehistory of Utah and the Eastern Great Basin*, 32 and 35, fig. 16.

24. H. M. Wormington, "Reappraisal of the Fremont Culture," *Denver Museum of Natural History*, no. 1 (1955): 61.

25. Demitri B. Shimkin, "Eastern Shoshone," in *Great Basin*, ed. Warren L. D'Azevedo, vol. 11, *Handbook of North American Indians,* ed. W. C. Sturtevant (Washington, D.C.: Smithsonian Institution, 1986), 324, fig. 16c.

26. Ibid., 309.

27. Cummings and Puseman, "Pollen, Starch, Phytolith, and Macrofloral Analysis."

28. Blaine Miller, Bureau of Land Management, personal communication, dates on file at the BLM, Price Field Office. 840+/- 70 BP, 830+/- 60 BP. Calibrated date (two sigma range), AD 1050–1150.

29. James H. Gunnerson, "Three Wooden Shovels from Nile Mile Canyon," in *Miscellaneous Collected Papers*, ed. James H. Gunnerson, David M. Pendergast, and Keith M. Anderson, University of Utah Anthropological Papers No. 60 (Salt Lake City: University of Utah, 1962), 3–4.

30. Ibid., 4.

31. Pamela Miller, Curator of Archaeology, College of Eastern Utah Prehistoric Museum, personal communication, June 1, 2001.

32. Kay Sargent, "On a Dig in Southeastern Utah," in Beehive History 3, ed. Miriam B. Murphey (Salt Lake City: Utah Historical Society, 1978), 6. Platters now held at the Utah Division of State History in Salt Lake City.

33. Otis Tufton Mason, "A Primitive Frame for Weaving Narrow Fabrics," Annual Report of the Board of Regents of the Smithsonian Institution, Showing the Operations, Expenditures, and Condition of the Institution for the Year Ending June 30, 1899, report of the U.S. National Museum" (Washington, D.C.: Government Printing Office, 1901), 487–511, pl. 9: Pueblo Batten Knives for Beating Home the Weft, esp. second from the top.

34. Elizabeth Morris, "Anasazi Textiles," in *Treading in the Past: Sandals of the Anasazi*, ed. Kathy Kankainen (Salt Lake City: University of Utah Press, 1995), 6.

35. Allen and Baker, eds., *Of Earth, Stone, and Corn*, 151, cat. nos. 34–35 (MPC 95.2.105.1, MPC 98.10.14.1).

36. James Adovasio, *Basketry Technology*, 154–155, fig. 166, a–b (b is the closest match).

37. Ibid., 154.

38. Shimkin, "Eastern Shoshone," 322, fig. 14.

39. Joel C. Janetski, "Wood and Reed Artifacts," in Jesse D. Jennings, *Cowboy Cave*, University of Utah Anthropological Papers No. 104 (Salt Lake City: University of Utah Press, 1980), 82, fig. 36, esp. b; and 87 (discussion).

40. Phil R. Geib, Archaeology Department, NAU Branch, The Navajo Nation, Flagstaff, Arizona, personal communication, July 12, 2001.

41. The Museum is grateful to Phil R. Geib of the Archaeology Department, NAU Branch, The Navajo Nation, Flagstaff, Arizona, for examining this horn tool and the tool listed in the ensuing entry for micro-chert traces. His descriptive information and comments are included through his permission. The condition report and observations regarding the use wear as suggested by warping, discoloration, and indentations were the editor's.

42. Pamela Miller, "Radiocarbon Dating of Leather Samples from Prehistoric Robes," Division of History 1992 Grant to the CEU Prehistoric Museum Final Report (unpublished manuscript, College of Eastern Utah Prehistoric Museum, 1993), 1–2.

43. Personal communication, June 2001. Cf. also, Miller, "Radiocarbon Dating of Leather Samples from Prehistoric Robes," 1–2.

44. Beta 152521, AMS (animal hide), 920 +/- 40 BP. Calibrated date (two sigma range), AD 1020 –1210.

45. Lanford and Miller in "Late Prehistoric Painted Rawhide and Leather Artifacts from Utah," 38–47.

46. Cf., for example, Robert F. Murphy and Yolanda Murphy, "Northern Shoshone and Bannock," in *Great Basin*, ed. Warren L. D'Azevedo, vol. 11, *Handbook of North American Indians,* ed. W. C. Sturtevant (Washington, D.C.: Smithsonian Institution, 1986), 304, fig. 13.

47. E. P. Pectol, "Wayne County: Wayne Wonderland and Its Ancient Culture" (unpublished manuscript in possession of Neal Busk, Richfield, Utah, 1947), 5. Pectol apparently intended this manuscript eventually to become a chapter of a book on the history of Wayne County.

48. Lanford and Miller, "Late Prehistoric Painted Rawhide," 42–43 with figs. 8–11.

49. Pauline Turner Strong, "Santa Ana Pueblo," in *Southwest*, ed. Alfonso Ortiz, vol. 9, *Handbook of the North American Indians,* ed. W. C. Sturtevant (Washington, D.C.: Smithsonian Institution, 1979), 402, fig. 7. The practice of attaching things to fringed leather may have a long history: cf. C. Melvin Aikens and David B. Madsen, "Prehistory of the Eastern Area," in *Great Basin*, ed. Warren L. D'Azevedo, vol. 11, *Handbook of North American Indians,* ed. W. C. Sturtevant (Washington, D.C.: Smithsonian Institution, 1986), 157, fig. 10e (Hogup Cave, AD 400).

50. Capitol Reef Park does not retain a record of the full name of the cataloguer Clark.

51. James D. Wilde, employed by the Brigham Young University Office of Public Archaeology in 1986, examined the Pectol-Lee collection at the request of Capitol Reef staff.

52. Winston Hurst and Bruce D. Louthan, *Survey of Rock Art in the Central Portion of Nine Mile Canyon*, Publications in Archaeology, New Series No. 4, Department of Anthropology (Provo, Utah: Brigham Young University, 1979), 76, fig. 33.

53. Polly Schaafsma, *Rock Art of Utah: A Study from the Donald Scott Collection* (Salt Lake City: University of Utah Press, 1994), 44, pl. 22.

54. Ibid., 52, fig. 52.

55. John Noxon and Deborah Marcus, "A Preliminary Report on the Rock Art of Capitol Reef National Park in Utah: A Project granted by the Youthgrants in the Humanities, July 30, 1978" (unpublished manuscript, College of Eastern Utah Prehistoric Museum J. Eldon Dorman Research Library, 1978), 6, figs. 1 and 2.

56. Beta 152520, AMS date (animal hide), 920 +/- 40 BP. Calibrated dates (two sigma range) AD 980–1050 and AD 1100–1140.

57. James A. Maxwell, ed., "America's Fascinating Indian Heritage," *Readers Digest* (Pleasantville, New York: The Reader's Digest Association, Inc., 1978), 174.

58. Richard N. Holmer, "Projectile Points of the Intermountain West," in *Anthropology of the Desert West*, eds. Carol Condie and Don Fowler, University of Utah Anthropological Papers No. 110 (Salt Lake City: University of Utah Press, 1986), 105.

59. W. H. Wills and Bruce B. Huckell, "Economic Implications of Changing Land-Use Patterns in the Late Archaic," in *Themes in Southwest Prehistory*, ed. George J. Gummerman (Santa Fe: School of American Research, 1994), 35; and, Debra Martin, "Patterns of Diet and Disease: Health Profiles for the Prehistoric Southwest," in *Themes in Southwest Prehistory*, ed. George J. Gummerman (Santa Fe: School of American Research, 1994), 98.

BIBLIOGRAPHY

Adovasio, James M.

1970 Origin, Development and Distribution of Western Archaic Textiles. *Tebiwa* 13(2):1–40.

1974 Prehistoric North American Basketry. In *Nevada State Museum Anthropological Papers Number 16,* Collected Paper No. 5, pp. 99–148. Nevada State Museum, Carson City.

1975 Fremont Basketry. *Tebiwa* 17(2):67–76.

1977 *Basketry Technology: A Guide to Identification and Analysis.* Aldine, Chicago.

1979 Comment by Adovasio. *American Antiquity* 44(4):723–731.

1986a Prehistoric Basketry. In *Great Basin,* edited by Warren L. d'Azevedo, pp. 194–205. *Handbook of American Indians*, vol. 11, William C. Sturtevant, general editor. Smithsonian Institution, Washington, D.C.

1986b Artifacts and Ethnicity: Basketry as an Indicator of Territoriality and Population Movements in the Prehistoric Great Basin. In *Anthropology of the Desert West: Essays in Honor of Jesse D. Jennings,* edited by Carol J. Condie and Don D. Fowler, pp. 45–88. University of Utah Press, Salt Lake City.

Allen, Marti L., and Shane A. Baker (editors)

2000 *Of Earth, Stone, and Corn: The Anasazi and Their Puebloan Descendants.* Museum of Peoples and Cultures Popular Series 2. Brigham Young University, Provo, Utah.

Bean, Lowell John, and Dorothea Theodoratus

1986 Eastern Pomo and Southeastern Pomo. In *California*, edited by Robert F. Heizer, pp. 289–305. *Handbook of North American Indians,* vol. 8, William C. Sturtevant, general editor. Smithsonian Institution, Washington, D.C.

Beckwith, Frank

1927 The High Priest's Vestments Used by the Ancient Cliff Dwellers of Wayne County Centuries Ago. *Improvement Era* (September):1029–1037.

Bee, Robert L.

1983 Quechan. In *Southwest*, edited by Alfonso Ortiz, pp. 86–98. *Handbook of Native American Indians*, vol. 10, William C. Sturtevant, general editor. Smithsonian Institution, Washington, D.C.

Brody, J. J.

1991 *Anasazi and Pueblo Painting.* University of New Mexico Press, Albuquerque.

1997 *Pueblo Indian Painting: Tradition and Modernism in New Mexico, 1900–1930.* School of American Research Press, Santa Fe.

Brooks, Juanita

1970 *The Mountain Meadow Massacre.* University of Oklahoma Press, Norman.

1992 *John Doyle Lee: Zealot, Pioneer Builder, Scapegoat.* Utah State University Press, Logan.

Bunzel, Ruth L.

1992 *Zuni Ceremonialism.* University of New Mexico Press, Albuquerque.

Burgh, Robert F., and Charles R. Scoggin

1948 *The Archaeology of Castle Park Dinosaur National Monument.* University of Colorado Studies Series in Anthropology No. 2. University of Colorado Press, Boulder.

Callaway, Donald G., Joel C. Janetski, and Omer C. Stewart

1986 Ute. In *Great Basin,* edited by Warren L. d'Azevedo, pp. 336–367. *Handbook of North American Indians*, vol. 11, William C. Sturtevant, general editor. Smithsonian Institution, Washington, D.C.

Christensen Southwick, Elaine (arrangers)

1971 *". . . And I Went Home Rejoicing:" The Background, Life and Posterity of Edward Southwick III.* J. Grant Stevenson, Provo, Utah.

Coltrain, Joan Brenner

1994 Fremont Foragers and Farmers: A Stable Carbon Isotope Study. Paper presented at the 24th Great Basin Anthropological Conference, Elko, Nevada. n.d.

1996 Stable Carbon and Radioisotope Analyses. In *Steinaker Gap: An Early Fremont Farmstead*, by Richard K. Talbot and Lane D. Richens, pp. 115–122. Museum of Peoples and Cultures Occasional Papers No. 2. Brigham Young University, Provo, Utah.

Copeland, James M., and Richard E. Fike

1988 "Fluted Projectile Points in Utah." *Utah Archaeology 1988* 1(1):5–28.

Davis, William E., Dorothy Sack, and Nancy Shearin

1996 "The Hell'N Moriah Clovis Site." *Utah Archaeology 1996* 9(1):55–70.

d'Azevedo, Warren L.

1986 Washoe. In *Great Basin*, edited by Warren L. d'Azevedo, pp. 466–489. *Handbook of North American Indians,* vol. 11, William C. Sturtevant, general editor. Smithsonian Institution, Washington, D.C.

De Ved, L., and R. De Ved

1994 Prehistoric Baskets from the Leo C. Thorne Collection, Part 1. *Utah Archaeology 1994* 7(1):117–126.

Dumarest, Father Noel

1919 Notes on Cochiti, New Mexico, translated and annotated by Elsie Clews Parsons, pp. 137–236. In *Memories of the American Anthropological Association*, vol. 6, no. 3.

Dwyer, James, and David Rattray (senior editors)

1997 *Magic and Medicine of Plants,* 9th edition. The Reader's Digest Association, Inc., Pleasantville, New York.

Euler, Robert C.

1966 *Southern Paiute Ethnohistory.* Glen Canyon Series No. 28, Anthropological Papers No. 78. University of Utah Press, Salt Lake City.

Fewkes, J. Walter

1926 *An Archaeological Collection from Young's Canyon, Near Flagstaff, Arizona.* Smithsonian Miscellaneous Collections, vol. 77, no. 10.

Fowler, Catherine S.

1986 Subsistence. In *Great Basin*, edited by Warren L. d'Azevedo, pp. 64–97. *Handbook of North American Indians,* vol. 11, William C. Sturtevant, general editor. Smithsonian Institution, Washington, D.C.

2000 Great Basin Affiliations of the Ute Peoples of Colorado. In *Ute Indian Arts and Culture from Prehistory to the New Millennium,* edited by William Wroth, pp. 89–106. Colorado Springs Fine Arts Center, Colorado Springs.

Fowler, Catherine S., and Lawrence E. Dawson

1986 Ethnographic Basketry. In *Great Basin*, edited by Warren L. d'Azevedo, pp. 705–737. *Handbook of North American Indians,* vol. 11, William C. Sturtevant, general editor. Smithsonian Institution, Washington, D.C.

Fowler, Catherine S., and Sven Liljeblad

1986 Northern Paiute. In *Great Basin*, edited by Warren L. d'Azevedo, pp. 435–465. *Handbook of North American Indians,* vol. 11, William C. Sturtevant, general editor. Smithsonian Institution, Washington, D.C.

Geib, Phil R.
1996 *Glen Canyon Revisited.* Anthropological Papers No. 119. University of Utah Press, Salt Lake City.

Griffith, James Seavey
1983 Kachinas and Masking. In *Southwest*, edited by Alfonso Ortiz, pp. 368–392. *Handbook of North American Indians,* vol. 10, William C. Sturtevant, general editor. Smithsonian Institution, Washington, D.C.

Gunnerson, James H.
1969 *The Fremont Culture: A Study in Culture Dynamics on the Northern Anasazi Frontier*. Papers of the Peabody Museum of Archaeology and Ethnology, vol. 59, no. 2. Harvard University, Cambridge.

Haas, Jonathan, Edmund J. Ladd, Jerrold E. Levy, Randall H. McGuire, and Norman Yoffee
1994 Historical Processes in the Prehistoric Southwest. In *Understanding Complexity in the Prehistoric Southwest*, edited by George J. Gumerman and Murray Gell-Mann, pp. 203–232. SFI Studies in the Sciences of Complexity, Proceedings, vol. 16. Addison-Wesley, Reading, Massachusetts.

Harrington, Mark R.
1937 Excavation of Pueblo Grande de Nevada. *Bulletin of the Texas Archaeological and Paleontology Society* 9:130–145.

Haviland, William A.
2002 *Cultural Anthropology,* 10th edition. Harcourt College Publishers, Orlando.

Janetski, Joel C., and Lee Kreutzer
1997 Contrasts in Forager and Farmer Land Use along the Waterpocket Fold, Capitol Reef National Park. Paper presented at the 62nd Annual Conference, Society for American Archaeology, Nashville. April 5, 1997.

Janetski, Joel C., Richard K. Talbot, Deborah E. Newman, Lane D. Richens, James D. Wilde, Shane A. Baker, and Scott E. Billat
1997 *Clear Creek Canyon Archaeological Project Volume Five: Results and Synthesis*. Museum of Peoples and Cultures Technical Series 95-9. Brigham Young University, Provo, Utah.

Jennings, Jesse D.
1974 *Prehistory of North America*, 2nd edition. McGraw-Hill, New York.

1978 *Prehistory of Utah and the Eastern Great Basin.* Anthropological Papers No. 98. University of Utah Press, Salt Lake City.

1980 *Cowboy Cave*. Anthropological Papers No. 104. University of Utah Press, Salt Lake City.

Jennings, Jesse D., Alan R. Schroedl, and Richard N. Holmer
1980 *Sudden Shelter*. Anthropological Papers No. 103. University of Utah Press, Salt Lake City.

Jennings, Jesse D., and Dorothy Sammons-Lohse
1981 *Bull Creek*. Anthropological Papers No. 105. University of Utah Press, Salt Lake City.

Jennings, Jesse D., Erik K. Reed, James B. Griffin, J. Charles Kelley, Clement W. Meighan, Stanley Stubbs, Joe Ben Wheat, and Dee C. Taylor
1956 The American Southwest: A Problem in Cultural Isolation. In *Seminars in Archaeology: 1955*, edited by R. Wauchope, pp. 50–128. Memoirs of the Society for American Archaeology, Salt Lake City.

Johnson, Judi
1983 *Native American Dolls and Cradleboards*. Illinois State Museum Handbook of Collections, No. 4. Illinois State Museum, Springfield.

Kaestle, Frederika A., and David Glenn Smith
2001 Ancient Mitochondrial DNA Evidence for Prehistoric Population Movement: The Numic Expansion. *American Journal of Physical Anthropology* 115:1–12.

Kelly, Isabel T.
1964 *Southern Paiute Ethnography*. Glen Canyon Series No. 21, Anthropological Papers No. 69. University of Utah Press, Salt Lake City.

Kinnear-Ferris, S. A.
1999 "Analysis of Canyonlands Region Woven Perishables and a Comparison with Those of Surrounding Regions." Unpublished M.A. thesis, Regis University, Denver.

Kreutzer, Lee Ann
1994 The Pectol Collection, Capitol Reef National Park, Utah. *Utah Archaeology 1994* 7(1):104–116.

Kreutzer, Lee Ann, and M. R. Shaw
2001 Survey for Cultural Resources of Little Sand Flat in Capitol Reef National Park, Utah. Manuscript on file, Capitol Reef National Park, Utah.

Lamphere, Louise

1983 Southwestern Ceremonialism. In *Southwest*, edited by Alfonso Ortiz, pp. 743–763. *Handbook of North American Indians,* vol. 10, William C. Sturtevant, general editor. Smithsonian Institution, Washington, D.C.

Lange, Charles H.

1959 *Cochiti: A New Mexico Pueblo Past and Present.* University of Texas Press, Austin.

Lapena, Frank R.

1986 Wintu. In *California*, edited by Robert F. Heizer, pp. 324–340. *Handbook of North American Indians,* vol. 8, William C. Sturtevant, general editor. Smithsonian Institution, Washington, D.C.

Liljenquist, Mauri

2001 "The Commodification of Twentieth-Century Hopi Kachina Dolls." M.A. Thesis, Brigham Young University, Provo.

Lindsay, Alexander J., Jr., J. Richard Ambler, Mary Anne Stein, and Philip M. Hobler

1968 *Survey and Excavation North and East of Navajo Mountain, Utah, 1959–1962.* Museum of Northern Arizona Bulletin No. 45. Flagstaff.

Loeb, E. M.

1926 Pomo Folkways. *University of California Publications in American Archaeology and Ethnology* 19(2):149–405.

Lyneis, Margaret M.

1995 Virgin Anasazi, Far Western Puebloans. *Journal of World Prehistory* 9(2):199–241.

Madsen, David B.

1994 Mesa Verde and Sleeping Ute Mountain: The Geographical and Chronological Dimensions of the Numic Expansion. In *Across the West: Human Population Movement and the Expansion of the Numa*, edited by David B. Madsen and David Rhode, pp. 24–31. University of Utah Press, Salt Lake City.

Madsen, David B., and Steven R. Simms

1998 The Fremont Complex: A Behavioral Perspective. *Journal of World Prehistory* 12(3):255–336.

Madsen, David B., and David Rhode (editors)

1994 *Across the West: Human Population Movement and the Expansion of the Numa.* University of Utah Press, Salt Lake City.

Madsen, Rex E.

1977 *Prehistoric Ceramics of the Fremont.* Ceramic Series No. 6. Museum of Northern Arizona, Flagstaff.

Margolin, Malcom (editor)

1993 *The Way We Lived.* Heydey Books, Berkeley.

Mason, O. T.

1988 *American Indian Basketry.* Dover, New York.

Matheny, Ray T., Thomas S. Smith, and Deanne G. Matheny

1997 Animal Ethology Reflected in the Rock Art of Nine Mile Canyon, Utah. *Journal of California and Great Basin Anthropology* 19(1):70–103.

McGavin, Elmer C.

1947 *"Mormonism" and Masonry.* Bookcraft, Salt Lake City.

McKenzie, Jean McConkie

n.d. *Rock Art: Dry Fork Canyon, Vernal, Utah.* Mansfield Publishing, Vernal, Utah.

McLendon, Sally, and Michael J. Lowy

1986 Eastern Pomo and Southeastern Pomo. In *California*, edited by Robert F. Heizer, pp. 306–323. *Handbook of North American Indians,* vol. 8, William C. Sturtevant, general editor. Smithsonian Institution, Washington, D.C.

McQuiston, Don and Debra McQuiston

1995 *Dolls and Toys of Native America: A Journey through Childhood.* Chronicle Books, San Francisco.

Miller, Wick R.

1986 Numic Languages. In *Great Basin,* edited by Warren L. d'Azevedo, pp. 98–106. *Handbook of North American Indians*, vol. 11, William C. Sturtevant, general editor. Smithsonian Institution, Washington, D.C.

Montgomery, Keith R., and Jackie A. Montgomery

1993 *Utah Department of Transportation State Route-31 Huntington Canyon Project: Archaeological Excavations at Sites 42Em2109 and 42Em2095 Emery County, Utah.* Abajo Archaeology, Bluff, Utah.

Moorman, Donald R., and Gene A Sessions
1992 *Camp Floyd and the Mormons: The Utah War.* University of Utah Press, Salt Lake City.

Morss, Noel
1931 *The Ancient Culture of the Fremont River in Utah: Report on the Explorations under the Claflin-Emerson Fund, 1928–1929.* Papers of the Peabody Museum of American Archaeology and Ethnology, vol. 12, no. 3. Harvard University, Cambridge.

1954a *Clay Figurines of the American Southwest.* Papers of the Peabody Museum of American Archaeology and Ethnology, vol. 49, no. 1. Harvard University, Cambridge.

1954b *The Ancient Culture.* Papers of the Peabody Museum of American Archaeology and Ethnology, vol. 49, no. 1. Harvard University, Cambridge.

Murphy, Miriam B.
A History of Wayne County. Utah State Historical Society, Salt Lake City.

Murphy, Robert F., and Yolanda Murphy
1986 "Northern Shoshone and Bannock." In *Great Basin*, edited by Warren L. d'Azevedo, pp. 284–307. *Handbook of North American Indians,* vol. 11, William C. Sturtevant, general editor. Smithsonian Institution, Washington, D.C.

Office of Public Archaeology
1996 *Capitol Reef National Park Research Design: Phase 1.* Museum of Peoples and Cultures Technical Series No. 96.5. Brigham Young University, Provo, Utah.

Opler, Morris
1983a Chiricahua Apache. In *Southwest*, edited by Alfonso Ortiz, pp. 401–418. *Handbook of North American Indians,* vol. 10, William C. Sturtevant, general editor. Smithsonian Institution, Washington, D.C.

1983b Mescalero Apache. In *Southwest*, edited by Alfonso Ortiz, pp. 419–439. *Handbook of North American Indians,* vol. 10, William C. Sturtevant, general editor. Smithsonian Institution, Washington, D.C.

O'Rourke, Dennis H., M. Geoffrey Hayes, and Shawn W. Carlyle
2000 Ancient DNA Studies in Physical Anthropology. *Annual Review of Anthropology* 29(2000):217–242.

O'Rourke, Dennis H., Ryan L. Parr, and Shawn W. Carlyle

1999 Molecular Genetic Variation in Prehistoric Inhabitants of the Eastern Great Basin. In *Understanding Prehistoric Lifeways in the Great Basin Wetlands: Bioarchaeological Reconstruction and Interpretation*, edited by B.E. Hemphill and C. S. Larsen, pp. 84–102. University of Utah Press, Salt Lake City.

Ortiz, Alfonso

1979 San Juan Pueblo. In *Southwest*, edited by Alfonso Ortiz, pp. 278–295. *Handbook of the North American Indians,* vol. 9, William C. Sturtevant, general editor. Smithsonian Institution, Washington, D.C.

Parson, Elsie Clews

1919 Increase by Magic: A Zuni Pattern. *American Anthropologist* 21(3):279–286.

1939 *Pueblo Indian Religion.* University of Chicago Press, Chicago.

Peterson, Kenneth Lee

1988 *Climate and the Dolores River Anasazi.* Anthropological Papers No. 113. University of Utah, Salt Lake City.

Placc, Chuck

1992 *Ancient Walls: Indian Ruins of the Southwest.* Fulcrum Publishing, Golden, Colorado.

Potter, James M.

1997 Communal Ritual and Faunal Remains: An Example from the Dolores Anasazi. *Journal of Field Archaeology* 24(3):353–364.

Rozaire, Charles E.

1974 Analysis of Woven Materials from Seven Caves in the Lake Winnemucca Area, Pershing County, Nevada. In *Nevada State Museum Anthropological Papers Number 16,* Collected Paper No. 4, pp. 61–97. Nevada State Museum, Carson City.

Schaafsma, Polly

1980 *Indian Rock Art of the Southwest.* University of New Mexico Press, Albuquerque.

1986 Rock Art. In *Great Basin,* edited by Warren L. d'Azevedo, pp. 215–226. *Handbook of North American Indians*, vol. 11, William C. Sturtevant, general editor. Smithsonian Institution, Washington, D.C.

1994 *The Rock Art of Utah: A Study from the Donald Scott Collection.* Reprinted. University of Utah Press, Salt Lake City. Originally published 1971, Papers of the Peabody Museum of Archaeology and Ethnology, vol. 65. Harvard University, Cambridge.

Schroedl, Alan R.
1991 Paleo-Indian Occupation in the Eastern Great Basin and Northern Colorado Plateau. *Utah Archaeology 1991* 4(1):1–15.

Simmons, Leo W.
1970 *Sun Chief: The Autobiography of a Hopi Indian.* Yale University Press, New Haven.

Smiley, Francis E.
1997 Regional Packing, Group Dynamics, and the Diffusion of Innovation. In *Early Farmers in the Northern Southwest: Papers on Chronometry, Social Dynamics, and Ecology*, edited by F. E. Smiley and M. R. Robbins, pp. 59–71. Animas-La Plata Archaeological Project Research Paper No. 7. Flagstaff, Arizona.

Smiley, Francis E., and Michael R. Robins (editors)
1997 *Early Farmers in the Northern Southwest: Papers on Chronometry, Social Dynamics, and Ecology.* Animas-La Plata Archaeological Project Research Paper No. 7. Flagstaff, Arizona.

Smith, Anne M.
1974 *Ethnography of the Northern Utes*. Papers in Anthropology No. 17. Museum of New Mexico Press, Albuquerque.

Steward, Julian H.
1936 *Pueblo Material Culture in Western Utah.* The University of New Mexico Bulletin, No. 287, Anthropological Series, vol. 1, no. 3. Albuquerque.

1938 *Basin-Plateau Aboriginal Sociopolitical Groups.* Bulletin No. 120. Bureau of American Ethnology, Smithsonian Institution, Washington, D.C.

Stewart, Kenneth M.
1983 Mohave. In *Southwest*, edited by Alfonso Ortiz, pp. 55–70. *Handbook of Native American Indians*, vol. 10, William C. Sturtevant, general editor. Smithsonian Institution, Washington, D.C.

Stewart, Omer C.
1942 *Culture Element Distributions: XVIII Ute-Southern Paiute*. University of California Anthropological Records, vol. 6, no. 4. University of California Press, Berkeley.

1966 Tribal Distributions and Boundaries in the Great Basin. In *The Current Status of Anthropological Research in the Great Basin: 1964*, edited by Warren L. d'Azevedo, Wilbur A. Davis, Don D. Fowler, Wayne Suttles, pp. 167–237.

Technical Report Series S-H, Social Sciences and Humanities Publications No. 1. Desert Research Institute, Reno.

Strong, Pauline Turner
1979 Santa Ana Pueblo. In *Southwest*, edited by Alfonso Ortiz, pp. 398–406. *Handbook of the North American Indians,* vol. 9, William C. Sturtevant, general editor. Smithsonian Institution, Washington, D.C.

Talbot, Richard K.
2000 Fremont Farmers: The Search for Context. In *The Archaeology of Regional Interaction: Religion, Warfare, and Exchange across the American Southwest and Beyond*, edited by Michelle Hegmon, 275–293. University Press of Colorado, Boulder.

Talbot, Richard K., and Lane D. Richens
1996 *Steinaker Gap: An Early Fremont Farmstead.* Museum of Peoples and Cultures Occasional Papers No. 2. Brigham Young University, Provo, Utah.

Talbot, Richard K., Lane D. Richens, Shane A. Baker, and Joel C. Janetski
1999 *Broken Arrow Cave (42Ka4356): 1997 Testing Results.* Museum of Peoples and Cultures Technical Series No. 99-5. Brigham Young University, Provo, Utah.

Taylor, Dee C.
1957 *Two Fremont Sites and Their Position in Southwestern Prehistory.* University of Utah Anthropological Papers No. 29. University of Utah Press, Salt Lake City.

Teiwes, Helga
1991 *Kachina Dolls: The Art of Hopi Carvers.* University of Arizona Press, Tucson.

Thomas, David Hurst, Lorann S. A. Pendleton, and Stephen C. Cappannari
1986 Western Shoshone. In *Great Basin,* edited by Warren L. d'Azevedo, pp. 262–283. *Handbook of North American Indians*, vol. 11, William C. Sturtevant, general editor. Smithsonian Institution, Washington, D.C.

Wallace, William J.
1986 Hupa, Chilula, and Whilkut. In *California*, edited by Robert F. Heizer, pp. 164–179. *Handbook of North American Indians,* vol. 8, William C. Sturtevant, general editor. Smithsonian Institution, Washington, D.C.

Wheat, Margaret M.
1986 *Survival Arts of the Primitive Paiute*, 4th edition. University of Nevada Press, Reno.

White, Leslie A.
1942 *The Pueblo of Santa Ana, New Mexico.* Memories of the American Anthropology Association 60. Menasha, Wisconsin.

Wormington, H. Marie
1955 *A Reappraisal of the Fremont Culture.* Denver Museum of Natural History, No. 1. Denver.

1970 *Prehistoric Indians of the Southwest.* The Denver Museum of Natural History, Popular Series No. 7. The Denver Museum of Natural History, Denver.

Wyman, Leland C.
1983 Navajo Ceremonial System. In *Southwest*, edited by Alfonso Ortiz, pp. 536–557. *Handbook of Native American Indians*, vol. 10, William C. Sturtevant, general editor. Smithsonian Institution, Washington, D.C.

Young, M. Jane
1998 *Signs from the Ancestors: Zuni Cultural Symbolism and Perceptions of Rock Art.* University of New Mexico Press, Albuquerque.

Zigmond, Maurice L.
1986 Kawaiisu. In *Great Basin,* edited by Warren L. D'Azevedo, pp. 398–411. *Handbook of North American Indians*, vol. 11, William C. Sturtevant, general editor. Smithsonian Institution, Washington, D.C.